THE CHURCH AT PRAYER

THE CHURCH AT PRAYER

An Introduction to the Liturgy

New Edition

Edited by Aimé Georges Martimort
with the Collaboration of R. Cabié, I. H. Dalmais
J. Evenou, P. M. Gy, P. Jounel, A. Nocent, and D. Sicard

Volume III

THE SACRAMENTS

by

Robert Cabié, Jean Evenou, Pierre Marie Gy,
Pierre Jounel, Aimé Georges Martimort,
Adrien Nocent, and Damien Sicard

Translated by Matthew J. O'Connell

THE LITURGICAL PRESS
Collegeville, Minnesota

Cover design by Donald A. Molloy

THE CHURCH AT PRAYER—VOLUME III: THE SACRAMENTS is the authorized English translation of *L'Eglise en Prière: Les Sacrements*, published by Desclée, Paris-Tournai, 1984.

Nihil obstat: Rev. Robert C. Harren, J.C.L., *Censor deputatus.*

Imprimatur: ✛ Jerome Hanus, O.S.B., Bishop of St.Cloud, November 5, 1987.

Excerpts from the English translation of *The Roman Missal* © 1973, 1985, International Committee on English in the Liturgy, Inc. (ICEL); excerpts from the English translation of *The Liturgy of the Hours* © 1974, ICEL; excerpts from the English translation of General Norms for the Liturgical Year and the Calendar (1969), the General Instruction of the Liturgy of the Hours (1974), and the General Instruction of the Roman Missal (1975) from *Documents on the Liturgy 1963–1979: Curial, Papal, and Conciliar Texts* © 1982, ICEL. All rights reserved.

Excerpts of prayers translated from the old Latin Roman Missal (Canon) are from *The Maryknoll Missal* edited by the Maryknoll Fathers (New York: Kenedy, 1964). All rights reserved.

Library of Congress Cataloging-in-Publication Data

Sacraments. English.

    The sacraments.

    (The Church at prayer ; v. 3)
    Translation of: Les sacrements.
    Includes bibliographies and index.
    1. Sacraments—Catholic Church. 2. Catholic
Church—Doctrines. I. Cabié, Robert. II. Title.
III. Series: Eglise en prière. English ; v. 3.
BX1970.E313 1987 vol. 3   264'.02 s   87-33897
[BX2200]   [265]
ISBN 0-8146-1365-9

Contents

Contributors to Volume III

Robert Cabié, *Professor in the Faculty of Theology of Toulouse*

Jean Evenou, *Editor-in-Chief of La Maison-Dieu*

Pierre Marie Gy, O.P., *Director of the Institut Supérieur de Liturgie in Paris, Consultor of the Congregation for Divine Worship*

Pierre Jounel, *Honorary Professor of the Institut Catholique of Paris, Consultor of the Congregation for Divine Worship*

Aimé Georges Martimort, *Honorary Dean of the Faculty of Theology in Toulouse, Consultor of the Congregation for Divine Worship*

Adrien Nocent, O.S.B., *Professor of the Pontifical Liturgical Institute at San Anselmo, Rome*

Damien Sicard, *Secretary of the Provence-Mediterranean Apostolic Region of France*

Preface

The third French edition of the present work was published in 1965, less than two years after the promulgation of the Constitution on the Liturgy of Vatican II. It was clear, of course, that this solemn document was but the starting piont of a work of restoration and reform that could be carried out only gradually.

Now, twenty-five years after the Constitution *Sacrosanctum Concilium*, the reform of the liturgy is virtually complete. A task of immense scope, unparalleled in the history of the Church, brought bishops and liturgists together from all over the world, first in the Council for the Implementation of the Constitution on the Sacred Liturgy (1964–69) and then in the Congregation for Divine Worship (1969–75). The problems that the contemporary world and its culture (or, rather, its varied cultures) raise for the prayer of the Church were pointed out with great clarity by the Council, which also enunciated the principles to be followed in solving them. The application of these principles, however, led to a revision of perspectives and to decisions that we could not have clearly anticipated in 1965.

The new liturgical books take, in fact, a new approach to the act of celebrating: they always begin with instructions or introductions that are quite different in character from the rubrics of old, since they include doctrinal and spiritual guidelines, the pastoral aspect, and possible ways of adapting the rites in question.

This bold new approach would not have been possible without the work done, especially in the twentieth century, by the historians of liturgy and the theologians. The first French edition of *The Church at Prayer* was an attempt at a summary assessment of all that labor. But far from putting an end to research, the liturgical reform gave it a new stimulus because it raised new problems or called for a more profound and scholarly grasp of the tradition. Moreover, it was no longer isolated pioneers, as in the days of Duchesne and Batiffol, Baumstark and Andrieu, who ventured into this field. On the contrary: teams now meet periodically, as at the Semaines de Saint-Serge, and liturgical schools train students (the

Liturgical Institutes of Paris and of San Anselmo in Rome have celebrated the twentieth anniversary of their foundation).

Scholars have been devoting their efforts especially to the prehistory of the Christian liturgy and to its beginnings and its relation to Jewish prayer. In addition, the comparative method initially developed by Baumstark has given a splendid impulse to the study of the Eastern and Western liturgies. It is no longer possible to reconstruct the history of the Roman liturgy without locating it in this broader framework. That same larger perspective is indispensable especially for answering doctrinal questions about the sacraments and for resolving the sensitive problem of adaptation to local Churches, as well as for inspiring the creative responses that adaptation calls for. The controversies to which the liturgical reform has given rise in various places are to be explained by an ignorance of the tradition and of the diversity it allows.

For all these reasons it has not been possible simply to correct and reprint *The Church at Prayer.* An entirely new edition is called for that will, on the one hand, highlight the spiritual and pastoral directions taken in the liturgical reform with which the name of Pope Paul VI will be permanently linked, and that will, on the other, set forth more fully than in earlier editions what we know of the varied expressions the Church has given to its prayer according to historical and geographical circumstances.

Several of the contributors to Volume III of earlier editions have been unable to aid in this revision, for reasons of health or because of other commitments. This has required a new division of labor: Monsignor Jounel, Father Gy, Dom Nocent, and I have now been joined by three new contributors to Volume III: Robert Cabié, who has already written the whole of Volume II on the Eucharist; Jean Evenou, of the diocese of Vannes, editor of *La Maison-Dieu;* and Canon Damien Sicard, Secretary of the Provence-Mediterranean Apostolic Region and author of an important study of the liturgy of death.

Finally, let me remind the reader of the limits of this work; they are the same as those mentioned in 1961 in the very first French edition. Readers will not find here a complete exposition that includes the entire content of the instructions and introductions to the new liturgical books, any more than they would have found in earlier editions a complete course in rubrics. For that kind of information they must turn to the practical instruction that is given to students in institutions of priestly formation.

In addition, the contributors always suppose that their readers have at hand at least the main liturgical texts now in use. We urge them to be constantly rereading these texts and, even more, to discover the meaning of the rites by participating in them. It is by meditating on the texts, those now in use and those of the past, and by participating as fervently as possible in the liturgical celebration, that we will be able to enter with understanding into the mysteries of the praying Church, in which Christ himself is present and active.

Aimé Georges Martimort

Abbreviations

SCRIPTURE

Gen	Genesis	Dan	Daniel
Exod	Exodus	Ezra	Ezra
Lev	Leviticus	Neh	Nehemiah
Num	Numbers	1–2 Chr	1–2 Chronicles
Deut	Deuteronomy	Bar	Baruch
Josh	Joshua	Jdt	Judith
Judg	Judges	1–2 Mac	1–2 Maccabees
1–2 Sam	1 and 2 Samuel	Sir	Sirach
1–2 Kgs	1 and 2 Kings	Tob	Tobit
Isa	Isaiah	Wis	Wisdom
Jer	Jeremiah	Matt	Matthew
Ezek	Ezekiel	Mark	Mark
Hos	Hosea	Luke	Luke
Joel	Joel	John	John
Amos	Amos	Acts	Acts of the Apostles
Obad	Obadiah	Rom	Romans
Jonah	Jonah	1–2 Cor	1–2 Corinthians
Mic	Micah	Gal	Galatians
Nah	Nahum	Eph	Ephesians
Hab	Habakkuk	Phil	Philippians
Zeph	Zephaniah	Col	Colossians
Hag	Haggai	1–2 Thess	1–2 Thessalonians
Zech	Zechariah	1–2 Tim	1–2 Timothy
Mal	Malachi	Titus	Titus
Ps (Pss)	Psalm(s)	Phlm	Philemon
Job	Job	Heb	Hebrews
Prov	Proverbs	Jas	James
Ruth	Ruth	1–2 Pet	1–2 Peter
Cant	Canticle of Canticles	1–3 John	1–3 John
Eccl	Ecclesiastes	Jude	Jude
Lam	Lamentations	Rev	Revelation
Esth	Esther		

WORKS MOST FREQUENTLY CITED

AAS	*Acta Apostolicae Sedis* (Rome, then Vatican City, 1909ff.)
Acta sanctorum	*Acta sanctorum collecta . . . a Sociis Bollandianis* (3rd ed.; Paris: Palme, 1863ff., then Brussels: Bollandistes).
ALW	*Archiv für Liturgiewissenschaft* (Regensburg: F. Pustet, 1950ff.).
Andrieu, *OR*	M. Andrieu, *Les Ordines Romani du haut moyen âge* (5 vols. Spicilegium Sacrum Lovaniense 11, 23, 24, 28, 29; Louvain: Spicilegium, 1931ff.). A sixth volume is in preparation.
Andrieu, *PR*	M. Andrieu, *Le Pontifical Romain au moyen âge* (4 vols. ST 86, 87, 88, 99; Vatican City, 1938–41).
Brightman	F. E. Brightman, *Liturgies Eastern and Western* I. *Eastern Liturgies* (Oxford: Clarendon Press, 1896). Only Volume I was published.
CCL	Corpus Christianorum collectum a monachis O.S.B. abbatiae S. Petri in Steenbrugge, Series Latina (Turnhout: Brepols, 1954ff.).
CECSL	Consilium ad exsequendam Constitutionem de sacra liturgia (Council for the Implementation of the Constitution on the Sacred Liturgy).
CSCO	Corpus Scriptorum Christianorum Orientalium editum consilio Universitatis Catholicae Americae et Universitatis Catholicae Lovaniensis (Louvain, 1903ff.).
CSEL	Corpus scriptorum ecclesiasticorum Latinorum editum consilio et impensis Academiae litterarum . . . Vindobonensis (Vienna: Tempsky, 1866ff.).
DACL	*Dictionnaire d'archéologie chrétienne et de liturgie,* edited by F. Cabrol, H. Leclercq [and H. Marrou] (Paris: Letouzey et Ané, 1907–53). 5 vols.
DBS	*Dictionnaire de la Bible: Supplément* (Paris, 1928ff.).
Denz	H. Denzinger, *Ritus orientalium . . . in administrandis sacramentis . . .* (2 vols. Würzburg: Stahel, 1863; repr., Graz: Akademische Druck, 1961).
DOL	*Documents on the Liturgy 1963–1979. Conciliar, Papal, and Curial Texts.* Edited by the International Commission on English in the Liturgy (Collegeville: The Liturgical Press, 1982).
DS	*Enchiridion symbolorum, definitionum et declarationum de rebus fidei et morum,* edited by H. Denzinger. 32nd ed. by A. Schönmetzer (Barcelona: Herder, 1963).
EDIL	*Enchiridion documentorum instaurationis liturgicae* I. *1963–1973* (Turin: Marietti, 1976).
EL	*Ephemerides liturgicae* (Rome: Edizioni liturgiche, 1887ff.). For years with two series the references are to the series *Analecta ascetico-historicae*, without this being expressly stated.

Fabre-Duchesne	P. Fabre and L. Duchesne, *Le Liber censuum de l'Eglise romaine* (3 vols. Fontemoing: E. de Boccard, 1910–52).
GCS	Die griechischen christlichen Schriftsteller der ersten Jahrhunderte, edited by the German Academy of Sciences in Berlin (Berlin: Akademie Verlag, 1897ff.).
Ge	Old Gelasian Sacramentary = Ms. Reginen. Lat. 316 in the Vatican Library, ed. L. K. Mohlberg, P. Siffrin, and L. Eizenhöfer, *Liber sacramentorum Romanae aeclesiae ordinis anni circuli* (REDMF 4; Rome: Herder, 1960).
Gell	Sacramentaire de Gellone, Paris, Bibl. Nat., ms. lat. 12048, ed. A. Dumas (CCL 159; Turnhout: Brepols, 1981).
GILH	*General Instruction of the Liturgy of the Hours*, trans. in *DOL*.
GIRM	*General Instruction of the Roman Missal*, trans. in *DOL*.
GNLYC	*General Norms for the Liturgical Year and the Calendar*, trans. in *DOL*.
GR	Gregorian Sacramentary, ed. J. Deshusses (Spicilegium Friburgense 16; Freiburg: Universitätsverlag, 1971, 1979²).
Hänggi-Pahl	A. Hänggi and I. Pahl, *Prex eucharistica. Textus e variis liturgiis antiquioribus selecti* (Spicilegium Friburgense 12; Freiburg: Universitätsverlag, 1968).
HBS	Henry Bradshaw Society for Editing Rare Liturgical Texts. London, 1891ff.
JLW	*Jahrbuch für Liturgiewissenschaft*, ed. O. Casel (Münster: Aschendorff, 1921–41).
JTS	*Journal of Theological Studies* (London: Macmillan, and then Oxford: Clarendon Press, 1900ff.).
Le	The sacramentary formerly known as the Leonine Sacramentary. Manuscript of Verona, Bibl. Capitolare, LXXXV [80]. — Ed. L. K. Mohlberg, L. Eizenhöfer, and P. Siffrin, *Sacramentarium Veronense* (REDMF 1; Rome: Herder, 1955–56).
LH	*The Liturgy of the Hours* (4 vols.; New York: Catholic Book Publishing Co., 1975ff.). Latin: *Liturgia Horarum* (Rome, 1971).
LMD	*La Maison-Dieu. Revue de pastorale liturgique* (Paris: Cerf, 1945ff.).
LO	Lex orandi (Paris: Cerf, 1944–70).
LP	L. Duchesne, *Le Liber pontificalis. Texte, introduction, et commentaire*. 2nd ed. by C. Vogel (3 vols.; Paris: E. de Boccard, 1955–57).
LQF	Liturgiegeschichtliche (later: Liturgiewissenschaftliche) Quellen und Forschungen (Münster: Aschendorff, 1919ff.).
LXX	The Septuagint. — Ed. A. Rahlfs, *Septuaginta id est Vetus Testamentum graece iuxta LXX interpretes* (3rd ed., 2 vols. Stuttgart: Württembergische Bibelanstalt, 1935).
Mansi	J. D. Mansi, *Sacrorum conciliorum nova et amplissima collectio* (31 vols.; Florence-Venice, 1757–98. Reprint and

	continuation, vols. 1–53; Paris, Leipzig, and Arnheim, 1901–27).
Martène	E. Martène, *De antiquis Ecclesiae ritibus.* (References to the various editions are given in A. G. Martimort, *La documentation liturgique de dom Edmond Martène* [ST 279; Vatican City, 1978]).
MGH	Monumenta Germaniae historica (Hannover: Hahn, and Berlin: Weidmann, 1826ff.).
MR	*Missale Romanum,* 2nd typical ed., March 27, 1975.
MTZ	*Münchener theologische Zeitschrift* (Munich, 1950ff.).
OC	*Oriens christianus. Halbjahrshefte für die Kunde des christlichen Orients* (Wiesbaden, 1901ff.).
OCA	Orientalia christiana analecta (Rome: Pontificio Istituto Orientale, 1923ff.) (1923–34: Orientalia christiana; 1935ff.: Orientalia christiana analecta).
OCP	*Orientalia christiana periodica* (Rome: Pontificio Istituto Orientale, 1935ff.).
OR I, etc.	*Ordo Romanus.* Unless the contrary is indicated, the number accompanying this abbreviation is the one assigned in Andrieu, *OR.*
OR Mab	*Ordo Romanus* according to the numbering in J. Mabillon, *Musaei Italici* II (Paris, 1969) = PL 78:851-1372.
OS	*L'Orient syrien* (Paris, 1956–67).
PG	J. P. Migne, Patrologiae cursus completus, Series graeca (Paris-Montrouge, 1857–66). 161 volumes.
PL	J. P. Migne, Patrologiae cursus completus, Series latina (Paris-Montrouge, 1844–64). 221 volumes.
PLS	A. Hamann, *Supplementum Patrologiae Latinae* (Turnhout: Brepols, 1958–74). 5 volumes.
PO	Patrologia orientalis. First editors: R. Graffin and F. Nau (Paris: Firmin-Didot, then Turnhout: Brepols, 1903ff.).
POC	*Proche-Orient chrétien* (Jerusalem: Ste. Anne, 1951ff.).
PR	Pontificale Romanum (Roman Pontifical).
PRG	C. Vogel and R. Elze, *Le pontifical romano-germanique du* X^e *siecle* (ST 226, 227, 269; Vatican City, 1963–72). 3 volumes.
QL	*Questions liturgiques et paroissiales,* then simply *Questions liturgiques* (Louvain: Abbaye du Mont Cësar, 1910ff.).
RAC	*Reallexikon für Antike und Christentum,* ed. T. Klauser (Stuttgart: Hiersemann, 1950ff.).
RBén	*Revue bénédictine* (Abbaye de Maredsous, 1884ff.).
RechSR	*Recherches de science religieuse* (Paris, 1910ff.).
REDMF	Rerum ecclesiasticarum documenta, Series maior: Fontes (Rome: Herder, 1955ff.).
Renaudot	E. Renaudot, *Liturgiarum orientalium collectio* (Paris, 1716. More accurate 2nd ed.: Frankfurt: E. Baer, 1847, in 2 volumes).

RevSR	*Revue des sciences religieuses* (Strasbourg: Palais Universitaire, 1921ff.).
RHE	*Revue d'histoire ecclésiastique* (Louvain, 1900ff.).
ROC	*Revue de l'Orient chrétien* (Paris: Leroux, then Paris: Picard, 1896ff.).
RR	Rituale Romanum (Roman Ritual).
RTAM	*Recherches de théologie ancienne et médiévale* (Louvain: Abbaye du Mont César, 1929ff.).
Sacramentary	*The Sacramentary*, revised according to the second typical edition of the *Missale Romanum*, March 27, 1975 (Collegeville: The Liturgical Press, 1985).
SC	Sources chrétiennes. Collection ed. by H. de Lubac and J. Daniélou (later: C. Mondésert) (Paris: Cerf, 1942ff.).
SCDW	Sacred Congregation for Divine Worship (May 8, 1969, to July 11, 1975, and from April 5, 1984).
SCR	Sacred Congregation of Rites. When this abbreviation is followed by a number, the reference is to *Decreta authentica Congregationis sacrorum rituum* (Rome, 1898–1927). 7 volumes or, more accurately, 5 volumes and 2 of appendixes.
SCSDW	Sacred Congregation for the Sacraments and Divine Worship (from July 11, 1975, to April 5, 1984).
SE	*Sacris erudiri. Jaarboek voor Godsdienstwetenschappen* (Steenbrugge: St.-Pietersabdij, 1948ff.).
ST	Studi e testi (Rome, then Vatican City, 1900ff.).
TA	Texte und Arbeiten, published by the Archabbey of Beuron, 1917ff. (Unless there is an indication to the contrary, the references are to the first section of this series.)
TS	Texts and Studies. Contributions to Biblical and Patristic Literature (Cambridge: Cambridge University Press, 1882ff.).
TU	Texte und Untersuchungen zur Geschichte der altchristlichen Literatur (Leipzig, then Berlin: Akademie Verlag, 1882ff.).
VSC	Vatican Council II, Constitution *Sacrosanctum Concilium* on the Sacred Liturgy. Latin text: *AAS* 56 (1964) 97–138. The translation of this document is that found in *DOL* (above).
ZKT	*Zeitschrift für katholische Theologie* (Innsbruck, 1877ff.).

The Pontifical and the Ritual

P. Jounel

Between 1968 and 1977 the Apostolic See published all the *ordines* for the celebration of the sacraments and the major blessings, as well as for funerals.[1] Seven of these rites belong to the *Pontificale Romanum* and seven to the *Rituale Romanum*, both *ex decreto oecumenici Concilii Vaticani II instauratum*, but in their Latin form they have not yet been collected into volumes. The manner of publication has its problems, since while the Pontifical is the bishop's book and the Ritual the priest's, some rites can be celebrated by either bishop or priest and even by a deacon or a layperson. Not only does the bishop, as "the high priest of his flock,"[2] celebrate all the sacraments, but he may also give priests the right, or delegate them, to celebrate any of the rites properly his, except for ordinations and the consecration of chrism. Thus since 1952 confirmation has been included in the Ritual as well as in the Pontifical. It is possible therefore that the distinction between Pontifical and Ritual cannot be sustained; it did not exist before the eleventh century and is still for practical purposes unknown in the East, where all the sacramental rites and blessings are collected in the Euchologion. In the beginning, the book proper to the celebrant, whether bishop or priest, was the Sacramentary; this contained not only the presidential prayers of the Mass, but also those of the other sacraments, the various blessings, and the ending of the Liturgy of the Hours.[3]

---

1. See the list in *The Church at Prayer* I: pp. 80–84.

2. *VSC* 41 (*DOL* 1 no. 41).

3. All sacramentaries of the Gregorian type begin with the *Ordo missae*, which is immediately followed by the ordinations of bishop, priest, and deacon.

Beginning in the seventh and eighth centuries booklets were gradually developed that described the various liturgical rites in more or less detail. Most of these guidebooks for celebration were produced in the Frankish countries by clerics or monks who had seen how the Mass and other services were celebrated at Rome; they claimed therefore to show the Roman manner of celebration and came to be known as *Ordines Romani.*[4] In many cases, however, this name concealed more or less extensive adaptations of Roman usage so as to harmonize it with the usages of the local liturgies. The time came when for convenience the corresponding prayers in the Sacramentary were included with these descriptions of ceremonies (ordinations, for example, or the dedication of a church). Soon after, the several booklets were brought together into a single volume. As a result, alongside the Mass-book or Missal, there was a book for the other sacraments, the blessings, and connected rites. At the end of the thirteenth and beginning of the fourteenth centuries this book was given the name "Pontifical."

I. THE PONTIFICAL

BIBLIOGRAPHY

Pontificalis ordinis liber, ed. A. Patrizi Piccolomini and J. Burckard (Rome: St. Plannck, 1485) (Hain-Copinger 13285).

Pontificale Romanum, published by authority of Pope Gregory XIII (Venice, 1582).

Pontificale Romanum Clementis VIII P. M. iussu restitutum atque editum (Rome, 1596). First official edition of the Roman Pontifical. The final edition, with a revised Book II, was published by Pope John XXIII in 1962.

V. Leroquais, *Les Pontificaux manuscrits des bibliothèques publiques de France* (Mâcon: Protat, 1937). 3 volumes and a volume of plates.

C. Vogel and R. Elze, *Le Pontifical romano-germanique du dixieme siècle* (3 vols.; ST 226, 227, 269; Vatican City, 1963–72).

N. K. Rasmussen, *Les Pontificaux du haut moyen âge* (in the press).

M. Andrieu, *Le Pontifical Romain au moyen âge* 1. *Le Pontifical Romain du XIIe siècle;* 2. *Le Pontifical de la Curie romaine au XIIIe siècle;* 3. *Le Pontifical de Guillaume Durand;* 4. *Tables* (ST 86, 87, 88, 99; Vatican City, 1938–41).

J. Catalani, *Pontificale Romanum . . . commentariis ornatum* (Rome, 1738).

W. Greenwell, *The Pontifical of Egbert, Archbishop of York* (Publications of the Surtees Society 27; Durham: Andrews, 1893).

H. A. Wilson, *The Benedictional of Archbishop Robert* (HBS 24; London, 1902).

_____, *The Pontifical of Magdalen College* (HBS 39; London, 1910).

M. J. Metzger, *Zwei karolingische Pontifikalien vom Oberrhein* (Freiburg: Herder, 1914).

G. H. Doble, *The Lanalet Pontifical* (HBS 74; London, 1935).

---

4. M. Andrieu, *Les Ordines Romani du haut moyen âge* (5 vols.; Spicilegium Sacrum Lovaniense 11, 23, 24, 28, 29; Louvain, 1931–61).

B. Stromberg, *Den Pontifikala liturgin i Lund och Roskilde under medeltiden* (Studia theologica Lundensia; Lund, 1955).

Fr. Unterkircher, *Das Kollektar-Pontifikale des Bischofs Baturich von Regensburg (817–848)* (Spicilegium Friburgense 8; Fribourg, 1962).

A. Martini, *Il cosidetto Pontificale di Poitiers* (REDMF 14; Rome, 1979).

a) *The Romano-German Pontifical*

The name *Liber pontificalis* was originally given to the *Gesta pontificum* of the Roman Church, a chronicle begun in the first quarter of the sixth century and continued down to the fifteenth.[5] The compilation of non-eucharistic *Ordines*, moreover, did not include only specifically episcopal rites; it also contained a whole collection of blessings that a priest could give, monastic prayers, and, at times, even didactic treatises. This description fits the most important of these collections, which a monk of Saint Alban in Mainz compiled in the middle of the tenth century. M. Andrieu showed its singular importance for the history of the medieval liturgy and gave it the name "Romano-German Pontifical" by which it has been known ever since.[6] When the *Ordines* used by priests throughout the year were removed from the collection, the resulting book contained only the rites proper to bishops and thus became a *Liber pontificalis*.

The Romano-German Pontifical[7] was not the direct ancestor of all pontificals later than the tenth century, but it was certainly the ancestor of the Roman Pontifical. As a result, the continuing romanization, beginning in the thirteenth century, of the pontificals of the local Churches gave the Romano-German Pontifical a multitudinous posterity. It contains 258 *Ordines* arranged as follows: rites of ordination, from tonsure to priestly ordination (1–19); consecration of a virgin, ordination of a deaconness, consecration of a widow, ordination of an abbot and of an abbess, profession of a monk (20–32); dedication of a church and associated blessings (33–55); ordination of a bishop and of the Roman Pontiff (56–71); blessing of a king, an emperor, a queen (72–78); *Ordo* for a council, and associated rites (79–90); *Ordines* and explanations for the celebration of Mass (92–98); *Ordo* of the liturgical year (99); other *Ordines* for Mass (100–103), ordinations (104), and the reconciliation of penitents (106); rites of baptism (107–11) and treatises on baptism (112–13); exorcisms (114–23), reconciliation of a heretic (124–27); various blessings (128–35); individual confession (136–37); visitation and anointing of the sick (138–49); liturgy of the dead (150–70); prayers concerned with monastic life (171–211); bless-

---

5. L. Duchesne, *Le Liber Pontificalis* (2 vols.; Paris, 1886–92; reprinted: Paris: E. de Boccard, 1955); vol. 3 by C. Vogel (Paris: E. de Boccard, 1957).

6. Andrieu, *OR* 4:496–548.

7. C. Vogel and R. Elze, *Le Pontifical romano-germanique du dixième siècle* (3 vols.; ST 226, 227, 269; Vatican City, 1963–72).

ings of various objects (212–45); *Ordines* for the "judgment of God" (246–52); nuptial blessing and prayers for the fertility of the wife (253–58).

The Romano-German Pontifical is remarkable not only for its scope but for its euchological content. The essential formularies were taken from the earlier sacramentaries, but many prayers and rites (those, for example, for the imposition of ashes or the beginning of Lent or the procession with the palms) appeared here for the first time and had nothing to do with the liturgy of Rome. The fusion of the two traditions gave birth in fact to a new liturgy, the Romano-German, that subsequently was to be accepted in Rome itself and, via Rome, in the entire West.

b) *The Roman Pontifical in the Twelfth and Thirteenth Centuries*

After being brought to Rome by the chances of history as early as the end of the tenth century, the Romano-German Pontifical soon underwent modifications. It needed, first of all, to be adapted to the local situation. Thus variants were introduced into the ordination of a bishop, and an *ordo* was included for the specifically Roman nocturnal procession of August 15. Above all, however, the book had to be made easier to use. To this end, all the rites dealing with the daily life of monasteries were removed; of the *ordines* for the liturgical year the only ones kept were for February 2, Ash Wednesday, and Holy Week. In addition to strictly episcopal rites, a good many blessings were kept, among them the blessing of a wife, as were the anointing of the sick, the liturgy of the dying, and the liturgy of funerals.[8] But almost all of the euchological formularies came from the Mainz compilation.

From the time of Innocent III (1198–1216) to that of Boniface VIII (1294–1303) the Pontifical used by the Roman Curia underwent appreciable change, not in the number of its *ordines* (there were forty-three in the twelfth century and fifty-four in the thirteenth), but in the content of each. The basic material taken from the Pontifical of Mainz remained intact, but the rites became ever fuller and the ceremonial directions ever more detailed, especially for those functions celebrated by the pope in person.[9]

c) *The Pontifical of William Durandus*

The travels of the popes in the twelfth and thirteenth centuries helped spread outside of Rome the liturgical books compiled for papal use. The Pontifical of the Roman Curia was, however, to be replaced during the fourteenth century by one that a bishop, formerly of the Curia, compiled in about 1294. William Durandus (1230–1296) was a well-known liturgist

---

8. M. Andrieu, *Le Pontifical romain au moyen âge 1. Le Pontifical romain du XIIᵉ siècle* (ST 86; Vatican City, 1938).

9. See volume 2 of Andrieu's *PR* (see the bibliography).

and an important officer of the pontifical court, when he was chosen bishop of Mende. Anxious to carry out his episcopal functions in a dignified manner, he compiled a book for his personal use, basing it on the Pontifical of the Curia.[10]

Durandus began by eliminating rites that a bishop did not usually perform, such as those connected with the visitation and anointing of the sick or with funerals, or those of the catechumenate; on the other hand, he added a number of *ordines* for, among other things, the visitation of a parish and the reception of a prelate or a prince of noble lineage. His most noteworthy innovation was to group the rites in three books. The first book dealt with persons (I, 1–28), the second with places or objects (II, 1–39), and the third with special rites occurring through the year and with ceremonial aspects of episcopal celebrations (III, 1–30). The formularies were taken basically from the Pontifical of the Curia, but Durandus did not hesitate to innovate, to overburden the rites, and to introduce texts from local liturgies or that he himself composed.

Although Durandus compiled his Pontifical for his own use, it soon gained lasting success. It was better composed, more complete, and more coherent than that of the Curia, and these qualities won it acceptance.

d) *The Roman Pontifical of 1595*

In 1485, A. Patrizi Piccolomini, bishop of Chiusi, published the first printed edition of the Roman Pontifical, which he had prepared at the request of Pope Innocent VIII and with the help of Johannes Burckard, papal master of ceremonies.[11] The bishop was satisfied with a few adaptations of the Pontifical of William Durandus; he suppressed, among other things, some rites that had fallen into disuse or were habitually celebrated by priests.

During the sixteenth century the *Pontificalis liber* of 1485 underwent several reprintings, each with minor changes. The definitive title *Pontificale Romanum* first appeared in the edition authorized by Gregory XIII (Venice, 1582). The Roman Pontifical was carefully revised and promulgated as an official book by Clement VIII in 1595. This pope showed himself stricter than Pius V had been in promulgating the Breviary and Missal, for he abolished all the Pontificals of the local Churches and authoritatively required the exclusive use of the Roman Pontifical. The book was re-edited several times more after 1595; the most notable of these new editions was that of John XXIII, who radically altered the second book by simplifying the rites for the dedication of churches and the consecration of altars (1962).

---

10. See volume 3 of Andrieu's *PR*.

11. P. de Puniet, *Le Pontifical romain* (Louvain: Mont César, 1930), 1:55-62. The text of Patrizi's preface is given on 67-78. ET: *The Roman Pontifical: A History and Commentary*, trans. M. V. Harcourt (New York: Longmans, Green 1932f.), 56–57.

II. THE RITUAL

BIBLIOGRAPHY

A. Castellani, *Liber sacerdotalis* (Venice, 1523). After 1537 the book was entitled *Sacerdotale iuxta S. R. E. ritum* and then *Sacerdotale Romanum*.

J. A. Santori, *Rituale sacramentorum Romanum Gregorii XIII iussu editum* (Rome, 1584). The title is inaccurate, since the book was not in fact promulgated.

Rituale Romanum Pauli V P. M. iussu editum (Rome, 1614). First official edition of the Roman Ritual. The final edition, published in 1953, was modified to some extent by the promulgation of the *Ordo Baptismi adultorum per gradus catechumenatus dispositus* in 1962.

J. Catalani, *Rituale Romanum Benedicti XIV perpetuis commentariis exornatum* (Padua, 1760).

F. A. Zaccaria, *Bibliotheca ritualis* (Rome: Manaldini, 1776), 1:144–60.

A. Franz, *Die kirchliche Benediktionen im Mittelalter* (Freiburg: Herder, 1909).

B. Loewenberg, *Das Rituale des Kard. Julius Antonius Sanctorius. Ein Beitrag zur Entstehungsgeschichte des Rituale Romanum* (Munich, 1937).

Estudios sobre el ritual. Special volume of *Liturgia* (Santo Domingo de Silos, 1958).

J. B. Molin, "Un type d'ouvrage mal connu, le Rituel, son intérêt et ses caractéristiques bibliographiques," *EL* 63 (1959) 218–24.

_____, "Introduction à l'étude des Rituels anciens," *Bulletin du Comité des études* (of the Compagnie de Saint-Sulpice) 3 (1959) 675–95.

P. M. Gy, "Collectaire, Rituel, Processionnal," *Revue des sciences philosophiques et théologiques* 44 (1960) 441–69.

C. Vogel, *Medieval Liturgy: An Introduction to the Sources,* trans. and rev. W. Storey and N. Rasmussen (Washington, D.C.: Pastoral Press, 1986), 257–65.

E. Cattaneo, "Il Rituale romano di Alberto Castellani," in *Miscellanea liturgica . . . Lercaro* 2 (Rome: Desclée, 1967) 629–47.

J. B. Molin and A. Aussedat-Minvielle, *Repertoire des rituels et processionnaux imprimés conservés en France* (Paris: Ed. du C.N.R.S., 1984).

We know almost nothing about the abridged sacramentaries and booklets for the celebration of the sacraments and funerals that may have been used in rural parishes before the final centuries of the Middle Ages. The monasteries, which had a wealth of liturgical books, began making extracts of these books from the ninth and tenth centuries on. They compiled, among others, collections of prayers for the Office (Collectaries), often adding to them a certain number of blessings as well as the formularies absolutely necessary for the celebration of the sacraments (baptism, penance, anointing of the sick), for attending to the dying, and for funerals. These were the first rituals. Finally, booklets were often compiled for the processions that played such a large part in the monastic liturgy (the Processional). Parish rituals appeared especially from the thirteenth century on, so that the regulations issued by diocesan synods could be implemented. At the same period, there was a tendency to eliminate from the compilation of non-Eucharistic *ordines* all those not reserved to the bishop, in order to produce a book for his exclusive use (the Pontifical).

It was appropriate, therefore, to collect in a separate volume the formularies intended more specifically for priests.

This book for presbyters was given various names, with one name usually prevailing throughout a region. In some areas it was called *Rituale*, in others *Manuale, Agenda, Obsequiale, Ordinarium, Sacerdotale, Sacramentale,* or *Parochiale.* The variety of names persisted in diocesan rituals for a long time after the publication of the Roman Ritual of 1614.

a) *The First Printed Rituals*

In the preface to the Roman Pontifical of 1485, Piccolomini announced his intention of collecting "in a separate volume all that pertained to priests." He was unable to do so; his plan was carried out instead by Alberto Castellani, O.P., who published a *Liber sacerdotalis* (Venice, 1523). Although this book, which was eventually entitled *Sacerdotale Romanum,* always remained an unofficial work, it quickly spread far and wide, not only in Italy but also in France. It was continually republished until the Ritual of Paul V appeared. After the Council of Trent it was adapted to reflect the conciliar decrees.

Castellani's ritual had three sections, in which each chapter was prefaced by remarks of a juridico-pastoral kind. The first section dealt with the sacraments: baptism, marriage, penance, Eucharist (with the *Ordo Missae* and the treatise *De defectibus*), extreme unction, visitation of the sick, attendance on the dying, and office of the dead; this last was very extensive. The second section contained the blessings (seventy formularies). The third was for processions. Particularly to be noted in this third part is the procession for the *depositio* of the Eucharist in the "tomb" on Good Friday and its removal (*elevatio*) on Easter morning, as well as Easter Vespers with the procession *ad fontes.* The book concluded with the table for calculating the dates of Church feasts, the exorcisms, the text of five sermons for the major feasts (as an aid to preachers), and the tables for the translation and concurrence of feasts.

Cardinal Giulio Antonio Santori, bishop of Santa Severina, subsequently devoted himself to producing a ritual. In the judgment of Pope Paul V, he did so "with lengthy study and great energy." His work was printed only after his death (1601) and, for reasons not very clear,[12] it was not distributed. It contained seven hundred and twelve pages, or twice as many as Castellani's book. One point especially is to be noted in this vast and learned compilation: the author wanted to restore the stages of the catechumenate in accordance with ancient practice. After all, had not

---

12. F. A. Zaccaria, *Bibliothesa ritualis* (Rome: Monaldini, 1776), 1:145–46. The work contains a list of the rituals printed in the various countries in the sixteenth and seventeenth centuries.

the sixteenth century brought a new missionary outreach of the Church both in the Americas and in the Far East?

b) *The Ritual of Paul V*

The *Rituale Romanum* was promulgated by Pope Paul V in 1614. In his decree of promulgation the pope said that the commission entrusted with preparing it had chiefly (*in primis*) consulted the ritual of Santori. The first concern of the commission was to simplify Santori's work. Like Castellani's, the Roman Ritual contained three parts: sacraments, blessings, and processions, each *ordo* being preceded by *praenotanda.* The entire canonical apparatus was removed from the chapter on penance, while the chapter on the Eucharist was reduced to the rite of communion outside of Mass. The blessings were reduced to thirty. In the third part, the non-Roman procession on Easter morning was eliminated, as was the procession *ad fontes* at Easter Vespers. On the other hand, directives were added at the end on how to keep the parish books on baptisms, confirmations, marriages, the *status animarum*, and the dead. Whereas Clement VIII had abolished all existing pontificals, Paul V was satisfied to exhort bishops, abbots, and parish priests to adopt the new ritual he was offering them.

The Ritual of Paul V went through numerous editions. In the nineteenth century an overabundant appendix, containing a mass of blessings, was added to it. Pius XII inserted these into the body of the Ritual in 1952.[13] Pius XI had adapted the *praenotanda* to the Code of Canon Law for inclusion in the edition of 1925. The year 1962 brought the final addition to the Roman Ritual: the *Ordo* for the several-stage catechumenate, and thus a long-delayed victory for Cardinal Santori.

c) *The Diocesan Rituals*

Outside of Italy, the integral Roman Ritual was received hardly anywhere before the middle of the nineteenth century, and down to Vatican II many dioceses had their local appendixes to it in the form of a *Collectio rituum* or *Enchiridion rituum specialium*. On the other hand, all the bishops took care to revise their diocesan rituals in accordance with the model promulgated by Paul V. In France the ritual became a real pastoral handbook of sacramental practice. Not only were the titles and rubrics translated, but each rite was accompanied by detailed instructions. The chapter on the Eucharist, for example, contained the prayers of prone, which were the last vestige of the old general intercessions. The chapter on marriages gave the rules for the validity of engagements.

---

13. On this final *editio typica* of the Ritual of Paul V see E. Viale, "Rituale Romanum . . .," *LMD* no. 34 (1953) 164–66.

III. THE EUCHOLOGION

BIBLIOGRAPHY

Euchologion to mega (Rome, 1873).
J. Goar, *Euchologion, sive Rituale Graecorum* (Paris: S. Piget, 1647; 2nd ed., Venice:
   B. Javarina, 1730; reprinted: Graz, 1960).
Euchologe ou Rituel de l'Eglise orthodoxe. Texts selected and translated by A. Nelidow
   and A. Nièvre (Le Bousquet-sur-Orb [Hérault], 1979). Extracts from the Eucho-
   logion.
J. A. Assemani, *Codex liturgicus Ecclesiae universae* (13 vols.; Rome: Bizzarini,
   1749–66; reprinted: Welter, 1902).
H. Denzinger, *Ritus orientalium Coptorum, Syrorum et Armenorum in adminis-
   trandis sacramentis* (2 vols.; Würzburg: Stahel, 1863–64; reprinted: Graz, 1961).
A. Baumstark, *Comparative Liturgy*, 3rd ed. by B. Botte, trans. F. L. Cross
   (Westminster, Md.: Newman, 1958).

The Churches of the East have, as a whole, kept the usage followed by the Western Church in the high Middle Ages. Not only do they not distinguish between pontifical and ritual, but they put the entire content of the ancient sacramentaries in a single book.[14] Only in a very broad sense, therefore, is "Ritual" a legitimate translation of the Greek *Euchologion*.

The Euchologion[15] is the best known of the Byzantine liturgical books. As early as the seventeenth century J. Goar, a Dominican, made a complete Latin translation with valuable annotations. In size the volume is comparable to the Romano-German Pontifical: the Greek Euchologion contains two hundred and eighty-six formularies, the Mainz Pontifical two hundred and fifty-eight. Here, briefly, is the organization of the book: It opens with the offices for evening (*lucernarium*, vespers) and morning, then the liturgy of the Presanctified for Lent. These are followed by ordinations from lector to bishop, baptism, marriage (betrothal and crowning), and anointing of the sick. After the blessing of water on the feast of the Theophany come the monastic rites, funeral rites, and a good many blessings. Among the last-named the confection of myron occupies a prominent place. Then come the rites of penance and various prayers. The dedication of churches (*enkainia*) and the liturgy for the installation of the emperor and his major officials close the book.[16]

---

14. The Hieratikon, which contains the functions performed by priests, is an extract from the Euchologion.

15. A list of the contents of the Euchologion is given in *DACL* 6:1368–74.

16. The Pontifical of the Western Syrians was compiled by Patriarch Michael the Great (1166–99); I. Vosté, *Pontificale iuxta ritum Ecclesiae Syrorum occidentalium . . . versio latina* (Vatican Polyglot Press, 1941). The Pontifical of the Eastern Syrians is known to us only in much later recensions (end of the fifteenth and the sixteenth centuries): I. Vosté, *Pontificale iuxta ritum Ecclesiae Syrorum orientalium . . . versio latina* (Vatican Polyglot

Press, 1937). The Copts have had a printed Pontifical (published by R. Tuki) since 1761;
the Vatican Library has two manuscript Coptic euchologia dating from the first decades
of the fourteenth century. For the Armenians: F. Conybeare, *Rituale Armenorum . . .* (Oxford: Clarendon, 1905).

Chapter I

Christian Initiation

R. Cabié

GENERAL BIBLIOGRAPHY

C. Chardon, *Histoire des sacrements* I, 1, sect. 1 and 2 (1st ed., 1745); reprinted in J. P. Migne, *Theologiae cursus completus* 20 (Paris, 1840) 11–218.

P. de Puniet, "Catéchuménat," *DACL* 2 (1909) 2579–2621.

H. Leclercg, "Catéchèse, catéchisme, catéchumenat," *DACL* 2 (1910) 2530–79.

P. de Puniet, "Baptême," *DACL* 2 (1910) 251–346.

L. Andrieux, *La première communion des origines au XXe siècle* (Paris: Beauchesne, 1911).

P. de Puniet, "Confirmation," *DACL* 3 (1914) 2515–44.

L. Duchesne, *Origines du culte chrétien* (Paris: E. de Boccard, 1920⁵), 309–60. [The fifth French edition was considerably changed from the earlier edition translated into English as: *Christian Worship: Its Origin and Evolution,* trans. M. L. McClure (London: SPCK, 1903). I shall give references henceforth only to the French fifth edition. — Tr.]

A. Raes, *Introductio in liturgiam orientalem* (Rome: Pontifical Oriental Institute, 1947), 120–43.

P. Paris, *L'initiation chrétienne* (Paris: Beauchesne, 1948).

J. Daniélou, "Le symbolisme des rites baptismaux," *Dieu vivant* 1 (1949) 17–43.

A. Chavasse, "Histoire de l'initiation chrétienne des enfants de l'antiquité à nos jours," *LMD* no. 28 (1951) 26–44.

A. G. Martimort, "La confirmation," in *Communion solennelle et profession de foi* (LO 14; Paris: Cerf, 1952), 159–201.

L. Bouyer, "La signification de confirmation," *Vie Spirituelle: Supplément* no. 29 (1954) 162–79.

H. Schmidt, *Hebdomada sancta* (Rome: Herder, 1957), 274–75 and 758–62 (bibliography).

A. Stenzel, *Die Taufe. Eine genetische Erklärung der Taufliturgie* (Innsbruck: Rauch, 1957).

J. Lécuyer, "Théologie de l'initiation chrétienne chez les Pères," *LMD* no. 58 (1959) 5–28.

P. Camelot, *Spiritualité du baptême* (LO 30; Paris: Cerf, 1960).

H. Schmidt, *Introductio in liturgiam occidentalem* (Rome: Herder, 1960), 238–321 (with detailed bibliography).

M. Righetti, *Manuale di storia liturgica* 4 (Milan: Ancora, 1959²), 21–146.

G. Kretschmar, "Die Geschichte des Taufgottesdienstes in der alten Kirche," in *Leitourgia. Handbuch des evangelischen Gottesdienstes* 5 (Kassel: Stauda, 1970) 1–348.

E. C. Whitaker, *Documents of the Baptismal Liturgy* (Alcuin Club Collections 42; London: SPCK, 1970²).

I simboli dell'iniziazione cristiana. Atti del I° Congresso internazionale di liturgia (Studia Anselmiana 87, Analecta liturgica 7; Rome, 1983).

According to its etymology, "initiation" has to do with a beginning; but in its current Western use it suggests rather a formation, often primarily intellectual, that extends over a certain period of time. This meaning of the term may well lead to misunderstanding of Christian initiation, for the latter is accomplished by means of sacramental actions: baptism, confirmation, and Eucharist.[1] These actions may be separated and celebrated at different times; they suppose a preparation; and baptism itself can have various stages. But it is not these elements that turn the actions into an initiation, but rather the fact that the recipients of these actions thereby gain entry into the "new people" that is the Church of Jesus Christ. It can be said that to be fully a member of the visible community of Christians one must have passed through these three stages. Initiation can thus be experienced in its entirety at a single liturgical gathering, as happens usually in the East and even in the West when the recipients are adults. The Eucharist is distinguished from the other two sacraments in that it can be repeated throughout one's life, in order as it were to make the initiation begun by baptism and confirmation last until the death of the believer.

---

1. See P. M. Gy, "La notion chrétienne d'initiation. Jalons pour une enquête," *LMD* no. 132 (1977) 33–54.

Article I: **The Origins of Christian Initiation**
(To the Middle of the Second Century)

BIBLIOGRAPHY

P. Coppens, "Baptême," *DBS* 1 (1928) 852–924.
H. Chirat, *L'assemblée chrétienne à l'âge apostolique* (LO 10; Paris: Cerf, 1949), 126–49.
J. Schmitt, "Baptême et communauté d'après la primitive pensée apostolique," *LMD* no. 32 (1952) 53–73.
A. Benoît, *Le baptême chrétien au second siècle. La théologie des Pères* (Paris: Presses Universitaires, 1953).
J. Daniélou, *The Theology of Jewish Christianity*, trans. J. A. Baker (Westminster, Md.: Newman, 1964), 315–38.
L. Gerhard, "Der Ursprung der christlichen Taufe," *Theologische Quartalschrift* 156 (1956) 35–54.

§1. The New Testament

From the outset people entered the Church by way of a rite with water; baptism made its appearance simultaneously with the Christian community. St. Paul says that all the faithful were baptized, including himself: "Do you not know that all of us who have been baptized into Christ Jesus were baptized into his death?"[1] This initiation was expressly connected with the paschal mystery of the Lord. In the minds of believers this symbolic act was even regarded as a requirement of the risen Lord himself, for it was on his lips that the order to act in this manner was placed: "Go therefore and make disciples of all nations, baptizing them in the name of the Father and of the Son and of the Holy Spirit."[2] This Trinitarian formula does not directly tell us what precise words were used in the

---

1. Rom 6:3. See 1 Cor 12:13.
2. Matt 18:28.

celebration, and we are not even certain that Jesus really spoke the words himself; on the other hand, the text leaves no doubt about the significance that the first Christians attributed to this rite of initiation.[3]

The reason for their attitude was that the Lord himself had received baptism; the Synoptic Gospels highlight that event which marked the beginning of his ministry among human beings. The baptism he received was that of John, but it was made special by a theophany that asserted the Messiah's divine sonship.[4] This sonship was to be communicated to all of the Messiah's brothers and sisters through the grace of adoption that came with their initiation. But Jesus was not only a recipient of baptism; he was and is, above all, the giver of baptism. The Fourth Gospel emphasizes this aspect: "This is he who baptizes with the Holy Spirit."[5]

Christian baptism came into existence in a religious setting that was familiar with ritual baths, and this fact doubtless influenced the new practice. The latter was nonetheless original.[6] Its special character was strongly emphasized in the Acts of the Apostles: it was always celebrated "in the name of Jesus" and this historical reference to Christ made it an unprecedented phenomenon. The cited words were not a liturgical formula, and the New Testament hardly enables us to reconstruct the ceremonial. It must be emphasized, moreover, that in the Christian rite, as in the rite of John, recipients never purified themselves, as people customarily did at that time; there was always someone who gave baptism to them, and even the Lord himself willed to receive his baptism. Furthermore (the reference is still to Acts), just as the Church came to birth in a twofold passage through Easter and Pentecost, so the initiation of the disciples was seen as including both a baptism in the name of Jesus (in water and the Spirit) and a gift of the Spirit that on more than one occasion is connected with

---

3. But "it may be that this formula, as far as the fullness of its expression is concerned, is a reflection of the liturgical usage established later in the primitive community" (*The Jerusalem Bible* [New Testament] [New York: Doubleday, 1966], 64, note g). See Mark 16:16: "He who believes and is baptized will be saved." Everyone is aware of the difficulties regarding the origin of the ending of Mark; in any case, the passage does not seem to be derived from the First Gospel.

4. Matt 3:13-17; Mark 1:9-11; Luke 3:21-22.

5. John 1:29-34; see 3:22-26: "Jesus . . . baptized. . . . Now a discussion arose between John's disciples and a Jew over purifying. And they came to John, and said to him, 'Rabbi, he who was with you beyond the Jordan, to whom you bore witness, here he is, baptizing' "; 4:1-2: "The Pharisees had heard that Jesus was making and baptizing more disciples than John (although Jesus himself did not baptize, but only his disciples)." See S. Légasse, "Le baptême administré par Jésus," *Bulletin de littérature ecclésiastique* 78 (1977) 3-30.

6. Reference is usually made especially to the baths of purification practiced at Qumran and to "proselyte baptism." See S. Légasse, "Baptême juif et baptême chrétien," *Bulletin de littérature ecclésiastique* 77 (1976) 3-40.

a laying on of hands by the apostles.[7] The information given is too vague for us to reconstruct the details of a ceremony, still less to make a fully developed distinction between baptism and confirmation. It is significant, however, that these two aspects of the entrance of believers into the community are mentioned in several passages.

It is to be noted, finally, that while initiation seems to have been given without any lengthy preparation and at times even very speedily (as in the case of the eunuch of Queen Candace, whom Philip baptized[8]), it was nonetheless always preceded by a proclamation of the Word and supposed an acceptance of the gospel that led to a conversion.[9]

§2. The *Didache*

The oldest text on initiation to be found outside the Bible is in the *Didache*, a little book of Syrian origin that is a compilation of various documents that may go back to the end of the first or the beginning of the second century:

> As for baptism, baptize in this way: After having said all that precedes, baptize in running water, in the name of the Father and of the Son and of the Holy Spirit. If you do not have running water, baptize in some other water, and if you cannot do it in cold water, do it in warm. If you are without either, then pour water on the head three times in the name of the Father and of the Son and of the Holy Spirit. Let the baptizer, the one to be baptized, and others who can, fast before the baptism; but order the candidate to fast one or two days beforehand.[10]

The words *tauta panta proeipontes* ('after having said all that precedes") is a reference to the teaching of the "Two Ways" that has been explained in the preceding chapters and is regarded here as a preparation of the candidates for baptism. These transitional words are doubtless from the pen of the compiler, but the remainder of the sentence displays very archaic traits with its mention of running water and of the Trinitarian formula

---

7. Acts 8:15-17; 19:1-7; see 3:28. In Acts 10:44-48 the coming of the Spirit precedes baptism. Note that when the action of the apostles is described, it consists in a laying on of both hands, contrary to the usual liturgical rite: "epetithesan tas cheiras . . . dia tēs epitheseōs tōn cheirōn" (8:17-18); "epithentos autois tou Paulou cheiras" (19:6).

8. Acts 8:26-38.

9. Acts 3:28 and 41; 8:12; 16:14-15; 16:31-33. Conversion was quickly followed by an explicit profession of faith, as seems to be indicated by the ancient interpolation in Acts 8:37: "Dixit autem Philippus: Si credis ex toto corde, licet. Et respondens ait: Credo Filium Dei esse Iesum Christum" ("And Philip said, 'If you believe with all your heart, you may.' And he replied, 'I believe that Jesus Christ is the Son of God' ").

10. *Didache* 7, 1-4, ed. and trans. W. Rordorf and A. Tuiler (SC 248; Paris: Cerf, 1978), 170-73.

that may already have been in use in the liturgy of baptism. The same is doubtless true of the preceding fast in which at least some of the community take part.[11]

§3. Saint Justin

In the mid-second century Justin's *First Apology* has a section on initiation. It states in particular:

> Those who believe wholeheartedly that what we have taught and explained to them is true begin by professing that they can live in accordance with it; they are then taught to pray and to ask God, amid fasting, for the forgiveness of their past sins; we ourselves pray and fast with them. Then we bring them to a place where there is water, and they are reborn with the same kind of rebirth with which we ourselves have been reborn. They are then bathed in the water in the name of God, the Father and Master of the universe, and of our Savior, Jesus Christ. . . .[12]

Baptism is presented here as the sacrament of the forgiveness of sins and of new birth (a theme that Justin develops in the continuation of the passage cited); he also speaks of baptism as an "illumination." He further emphasizes the necessity of accepting the faith of the Church. The candidates therefore received instruction on Christian teaching and on the Christian way of life; they also underwent a preparation (in which the entire community joined) that consisted of prayer and fasting. There was as yet no organized catechumenate.

---

11. The shift from "you" in the plural ("baptize") to "you" in the singular ("if you do not have . . .") is perhaps a sign that several sources are being used, the second providing instructions on the water to be used and on the strict requirement of fasting by the candidates. The Coptic version adds a prayer over perfumed oil, thus presupposing an anointing that is not present in the primitive redaction.

12. St. Justin, *Apologia I* 61, 2–3, ed. L. Pautigny (Textes et documents 1; Paris: Picard, 1904), 126–28; see also 65, 1 and 66, 1 (pp. 138 and 140).

Article II: The Organization of the Ritual of Initiation Until the Spread of Infant Baptism
(From the Mid-second to the Sixth Century)

When the ritual of baptism did become organized, it took appreciably different forms in the various Churches and underwent many changes in the space of four centuries.[1] In sketching the main lines of this development I can only call attention to the essential convergences among the various usages and to the most important variants. I shall proceed by studying in order the parts making up the liturgy of initiation, after first describing the principal sources of the information available to us.

§1. The Sources

BIBLIOGRAPHY

Hippolytus, *La Tradition apostolique* 15–21, ed. B. Botte (LQF 39; Münster: Aschendorff, 1963), 32–39.

Didascalia apostolorum 16, ed. R. H. Connolly, *Didascalia Apostolorum. The Syriac Version Translated and Accompanied by the Verona Latin Fragments* (Oxford: Clarendon, 1926), 146.

St. Cyril of Jerusalem, *Catéchèses mystagogiques,* ed. A. Piédagnel, trans. P. Paris (SC 126; Paris: Cerf, 1966).

St. John Chrysostom, *Baptismal Instructions,* trans. P. W. Harkins (Ancient Christian Writers 31; Westminster, Md.: Newman, 1963). Ed. and French trans. A. Wenger (SC 50; Paris: Cerf, 1957).

Theodore of Mopsuestia, *Homélies catéchétiques* 12–14, ed. and trans. R. Tonneau and R. Devreesse (ST 145; Vatican City, 1949), 321–461.

Constitutiones Apostolorum III, 16; VII, 22 and 39–45, ed. F. X. Funk, *Didascalia et Constitutiones apostolorum* (Paderborn: Schöningh, 1905), 1:209–11, 404–8, and 440–52.

Euchologium Serapionis 19–25, ed. Funk, *ibid.,* 2:180–87.

---

1. It must be kept in mind that each document provides information only for the place and time of its origin. Even neighboring Churches might have different customs.

17

St. Ambrose, *De sacramentis, De mysteriis,* ed. B. Botte (SC 25bis; Paris: Cerf, 1961²).

St. Augustine, *Sermons pour la Pâque,* ed. and trans. S. Poque (SC 116; Paris: Cerf, 1966).

Testamentum Domini Nostri Iesu Christi II, 1–10, ed. I. E. Rahmani, with Latin translation (Mainz: Kirchheim, 1899), 110–13.

John the Deacon, *Epistula ad Senarium,* ed. A. Wilmart, *Analecta Reginensia* (ST 59; Vatican City, 1933), 170–79 (PL 59:399–408).

Liber sacramentorum Romanae Aeclesiae ordinis anni circuli (Gelasian Sacramentary), nos. 193–99, 225–28, 254–57, 283–327, 419–24, 444–52, ed. L. C. Mohlberg (REDMF 4; Rome: Herder, 1960), 38–74.

Liber ordinum, ed. M. Férotin (Monumenta Ecclesiae liturgica 5; Paris: Didot, 1904), cols. 24–36.

Missale Bobbiense, fol. 112v–119r, ed. E. A. Lowe (HBS 61; London, 1920).

Missale Gothicum, nos. 252–65, ed. H. M. Bannister, vol. 1 (HBS 52; London, 1917).

Missale Gallicanum vetus, nos. 159–77, ed. L. C. Mohlberg (REDMF 3; Rome: Herder, 1958).

Our information comes from works that differ widely in genre:

1) *"Canonico-liturgical" literature* includes, first of all, the *Apostolic Tradition* of Hippolytus,[2] written at Rome in about 225. It also includes the various revisions that the *Apostolic Tradition,* and the *Didache,* underwent in the East. Among these revisions, the most important are *The Didascalia of the Apostles,*[3] which originated in regions east of the Roman Empire and goes back very probably to the first half of the third century; the *Apostolic Constitutions,* a compilation of disparate pieces that the author (writing in about 380 and probably at Antioch) did not attempt to harmonize;[4] and the *Testament of Our Lord,* which has been traced to the fifth century and the eastern part of Syria.[5] These documents, which are interdependent, provide information about local usages only to the extent that they depart from the model that inspires them.

---

2. The Greek original has been lost. The surviving parts of the Latin translation in the Verona manuscript include only some of the passages that concern us here. The text must therefore be reconstructed from the Coptic (Sahidic and Bohairic), Ethiopic, and Arabic versions.

3. The divergences have been dealt with as they concern deaconesses and their role in the baptism of women; see A. G. Martimort, *Les diaconesses, essai historique* (Bibliotheca EL, Subsidia 24; Rome: Edizioni liturgiche, 1982), 33 and 38–40.

4. The *Constitutiones Apostolorum* contain three passages on baptism: a revised version of the *Didascalia* in Book III; in Book VII a fairly brief adaptation of the *Didache* and a detailed ritual, the sources of which are uncertain. Note that Book VIII contains no ritual of initiation, although it has an extensive development of the text of Hippolytus on ordinations and the Eucharist.

5. The *Testamentum* makes up the first two books of the collection known as the *Octateuch of Clement.* The baptismal ritual is based on Hippolytus, but with important changes, especially in what concerns the baptism of women.

2) *Mystagogical catecheses* are among the most valuable sources for the ceremonial of initiation. These homilies were delivered during the days after the celebration and addressed to the neophytes; they commented on the liturgy that the latter had experienced but of which they had known little beforehand because of the "discipline of the secret." The best known of these catecheses date to around the end of the fourth century and include those of Ambrose of Milan,[6] Cyril of Jerusalem or his successor John,[7] Theodore of Mopsuestia[8] and John Chrysostom[9] at Antioch, and Augustine[10] in Africa. To these must be added the prebaptismal catecheses given to the candidates for baptism during Lent; some of these have come down to us.[11] Also deserving of mention from a slightly later period are the sermons of Severus of Antioch,[12] the works of Pseudo-Dionysius,[13] and, for the eastern part of Syria, the homilies attributed to Narsai of Nisibis[14] and, for Gaul, those of Caesarius of Arles.[15]

---

6. The *De sacramentis* reproduces the homilies of Ambrose from the notes of stenographers; the *De mysteriis* seems to be a treatise in which the author covers the same ground but for publication.

7. The mystagogical catecheses are the last five of a collection that includes a "procatechesis" and eighteen prebaptismal instructions. The problem of authenticity arises only in connection with the mystagogical catecheses; see A. Piédagnel in SC 126:18–40.

8. The Greek text has been lost, but there is a Syriac version of eleven prebaptismal and five mystagogical homilies that Theodore delivered before he was raised to the episcopate; they were probably delivered at Antioch, but not in the church where Chrysostom preached, since there are variations in the rites.

9. We have some instructions given by Chrysostom when he was a priest at Antioch: the second of the two published by Montfaucon (PG 49:231–40), the four discovered at Moscow (A. Papadopoulos-Kerameus, *Varia graeca sacra* [Receuil de textes grecs inédits, du IVe and XVe siècle; St. Petersburg, 1909), and the eight from Mount Athos (Harkins, ACW 31; A. Wenger, SC 50). But points of information on the liturgy of initiation are to be found throughout the sermons of Chrysostom.

10. Augustine's remarks about initiation are scattered throughout his writings, especially in the sermons on the Easter cycle. In *Sermons pour la Pâque* (SC 116; Paris: Cerf, 1966), S. Poque gives an example of each stage in the cycle. The bishop of Hippo explained the rites of baptism especially during the Easter Vigil, and the rites of the Eucharist on Easter day itself. There were no mystagogical catecheses proper during the days of the octave.

11. See above, notes 7, 8, 9.

12. Severus speaks of baptism in numerous passages of his 125 *Homélies cathédrales*, which were published, with a French translation, in many fascicles of the PO from 1906 to 1912 (M. Brière gives the title and date of each homily in PO 29/1 [1960] 50–62).

13. Pseudo-Dionysius, *Hierarchia ecclesiastica* (PG 1:585–1120; French trans. by M. Gandillac in *Oeuvres complètes du Pseudo-Denys l'Aréopagite* (Bibliothèque philosophique; Paris: Aubier, 1943).

14. A. Mingana, *Narsai doctoris Syri homiliae et carmina* (Mossoul, 1905), Homilies 22 and 21 (the order needs to be revised); English translation by R. H. Connolly (TS VIII/1; Cambridge, 1909). There is a French translation of Homily 22 by A. Guillaumont in OS 1 (1956) 190–207, and of Homily 21 by P. Gignoux in A. Hamman, *L'initiation chrétienne* (Paris: Grasset, 1963), 195–213. [This Homily is not included in the English translation of Hamman's book (see the next bibliography in the text). — Tr.]

15. *S. Caesarii Arlatensis sermones*, ed. G. Morin (CCL 103 and 104; Turnhout: Brepols.

3) Various *treatises, letters, and short works* dealing with initiation often contain scattered remarks or even simple allusions to the rites.[16] Since the purpose of these authors was not to describe the rite, it is sometimes difficult to reconstruct its detailed organization from what they say. This is the case, for example, with the second and third century writings of Tertullian and Cyprian in Africa and Origen at Alexandria; it is also true of the travel diary of Egeria at Jerusalem in about 400 and of the sixth-century writings of Avitus of Vienne in Gaul and John the Deacon at Rome.

4) The *liturgical books*—if we exclude some earlier documents, such as the Euchologion of Serapion in Egypt (though this is doubtless not authentic but does go back to the fourth century)—were composed at a later period than the one I am discussing here; however, the formularies they contain are usually older. From Rome comes the Gelasian Sacramentary, from Gaul the Bobbio Missal, the Gothic Missal, and the old Gallican Missal,[17] and from Spain the *Liber ordinum*.[18] The East has bequeathed us very little from this period.[19]

§2. Preparation for Baptism

BIBLIOGRAPHY

F. J. Dölger, *Der Exorzismus im altchristlichen Taufritual* (Studien zur Geschichte und Kultur des Altertums 3; Paderborn: Schöningh, 1909).

P. Dondeyne, "La discipline des scrutins dans l'Eglise latine avant Charlemagne," *RHE* 28 (1932) 1–33, 751–87.

B. Capelle, "L'introduction du catéchuménat à Rome," *RTAM* 5 (1933) 129–54 (= his *Travaux liturgiques* 3 [Louvain: Mont César, 1967], 186–210).

E. Dick, "Das Pateninstitut im altchristlichen Katechumenat," *ZKT* 63 (1939) 1–49.

A. Chavasse, "Les deux rituels romain et gaulois de l'admission au catéchuménat que renferme le Sacramentaire gélasien," in *Etudes de critique et d'histoire religieuse (offerts à L. Vaganay)* (Bibliothèque de la Faculté de Théologie de Lyon; Lyons: Vitte, 1948), 79–98.

---

16. Since these testimonies are so widely scattered, I shall give references to them only as I make use of them.

17. These books are contaminated by Roman usage, but their ritual of initiation preserves many Gallican peculiarities.

18. In addition to the *Ordo baptismi celebrandus quolibet tempore* (reference in the bibliography), the book also locates initiation in the Easter Vigil (cols. 217ff.).

19. To be noted, however, is the fifth- or sixth-century Constantinopolitan *Ordo* published in J. Goar, *Euchologion, sive Rituale Graecorum* (2nd ed.; Venice: Javeriana, 1730), 279–81, and F. Conybeare, *Rituale Armenorum* (Oxford: Clarendon, 1905), 438–42. See A. Wenger, SC 50:83–90. For Egypt: Arabic manuscript Museo Borgiano K IV 24 (= Vat, Borgia arab. 22), ed. A. Baumstark, "Eine aegyptische Mess- und Taufliturgie vermutlich des 6. Jahrhunderts," *OC* 1 (1901) 1–45.

C. Lambot, "Les sermons de saint Augustin pour les fêtes de Pâques," in *Mélanges M. Andrieu* (Strasbourg, 1950), 263–78.

B. Botte, "L'interprétation des textes baptismaux," *LMD* no. 32 (1952) 18–39.

A. Chavasse, *Le Sacramentaire gélasien* (Tournai: Desclée, 1958), 156–76.

E. Graffin, "La Catéchèse de Sévère d'Antioche," *OS* 5 (1960) 137–55.

T. Maertens, *Histoire et pastorale du rituel du catéchuménat et du baptême* (Paroisse et Liturgie 56; Bruges: Abbaye Saint-André, 1962).

M. Dujarier, *Le parrainage des adultes aux trois premiers siècles de l'Eglise. Recherche historique sur l'évolution des garanties et des étapes du catéchuménat avant 313* (Parole et mission 4; Paris: Cerf, 1962).

_____, "L'évolution de la pastorale du catéchuménat aux six premiers siècles de l'Eglise," *LMD* no. 71 (1962) 46–61.

A. Hamman, *Baptism: Ancient Liturgies and Patristic Texts*, English ed. T. Halton (Staten Island: Alba House, 1967).

T. M. Finn, *The Liturgy of Baptism in the Baptismal Instructions of St. John Chrysostom* (Studies in Christian Antiquity 15; Washington, D.C.: The Catholic University of America, 1967).

H. M. Riley, *Christian Initiation. A Comparative Study of the Interpretation of the Baptismal Liturgy in the Mystagogical Writings of Cyril of Jerusalem, John Chrysostom, Theodore of Mopsuestia and Ambrose of Milan* (Studies in Christian Antiquity 17; Washington, D.C.: The Catholic University of America, 1974).

G. Kretschmar, "Nouvelles recherches sur l'initiation chrétienne," *LMD* no. 132 (1977) 7–32.

B. Fischer, "Der patristische Hintergrund der drei grossen Johanneischen Taufperikopen . . .," in *I simboli dell'iniziazione cristiana. Atti del I° Congresso internazionale di liturgia* (Studia Anselmiana 87, Analecta liturgica 7; Rome, 1983), 61–79.

P. Verbraken, Le sermon LVIII de S. Augustin pour la tradition du Pater, in *Ecclesia orans* I (1984), 113–32.

S. Poque, au sujet d'une singularité romaine de la "Redditio symboli" (Conf. 8, 2–5) in *Augustinianum* 25 (1985), 113–43.

I. THE FIRST EVIDENCE OF THE CATECHUMENATE

The first attestations of the catechumenate appear at the end of the second century. The spread of Christianity and the influx of candidates required greater care in the formation of those coming to the faith at a time when persecutions on the one side and heterodox sects on the other had already caused not a few apostasies. Tertullian speaks of the "apprenticeship of the hearers" (*auditorum tirocinia*)[20] and rebukes heretics for making no distinction between catechumens and faithful.[21] In Africa we

---

20. Tertullian, *De paenitentia* VI, 14–15, ed J. G. P. Borleffs (CCL 1; Turnhout: Brepols, 1954), 331. In this passage "hearers" are a group parallel to the baptized (*intincti*); they are called both *auditores* and *audientes*, terms that seem to be equivalent to *catechmeni*. See *De corona* II, 1, ed. A. Kroymann (CCL2), 1041.

21. Tertullian, *De praescriptione haereticorum* XLI, ed. R. F. Refoulé (CCL 1), 221: ". . . quis catechumenus, quis fidelis incertum est, pariter adeunt, pariter audiunt, pariter orant." There is reference to Marcion's catechumens in *Adversus Marcionem* V, 7, 6, ed. A. Kroymann (CCL 1), 683.

also find St. Cyprian several times mentioning *catecumeni* or *audientes*.[22] Origen, for his part, calls for a waiting period before initiation; he observes that people do not listen to the teachings of the Church as they would to those of the philosophers, since "Christians previously examine the souls of those who want to hear them" (i.e., who want to be *audientes*, "hearers"). He even seems to distinguish between beginners and candidates proper.[23] In any case, Hippolytus of Rome does speak of these two stages in preparation for baptism: chapters 15–19 of the *Apostolic Tradition* deal with "those who present themselves for the first time in order to hear the word," and only in chapter 20 are "they chosen who will receive baptism."

II. REMOTE PREPARATION: THE CATECHUMENS

1. *Admission to the Catechumenate*

Hippolytus does not speak, any more than Tertullian did, of a rite of admission to the catechumenate. Those who present themselves are simply brought to "teachers," and inquiry is made into their state of life and the trades they follow, since they must renounce anything that would be contrary to the way of life befitting Christ's disciples.[24]

Only toward the end of the fourth century, and in the West, is mention found of a celebration to hallow the first step toward initiation. Augustine makes clear that an essential part of this celebration was the making of the sign of the cross on the person's forehead.[25] In this way Christ began to signify his hold on those who desired to follow after him; at the same time, the action already established a bond with the community that

---

22. See V. Saxer, *Vie liturgique et quotidienne à Carthage au milieu du IIIe siècle* (Studi di antichità cristiana 29; Vatican City: Pont. Istituto di archeologia cristiana, 1969), 107–16.

23. Origen, *Contre Celsum*, III, 59, trans. H. Chadwick (Cambridge: Cambridge University Press, 1953), 168: "At the beginning when we call men to be cured we encourage. . . . But when some of those who have been thus encouraged make progress and show that they have been purified by the Logos, and do all in their power to live better lives, then we call them to our mysteries." — See *Contre Celsum* III, 51 (p. 163); scholars have queried the distinction made here between "those who have not yet received the sign that they have been purified" and "those who, as far as they are able, make it their set purpose to desire nothing other than those things of which Christians approve."

24. *Traditio apostolica* 15–16 (Botte, LQF 39), 32–39.

25. St. Augustine, *In Johannis evangelium* 11, 3, ed. R. Willems (CCL 36; 1954), 111: "If we ask catechumens, 'Do you believe in Christ?,' they will answer 'Yes' and sign themselves with the cross. They already carry the cross of Christ on their foreheads and are not ashamed of their Lord's cross." — See *Serm. Denis* 17, 8, ed. G. Morin, *S. Augustini sermones post Maurinos reperti* (*Miscellanea Agostiniana* I; Rome: Vatican Polyglot Press, 1930), 88–89, etc.

invoked his name.[26] The celebration also included the rite of salt[27] and a laying on of the hand.[28] This liturgy seems to have been a relatively private affair, and the catechist himself could preside at it; this is perhaps why we have hardly any description of it for the East. The ceremony also seems to have been repeated, at least partially, throughout the period of probation of the future baptizands. The Gelasian Sacramentary,[29] which in this area is witness to Roman usage of the fifth century, presents an organized celebration that begins with an exsufflation[30] and ends with a blessing. The prayer formulas speak of the "first elements" or rudiments of doctrine, but also of a new life: *rudimenta fidei . . . gloriae.*

2. Role of the Sponsors

Throughout the entire period of preparation catechumens were aided by seasoned believers who communicated to them their own experience of the Christian life and would attest to their progress before the Church authorities. The faithful who accepted this role were known by various names. Tertullian calls them "sponsors" (*sponsores*),[31] as does Theodore of Mopsuestia at a later time; Egeria calls them "fathers" or "mothers"; John Chrysostom uses the term "spiritual father" (*patēr pneumatikos*) or "receiver" (*anadeichomenos*), this last being often found in the West in its Latin form (*suscepturus, qui suscipit,* etc.). Not infrequently the sponsor was the person who had awakened faith in the soul of the new recruit. In speaking of "those who present themselves for the first time," Hippolytus says: "Those who have brought them give evidence as to whether they are capable of hearing [the word]."[32]

Here is how John Chrysostom speaks to sponsors:

---

26. The forehead is the place where God marks his chosen ones: see Ezek 9:4; Rev 7:3; 9:4; 14:1. In the present context the sign is one by which the Church recognizes its own and by which the world also recognizes them.

27. See B. Botte, "Sacramentum catechumenorum," *QL* 43 (1962) 322–30. The salt is the first food the Church gives and it prefigures the Eucharistic meal. See Augustine, *Confessions* I, 11: ". . . adhuc puer . . . et signabar iam signo crucis eius, et condiebar eius sale."

28. St. Augustine, *De peccatorum meritis et remissione* II, 26 (PL 44:176): ". . . et catechumenos secundum quemdam modum suum per signum Christi et orationem manus impositionis puto sanctificari et quod accipiunt, quamvis non sit corpus Christi, sanctum est tamen et sanctius quam cibi quibus utimur quoniam sacramentum est."

29. *Ge* nos. 285–90 (pp. 42–44). — John the Deacon, *Epistula ad Senarium,* ed. A. Wilmart, *Analecta Reginensia* (ST 59; Vatican City, 1933), 17–78.

30. The exsufflation, which calls to mind the breath of God at work in the creation of man, came to be interpreted as exorcistic, a gesture of contempt for the powers of evil operative in creatures.

31. Tertullian, *De baptismo* 18, 4, ed. J. G. P. Borleffs (CCL 1; Turnhout: Brepols, 1954), 293; ed. and trans. E. Evans, *Tertullian's Homily on Baptism* (London: S.P.C.K., 1964), 39; ed. and French. trans. Refoulé and Drouzy (SC 35; Paris: Cerf, 1952), 92.

32. *Traditio apostolica* 15 (Botte 33).

Consider . . . how those who go surety for someone in a matter of money set up for themselves a greater risk than the one who borrows the money and is liable for it. If the borrower be well disposed, he lightens the burden for his surety; if the dispositions of his soul be ill, he makes the risk a steeper one. . . . If, then, those who go surety for others in a matter of money make themselves liable for the whole sum, those who go surety for others in matters of the spirit and on an account which involves virtue should be much more alert. They ought to show their paternal love by encouraging, counseling, and correcting those for whom they go surety. . . . You, the sponsors, have learned that no slight danger hangs over your head if you are remiss.[33]

3. *Exercises of the Catechumenate*

The very word "hearers" shows the importance of catechesis or instruction during this preparation for initiation. According to Hippolytus, the instructor may be a cleric or a layperson,[34] just as catechists today may be. At the request of a deacon of Carthage, St. Augustine wrote a short work, *De catechizandis rudibus*, as a help in this "instruction of beginners";[35] in it he explains the history of salvation, from the first verse of Genesis down to the present period of Church history ("ab eo quod scriptum est 'In principio fecit Deus caelum et terram' usque ad praesentia tempora Ecclesiae," III, 5), expounding it in such a way that the hearers "by hearing may believe, and by believing may hope, and by hoping may love" (IV, 8). As he points out, this supposes that the instructor takes into account the person's earlier education and real intentions.

In addition, the *audientes* attended the Sunday assemblies, but apart from the faithful and for only the first part of the Mass. They did not yet associate themselves with the prayer of the baptized,[36] although the latter constantly commended them to the Lord. This practice continued even after they had advanced to the next stage of preparation and until the very day of their initiation. Beginning in the fourth century, the East, too, provides numerous attestations of a dismissal of the catechumens after the liturgy of the Word.[37]

---

33. St. John Chrysostom, *Baptismal Instructions* II, 15–16, ed. and annotated P. W. Harkins (Ancient Christian Writers 31; Westminster, Md.: Newman, 1963), 49; text and French trans. in SC 50:141–43.

34. *Traditio apostolica* 19 (Botte 40–41).

35. St. Augustine, *The First Catechetical Instruction*, trans. J. P. Christopher (Ancient Christian Writers 2; Westminster, Md.: Newman, 1946), 24; Latin text in CCL 46, ed. I. B. Bauer (Turnhout: Brepols, 1969), 115–78.

36. *Traditio apostolica* 18 (Botte 40–41): "When the teacher has finished his instruction, the catechumens are to pray apart, separated from the faithful. . . . When they have finished praying, they are not to exchange the kiss of peace, because their kiss is not yet holy."

37. Book VIII of the *Constitutiones Apostolorum* gives two prayers, one for ordinary catechumens and the other for those who have enrolled for baptism; the Euchologion of

4. *Duration of the Catechumenate*

According to Hippolytus, "the catechumens are to hear the word for three years. But if individuals are zealous and apply themselves seriously to the work, they are to be assessed not by length of time but by their behavior."[38] Custom in this matter must have varied from place to place, since the Council of Elvira (Spain) in about 300 speaks of only two years and allows for cases of serious illness in which baptism is to be given sooner.[39]

Serious abuses soon appeared: some persons enrolled in the catechumenate but kept putting off the date of their initiation, sometimes until they were on their deathbeds, because the demands of Christian life made them hesitate. For this reason we find the Fathers often exhorting catechumens not to put off their initiation; they complain that many individuals celebrate Lent every year but never celebrate Easter. Thus St. Augustine begins Lent by urging the *audientes* to become candidates: "Easter is at hand; put down your name for baptism"[40]; or "Yesterday, beloved, I encouraged all of you who are catechumens to put aside every excuse for delaying and to hasten to the bath of rebirth."[41]

III. PROXIMATE PREPARATION: THE "CHOSEN"

The celebration of Easter was regarded as the most appropriate setting for the celebration of initiation. Tertullian says this in so many words,[42] and the same idea is found in Hippolytus, who attests to a more

---

Serapion begins with a prayer and blessing for catechumens (F. X. Funk, *Didascalia et Constitutiones apostolorum* [Paderborn: Schöningh, 1905], 1:478–85; 2:160–63); St. John Chrysostom reports a lengthy prayer of this kind (PG 61:399–404). It seems that in some Western Churches the catechumens used to be dismissed before the gospel, at least during the time of their remote preparation, but this custom was rejected by the Council of Orange of 441, can. 17; ed. C. Munier, *Concilia Galliae* 1 (CCL 148), 83.

38. *Traditio apostolica* 17 (Botte 38–39).

39. Council of Elvira, can. 42; ed. J. Vives, *Concilios visigóticos e hispano-romanos* (España cristiana, Textos 1; Barcelona-Madrid: Instituto Enrique Florez, 1963), 9: "Eos qui ad primam fidem credulitatis accedunt, si bonae fuerint conversationis intra biennium temporum placuit ad babtismi gratiam admitti debere, nisi infirmitate compellente coegerit ratio velocius subvenire periclitanti vel gratiam postulanti."

40. St. Augustine, *Serm.* 132, 1 (PL 38:734–35).

41. St. Augustine, in C. Lambot, "Nouveaux sermons de saint Augustin," *RBén* 62 (1952) 103.

42. Tertullian, *De baptismo* 19, 2 (CCL 1:293–93; SC 35:93–94; Evans 41): although baptism may be celebrated at any time, Easter and Pentecost must be regarded as privileged seasons. By "Pentecost" is meant here the entire fifty-day period beginning on Easter; but once a feast was established on the fiftieth day, it, too, became a special day for baptism. In the East, Epiphany was added to the preferred days, and this custom tended to spread

intense preparation as Easter drew near.[43] When Lent acquired an organized form in the Christian Churches at the beginning of the fourth century, it also took on the aspect of a lengthy retreat before baptism: the whole community advanced with the future initiates, reliving its own journey toward rebirth and the solemn Eucharist during the night of the resurrection.

1. *Registration*

According to the *Apostolic Tradition* the catechumens were presented to the bishop by their sponsors, who assured him of their good dispositions. The ceremony was a declaration of candidacy for the catechumens and an acceptance on the part of the Church that chose them in the name of the Lord. This step became increasingly important once there were more and more "hearers" who did not hasten on to the fountain of grace. Much more than the entrance into the catechumenate, it became the moment when the true disciples of Christ declared themselves. Once the catechumens committed themselves in this way, they were given a new name: *electus* (chosen) at Rome, *competens* (candidate) elsewhere in the West, and *mellōn phōtizesthai* (on the way to being enlightened) or simply *phōtizomenos* in the East generally.

Lent varied in length at different periods and in different Churches, but in any case the passage of the catechumens to this more intense preparation usually took place at the beginning of the period of fasting.[44] Egeria the pilgrim has left us a description of the event as celebrated in Jerusalem around the year 400:

> Names must be given in before the first day of Lent, which means that a presbyter takes down all the names before the start of the eight weeks

---

and, in addition, to include other solemnities in Gaul and Spain; opposition arose, however: Siricius, *Ep. ad Himerium Tarraconensem* (385) (PL 13:1134–35 and 56:555–56); later on, the Council of Auxerres (between 561 and 605), can. 18, in *Concilia Calliae* (CCL 148A), 267: "Non licet absque paschae solemnitatem ullo tempore baptizare nisi illos, quibus mors vicina est."

44. *Traditio apostolica* 20 (Botte 43): "When the choice is made of those who are to receive baptism, inquiry is to be made into their lives: Have they lived virtuously while they were catechumens? Have they honored widows and visited the sick? Have they done good works of all kinds? If those who bring them can give 'Yes' for an answer, these catechumens are to hear the gospel. From the time when they are thus set apart, hands are to be laid on them every day in exorcism."

44. At Milan, registration seems to have taken place at Epiphany: see S. Ambrose, *In Lucam* IV, 76, ed. M. Adriaen (CCL 14; 1957), 134 (where Ambrose is commenting on Luke 5:5: "Master, we toiled all night and took nothing!"): "Et ego, Domine, scio quod nox mihi est, quando non imperas. Nemo adhuc dedit nomen suum, adhuc noctem habeo. Misi iaculum vocis per epifania et adhuc nihil cepi, misi per diem. Exspecto ut iubeas: in verbo tuo laxabo retia."

for which Lent lasts here, as I have told you. Once the presbyter has all the names, on the second day of Lent at the start of the eight weeks, the bishop's chair is placed in the middle of the Great Church, the Martyrium, the presbyters sit in chairs on either side of him, and all the clergy stand. Then one by one those seeking baptism are brought up, men coming with their fathers and women with their mothers. As they come in one by one, the bishop asks their neighbours about them: "Is this person leading a good life? Does he respect his parents? Is he a drunkard or a boaster?" He asks about all the serious human vices. And if his inquiries show him that someone has not committed any of these misdeeds, he himself puts down his name.[45]

The Gelasian Sacramentary tells us that in Rome an acolyte registered the names of the candidates; these were then called by name, and a priest pronounced a prayer: ". . . Enroll in the new covenant the offspring of a new race [subolem noui prolis] so that as children of the promise they may rejoice to receive through grace what they could not have obtained through natural birth."[46]

2. *The Final Lent of the Candidates for Baptism*

The preparation that took place during the weeks before baptism was threefold: catechetical, liturgical, and ascetical. The three aspects were closely interconnected and worked together to form the candidates in a final struggle before their rebirth: "Et exorcismis scrutandi," says St. Leo, "et ieiuniis sanctificandi et frequentius sunt praedicationibus imbuendi."[47]

a) *Catechetical Preparation*

Lent was from the outset regarded as an especially appropriate time for dispensing the word of God more abundantly. Communities were exhorted to attend the frequent, sometimes daily,[48] gatherings at which the bishops commented on the Sacred Scriptures (unless they entrusted this

---

45. *Egeria's Travels*, trans. J. Wilkinson (London: S.P.C.K., 1971), 143–44 (slightly altered); Latin text ed. A. Franceschini and R. Weber (CCL 175; Turnhout: Brepols, 1965), 87.

46. *Ge* nos. 284 and 287 (pp. 42 and 43). The two formularies are not now in their original place; the book was revised to adapt it to the later organization of the catechumenate when the focus was on infants.

47. St. Leo, *Ep.* 16, 6 (PL 54:702): "they must be tested by exorcisms, sanctified by fasts, and instructed by frequent sermons."

48. See *Egeria's Travels* 46 (Wilkinson 144–45): "Those who are preparing for baptism during the season of the Lenten fast go to be exorcized by the clergy first thing in the morning. . . . As soon as that has taken place, the bishop's chair is placed in the Great Church, the Martyrium, and all those to be baptized, the men and the women, sit round him in a circle. . . . During the forty days he goes through the whole Bible" (CCL 175:87; SC 296:306). — For Antioch see below, n. 54. — During Lent Augustine commented at length on an entire book of the Bible, a feat that supposed frequent instructions. In other Churches (as at Rome) the instructions doubtless followed a more relaxed schedule.

responsibility to priests selected for their competence). The "chosen" took part with the faithful in these gatherings that, in some Churches, began or ended with rites especially geared to the candidates, as we shall see further on. But the candidates were also brought together for catecheses reserved specifically to them; these instructions covered all the articles of the Creed. When this teaching was completed, and on days that differed according to local customs, the *traditio symboli* took place, that is, the symbol of faith (the Creed) was "handed over" to them; they were to learn it by heart and be able to recite it publicly at the end of Lent; they would then "give back" the Creed (the *redditio symboli*), that is, they would profess their personal acceptance of the faith that had been handed on to them. As St. Augustine said:

> In eight days' time you will give back what you have received today. . . . They have given you the symbol itself so that you may keep it carefully. Let no one be afraid; let fear not keep anyone from giving it back. Trust us: we are your fathers and do not carry the schoolmaster's cane or birch. A person may be mistaken about a word, provided he does not err in the faith.[49]

The catechetical instructions thus did not convey purely intellectual teaching; still less were they a scholastic exercise. They were incorporated into the celebration. Cyril of Jerusalem would allow his listeners to copy down his instructions only if they did so in the presence of God.[50] The commentary on the Creed was usually followed by one on the Our Father; the latter, too, was the object of a *traditio* and a *redditio*.

In Roman practice this Lent of the "chosen" was punctuated by three especially important gatherings that were celebrated on Sundays. On these three days the liturgy of the word consisted of passages regarded as basic to instruction for baptism: the gospel of the Samaritan woman (John 4:16-42) with the incident at the spring of Meribah (Num 20:1-13), the gospel of the man born blind (John 9:1-41) with the exhortation of Isaiah, "Wash yourselves; make yourselves clean" (Isa 1:16-19), and the gospel of the resurrection of Lazarus (John 11:1-45) with the story of Elijah restoring life to the son of the widow with whom he was staying (1 Kgs 17:17-24). The homiletic tradition was skilled in drawing out the connections between these pericopes and gradually leading the candidates for initiation into the mystery of their rebirth. The "living water" that Jesus promised at the Well of Jacob and that springs from the rock symbolizing Christ (1 Cor 10:4); the water of Siloam, whose name ("sent") echoes that of

---

49. St. Augustine, *Serm Guelf.* 1, 11 (PLS 1:543).

50. At least this is the warning that ends the *procatechesis* in some manuscripts (PG 32:364).

the Savior and from which light comes for those who were dwelling in darkness; the water of the Jordan, by which Naaman was cleansed of his leprosy when he bathed in it at the prophet's command: these are waters that become capable of giving life after death, as to Lazarus at Bethany and even to the pagan nations represented by the widow of Zarephath.

b) *Liturgical Preparation*

In the Latin tradition these moments of more intense Lenten preparation were called "scrutinies," a term that suggests a testing in two senses: testing by a struggle to face and overcome obstacles, and testing by an examination that ascertains and clarifies the dispositions of the candidates.[51] Hippolytus writes: "The bishop is to exorcise each of them to see whether he or she is pure."[52] From the fourth century on, formulas of exorcism acquired a prominent place in the prebaptismal celebrations. They are mentioned by Egeria for Jerusalem,[53] Theodore of Mopsuestia and Chrysostom for Antioch,[54] pseudo-canon 7 of the Council of Constantinople in 381,[55] the letter of Pope Siricius (384–95) to Himerius of Tarragona,[56] Augustine in Africa, and so on. As Augustine puts it, "Exorcismi sacramento quasi molebamini."[57] Exorcism operated in a quasi-sacramental manner, and it prepared the *competentes* for their initiation as the grinding of the wheat constitutes the first stage in the making of bread. It did not of itself effect the forgiveness of sins, which came through the initiation proper, but it did commit the candidates to a process of conversion that they would not be able to bring about by their own resources. Christian life is a struggle against evil, and one must participate in it by enter-

---

51. John the Deacon in his letter to Senarius lays an inordinate stress on this second element, so that in his view the scrutiny means primarily the giving back of the Creed, and he adduces various purposes for this action in order to justify three sessions. Most of the ancient authors strike a balance between the two elements.

52. *Traditio apostolica* 20 (Botte 42).

53. See above, n. 48.

54. St. John Chrysostom, *Baptismal Instructions* II, 12–13 (Harkins 47): "You must understand why, after this daily instruction, we send you along to hear the words of the exorcists. . . . They cleanse your minds by these awesome words, putting to flight every device of the wicked one and making your hearts worthy of the royal presence. . . . This rite does away with all difference and distinction of rank." For Theodore see below at n. 59.

55. H. T. Bruns, *Canones apostolorum et conciliorum* 1 (Berlin: Reimer, 1839), 23 (with regard to those heretics who must be rebaptized): "We exorcize (*exorkizomen*) them with a triple exsufflation on face and ears." This canon of the Council of Constantinople is not authentic; it was probably from the pen of a fifth-century patriarch.

56. Siricius, *Ep. ad Himerium* 2 (PL 13:1135): ". . . his electis qui ante quadraginta vel eo amplius dies nomen dederint et exorcismis, quotidianis orationibus atque ieiuniis fuerint expiati."

57. St. Augustine, *Serm*, 227, in SC 116:236.

ing into the victorious struggle of Christ in his passion. Renunciation of the "old self" means distancing oneself from a world branded by sin, the world of the "prince of darkness." This accounts for the references and even solemn charges to the demon that acquired an increasingly large place in these formulas. The chief emphasis nonetheless was on the action of the Savior. St. John Chrysostom characterizes this action nicely when he compares Christ with an impartial judge:

> In the Olympic combats the judge stands impartially aloof from the combatants, favoring neither the one nor the other, but awaiting the outcome. He stands in the middle because his judgment is impartial. But in our combat with the devil, Christ does not stand aloof but is wholly on our side. . . . He anointed us as we went into the combat, but He fettered the devil . . . to keep him shackled hand and foot for the combat. But if I happen to slip, He stretches out His hand, lifts me from my fall, and sets me on my feet again.[58]

The rite itself could even be too expressive. Theodore of Mopsuestia says, "the employment of people known as 'exorcists' is indispensable. When a case is being argued, the accused must stand in silence. You keep your arms extended in the posture of prayer and your eyes lowered. For this reason you doff your outer garment and go barefoot. You stand on haircloth."[59]

The Gelasian Sacramentary contains the liturgy for the three scrutinies. The text that has come down to us has been altered, but it still enables us to reconstruct the practice of the fifth century. The Sacramentary contains two series of formularies, one for men, the other for women, each with a presidential prayer, an exorcism spoken by acolytes, and an imposition of hands on the "chosen." In the first of the three gatherings the opening prayer calls upon "the God of Abraham, Isaac, and Jacob," a title that is uncommon in the Roman tradition but is here attributable to the mention of the Exodus: the advance of the candidates to baptism is compared to the journey of the children of Israel—to whom the Lord sent his "holy angel" (Exod 23:20)—to the Promised Land.[60] The second

---

58. St. John Chrysostom, *Baptismal Instructions* III, 9 (Harkins 58).

59. Theodore of Mopsuestia, *Homélies catéchétiques* 12, ed. and trans. R. Tonneau and R. Devreesse (ST 145; Vatican City, 1949), 322–23. See St. Augustine, *Serm.* 216, 10 (PL 38:1082): "Et vos quidem cum scrutaremini . . . non estis induti cilicio, sed tamen vestri pedes in eodem mystice constiterunt."

60. *Ge* no. 291 (p. 44): ". . . Deus qui Moisi famulo tuo in monte Synai apparuisti et filios Israhel de terra Aegypti eduxisti, deputans eis angelum pietatis tuae, qui custodiret eos die ac nocte; te quaesumus, domine, ut mittere digneris sanctum angelum tuum, ut similiter custodiat et hos famulos tuos et perducat eos ad gratiam baptismi tui." Trans. in *Collectio rituum*, ed. W. J. Schmitz (Milwaukee: Bruce, 1964), 85: "O God of Abraham, God of Isaac, God of Jacob, you appeared on Mount Sinai to your servant, Moses; you led the children of Israel out of Egypt, graciously appointing an angel to guard them day and night. We ask you, Lord, to send your holy angel from heaven to guard in the same way your servants, N. and N., and to lead them to the grace of your baptism."

has a still more unusual beginning and is based on Phil 2:10-11.[61] The exorcism is the same for men and women; it is addressed to the devil, whose condemnation it recalls, since according to the gospel "the ruler of this world is already "judged."[62] The cross is the sign of Christ's victory: when set on the foreheads of the servants of God it establishes as it were a boundary that evil may not cross:

> Therefore, accursed devil, acknowledge your condemnation, and pay homage to the living and true God; pay homage to Jesus Christ, his Son, and to the Holy Spirit, and depart from these servants of God, N. and N.,[63] for Jesus Christ, our God and Lord, has called them to his holy grace and to the font of baptism. Accursed devil, never dare to desecrate this sign of the holy cross, that we are tracing on their foreheads.[64]

For each scrutiny the Sacramentary also gives a Mass formulary. A prayer introduces the entire celebration and another, the same on all three Sundays, effects a transition between exorcisms and Eucharist. This second prayer asks that God would bestow on "his servants, these men and women," the light of his wisdom, so that they may be sanctified, have "true knowledge," and keep "firm hope, right judgment, and irreproachable doctrine, in order that they may be ready to receive grace." The mystery of the Lord's body and blood, which the "chosen" have not yet received, will win for them these dispositions, the list of which echoes Pauline themes: "firmam spem, consilium rectum, doctrinam sanctam."[65]

---

61. *Ibid.*, no. 293 (pp. 44–45): "Deus caeli, deus terrae, deus angelorum, deus archangelorum, deus prophetarum, deus martyrum, deus omnium bene viventium, deus cui omnis lingua confitetur caelestium terrestrium et infernorum; te invoco, domine, ut has famulas tuas perducere et custodire digneris ad gratiam baptismi tui." Trans. Schmitz (n. 60), 103–5: "O God of the heavens and the earth, God of the angels and the archangels, God of the patriarchs and the prophets, God of the apostles and the martyrs, God of the confessors and the virgins, God of all who live holy lives, God whom every tongue confesses . . . of those in heaven, on earth, and under the earth: I beg you, Lord, to protect these your servants, N. and N., and to lead them to the grace of your baptism."

62. John 16:11.

63. This manner of speaking did not mean that the catechumens were thought of as possessed. The early liturgical books had special prayers for catechumens who were considered to be under demonic influence; this shows that there was no confusion.

64. *Ge* no. 92 (p. 44), trans. Schmitz (n. 60) 87. — The formularies for the other two scrutinies are incomplete; the prayers are missing, except the one for women at the second gathering; this refers to Susanna "who was rescued from a false accusation" (Dan 13:1-62) (no. 295; p. 45). The exorcism pronounced over men on this second occasion is lengthier (no. 294; p. 45); in it the Spirit is said to thwart the trickery of Satan and turn the baptized into temples. The exorcism over women is repeated from the preceding Sunday, as are those of the third scrutiny, although with variants: the one over men refers to Christ holding Peter's hand so that the latter may walk on the water (Matt 14:38), that over women to the man born blind and the raising of Lazarus (nos. 296–97; p. 45); the first of these two references in the exorcism of women perhaps belonged originally to the preceding Sunday.

65. 2 Cor 1:7; Titus 1:1–2; 2 Tim 4:3; etc.

Their names will therefore be read out in the intercessions, but not in the *Memento*, since they are as yet not capable of "offering" themselves; in the *Memento* their godparents will be mentioned, because these make offerings for the candidates.[66]

All these prayers make it clear that the choice of the candidates for baptism is made both by God and by the Church ("electis nostris, electos tuos");[67] the *electio* even embraces without distinction those who will be reborn and those who have already attained to the new birth ("respice ad electionem tuam . . . et regenerandos . . . et renatos").[68] Because of the scrutinies the postulants are already subject to the action of "sacramenta aeternitatis," but they have yet to be made "ready" ("aptandos")[69] for attaining to the "confession of the glory" of God ("ad confessionem tuae laudis accedere") and recovering their ancient dignity, that which the first parents had in paradise ("dignitati pristinae . . . reformentur").[70] When they have received the symbol (creed) which is "the first fruits of faith" ("quos fidei christianae primitiis imbuisti")[71] they are to some extent already "instructed in the holy mysteries" ("sanctis edocti mysteriis").[72] However, they must still attain to the gift of "grace," a term that, whether or not it is accompanied by descriptions or additions that perhaps were not all part of the primitive redaction, here signifies initiation. Those who are "earthly" through birth ("generatione terreni") will be made "heavenly" through rebirth ("regeneratione caelestes").[73] This rebirth is the result of the spiritual fruitfulness that makes the Church grow ("Ecclesiam tuam spirituali fecunditate multiplica"),[74] for the Church is wholly involved in this adventure of the "chosen": "Let your people come together, Lord,

---

66. *Ge* nos. 195–97 (p. 33): "Memento, domine, famulorum famularumque tuarum, qui electos tuos suscepturi sunt ad sanctam gratiam baptismi tui, et omnium circumadstantium (*Et tacis. Et recitantur nomina virorum et mulierum qui ipsos infantes suscepturi sunt. Et intras:*) Quorum tibi fides cognita. . . . — Hanc igitur oblationem, domine, ut propitius suscipias deprecamur quam tibi offerimus pro famulis et famulabus tuis quos ad aeternam vitam et beatum gratiae tuae dinumerare elegere atque vocare dignatus es, per Christum. (*Et recitantur nomina electorum. Postquem recensita fuerint dicis:*) Hos domine fonte baptismatis innovandos spiritus tui munere ad sacramentorum tuorum plenitudine poscimus praeparai."

67. *Ibid.*, nos. 193 and 195 (pp. 32 and 33).

68. *Ibid.*, no. 257 (p. 39).

69. *Ibid.*, no. 198 (p. 33).

70. *Ibid.*, no. 193 (p. 32).

71. *Ibid.*, no. 255 (p. 39).

72. *Ibid.*, no. 254 (p. 39).

73. These are the points developed in the presentation of the Creed to the chosen; the address is certainly old and some scholars see St. Leo as its source: ". . . Vos, itaque, dilectissimi, ex vetere homine in novum reformamini, et de carnalibus spiritales, de terrenis incipitis esse caelestes" (no. 316; p. 50).

74. *Ibid.*, no. 225 (p. 36).

and let them, being wholly submissive to you, be safeguarded against all unrest; let them give themselves fervently to the joys of their salvation and in their kindness pray for those still to be reborn."[75]

c) *Ascetical Preparation*

Even before the catechumenate reached an organized stage, fasting was already regarded as a preparation for baptism, as we saw in the *Didache* and St. Justin;[76] in these writings it was proposed that other Christians fast with the candidates. The same custom is found in the third century in both East and West. Tertullian, for example, speaks of prayer, fasting, genuflections, vigils, and the confession of past sins.[77] Once Lent was established, asceticism became an essential element of it, and the *competentes* submitted to it no less than the faithful: the former were urged to abstain from wine, food, and the baths, to practice nocturnal prayer, continence if they were married, the sharing of their goods with the poor, and so on. In the case of the candidates these observances were linked to the exorcisms,[78] to which, according to St. Augustine, they were an indispensable complement:

> What I, invoking the name of your Redeemer, am doing for you, do you complete by a careful examination and by compunction of heart. I resist the wiles of the old Enemy by prayers and complaints to God; do you continue steadfast in your petitions and in the compunction of your heart so that you may be rescued from the power of darkness and transferred into the kingdom of God's brightness. This is now your work; this, your task.[79]

The time before baptism is, moreover, in the words of John Chrysostom,[80] a "school for training and exercise" (*palaistra kai gymnasion*) for the struggle that is Christian life. Far from ending with initiation, this struggle will, on the contrary, require of those who have become

---

75. *Ibid.*, no. 256 (p. 39).

76. See above, pp. 15-16.

77. Tertullian, *De baptismo* 20, 1 (CCL 1:294): "Ingressuros baptismum orationibus crebris, ieuniis et geniculationibus et pervigiliis orare oportet cum confessione omnium retro delictorum." Evans 41: "Those who are on the point of entering upon baptism ought to pray, with frequent prayers, fastings, bendings of the knee, and all-night vigils, along with the confession of all their former sins."

78. See Siricius, above, n. 66. — Augustine, *Serm.* 227 (SC 116:236): "Ieunii humiliatione et exorcismi sacramento, quasi molebamini." — St. Leo, above, n. 58.

79. St. Augustine, *Serm.* 216, 6 (PL 38:1080), trans. in Hamman, *Baptism*, 209. In the same homily Augustine establishes a similar connection with his instructions: "I instruct by discourses; do you advance in good works. I scatter the teaching of the word; do you render the fruit of faith" (*Serm.* 216, 1 [PL 38:1077]; Hamman 205).

80. St. John Chrysostom, *Baptismal Instructions* III, 8 (Harkins 58).

"the light of the world" a sustained watchfulness lest they fall back under the control of the evil one.[81]

§3. The Rites of Baptism

I. THE FINAL PREPARATION

BIBLIOGRAPHY

P. Lundberg, *La typologie baptismale dans l'ancienne Eglise* (Uppsala: Lundequist, 1942).

J. Daniélou, *The Bible and the Liturgy* (Notre Dame: University of Notre Dame Press, 1956), 35–113.

J. Rogues, "La prefáce consécratoire du chrême," *LMD* no. 49 (1957) 35–49.

J. Daniélou, "The Sacraments and the History of Salvation," in *The Liturgy and the Word of God* (Collegeville: The Liturgical Press, 1959), 21–32.

H. Kirsten, *Die Taufabsage. Eine Untersuchung zur Gestalt and Geschichte der Taufe nach den altkirchlichen Taufliturgien* (Berlin: Verlagsanstalt, 1960).

L. de Bruyne, "L'initiation chrétienne et ses reflets dans l'art paléochrétien," *RevSR* 36 (1962) 27–86.

L. L. Mitchell, *Baptismal Anointing* (London: S.P.C.K, 1966).

E. J. Lengeling, "Vom Sinn der präbaptismalen Salbung," in *Mélanges B. Botte* (Louvain: Mont César, 1972), 326–57.

G. Winkler, "The Original Meaning of the Prebaptismal Anointing and Its Implications," *Worship* 52 (1978) 24–25.

S. Brock, "Die Taufordines der altsyrischen Kirche, insbesondere die Salbung der Taufliturgie," *Liturgisches Jahrbuch* 28 (1978) 11–18.

B. Botte, "Le symbolisme de l'huile et de l'onction," *QL* 62 (1981) 196–208.

B. Bobrinskoy, "Onction baptismale et Trinité dans la tradition syrienne ancienne," in *Mens concordet voci. Pour Mgr A. G. Martimort* (Paris: Desclée, 1983), 559–68.

This series of rites may be regarded as the conclusion and climax of the Lenten preparation. It included in particular the *redditio symboli* and sometimes that of the Our Father: on this occasion each of the *competentes* publicly proclaimed the faith he or she had received from the Church by reciting before the assembly the formulas previously commented on and "handed over" during the instructions. Most of these ceremonies, however, were older than Lent itself and are attested as early as the third century, especially by Tertullian and Hippolytus. They took place in the hours before the great vigil, during which initiation itself was to be celebrated; but, perhaps because of the large number of candidates, there was a growing tendency to perform at an earlier hour or on an earlier day those ceremonies that could easily be shifted since they did not require the com-

---

81. Matt 5:14; see Chrysostom, *Baptismal Instructions* IV, 17–22 (Harkins 72–74).

plete nakedness needed in the baptistery. Thus there was a liturgical assembly at Rome on Saturday morning,[82] at Antioch and Constantinople on Friday at the hour of Christ's death,[83] and, in other places, perhaps as early as the preceding Sunday.

Allowance must therefore be made for a rather wide diversity between Churches, and it will be indispensable, at least for the more important points, to note the provenance of the information gathered.

1. *The "Ephphetha"*

The first rite we meet, but only at Milan and Rome (and later on in Spain), is described as follows by St. Ambrose, who calls it the *apertio aurium*: "The priest touched your ears and nostrils . . . and said: *Effeta*, which is a Hebrew word meaning 'be opened.' "[84] Like the deaf mute of the gospel (Mark 7:32-35), the future initiates open their ears to the words addressed to them in the liturgy and receive the ability to "speak of the heavenly mysteries." Ambrose justifies the substitution of nostrils for mouth by a concern for propriety in the baptism of women; he refers to the breath of divine life and the spiritual perfume exhaled by those who renounce the scents of the world. He does not say that oil is used in making this gesture, as it was in the Roman practice reported by John the Deacon at the beginning of the sixth century,[85] or saliva, as attested at a later date by the Gelasian Sacramentary, which accompanies the action with a solemn charge to the devil.[86] Is this rite to be linked to the signing of the forehead, ears, and nostrils of which Hippolytus speaks in connection with the final exorcism?[87] If so, there would subsequently have been a fusion with the prebaptismal anointing (John the Deacon treats of the two rites at the same time), before the reference to the gospel caused the introduction of saliva. In like manner, the mouth and not the nostrils was touched in the *Ephphetha* rite according to the rubric in the Spanish *Liber ordinum*, where again there was question of an anointing.[88]

---

82. *Ge*, p. 67: "Sabbatorum die, mane. . . ."

83. St. John Chrysostom, third instruction in Papadopoulos-Kerameus, *Varia graeca sacra* (St. Petersburg, 1909), 171, and *Ordo* of Constantinople, above, n. 19.

84. St. Ambrose, *De sacramentis* I, 2-3, ed. B. Botte (SC 25bis; Paris: Cerf, 1959), 60; *De mysteriis* I, 3 (*ibid.*, 156).

85. John the Deacon, *Epistula ad Senarium* 4, 5 (Wilmart, *Analecta Reginensia* 173): "tanguntur sanctificationis oleo aures eorum, tanguntur et nares."

86. *Ge* no. 420 (p. 68): "Tanges ei nares et aures de sputo. . . . Effeta quod est adaperire in odorem suavitatis. Tu autem effugare diabole, adpropinquavit enim iudicium Dei."

87. *Traditio apostolica* 20 (Botte 44).

88. *Liber ordinum*, ed. M. Férotin (Monumenta Ecclesiae liturgica 5; Paris: Didot, 1904), col. 27: ". . . tangit ei sacerdos de oleo benedicto os et aures. . . . Effeta, effeta, cum Spiritu Sancto in odorem suavitatis, effeta. Bene omnia fecit: et surdos facit audire et mutos loqui."

2. *Renunciation of the Devil and Acceptance of Jesus Christ*

Unlike the *Ephphetha*, the renunciation of Satan was practiced in all the Churches. Hippolytus has it take place in the baptistery after the candidates have removed their clothing.[89] In Tertullian it seems to be repeated: "bis idolis renuntiamus": "As we are about to enter the water, on that very spot, and a little earlier in front of the assembly, while the bishop imposes his hand, we bear witness that we renounce the devil."[90] Later on, the rite was moved forward and often made part of an earlier gathering.

The *competens* renounces (*renuntio, abrenuntio, apotassomai*) the demon or devil or Satan (sometimes even addressing him, as in Hippolytus, Chrysostom, and Cyril), and his works (*operibus, ergois*) and seductions (*pompis, pompē*).[91] The East added "and his worship (*latreia*)," while "and his angels (*angelis, aggelois*)" is also found, as in Africa, Gaul, and Spain. These various expressions are intended to sum up all that can turn human beings away from the gospel: from the worship of false gods and all the superstitions of paganism to the lure of the theater, the games in the circus, and the deceptive delights offered by society, and including the favorite philosophies of the day and the doctrines of the heresiarchs and fomentors of schism. When the candidates for baptism answered with a firm *abrenuntio* to the questions addressed to them, as was the general practice in the West, or when they recited the formula whispered to them by a deacon or other minister, as was the most common usage in the East, they were experiencing a poignant moment in their spiritual journey: they were ending one way of looking at human life as they turned from the world and its pleasures ("saeculo et voluptatibus"), as it is put in the text supplied by Ambrose. A covenant was being sealed, a kind of oath being pronounced, the solemn nature of which was underscored by the rites, for the future initiates often stood or knelt on haircloth while wearing only their undergarments. In some Churches (Jerusalem, for example) they extended their hand and faced the West, "the region of darkness" and, immediately after the renunciation, turned their backs on it, thus providing an image of *conversio* in the most rigorous sense of this term.

In the patriarchate of Antioch, the renunciation (*apotaxis*) was followed by an acceptance of the Lord (*syntaxis*) and a profession of faith: "I join myself to Christ," or, according to Theodore of Mopsuestia, "I commit myself by vow, I believe and am baptized in the name of the Father, of the Son, and of the Holy Spirit."[92] It was at this point in the Roman

---

89. *Traditio apostolica* 21 (Botte 46).

90. Tertullian, *De spectaculis* 13, 1, ed. E. Dekkers (CCL 1), 239. — *De corona* 3, 2, ed. A. Kroymann (CCL 2), 1042.

91. See J. H. Waszink, "Pompa diaboli," *Vigiliae christianae* 1 (1947) 13–41.

92. Theodore of Mopsuestia, *Homélies catéchétiques* XIII, 14–15 (Tonneau-Devreesse 390–93).

ordo that the Creed was proclaimed.[93] If the candidates faced East during it (as they did in the liturgy of Jerusalem), it was in order to receive the light of Easter but also because "the paradise that God established in the East and from which our first ancestor was driven for his disobedience, is opening its gates."[94]

This last is a symbol we shall come across again. Here it expresses those dimensions of rebirth that are inaccessible to even the most generous efforts of the human will.

3. *The Oil and the Prebaptismal Anointings*

a) *The "Holy Oils"*

The use of oil in the liturgy of baptism is attested with certainty from the third century on. Some Churches, like the African or those of the East, except for Egypt and Jerusalem,[95] seem to have been familiar only with a kind of oil usually called *chrisma* by the Latins and *myron* by the Greeks. This last word refers beyond any possible doubt to a fragrant substance. In other Churches, however, there is mention of another oil: the "oil of exorcism" as distinct from the "oil of thanksgiving" in the *Apostolic Tradition*; the *eporkiston elaion* as distinct from *myron* in the Jerusalem catecheses; the *aleimma* (ointment) alongside the *chrisma* in the Euchologion of Serapion (the term used at times instead of the simple *elaion* or *oleum benedictum*).[96]

According to Hippolytus, "at the time set for baptism," the "oil of exorcism" was "exorcized" by the bishop, who also "gave thanks" over "the oil of thanksgiving."[97] The term *eucharistia* was understood as a consecration that, in Jerusalem, was effected by an epicletic prayer comparable to the epiclesis of the Mass: "Just as after the epiclesis of the Holy Spirit the bread of the Eucharist is no longer simple bread but the body of Christ, so also after the epiclesis this perfume is no longer perfume pure and simple

93. *Ge* no. 422 (p. 68).

94. Cyril of Jerusalem, *Catéchèses mystagogiques* I, 9, ed. A. Piédagnel, trans. P. Paris (SC 126; Paris: Cerf, 1966), 98. See Gen 2:8.

95. The third ritual in *Constitutiones Apostolorum* VII, 42 and 45 (Funk 1:448 and 450) seems to distinguish *elaion* from *myron*; although the ritual shows the general characteristics of the Syrian Church, it is in fact a compilation, and this detail may come from non-Syrian sources.

96. Note that Innocent I, in 416, uses *chrisma* as a name both for the oil with which neophytes were anointed and for the oil of the sick; see R. Cabié, *Lettre du pape Innocent Ier à Decentius de Gubbio* (Bibliothèque du RHE 58; Louvain: Publications universitaires, 1973), 24 and 30.

97. *Traditio apostolica* 21 (Botte 46).

or, one might say, ordinary perfume but a gift of Christ that through the presence of the Holy Spirit has become an instrument of his divinity."[98]

We may well think this analogy somewhat too narrowly conceived. In any event, we frequently find canonical rules specifically reserving confection of chrism to the bishop. At Rome, the rite was celebrated during the pope's final Mass before the Easter Vigil, that is, the Mass of Thursday. There, between the communion of the pope and the communion of the congregation, after a triple exsufflation on the combined oil and balm, the consecratory formula was pronounced.[99] After calling to mind the olive branch that had foretold the end of the flood, the prayer dwelt on the idea of olive oil as giving brightness to the face and a glow to the eyes of those who would receive a new birth in the baptismal waters. It also recalled the priestly anointing of Aaron and contemplated the anointing of Jesus by the Spirit at his baptism in the Jordan. It then turned to petition as it looked forward to the participation of Christians in this spiritual anointing of their Lord and asked God that the power of his Spirit might mingle with the chrism that bears the very name of Christ, so that the baptized might be consecrated as priests, kings, prophets, and martyrs and through their new birth might already receive eternal life and heavenly glory.[100] During a Eucharist on the morning of that same day (Thursday) the *oleum exorcizatum* was blessed by the priests attached to the titular churches.[101]

b) *The Anointing with the Oil of "Exorcism"*

At Jerusalem, everything up to this point took place in "the outer building";[102] those to be initiated now entered into the "Holy of Holies." At Milan, in like manner, the *Ephphetha* is followed by mention of entrance into the baptistery. The iconography of baptisteries, which often shows the shepherd surrounded by his flock in a setting of trees, flowers, and fountains, suggests a new paradisal symbolism behind the entrance of the candidates. Thus Gregory of Nyssa says: "Catechumen, you are outside of Paradise; you share the exile of Adam, our first father. But now the gate is opening. Enter the place from which you departed."[103]

According to the Jerusalem catecheses, as soon as the "chosen" had been brought in and had removed their clothing, they were "anointed with

98. Cyril of Jerusalem, *Catéchèses mystagogiques* III, 3 (SC 126:124).

99. *Ge* nos. 388–90 (pp. 61–63).

100. See A. Chavasse, "A Rome le jeudi-saint au VIIIe siècle d'après un vieil ordo," *RHE* 50 (1955) 23–24; see *OR* XXIV, nos. 8–18 (Andrieu, *OR* 3:289–301).

101. *Gr* no. 335 (1:173–74). (The Gelasian has a revised text.)

102. Cyril of Jerusalem, *Catéchèses mystagogiques* I, 11 (SC 126:102); see *ibid.*, I, 2 (SC 126:84): "eis ton proaulion tou baptismatos."

103. Gregory of Nyssa, *Adversus eos qui differunt baptismum oratio* (PG 46:417).

exorcised oil from the hair on the top of their head to the lower extremities. . . . This anointing puts to flight every trace of hostile power."[104] "We have reached the fountain," says St. Ambrose; "you have entered and been anointed . . . as an athlete of Christ, as though you were about to do combat in this world."[105] This unguent was truly that with which fighters rubbed themselves so that they might be more nimble in the competitions. But there was (in Cyril) another symbolism as well: "You have been cut from the wild olive tree and grafted onto the true olive tree." This allusion to Rom 11:17-24 was a reminder that the Christian struggle brings into play not only human powers but also those of Christ, who enters the members of his body like sap into a graft; such was the significance of this liturgical act that was, as it were, the finest jewel in the exorcisms. It was found in those Churches that made use of the two kinds of oil, and especially at Rome, from the *Apostolic Tradition*[106] down to the latest documents, although these show only vestiges of the complete anointing: an anointing on the breast according to John the Deacon,[107] on the breast and between the shoulders according to the Gelasian Sacramentary.[108] As for the Church of Egypt, the Euchologion of Serapion has preserved a prayer that reads:

> We apply this ointment to the men and women who draw near to this divine rebirth, and we pray that our Lord Jesus Christ will fill them with a power that heals and strengthens and that he will manifest himself through this anointing to rescue their souls, bodies, and spirits from every trace of sin and wickedness and every compromise with the devil. May he graciously grant them forgiveness, so that, dead to their sins, they may live for justice (1 Pet 2:24). Reformed by this ointment, purified by the bath, and renewed by the Spirit, may they be able in the future to overcome the hostile powers that assail them and all the powers of this life.[109]

c) *The Anointing with Perfumed Oil*

In the patriarchate of Antioch there was also a prebaptismal anointing, but this time with oil alone. St. John Chrysostom calls it *myron pneumatikon*. Syriac documents generally speak of "the oil of anointing," as,

---

104. Cyril of Jerusalem, *Catéchèses mystagogiques* II, 3 (SC 126:106–8).
105. St. Ambrose, *De sacramentis* 1, 4 (SC 25bis:62): "Venimus ad fontem, ingressus es, unctus es. . . . Unctus es quasi athleta Christi, quasi luctam huius saeculi luctaturus."
106. *Traditio apostolica* 21 (Botte 46): "After each person has made the renunciation, he [the priest] anoints him or her with the oil of exorcism, saying: 'Let every evil spirit depart from you.'"
107. John the Deacon, *Ep. ad Senarium* 6 (Wilmart 24).
108. *Ge* no. 421 (p. 68), just before the renunciation of Satan.
109. *Euchologium Serapionis* 22 (Funk 2:184). This prayer probably followed the one entitled "After the renunciation of the devil."

for example, the translation preserved in the *Homilies* of Theodore of Mopsuestia, but also in the *Didascalia of the Apostles*, since this anointing was practiced in the eastern parts of Syria as well.[110]

This last-named document, which doubtless goes back to the first half of the third century, instructs the bishop as follows: "As of old the kings and priests were anointed in Israel, do thou in like manner, with the imposition of hand, anoint the head of those who receive baptism, whether of men or of women"; this anointing of the head is followed by a complete anointing that, in the case of female candidates, is performed by deaconesses.[111] This rite seems to have been very closely connected with the baptismal immersion. The same close connection seems to emerge from the writings of St. Ephraem in the following century and in approximately the same part of the world. He develops the reference to the Old Testament more fully; the kingly and priestly anointing is, as it were, the brandmark that the Spirit places on his sheep so that he may recognize them (a meaning nicely brought out by the gesture of the celebrant on the heads of the candidates). The anointing is at the same time, however, a source of healing and cleansing, although it will produce its effect only when contact with the waters of baptism takes place, for the oil then impregnates the entire body of the person who descends into the pool. The baptized are thus united with Christ as he rises from the dwelling place of the dead.[112] Narsai of Nisibis, at the end of the fifth century, repeats the image of the branded sheep and develops that of the armor donned for exercise in the spiritual arena; the latter image is mingled with that of the seal that

---

110. Like the *Didascalia*, the apocryphal *Acts* from the same region have only the anointing before baptism. The texts have been collected by R. H. Connolly in his *The Liturgical Homilies of Narsai* (Texts and Studies 8/1; Cambridge, 1909), xlii–xlix. — See A. Raes, "Où se trouve la confirmation dans le rite syrien-oriental?" *OS* 1 (1956) 239–46.

111. *Didascalia Apostolorum*, ed. R. H. Connolly, *Didascalia Apostolorum. The Syriac Version Translated and Accompanied by the Verona Latin Fragments* (Oxford: Clarendon, 1929), 146–47: "When women go down into the water, those who go down into the water ought to be anointed by a deaconess with the oil of anointing." Latin trans., Funk 1:210.

112. St. Ephraem, *Sermo de domino nostro*, ed. Th. J. Lamy, *S. Ephraem Syri hymni et sermones* 1 (Mechlin, 1982), 263: "[The Spirit] used oil to put his mark on priests and kings. With oil the Holy Spirit puts his seal on his sheep. . . . When persons are anointed and signed in baptism, they are anointed with holy oil so that the body may be purified . . . for baptism becomes as it were a second womb for them. . . . Priests assist this womb in giving birth. Anointing precedes the birth. . . . Oil, the source of healing, is applied to the body, which is the source of sicknesses, because oil destroys sins as the flood did. . . . The oil lovingly accompanies the person who is immersed. . . . Oil, which by its nature penetrates within, unites itself to the body that is immersed, and when it is immersed it brings back from the depths a rich treasure. Christ, who by his nature is incapable of dying, put on a mortal body, immersed himself, and brought from the waters the treasure of life which our first parents had possessed."

is set upon the body refashioned by the oil and the water and shines out to be seen by angels and human beings.[113]

At Antioch we find this same anointing begun by the bishop and completed by another minister, but these are two stages separated in time. The first of them concludes the renunciation of Satan and the acceptance of Christ:

> As if you were a combatant chosen for the spiritual arena, the priest [= the bishop] anoints you on the forehead with the oil of the spirit and signs you [with the sign of the cross], saying: "So-and-so is anointed in the name of the Father, and of the Son, and of the Holy Spirit." . . . Next after this, in the full darkness of the night, he strips off your robe and, as if he were going to lead you into heaven itself by the ritual, he causes your whole body to be anointed with that olive oil of the spirit, so that all your limbs may be fortified and unconquered by the darts the adversary aims at you.[114]

The theme of struggle with the devil is predominant here, but the point emphasized is that the brightness of the oil, put on the forehead with a sign of the cross, blinds the enemy. The complete anointing suggests less the anointing of athletes to make them nimble than a protection that makes the baptized invulnerable. The emphasis is a little different in Theodore of Mopsuestia, who returns to the idea of a brand by which sheep or soldiers are recognized; the soldiers in this case are enrolled 'in the heavenly army." This is a service that delivers human beings from enslavement; whence the rite that concludes this first stage of the final rite: "Your sponsor, who is standing behind you, extends a linen *orarium* over your head and raises you up; he makes you stand upright. . . . This is a sign of the state of freedom to which you are called, for people in this state customarily wear a linen veil on their heads."[115] The oil then becomes the garment of those who have put aside their clothing, but it is "a garment of immortality."[116] No longer is there question simply of a final exorcism; the Trinitarian formula shows that we are dealing with "the first fruits of the sacrament," "as though to lead the candidates into heaven itself." Furthermore, in all these documents (doubt exists only with regard to Theodore) the absence of a postbaptismal anointing focuses all the more attention on this one,[117] which presents itself not as an exorcism but as a consecration.

---

113. Narsai of Nisibis, *Hom.* 22, trans. A. Guillemont, *OS* 1 (1956) 202–7.

114. St. John Chrysostom, *Baptismal Instructions*, II, 22 and 24 (Harkins 51–52). Theodore of Mopsuestia, *Homélies catéchétiques* XIII, 7 and XIV, 8 (Tonneau-Devreesse 396–97 and 418–18), has the bishop repeat the same formula before the complete anointing.

115. Theodore, XIII, 9 (pp. 398–401).

116. *Ibid.*, XIV, 8 (pp. 418–19).

117. In the *Constitutiones Apostolorum* the two rituals of Book VII have a postbaptismal anointing, but it seems to be less important than the prebaptismal. See VII, 22, 2, and below, n. 197. — See B. Botte, "Le baptême dans l'Eglise syrienne," *OS* 1 (1956) 137–55.

It is possible that the anointing of the head with chrism, which calls
to mind the inauguration of the mission of prophets and kings in the Old
Testament, is the oldest part of this rite[118] and that the act of spreading
oil over the entire body introduced new symbolisms and began a process
that ended with the repetition of this gesture after baptism.

4. *The Nakedness of the Baptized*

The anointing of the entire body already presupposed the complete
nakedness that would subsequently be required for the baptismal immersion. But this practical necessity suggested a whole range of symbolisms,
among which the Fathers made numerous connections in their sermons:
abandonment of one's past life and renunciation of the old self with its
mortality; assimilation to the Lord on the cross; equality of all in the mystery of rebirth; and so on. These various meanings, however, were all
rooted in the image of paradise, which cropped up here again with all
of its rich meaning: the garment of corruption that the baptized put off
in imitation of Christ is the garment that Adam was forced to put on when
he felt ashamed after his disobedience; it is the condition into which the
fall precipitated him. "O wonder of wonders!" exclaims the Jerusalem catechist, "you were naked in the sight of all but you did not blush. Truly,
you bore the image of the first human being who was naked in paradise
and did not blush."[119] According to Theodore, the need to wear clothing
is a sign of sin, and we must remove it if we are to understand the gift
of God and reach the grace of baptism: we must have conquered shame
if we are to regain the filial trust that simplicity and freedom (*parrhēsia*)
caused to reign in the Garden of Eden. St. Gregory of Nyssa writes: "You
did banish us from Paradise, and did recall us; You did strip off the fig-
tree leaves, an unseemly covering, and put upon us a costly garment. . . .
No longer shall Adam be confounded when called by you, nor hide himself convicted by his conscience, cowering in the thicket of Paradise. Having recovered his freedom, he steps forth in the full light of day."[120]

Sensibilities differ, however, from culture to culture, and the sense of
propriety of some peoples held in check the sense of wonder roused by

---

118. The apocryphal *Acts of Thomas*, the Syriac original of which seems to go back
to third-century Edessa, has baptisms celebrated by the apostles according to the following
pattern: anointing of the head, immersion in the name of the Trinity, Eucharist; see *Actes
de Thomas* 26–27, 120–21, 131–33, 157–58, in M. Bonnet, *Acta apostolorum apocrypha*
II/2 (Darmstadt: Wissenschaftliche Buchgesellschaft, 1959), 141–43, 229–31, 238–40, 266–68;
English trans. by R. McL. Wilson, in *New Testament Apocrypha*, ed. E. Hennecke and W.
Schneemelcher, English trans. ed. by R. Mcl. Wilson 2 (Philadelphia: Westminster, 1965),
425–531.

119. Cyril of Jerusalem, *Catéchèses mystagogiques* II, 2 (SC 126:106).

120. Gregory of Nyssa, *In diem luminum* (PG 46:600), trans. in Hamman 137 [except
for the final sentence, which is here translated from the author's French. — Tr.].

the nakedness in the baptisteries. This was the case in the eastern regions of Syria: "It is not fitting that women should be seen by men," says the *Didascalia of the Apostles*, while canonical regulations from the end of the fifth century in a Jacobite community in the Tigris region contain the following prescription: "Since it is not fitting that the priest who baptizes women should see their nakedness, he simply extends his hand, while a veil serves to screen them; a deaconess leads the woman to be baptized to the priest, who places his hand on her head without seeing her, and baptizes her."[121]

II. THE BATH OF NEW BIRTH

BIBLIOGRAPHY

B. Neunheuser, "De benedictione aquae baptismalis," *EL* 44 (1930) 194–207, 258–81, 369–412, 455–92.

H. Scheidt, *Die Taufwasserweihegebete* (LQF 29; Münster: Aschendorff, 1935).

P. Lundberg, *La typologie baptismale dans l'ancienne Eglise* (Uppsala: Lundequist, 1942).

M. Eliade, *Patterns in Comparative Religion*, trans. R. Sheed (New York: Sheed & Ward, 1958), 188–215.

L. Beirnaert, "The Mythic Dimension in Christian Sacramentalism," *Crosscurrents* 2 (1952) 68–86.

W. Bedard, *The Symbolism of the Baptismal Font in Early Christian Thought* (The Catholic University of America Studies in Sacred Theology, 2nd ser., 45; Washington, D.C., 1951).

B. Capelle, "Inspiration biblique de la bénédiction des fonts baptismaux," *Bible et vie chrétienne* 13 (1956) 30–40.

S. Benz, "Zur Vorgeschichte des Textes des römischen Taufwasserweihe," *RBén* 66 (1956) 213–55.

J. Lécuyer, "La prière consécratoire des eaux," *LMD* no. 49 (1957) 71–95.

J. Daniélou, "Le symbolisme de l'eau vive," *RevSR* 32 (1958) 335–46.

A. Olivar, "Vom Ursprung der römischen Taufwasserweihe," *ALW* 6 (1959) 62–78.

J. F. Ribera, "Le rite baptismal dans l'ancienne liturgie hispanique," *LMD* no. 58 (1959) 39–47.

J. P. De Jong, "Benedictio fontis. Eine genetische Erklärung der römischen Taufwasserweihe," *ALW* 8 (1963) 21–46.

C. Coebergh, "Problèmes de l'évolution historique et de la structure littéraire de la *Benedictio fontis* du rit romain," *SE* 16 (1965) 260–319.

E. Lanne, "L'acqua e l'unzione nelle Chiese orientali," in *I simboli dell'iniziazione cristana* (Studia Anselmiana 87, Analecta liturgica 7; Rome, 1983), 137–56.

---

121. *Didascalia apostolorum* (Connolly 146). — *L'Ordo et les canons des ordinations dans la sainte Eglise*, can. 18; Syriac text and Latin trans. in I. Rahmani, *Studia Syriaca*, fasc. 3: *Vetera documenta liturgica* (Scharfe, 1908), 29–31; French trans. and commentary in A. G. Martimort, *Les diaconesses* (above, n. 3), 49–51. There is even mention, with reference to the area of Seleucia-Ctesiphon at the end of the sixth century, of a wall with a window through which the priest reached his hand, which was guided by a deaconess, for the anointing and immersion; *ibid.*, 51–53.

1. *The Prayer over the Water*

According to the *Apostolic Tradition,* "at cockcrow the prayer over the water is to be said."[122] The first act in the solemn celebration of baptism thus took place at dawn on Easter, after lengthy preparation of the catechumens. Tertullian wrote: "At once [when God is invoked] the Spirit comes down from heaven and stays upon the waters, sanctifying them from within himself, and when thus sanctified they absorb the power of sanctifying."[123] As early as the third century, then, the baptismal ritual already contained a prayer said over the water into which the *competentes* were to descend. St. Ambrose goes so far as to say that "not all water heals, but only water that has the grace of Christ. Water is an instrument; it is the Holy Spirit who acts. Water heals only if the Spirit descends upon it to consecrate it." And he adds: "The bishop exorcizes water, a creaturely element; then he says the invocation and prayer that the font may be consecrated."[124] This distinction of two phases in the formulary corresponds to the twofold biblical symbolism on which the rite is based.

a) *The Symbolism of the Baptismal Water*

Water is the dwelling place of the wicked powers that stir up deadly storms at sea and the destructive floods that occur when torrents suddenly rush through dried up riverbeds. In his prebaptismal catecheses, Cyril of Jerusalem is reminded of the monster Behemoth swallowing the Jordan (Job 40:18): "Jesus descended into the water and chained up the strong one, so that we might receive the power to walk on serpents and scorpions. . . . Life ran before so that death might be curbed and all of us, the saved, might say: 'Death, where is your sting? Hell, where is your victory?' Baptism has destroyed the sting of death."[125]

But ever since creation, when the Spirit of God hovered over the waters (Gen 1:2), water has also, and above all, been the place from which life emerges. Christ can therefore rightly speak to Nicodemus of "being born again of water and the Spirit" (John 3:5). The dominant theme in the blessing of baptismal water is, therefore, the baptismal font as a maternal womb that is impregnated by the Spirit. Theodore of Mopsuestia, for example, makes this point clearly: "Just as the maternal womb receives the seed for a fleshly birth . . . so the water becomes a womb for those born of

---

122. *Traditio apostolica* 21 (Botte 44).

123. Tertullian, *De baptismo* 4, 4 (Evans 11). See St. Cyprian, *Ep.* 70, ed. L. Bayard (Paris: Les Belles Lettres, 1961), 2:253, who derives from this fact an argument against the validity of the baptism of heretics.

124. St. Ambrose, *De sacramentis* 1, 15 (SC 25bis:68).

125. Cyril of Jerusalem, *Catéchèses baptismales* III, 12 (PG 33:441); French. trans. by J. Bouvet (Les écrits des saints; Namur: Ed. du Soleil levant, 1962), 75–76.

it, but it is the grace of the Spirit that forms the baptized therein for a second birth." For this reason "the bishop . . . asks God that the grace of the Holy Spirit may come upon the water and make it capable of bearing. . . ."[126] A new creation takes place: the sin of Adam brought death, but the Savior has formed us anew; this can come about only by a configuration to the new Adam who died and rose from the dead; the image of the maternal womb is combined here with the image of the earth as a womb from which Christ arose on Easter morning. Repeating the teaching of St. Paul (Rom 6:3-11), the *Apostolic Constitutions* place this petition on the bishop's lips: "Sanctify this water so that those who are baptized may be crucified with Christ, die with him, be buried with him, and rise with him to be adopted children."[127]

b) *The Formularies for the Blessing of the Baptismal Font*

These two basic symbolisms provide the material of the liturgical prayers for the consecration of the font. In addition, the prayers take a number of images from Scripture: the rivers of Paradise (Gen 2:10-14), the flood (Gen 6:13—8:22; 1 Pet 3:19-21), the waters of Marah (Exod 15:23-25), the waters of Meribah that sprang from the rock (Exod 17:7); and so on. To these are added New Testament references derived from meditation on Christ as he extends his hand to Peter when the latter walks on the water (Matt 14:24-31) or as he pours blood and water from his side on the cross (John 19:34), and, of course, from the account of Christ's own baptism by John. All this material made possible a rounded catechesis on baptism as purification and return to Paradise, as deliverance and establishment of a new people, as unmerited gift of participation in the paschal mystery.

i) *The Roman Prayer*[128] was already in existence in the first half of the sixth century, for it belongs to the oldest stratum of the Gelasian Sacramentary; but it goes back beyond that time since Peter Chrysologus, in the middle of the fifth century, cites passages from it.[129]

After an introduction that speaks immediately of begetting and creating new peoples, the formulary calls to mind the primordial waters of Genesis and those of the flood, and then addresses this prayer to God:

> Lord, you give joy to your city with your floods of grace (see Ps 45:5)
> and you open the font of baptism to the entire world so that the pagan na-

---

126. Theodore of Mopsuestia, *Homélies catéchétiques* XIV, 9 (Tonneau-Devreesse 420-21).

127. *Constitutiones Apostolorum* VII, 43 (Funk 1:450).

128. *Ge* nos. 444-48 (pp. 72-74); *Gr* nos. 373-74 (pp. 186-88).

129. Peter Chrysologus, *Serm.* 117 (PL 52:521). Some scholars have even thought him to be the author of the prayer; see S. Benz, "Zur Vorgeschichte der römischen Taufwasserweihe," *RBén* 66 (1956) 218-55.

tions may be reborn in it. Look upon the face of your Church and multiply your children within her. By your majestic power may the Church receive from the Holy Spirit the grace of your only-begotten Son. May this Spirit make fruitful the water prepared for the rebirth of human beings by mingling with it the mysterious power of his light.

Exorcisms follow in which the Lord is asked to drive every unclean spirit from the font lest "any of them creep in by stealth and put in it the seeds of corruption." The tone then changes in a way that suggests an interpolation, perhaps of Gallican origin: the prayer addresses the water directly with "I bless you" and, after several biblical references, recalls the command of Jesus to baptize all nations in the name of the Father and of the Son and of the Holy Spirit. The prayer then returns to its earlier emphases as it calls on God to breathe on the water so that it may wash, cleanse, and produce a new creation.

> Let the power of your Spirit descend into the water that fills this font; let it make the whole mass of water fruitful so that it may bring rebirth. Let all stain of sin be wiped away here; let human nature, created in your image and reestablished in its original dignity, be here cleansed of all its staleness, so that all who enter into this sign of rebirth may be reborn as new and truly innocent children.

As the celebrant began this prayer, the two candles by which he was reading were dipped into the font to symbolize the gift of the Spirit coming in the form of light. This was the only gesture accompanying the formula at that time.[130]

ii) *Spain and Gaul* have left us some early texts, in particular a Gallican prayer that gives a lot of space to the Pool of Bethzatha (John 5:1-18; the "Probatica" of the Vulgate): the blessing of God descends on the water of baptism as the angel descended and troubled the water of the pool, in order to bring renewal to those who went down into it.[131] A Visigothic formulary first addresses the water itself, as though to remind it of the role it has played in the history of salvation; the prayer then turns to the Lord and develops especially the theme of Paradise:

> Break down the wall of Paradise with its protecting flames. Let those returning find open the gateways into a flowering land; let them receive again the image of God that was lost because of the serpent's trickery. . . . Let them rise for their rest . . . so that, renewed by this mystical water, they may know themselves redeemed and reborn.[132]

---

130. *OR* XXIII, no. 29 (Andrieu, *OR* 3:273); *OR* XXX-B, no. 46 (Andrieu *OR* 3:472).
131. *Missale Gothicum* no. 257, ed. H. M. Bannister (HBS 52; London, 1917), 72.
132. *Liber ordinum* 4 (Férotin, col. 29–30).

iii) For the *East* I shall cite part of a prayer still used by the Syrians of Antioch, certainly an ancient one,[133] since we find the same components, in very nearly the same form, among the Copts, the Byzantines, and the Armenians.[134]

> Lord, creator of all creatures visible and invisible, you made the heavens and the earth and all that is in them; you gathered the waters into a single mass and made the earth to appear; you locked up the abyss and keep it imprisoned; you divided the waters that are above the firmament; by your power you set bounds to the sea and crushed the heads of the dragons. . . . Look upon this water, which is your creature. Grant it the grace of your salvation, the blessing of the Jordan, the consecration of the Holy Spirit. . . . Let the sign of the glorious and holy cross smash the head of the murderous dragon; let the invisible spirits of the air depart; let the demon of darkness not conceal himself in the water nor the unclean spirit of darkness descend into the water with those to be baptized. . . . Grant that this water may become a water of rest, joy, and gladness, a water that symbolizes the death and resurrection of your only Son; may it bring cleansing from the stains of body and soul, the casting off of bonds, the forgiveness of sins, the enlightenment of souls. May it be a bath of rebirth, bestowing the grace of adoption, the garment of immortality, and renewal by your Holy Spirit. . . . Grant that those baptized in it may be transformed, so as to strip off the old self that is corrupted by the pleasures of error and to put on the new self that is renewed through knowledge in the image of its creator. Let those who are made like your only Son in his death . . . share also in his resurrection. . . . Let them be counted among the first-born whose names are written in heaven.[135]

The East and then Gaul and Spain seem to have had from a rather early period the custom of mingling a little chrism with the water; the original purpose of this action was simply to perfume the water.[136]

c) *The Opening of the Baptistery*

In Spain and in some Churches of Gaul it was customary to close and seal the doors of the baptistery and then open them again at the beginning of the Easter triduum when the time came to prepare the baptismal pool for the Easter Vigil. The Council of Toledo in 694 saw in this prac-

---

133. H. Scheidt, *Die Taufwasserweihegebete* (LQF 29; Münster: Aschendorff, 1935). See B. Botte, "Le baptême dans l'Eglise syrienne" (n. 117, above), 53–54.

134. Note that the Euchologion of Serapion 19 (Funk 2:180–82) has a "consecration of the waters" that is presented as a new descent of Christ into the Jordan.

135. G. Khouri-Sarkis, "Prières et cérémonies du baptême dans le rite de l'Eglise syrienne d'Antioche," *OS* 1 (1956) 173–76.

136. Only later on would this action be seen as a symbol of the Spirit sanctifying the water (see Ildephonsus of Toledo, *De cognitione baptismi* 109; PL 96:175) or as a link with the bishop who blesses the chrism.

tice a sign of how very suitable the Easter Vigil was for celebrating the Christian's rebirth. But the practice goes back a good deal earlier; Gregory of Tours, for example, refers to it several times.[137]

2. *The Profession of Faith and the Immersion*

Everything was ready for the solemn moment of baptism: the font had been consecrated and the candidates were standing beside the water, their bodies covered with the anointing they had just received. "You were led by the hand," says the Jerusalem catechist, "to the holy pool of God's baptism. . . . They asked each if he or she believed in the name of the Father and of the Son and of the Holy Spirit. And you professed the faith that saves and you were immersed three times in the water, and then you came out."[138]

In all probability it is this same rite that is attested for Africa,[139] Milan,[140] and Rome:[141] the candidate descended into the pool; the celebrant, his hand resting on the person's head, asked him or her three questions about their faith in the Trinity: "Do you believe . . . . ?"; then, each time that he heard the answer "I believe," he immersed the person in the water. At that time, then, the profession of faith (question and answer) served as the sacramental formula. This practice was very widespread in the West, since only Gaul and Spain seem to have departed from it.

The same rite was followed in Jerusalem (provided we have correctly interpreted the Jerusalem catecheses) but nowhere else in the East, at least in the patriarchate of Antioch (we are poorly informed about the patriarchate of Alexandria).[142] We saw this earlier in the discusssion of the pre-

---

137. Eighteenth Council of Toledo 3, ed. J. Vives (above, n. 39), 528–29; Gregory of Tours, *De gloria martyrum* 24, ed. B. Krusch, MGH, *Script. aev. Merov.*, 1 (1885) 502, says that the baptistery is closed on Holy Thursday and reopened on Saturday, and makes this a simple means of verifying a miracle; perhaps he did not properly grasp what was reported to him regarding Spain.

138. Cyril of Jerusalem, *Catéchèses mystagogiques* II, 4 (SC 126:110).

139. The African authors are reserved in speaking of this rite. Tertullian, *De corona* 3, 3 (CCL 2:1042): "We are immersed three times, while giving in answer something more than the Lord determined in the gospel." See his *De baptismo* 2, 1; *Ad martyres* 3, 1. — See St. Cyprian, *Ep.* 70 (Bayard 254); St. Augustine, *Ep.* 98, 7, ed. A. Goldbacher (CSEL 34; Vienna, 1898), 528–29.

140. St. Ambrose, *De sacramentis* 2, 20 (SC 25bis:84, 86): "Interrogatus es: Credis in deum patrem omnipotentem? Dixisti: Credo, et mersisti, hoc est sepultus es. Iterum interrogatus es: Credis in dominum nostrum Iesum Christum et in crucem eius? Dixisti: Credo, et mersisti. Ideo et Christo es consepultus. Qui enim Christo consepelitur cum Christo resurgit. Tertio interrogatus es: Credis et in Spiritum Sanctum? Dixisti: Credo, tertio mersisti ut multiplicem lapsum superioris aetatis ablueret trina confessio."

141. *Traditio apostolica* 21 (Botte 48–50). — *Ge* no. 49 (p. 74).

142. It is possible that the formula used there was the one found later in the West. Timothy of Alexandria (380–85), *Réponses canoniques*, ed. J. B. Pitra, *Iuris ecclesiastici Graecorum*

baptismal anointing. It is possible that Jerusalem, a pilgrimage city visited by many foreigners, was influenced by the Latins.

Theodore of Mopsuestia gives a detailed description of the rite followed in Syria:

> The bishop stands there and, extending his hand, places it on your head and says: "N. is baptized in the name of the Father and of the Son and of the Holy Spirit" . . . . He puts his hand on your head and says: "In the name of the Father," and as he does so he pushes you down into the water . . . and you bow your head as if to signify your assent . . . and you raise your head again; then he says, "And of the Son," and in the same way he forces you to immerse yourself. . . . You raise your head again, and then he says, "And of the Holy Spirit," and in the same way he pushes and immerses you. . . . Then you emerge completely from the water of baptism.[143]

This information matches what we find in other documents from the same region (in Chrysostom, for example) and even from the area farther East (as in Narsai).[144] To be noted is the fact that these three witnesses emphasize the impersonal formula. Chrysostom says: "It is not only the priest who touches the head, but also the right hand of Christ, and this is shown by the very words of the one baptizing. He does not say: 'I baptize so-and-so,' but: 'So-and-so is baptized,' showing that he is only the minister of grace." This is in contrast to the practice that would spread throughout the West later on and which we find first in Gaul and Spain in the form: "Ego te baptizo in nomine Patris et Filii et Spiritus Sancti, ut habeas vitam aeternam."[145]

Did this type of rite, then, contain no profession of faith? It is worth noting that Theodore speaks of the candidate giving assent by a bow of the head; and he adds: "If you could speak at that moment, you would say 'Amen.'" But it is also not impossible that credal questions were asked of the candidate just before the sacramental bath. In a homily that in all likelihood was preached in Antioch, Chrysostom speaks allusively (because noninitiates are present) of words "spoken on that evening" that

---

historia et monumenta 1 (Rome: Typis Collegii Urbani, 1864), 638, gives the following formula for a conditional baptism: "Baptizō se eis onoma tou Patros kai tou Huiou kai tou hagiou Pneumatos." In addition, the Canons of Hippolytus, ed. R. Coquin (PO 31, 2; Paris: Didot, 1966), 380–81, which have come down to us in Arabic and can be traced to mid-fourth century Egypt, after having repeated substantially the same questions as in the Traditio apostolica, add: "He says each time: I baptize you in the name of the Father and of the Son and of the Holy Spirit, the holy Trinity."

143. Theodore of Mopsuestia, Homélies catéchétiques XIV, 14 and 18–20 (Tonneau-Devreesse 430–31, 440–43).

144. St. John Chrysostom, Baptismal Instructions II, 26 (Harkins 53). — Narsai of Nisibis, Hom. 21, French trans. P. Gignoux, in Hamman, L'initiation chrétienne (above, n. 14), 201.

145. Liber ordinum (Ferotin, col. 32); Missale gothicum, no. 262 (Bannister 77).

ended with "I believe in the resurrection of the dead." "It is after we have confessed this and all the other articles that we descend into the fountain of sacred water."[146] In any case, this description fits what took place in the liturgies of Gaul and Spain.

The baptismal immersion is everywhere described, after St. Paul, as a sharing in the death and even the burial of the Lord: "sepultus es," says St. Ambrose. The Jerusalem catechist, who was speaking in the Anastasis rotunda, is quite specific: "You were three times immersed in the water and came up from it, thus signifying in a manner likewise symbolic the three-day burial of Christ" (*Mystagogical Catecheses* II, 4). This symbolism was added on to the original meaning of the triple immersion in the earlier tradition, namely, that the person is baptized in the name of the Trinity.

Some Churches of Spain, at least from the sixth century on, did not follow the practice of a triple immersion. Their intention in using but a single immersion of the baptized was to distinguish themselves from the Arians, who had become the dominant force in the Peninsula as a result of the Visigothic invasion.[147]

In any case, the theme of death and burial always led into that of birth and life. "This saving water was both your tomb and your mother," according to the Jerusalem catecheses. We are configured not only to the death of Christ but also to his resurrection, and "while this imitation is only symbolic, the salvation that comes through it is real" and can be attained only in the womb of Mother Church. Tertullian writes: "Therefore, you blessed ones, for whom the grace of God is waiting, when you come up from that most sacred washing of the new birth, and when for the first time you spread out your hands with your brethren in your mother's house, ask of your Father. . . ."[148]

§4. The Postbaptismal Rites

BIBLIOGRAPHY

J. Coppens, *L'imposition des mains et les rites connexes . . .* (Wetteren: De Meester, 1925).

146. St. John Chrysostom, *Homiliae in Primam ad Corinthios* 40 (PG 61:347, 349). The practice was doubtless the same at Constantinople, according to Proclus; see A. Wenger, Introduction in SC 50:94–96.

147. Writing to Leander of Seville in 591, Gregory the Great, *Ep.* 43 (PL 77:497–98; Jaffe 1111), considers both practices to be licit. But the matter was the subject of controversy, and in order to avert division, a council over which Isidore of Seville presided in 633 pronounced in favor of the single immersion: Fourth Council of Toledo, can. 6, in J. Vives, *Concilios visigóticos e hispano-romanos* (above, n. 39), 191–93.

148. Tertullian, *De baptismo* 20, 5 (CCL 1:295; SC 35:96; Evans 43).

B. Welte, *Die postbaptismale Salbung* (Freiburger theologische Studien 51; Freiburg: Herder, 1939).

L. de Bruyne, "L'imposition des mains dans l'art chrétien antique," *Rivista di archeologia cristiana* 19 (1943) 113-278.

J. Lécuyer, "La confirmation chez les Pères," *LMD* no. 54 (1958) 23-52.

B. Botte, "Le vocabulaire ancien de la confirmation," *LMD* no. 54 (1958) 5-22.

_____, "L'onction postbaptismale dans l'ancien patriarcat d'Antioche," in *Miscellanea liturgica . . . Lercaro* 2 (Rome: Desclée, 1967), 795-808.

P. M. Gy, "Histoire liturgique du sacrement de confirmation," *LMD* no. 58 (1959) 135-45.

J. P. Bouhot, *La confirmation, sacrement de la communion ecclésiale* (Parole et tradition; Lyons: Chalet, 1968).

N. Bux, "L'olio simbolo dello Spirito Sancto," in *I simboli dell'iniziazione cristiana* (Studia Anselmiana 87, Analecta liturgica 7; Rome, 1983), 123-35.

R. Cabié, "L'ordo de l'initiation chrétienne dans la Tradition apostolique d'Hippolyte de Rome," in *Mens concordet voci. Pour Mgr A. G. Martimort* (Paris: Desclée, 1981), 543-58.

I. THE "COMPLETION" OF BAPTISM IN THE VARIOUS CHURCHES

"You come up from the water of baptism to receive the completion," says Theodore of Mopsuestia. The Syriac word *šūlāmā* corresponds to the Greek *teleiōsis*, which suggests a fulfillment or consummation.[149] At this point in the rite there were such differences between local traditions that we must look at the practice of each separate Church.

1. *Africa*

Africa had at least two essential rites: an anointing and an imposition of the hand. According to Tertullian,

> . . . after that we come up from the washing and are anointed with the blessed unction, following that ancient practice by which, ever since Aaron was anointed by Moses, there was a custom of anointing them for priesthood with oil out of a horn. That is why priests are called christs, from "chrism" which is [the Greek for] "anointing": and from this also our Lord obtained his title, though it has become a spiritual anointing, in that he was anointed with the Spirit by God the Father. . . . Next follows the imposition of the hand in benediction, inviting and welcoming the Holy Spirit.[150]

These two actions, the first of which signifies priestly consecration and the second the gift of the Spirit, are also found in Cyprian[151] and Au-

---

149. Some critics think that *šūlāmā* corresponds rather to *telete*, the name for a ceremony of initiation in the mystery religions.

150. Tertullian, *De baptismo* 7, 1, and 8, 1 (CCL 1:282-83; SC 35: 76; Evans 17 [slightly altered]).

151. St. Cyprian, *Ep.*, 70, 2, 2, and 72, 1, 1 (Bayard 254 and 260): "It is required the person baptized be anointed . . . in order to be an anointed of God and possess within

gustine.[152] Tertullian also speaks of a "signing," which seems to be a distinct action (the neophyte is marked with the sign of the cross), since it has its place in a list that is intended as a summary of the entire initiation:

> The flesh is bathed so that the soul may be cleansed; the flesh is anointed so that the soul may be consecrated; the flesh is "signed" so that the soul may be strengthened; the flesh is overshadowed by the laying on of the hand, so that the soul may be enlightened by the Spirit; the flesh is fed with the body and blood of Christ, so that the soul itself may be fed by God.[153]

But the Carthaginian writer does not speak elsewhere of this signing, and anyone going on to read Cyprian[154] may ask whether the signing was not in fact combined with other rites.

In the period when Augustine was bishop of Hippo, the baptized donned white garments as symbols of the new life, the seed of which they had received[155] while they covered their heads with a veil, the sign of freedom. In addition, the ceremonial had been expanded to include a washing of feet, which would be attested later on in Africa after Augustine. Could this have been introduced from Milan where Augustine himself had been baptized?

2. Milan

St. Ambrose speaks of baptism proper being followed by an anointing, a washing of feet, new garments, and a *consignatio*.

As soon as the newly baptized came out of the font they approached the bishop who poured *myron* ("hoc est unguentum," Ambrose explains) on their heads while saying: "God the almighty Father, who has given you rebirth from water and the Spirit and has forgiven your sins, anoints you for eternal life."[156] Citations from the Bible recall the anointings of Aaron and Jesus.[157] Then, after the reading of John 13, the bishop begins,

---

himself the grace of Christ;" ". . . they imposed the hand on him that he may receive the Holy Spirit" (In both cases Cyprian is challenging the validity of initiation received in heresy).

152. St. Augustine, *Serm.* 224 (PL 38:1147): "Baptizatus est, sanctificatus est, unctus est, imposita est ei manus" (the reference is to an infant that had died unbaptized and was brought back to life that it might receive the sacraments). Elsewhere Augustine speaks of the anointing itself as "sacrament of the Holy Spirit" (*Serm.* 227 [SC 116:286]): The person has, like bread, been kneaded by baptism, but he still needs to be baked: "Quid ergo significat ignis, hoc est chrisma olei? Etenim ignis nutritor spiritus sancti est sacramentum."

153. Tertullian, *De resurrectione mortuorum* 8, 3, ed. J. G. P. Borleffs (CCL 2; Turnhout: Brepols, 1954), 931.

154. St. Cyprian, *Ep.* 73, 6, 2 (Bayard 266): ". . . and they impose a hand on him that he may receive the Spirit and be sealed (*signetur*)."

155. St. Augustine, *Ep.* 55, 33 (CSEL 33:55).

156. St. Ambrose, *De sacramentis* 2, 2; 3, 1; *De mysteriis* 28 (SC 25bis:88, 102, 171).

157. Ps 132:2; Cant 1:2–3.

and the priests continue, washing the feet of these new Christians.[158] These then receive a white garment.[159] Finally the *spiritale signaculum* is given: "At the invocation of the bishop the Spirit is poured out *quando consignaris*," but the commentator does not say whether oil is used in the sealing, although in the Roman use of the word it refers to an anointing.[160]

3. Rome

The *Apostolic Traditions* speaks of two anointings that are separated by an imposition of hands and followed by a signing:

> When he [the newly baptized] comes out of the pool, the priest will anoint him with the oil of thanksgiving while saying: "I anoint you with holy oil in the name of Jesus Christ." Then each after drying himself puts on his clothing, and they enter the church. The bishop imposes hands on them and says the invocation: "Lord God, who have made them worthy to obtain the forgiveness of sins through the bath of rebirth, make them worthy to be filled with the Holy Spirit, and send your grace upon them so that they may do your will and serve you". . . . Then, pouring the oil of thanksgiving from his hand and placing it [his hand] on the head of each, he says: "I anoint you with holy oil in God the almighty Father and in Christ Jesus and in the Holy Spirit." And after signing each on the forehead he gives him the kiss of peace and says: "The Lord be with you." And the person signed says, "And with your Spirit."[161]

a) *The Anointings and the Sealing*

The two anointings, which are not found elsewhere at this point, were to remain peculiar to the Roman liturgy, one of them being done by a priest and the other by the bishop.[162] The formulas given by Hippolytus are not especially meaningful, and those found later in the Gelasian Sacramentary are hardly more so.[163] Commenting on the action of the priest, John the Deacon says that "the baptized are to understand from

---

158. St. Ambrose, *De sacramentis* 3, 4–7 (SC 25bis:92–96). Ambrose justifies the practice of his Church which, he says, differs from that of Rome.

159. Idem, *De mysteriis* 34 (SC 25bis:174).

160. Idem, *De sacramentis* 3, 8–10; *De mysteriis* 42 (SC 25bis:96–98, 178). See P. Galtier, "La consignation dans les Eglises d'Occident," *RHE* 13 (1912) 263–65.

161. *Traditio apostolica* 21 (Botte 50–54).

162. Could this doubling be the result of Hippolytus combining two different rituals? This is the hypothesis of J. P. Bouhot, *La confirmation, sacrement de la communion ecclésiale* (Lyons: Chalet, 1968), 38–49. See R. Cabié, "L'ordo de l'initiation chrétienne dans la Tradition apostolique d'Hippolyte de Rome," in *Mens concordet voci. Pour Mgr A. G. Martimort* (Paris: Desclée, 1983), 543–58.

163. *Ge* nos. 450 and 451 (p. 74): "Deus . . . te linit chrismate salutis" and "Signum Christi in vitam aeternam."

this that kingship and the mystery of priesthood come together in them"[164]; John makes no explicit mention of a second anointing, but this may be simply because Senarius had not asked him about it.

The rite as described by Hippolytus was not a skimpy one: the bishop poured the oil from his cupped hand and spread it abundantly on the person's head, probably by rubbing it in, and then he signed the person on the forehead; the latter action complemented the anointing, since it was done with fingers still soaked in chrism, and not long after it would in fact be fused with the action of anointing and become the expression of the gift of the Spirit.[165] Innocent I, at the beginning of the fifth century, says that the bishop anoints the forehead and that his action is thus distinguished from that of the priest, who anoints the head; the word *consignare* is now the technical name for the bishop's anointing.[166]

b) *The Imposition of the Hand*

In Hippolytus it was the prayer accompanying the imposition of the hand that asked that the neophytes might be "filled with the Holy Spirit"; in this his liturgy resembled that of the Africans. John the Deacon does not mention the prayer, but at the end of his letter there are two references to the "blessing of the bishop."[167] In any case, the rite just described was to be a permanent part of the Roman tradition, although it shared its prerogatives with the anointing, and although even the name of the imposition (*consignatio*) came to be applied to the entire ceremony, as we can see from the Gelasian Sacramentary: "Ad consignandum imponit eis manus. . . . postea signat eos in fronte de chrismate." The imposition of the hand was still important by reason of the accompanying prayer for the "sevenfold" Spirit.[168]

---

164. John the Deacon, *Ep. ad Senarium* 6 (Wilmart 174): ". . . regnum in se ac sacerdotale convenisse mysterium."

165. This fusion had perhaps already been accomplished in 251, when Cornelius said of Novatian that he had received only emergency baptism: "He has not received the other things that must be received according to the regulations of the Church, and he has not been sealed by the bishop. How then can he have received the Holy Spirit?" This text has been preserved for us in Greek in Eusebius, *Historia ecclesiastica* VI, 53, 15, ed. G. Bardy, (SC 41; Paris: Cerf 1955), 41, where the verb used is *sphragisthēnai*. The other postbaptismal rites are mentioned in only a general way: "the other things."

166. Innocent I, *Ep. ad Decentium* (Cabié [above, n. 96] 22–24): 'De consignandis infantibus . . .: presbyteris unguere licet . . . non tamen in fronte, quod solis debetur episcopis cum tradunt Spiritum paraclitum."

167. John the Deacon, *Ep. ad Senarium* 9 and 14 (Wilmart 176 and 178), apropos of heretics who are not rebaptized and who "enter the bosom of Mother Church 'benedictione succedente pontificis'" and of the baptized who die "sine chrismatis unctione ac benedictione pontificis."

168. *Ge* no. 451 (p. 74).

c) *The White Garments*

As soon as they emerged from the font, the baptized donned a white garment that they were to wear throughout the octave; according to John the Deacon, they also wore a veil on their heads.[169]

4. *Gaul and Spain*

Here, too, there was an anointing and an imposition of the hand, while Gaul added a washing of feet.[170]

a) *The Anointing*

Chrismation is attested in Spain as early as the fourth century. Pacian of Barcelona formally connects it with a gift of the Spirit[171] and speaks of it as a *consignatio*.[172] In Gaul it is mentioned in particular at the beginning of the fifth century in the *De septem ordinibus Ecclesiae*, which was attributed to St. Jerome,[173] and, a century later, by Salvian of Marseilles.[174] Gregory of Tours reports that Clovis was "baptized . . . and anointed with holy chrism in the form of a sign of the cross."[175]

This postbaptismal anointing was the only one, at least before Roman influences came into play; it was normally an action of the bishop, but a priest was to do it after baptism whenever he presided at the celebration.[176] In southeastern Gaul the Council of Orange of 441 even extended this privilege to deacons and said explicitly: "It has been accepted among

---

169. John the Deacon, *Ep. ad Senarium* 6 (Wilmart 174): "It is in order to have a clearer image of priesthood that the head of the newly reborn receives a linen veil as an adornment. . . . They are clad in white garments to express the mystery of the Church which rises to life . . ."

170. If this rite ever existed in Spain, it very quickly disappeared. The Council of Elvira (about 300), can. 48 (Vives [n. 39] 10) says with regard to the baptized: "Neque pedes eorum lavandi sunt a sacerdotibus vel clericis."

171. Pacian of Barcelona, *Serm. de baptismo* (PL 13:1093): "Lavacro peccata purgantur, chrismate Spiritus Sanctus perfunditur."

172. Idem, *Ep.* 3 (PL 13:1065): "Vestrae plebi unde Spiritum, quam non consignat unctus sacerdos?" See his *Ep.* 2 (PL 13:1057).

173. Ps.-Jerome, *De septem ordiniibus Ecclesiae*, ed. H. W. Kalff (Inaugural-Dissertation der Universitat Würzburg; Würzburg, 1935), 77.

174. Salvian of Marseilles, *De gubernatione Dei* III, 2, 8, ed. F. Pauly (CSEL 8; Vienna: Trempsky, 1883), 44, lists "baptismi gratiam, divini chrismatis unctionem" among the blessings God bestows on Christians.

175. Gregory of Tours, *Historia Francorum* II, 31, ed. P. Poupardin (Paris: Picard, 1913), 63: "Delibutus sacro crismate cum signaculo sanctae crucis." — Avitus of Vienne, *Ep.* 66, ed. R. Peiper (MGH, *Auct. ant.* VI, 2), 75, writing to the king, speaks of the hair that has grown in under his helmet and covered "salutarem galeam sacrae unctionis."

176. See the Council of Toledo of 397–400, can. 20 (Vives 25): 'Statutum est diaconem non crismare, sed presbyterum absente episcopo, praesente vero si ab ipso fuerit praeceptum."

us that the anointing with chrism is done only once."[177] This was also the practice to be seen in the liturgical books.[178]

b) *The Imposition of the Hand*

In Spain the Council of Elvira explicitly mentions the imposition of the hand,[179] but we must wait almost three centuries for other testimonies to the practice.[180] The *Liber ordinum* contains the gesture and provides two formularies for the accompanying invocation of the Spirit, one in the *Ordo . . . quolibet tempore* and the other, which is fuller, for the Easter Vigil.[181] The Council of Seville in 619 mentions the rite among those reserved to the bishop,[182] and Isidore of Seville, after noting that "after baptism the Holy Spirit is bestowed by the bishops through an imposition of hands,"[183] justifies the reservation from the Acts of the Apostles.

As for Gaul, the liturgical books (which, it is true, are relatively recent) end the ceremony of initiation with the anointing and the washing of feet. But while documents later than the fifth century say nothing about the imposition of the hand, the rite is formally attested for that century and at least for the southern section of the country. According to the Council of Orange, already cited, the imposition is the action used in the *con-*

---

177. Council of Orange, can 2, in *Concilia Galliae* 2 (CCL 148), 78: "Nullum ministrorum, qui baptizandi recipit officium, sine chrismate usquam debere progredi, quia inter nos placuit semel chrismari. De eo autem qui in baptismate, quacunque necessitate faciente, non chrismatus fuerit, in confirmatione sacerdos commonebitur. Nam inter quoslibet chrismatis ipsius nonnisi una benedictio est, non ut praeiudicans quidquam, sed ut non necessaria habeatur repetita christmatio." See A. Chavasse, "Le deuxième canon d'Orange de 441, essai d'exégèse," in *Etudes de critique et d'histoire religieuses* (in honor of L. Podechard) (Bibliothèque de la Faculté de Théologie de Lyon 2; Lyons: Facultés catholiques, 1948), 103–20.

178. *Liber ordinum* (Ferotin, col. 33): ". . . crismat eum sacerdos faciens signum crucis in solo fronte, dicens: Signum vitae aeternae quod dedit Deus Pater omnipotens per Iesum Christum Filium suum credentibus in salutem." The formulas are different in the Gallican books.

179. Council of Elvira, can. 38 (Vives 8): ". . . ad episcopum eum [a baptized person in danger of dying] perducat, ut per manus impositionem perfici possit." Can. 77 (p. 15) likewise speaks of the bishop's blessing.

180. In the fourth century the work of the Luciferian who revised the *De Trinitate* of Eusebius of Vercelli contains the odd expression "manus impositionis chrismae" as an invocation of the sevenfold Spirit: *De Trinitate libri VII*, VII, 20, ed. V. Bulhart (CCL 9; Turnhout: Brepols, 1957), 97.

181. *Liber ordinum* (Férotin, cols. 33 and 36). In what is doubtless the oldest recension the rubric reads: "imponit ei manus impositionem."

182. Second Council of Seville, can. 7 (Vives 168): "per impositionem manus fidelibus baptizatis . . . Paraclitum Spiritum tradere."

183. Isidore of Seville, *De ecclesiasticis officiis* II, 27 (PL 83:824–26). At the end of this passage Isidore closely follows the letter of Innocent I to Decentius. Note that he uses the plural "manuum," which was not to be found hitherto. See also Ildephonsus of Toledo, *De cognitione baptismi* 128–29 (PL 96:164–65).

firmatio that the bishop administers, since the latter normally takes no part in the chrismation.[184] The same state of affairs emerges, in about 465, from a homily of Faustus of Riez on Pentecost: "What the imposition of the hand bestows on each individual at the confirmation of neophytes is what the Spirit bestowed upon all when he descended on the throng of believers."[185] During approximately these same years Gennadius of Marseilles says expressly that "the baptized person receives the Holy Spirit through the imposition of the [bishop's] hand."[186]

c) *The Other Rites*

The practice of wearing white garments was followed in Gaul and Spain. The liturgical books do not always mention it, but this is probably because the giving of the garment was not originally accompanied by any formula.

In the Gallican liturgy, as in that of Northern Italy, the washing of feet followed the chrismation; it is there that we find it in the sacramentaries. The formula introducing it says: "I wash your feet as our Lord Jesus Christ washed the feet of his disciples; do you the same to guests and strangers."[187]

5. *The East*

The Syrian Churches did not originally have either an anointing or an imposition of the hand after the baptismal bath. After leaving the pool the neophyte was required only to take part in the Eucharist. This is the discipline attested for the eastern regions by the *Didascalia of the Apostles*, Narsai, St. Ephraem, and so on, and it was still followed at Antioch in the time of St. John Chrysostom, who mentions only the kiss of peace and the recitation of the Our Father.[188] Theodore, on the other hand,

---

184. See above, n. 177. Only in cases in which chrismation was not performed at baptism is the bishop to be alerted at confirmation, in order that he may remedy the defect.

185. Faustus of Riez, *Homilia de Pentecoste*, ed. L. A. Van Buchem, *L'Homélie pseudoeusébienne . . .* (Nijmegen: Janssen, 1967), 40. In addition to a critical edition of the document, Van Buchem's work has a study of the dossier on confirmation in southeastern Gaul.

186. Gennadius of Marseilles, *Liber siue definitio ecclesiasticorum dogmatum* 40, ed. C. H. Turner in *JTS* 7 (1906) 97 (PL 58:997).

187. *Bobbio Missal*, ed. E. A. Lowe (HBS 58; London, 1920), no. 251 (p. 75): "Ego tibi lavo pedes sicut dominus noster Iesus Christus fecit discipulis suis, ita ut facias hospitibus et peregrinis." — See St. Caesarius of Arles, *Serm.* 64 and 204, ed. G. Morin (CCL 103 and 104; Turnhout: Brepols, 1953), 276 and 821.

188. St. John Chrysostom, *Baptismal Instructions* II, 27 (Harkins 53): "As soon as they come forth from the sacred waters, all who are present embrace them. . . . They are led to the awesome table . . . where they taste of the Master's body and blood." — See his *Homiliae in Ep. ad Colossenses* 6 (PG 62:342): "He who comes up [from the font] says immediately: 'Our Father who art in heaven . . .'"

speaks of a signing or sealing, which was perhaps done with oil;[189] in any case, the Canons of Laodicea, in the last years of the fourth century or the first years of the fifth, prescribe "an anointing with heavenly chrism after baptism,"[190] and we find it in the three rituals of the *Apostolic Constitutions.*[191] All these documents retain the prebaptismal anointing, which seems to be no less important; they do not reflect the practice of the eastern regions, which at this time were still faithful to ancient custom.

In the case of Egypt it is difficult to get back beyond the Euchologion of Serapion, which supposes a chrismation after the baptismal bath, since it provides a "prayer over the chrism (*chrisma*) with which the baptized (*baptisthentes*) are anointed": ". . . now that they are reborn and renewed by the bath of new birth, let them also have part in the gift of the Holy Spirit (*tēs dōreas tou hagiou pneumatos*) and, being strengthened by this seal, remain firm and unshakable."[192]

II. THE GIFT OF THE HOLY SPIRIT

Rebirth from water and the Spirit and the reception of the Holy Spirit are two aspects of Christian initiation that are grounded in the mysteries of Easter and Pentecost respectively. This thought is echoed in all the rituals, at least from the third century on; this does not mean, however, that it is always possible to say where one aspect ends and the other begins.

1. *In the West*

It is in the West that we find the clearest picture of two stages, for the gift of the Spirit was there celebrated after the baptismal bath. Initially the gift was given by a laying on of the bishop's hand, in imitation of the Acts of the Apostles; this is clear in Tertullian and Hippolytus and continues in the following centuries in Spain, southern Gaul, and at Rome itself. The gesture was related, however, to two others, one preceding and one following. Preceding it was the anointing that referred to the descent

---

189. Theodore of Mopsuestia, *Homélies catéchétiques* XIV, 27 (Tonneau-Devreesse 456–57): "When you have received grace . . . and donned a shining white robe, the bishop comes forward and signs you on the forehead, saying: 'N. is signed in the name of the Father and of the Son and of the Holy Spirit'. . . . Like those anointed with oil by other human beings, you must receive the sealing."

190. Council of Laodicea, can. 48, ed. H. T. Bruns, *Canones apostolorum et conciliorum* 1 (Berlin: Reimer, 1839), 78.

191. *Constitutiones Apostolorum* III, 16 (Funk 1:211): "After this [baptism], the bishop is to anoint the baptized with *myron*"; — VII, 22 (Funk 1:406): "Finally you are to anoint (*sphragiseis*) with *myron*." See below, n. 197. — VII, 44, 1 (Funk 1:450): '*Chrisatō myrō*' (the Our Father follows).

192. *Euchologion of Serapion* 25 (Funk 2:186).

of the Spirit on Christ at his baptism and to its interpretation in the New Testament: "God anointed Jesus of Nazareth with the Holy Spirit" (Acts 10:38). The Messiah is here shown as completing the mission of those who under the old covenant had been consecrated by having oil poured upon them: priests, prophets, and kings. Here was a twofold expression of one and the same mystery; it doubtless contributed to the introduction at Rome of two different chrismations. Following upon the imposition of hands was the "seal" (*sphragis, signaculum*): the sign of the cross on the forehead that signified Christ's taking possession of this individual.[193]

These two rites—the anointing and the sealing—would eventually be combined into one, with the perfumed chrism then signifying in a symbolic way that membership in Christ means a participation in the "good odor" that Christ spreads abroad. The anointing-sealing would then be in competition with the imposition of the hand, to the point of entirely replacing it in some rituals. We can only think here of the verse of St. Paul: "It is God who gives us, with you, a sure place in Christ and has both anointed us and marked us with his seal, giving us as pledge the Spirit in our hearts" (2 Cor 1:21 NJB).

The Latin Churches thus celebrated baptism and "confirmation" as two distinct, successive actions; the word "confirmation" made its first indubitable appearance in fifth-century Gaul.[194] By that time the practice was already widespread of reserving this second part of initiation to the bishop and therefore of separating it from the first in time whenever a priest presided at a baptism. This discipline, which was to remain the norm in the West,[195] is attested by Innocent I in a passage already cited; he justifies it from the story in Acts, according to which Peter and John were sent to bestow the Holy Spirit on the Samaritans whom Philip the Deacon had baptized (Acts 8:14-17).

2. *In the East*

In the Syrian East (since in regard to the anointings Egypt seems to have been closer to the West, at least from the point when its practice becomes known to us), the chrismation possessing the consecratory meaning that we have seen preceded baptism. The action proclaimed, as it were, the intention of bestowing baptism and the gift of the Spirit at the same

---

193. This gesture, which we saw earlier among the rites of the catechumenate, acquires a deeper meaning here when joined to the anointing as just described. One who is "signed" becomes "Christ."

194. See the Council of Orange, above, n. 177; Faustus of Riez, above at n. 185 (text and footnote); etc.

195. This is why John the Deacon, *Ep. ad Senarium* 14 (Wilmart 178–79), can raise the question of baptized persons who are living "sine chrismatis unctione ac benedictione pontificis."

time and in a single rite that included an imposition of the bishop's hand on the initiates while they were still in the water. The ceremony had two effects, but they were produced conjointly by the celebration as a whole. In western Syria, however, the need felt for more clearly distinguishing the two aspects caused the introduction of a second chrismation.

This development may be found surprising, since the East remained faithful to a single continuous ceremony, even in cases where the bishop was not present. There were indeed exceptional cases in which those admitted into the Church when in danger of death received the needed supplements later on, but these seem to have been a later application of the change of which I am speaking here. It is doubtless preferable therefore to accept B. Botte's hypothesis: We must take into account here a problem that preoccupied the early Church, namely, the reception into the Church of Christians who had been baptized in heresy. The position of the Council of Laodicea, as understood at Constantinople in the fifth century, was that while the baptism conferred in heresy was valid, it did not bring the gift of the Spirit and that this defect had to be made up for after baptism. The first appearance of the formula "Seal of the gift of the Holy Spirit" was precisely in this act of reconciliation. May we not think, therefore, that this kind of situation stimulated theological reflection by showing that the gift of the Spirit was separable from baptism and needed to be expressed in a rite that would follow upon baptism?[196] The first anointing, however, often kept its original meaning, as is clear from the second ritual in the *Apostolic Constitutions*:

> You shall first anoint with holy oil, then baptize with water, and finally sign with the myron, so that the anointing is a participation in the Holy Spirit, the water is the symbol of death, and the myron is the seal upon commitments.[197]

§5. The Baptismal Eucharist

BIBLIOGRAPHY

L. Andrieux, *La première communion des origines au XXe siècle* (Paris: Beauchesne, 1911).

J. Daniélou, "La catéchèse eucharistique chez les Pères de l'Eglise," in *La messe et sa catéchèse* (LO 7; Paris: Cerf, 1946), 73–85.

_____, "Baptême, Pâque, eucharistie," in *Communion solennelle et profession de foi* (LO 14; Paris: Cerf, 1952), 117–33.

---

196. B. Botte, "L'onction postbaptismale dans l'ancien patriarcat d'Antioche," in *Miscellanea liturgica . . . Lercaro* 2 (Rome: Desclée, 1967), 807–8.

197. *Constitutiones Apostolorum* VII, 22 (Funk 1:406).

Initiation was not yet completed: the candidates still had to share in the Eucharist.[198] They now took part for the first time (the "first" is emphasized in the *Apostolic Tradition*) in the prayer of the faithful;[199] for the first time, too, they presented their offerings at the altar and received the Body and Blood of the Lord. Their entrance into the assembly of the faithful was a solemn event; St. Gregory of Nazianzus says of it:

> The singing of psalms that will greet you is a prelude to the hymns of the other world. The candles you will hold in your hand are a sacrament of the lamps of heaven with which we shall go out to meet the Bridegroom.[200]

Psalms 43 (Vg 42) and 23 (Vg 22), which were sung at Milan, expressed the meaning of this procession to the Eucharist. According to Ambrose's commentary, Psalm 43 underscored the "renewed youth" of the "congregation that moves toward the altar of Christ while saying 'And I shall go in to the altar of God, the God who gives joy to my youth.' " Psalm 23 spoke of "the waters of rest . . . the anointing that perfumes the head . . . the overflowing cup"; the newly baptized, says the holy bishop, "hasten to draw near to the heavenly banquet; they come in and, seeing the holy altar made ready, they cry: 'You have prepared a table for me.' "[201] For these *infantes* who had just been born to the life of grace this was the climax of a long journey that began with their first acceptance of the faith; from now on they would be able to join with their brothers and sisters and with the elect of the Apocalypse in crying "Amen!"

According to Tertullian and Hippolytus, the first communion of the newly baptized was accompanied by a special rite: in addition to the bread and wine of the Eucharist they received a mixture of milk and honey. This custom was still practiced in Rome at the beginning of the sixth century, when John the Deacon interpreted it as a sign of the Promised Land.[202] For those who had just crossed the Jordan, "this was the land of resurrection. . . . It was they who were to receive this land." They were now the heirs of the promise, and the Eucharist gave them a foretaste of its fulfillment. They could now sing: "How sweet in my mouth are your words, O Lord, sweeter than honey from the comb!" (Ps 119[118]:103).

---

198. See Justin, *Apologia I* 65, 1, ed. L. Pautigny (Textes et documents 1; Paris: Picard, 1904), 138.

199. *Traditio apostolica* 21 (Botte 54): "Henceforth they will pray with the entire congregation, whereas before receiving all this they do not pray with the faithful."

200. Gregory of Nazianzus, *Oratio 40 In sanctum baptisma* 46 (PG 36:425).

201. St. Ambrose, *De mysteriis* 43 (SC 25bis:179–80). See J. Daniélou, "Le Psaume XXII et l'initiation chrétienne," *LMD* no. 23 (1959) 54–69.

202. John the Deacon, *Ep. ad Senarium* 12 (Wilmart 177). See Lev 20:24.

§6. The Initiation of Children

BIBLIOGRAPHY

> J. C. Didier, "Le pédobaptisme au IVe siècle," *Mélanges de science religieuse* 6
> (1946) 233–46.
> J. Jeremias, *Die Kindertaufe in den ersten vier Jahrhunderten* (Göttingen: Vanden-
> hoeck und Ruprecht, 1958); ET: *Infant Baptism in the First Four Centuries,* trans.
> D. Cairns (Philadelphia: Fortress, 1960).
> J. C. Didier, *Le baptême des enfants dans la tradition de l'Eglise* (Tournai: Desclée,
> 1960).
> _____, *Faut-il baptiser les enfants? La réponse de la tradition* (Chrétiens de
> tous les temps 21; Paris: Cerf, 1967).

The Church seems to have accepted at a very early date the legitimacy
of baptizing children. Origen, in any case, speaks of the practice as being
of apostolic origin,[203] and it existed in second-century Africa as we can
see from the reservations Tertullian expresses with regard to it.[204] But adults
and even infants received baptism in the same way and at one and the
same celebration, as the *Apostolic Tradition* makes clear: "They are to
undress, and baptism is to be administered first of all to the children. Those
children who can do so are to answer for themselves. In the case of those
who cannot, their parents or some member of the family are to answer
for them."[205]

The children in question were not all infants, since some could speak.
Gregory of Nazianzus advised delaying the baptism of children until they
were three years old, in order that they might be able "to understand something of the sacrament and give their own answers. Admittedly they do
not understand very clearly at that age, but at least they receive some
impression."[206] But there was no obligation to urge the baptism even of
children who had reached that age, and he himself, despite being the son
of a bishop, was not initiated in his early years. He made an exception,
however, for children in danger of death; there was no need, then, to wait
for the coming Easter, any more than in the case of adult catechumens
who were dangerously ill. The epitaphs in the graveyards show that the
advice was heeded: "Approprianus died aged one year, nine months and
nineteen days; he was baptized on the very day of his death at his grand-
mother's request."[207]

---

203. Origen, *In ep. ad Romanos commentaria* 5, 9 (PG 14:1047): "The Church received
from the apostles the tradition of baptizing even very young children."

204. Tertullian, *De baptismo* 18, 4–6 (CCL 1:293; SC 35:92–94; Evans 39).

205. *Traditio apostolica* 21 (Botte 44).

206. Gregory of Nazianzus, *Oratio 40 In sanctum baptisma* 28 (PG 36:400).

207. Third-century Roman epitaph, ed. E. Diehl, *Inscriptiones latinae christianae ve-
teres* (Berlin, 1961), no. 1343; see the fourth-century epitaph from Salona, *ibid.*, no. 1523:

Just as children were baptized with the adults, so, too, they received with them both confirmation and the Eucharist. Cyprian speaks of those who were carried in their parents' arms or led by their hand to sacrifice to idols in time of persecution; these children could later say: "We did not deliberately abandon the Lord's food and drink."[208] And in the fifth century Gennadius of Marseilles writes: "If there are little children or handicapped persons who cannot understand the teaching, those who present them are to answer for them like someone answering for himself at baptism; then, strengthened by the imposition of the hand and by the chrism they are to be admitted to the mysteries of the Eucharist."[209] In the West, whenever a priest presided at a baptism, the gift of the Spirit was postponed until later on, that is, until the first opportunity arose for the bishop to bestow it, at which time consideration of the subject's age played no part.

"Flavia received the grace of the glorious font in the usual way on the salutary day of Easter, and lived on for five months after baptism; her life-span was three years, ten months, and seven days."

208. St. Cyprian, *De lapsis* 9, ed. G. Hartel (CSEL 3/1; Vienna, 1868), 243: ". . . nec derelicto cibo et pabulo Domini ad profana contagia sponte properavimus."

209. Gennadius of Marseilles, *Liber siue definitio eclesiasticorum dogmatum* 21, ed. C. H. Turner, *JTS* 7 (1906) 93–94 (PL 58:993).

Article III: The Evolution of Christian Initiation
(From the Sixth to the Twentieth Century)

The proportion of adults and children presenting themselves for baptism was gradually reversed with the ongoing christianization of society; the point came when only rarely did individuals enter the Church except as very young children. Yet the Church did not on this account set aside the ritual that had been in use up to that time; it continued to conduct collective celebrations on set days of the year and to observe the several preparatory stages. The only changes were a few adaptations in the course of the sixth century. Thus the period preceding initiation was reduced to a few weeks, while entrance into the catechumenate coincided with the registration of the names of the *competentes* at the beginning of Lent.[1]

§1. Initiation in the West Until the Twelfth Century

BIBLIOGRAPHY

OR XI (Andrieu, OR 2:417–47).

Martène, Lib. I, cap. 1, M 361–432 (baptism) and Lib. I, cap. 2, M 433–67 (confirmation).

Comes de Murbach, ed. A. Wilmart, *RBén* 30 (1913) 25–69.

P. de Puniet, "La liturgie baptismale en Gaule avant Charlemagne," *Revue des questions liturgiques* 72 (1902) 382–423.

A. Chavasse, "La bénédiction du chrême en Gaule avant l'adoption intégrale de la liturgie romaine," *Revue du moyen-âge latin* 1 (1945) 109–28.

——————, "Le carême romain et les scrutins prébaptismaux avant le IXe siècle," *RechSR* 35 (1948) 325–81.

——————, "L'initiation à Rome dans l'antiquité et le haut moyen-âge," in *Communion solennelle et profession de foi* (LO 14; Paris: Cerf, 1952), 1–32.

---

1. This change is already attested by John the Deacon, *Ep. ad Senarium* 3 (Wilmart 172): the old rites of entrance into the catechumenate were combined with the first scrutiny. The registration of names was followed by the exsufflation, signing, and giving of salt, and then by the exorcism *super electos*.

J. Krinke, "Der spanische Taufritus im frühen Mittelalter," in *Aufsätze zur Kultur-geschichte Spaniens* (Spanische Forschungen der Görresgesellschaft 1/9; Münster, 1954), 33–116.

A. Chavasse, "La discipline romaine des sept scrutins baptismaux," *RechSR* 48 (1960) 227–40.

C. Vogel, "La reforme liturgique sous Charlemagne," in B. Bischoff, *Karl der Grosse* 2 (Düsseldorf, 1965), 217–32.

J. Deshusses, "Le 'Supplément' au sacramentaire grégorien: Alcuin ou saint Benoît d'Aniane?" *ALW* 9/1 (1965) 48–71.

J. D. C. Fischer, *Christian Initiation: Baptism in the Medieval West. A Study in the Disintegration of the Primitive Rite of Initiation* (Alcuin Club Collections 47; London: S.P.C.K., 1965).

T. C. Akeley, *Christian Initiation in Spain c. 300–1100* (London: Darton, Longman & Todd, 1967).

I. DOWN TO THE CAROLINGIAN PERIOD

1. *Rome*

a) *The Multiplication and Relocation of the Scrutinies*

The number of scrutinies rose to seven (including the gathering on Holy Saturday), as though to make up for the passivity of the subjects by a more intense activity of the Church in showing forth the unmerited character of God's gift. But since the community as a whole no longer felt involved to the same extent as in the days when it accompanied adults on their journey to baptism, it was no longer thought necessary to celebrate the scrutinies amid the assembled community. They were therefore moved to weekdays on which the biblical passages previously assigned to Sundays were now read; these were supplemented by other readings adapted to the preparation of catechumens.[2] At a second stage of the evolution the first two scrutinies alone remained tied to a specific day of Lent, namely the third Thursday and Saturday; the others could be moved as was found convenient. This is what we are told by *Ordo* XI, which dates from the seventh century or perhaps the end of the sixth and was intended for the use of Roman priests who had to baptize children in the titular churches or the basilicas.[3] The papal Sacramentary of Hadrian, which cannot date from before the end of the seven century, shows that the bishop presided in person only at the more important assemblies.[4]

---

2. A. Chavasse, "La discipline romaine des sept scrutins baptismaux," *RechSR* 48 (1960) 227–40.

3. *OR* XI (Andrieu, *OR* 2:415–47); see nos. 2, 37, 39–40, 76, 82.

4. This sacramentary has only the blessing of the salt and prayer *Omnipotens* of the first scrutiny, the closing formula of the third scrutiny, and the celebration of Holy Saturday: *Gr* nos. 356–61 (1:180–83).

b) *The Giving of the Gospels*

To the "handing over" of the Creed and the Our Father was now added the giving of the gospels.[5] This act replaced the old catechetical instructions that had now become useless since little children were not capable of profiting from them.

c) *The Formula for the Baptismal Bath*

A formula spoken by the celebrant alone replaced the dialogue in which those being baptized had professed their faith; the reason for this was that because of their age the baptizands now had a purely passive role. The new formula is attested in 744 by Pope Zachary in the corrupt form given it by priests in Germany who did not know Latin.[6] It is the formula that the Gregorian Sacramentary prescribes for the initiation of sick persons: "Ill. talis, baptizo te in nomine Patris et Filii et Spiritus Sancti."[7]

2. *Gaul and Spain*

As early as the first half of the fifth century, St. Caesarius of Arles seems to have already been dealing chiefly with little children, although he was still performing some adult baptisms. He exhorted parents to present their children for baptism at the beginning of Lent and to attend the vigils with them.[8] But these regulations were applied flexibly, since initiation could be celebrated on days other than Easter:

> As each feast draws near, especially the feasts of the saints, those who want one of their children baptized should come to the church ten days, or at least a week, in advance with those to be baptized and present them for the anointing with oil and the imposition of the hand. . . . Although it is preferable to celebrate baptisms at the paschal solemnity, nevertheless, because of human frailty and especially in the case of catechumens who are often ill, the gift of baptism is not to be refused.[9]

---

5. *Ge* nos. 299–309 (pp. 46, 48): reading by a deacon of the first verses of each of the Four Gospels, introduced by short explanations from the priest. On the other hand, in the handing over of the Creed the Nicene-Constantinopolitan Creed replaces the Apostles' Creed (the Gelasian gives it in Latin and in Greek): *Ge* no. 312 (pp. 48–49).

6. Zachary, *Ep. 7 ad Bonifacium* (PL 89:929): "Et dum baptizaret, nesciens latini eloquii, infringens linguam, diceret: Baptizo te in nomine Patria et Filia et Spiritu sancta."

7. *Gr* no. 982 (1:336). This is perhaps a late interpolation; the awkward redaction of the text suggests this hypothesis.

8. St. Caesarius of Arles, *Serm* 84:6 (CCL 103:348): "If parents are willing to present their children for baptism at the beginning of Lent and faithfully attend the vigils with them, their children will receive the sacrament of baptism in a rightful manner and they themselves will win the forgiveness of their sins."

9. Idem, *Serm*. 225, 6 (CCL 104:891). — Gregory of Tours speaks of baptisms on various feasts of the year; for example, an infant baptism several times put off was set first for Christmas, then Easter, then the feast of St. John (*Historia Francorum* VIII, 9, ed. P. Poupardin [Paris: Picard, 1913], 306).

The prebaptismal rites consisted of an anointing and an imposition of the hand that were to take place a certain time before baptism. Apart from this requirement, the authorities seemed ready to make not a few compromises. Elsewhere the same bishop of Arles makes his preference for the traditional date even clearer,[10] and the Council of Mâcon in 585 would bemoan the fact that "we no longer have more than two or three children being reborn of water and the Spirit on the holy day of Easter," a development that led it to remind the people of the old regulations.[11]

The role of the godparents took a new form: "Those who are to receive the little children are to say the Creed in their place or have others do this. . . . As for the children you receive: once they are baptized, correct them continually."[12]

The liturgical books bear the mark of this evolution, since practically all the rites are located together between Palm Sunday and the Easter Vigil. The same organization is found in the Spanish books. According to the *Liber ordinum*, the bishop and candidates go the baptistery after the third of the eleven Vigil readings; the candidates here can only have been children, since adults would not have been thus deprived of what was to be their final instruction. The rubric specifies that "the chrism and holy communion are on the altar of St. John," that is, in the baptistery. The neophytes therefore received communion there in the baptistery and were then taken home; adults would join the assembly for the Mass that followed.[13] As for the postbaptismal rites in Gaul, chrismation and the washing of feet were still practiced, but the imposition of the hand seems to have been forgotten, though it continued to be mentioned in the Peninsula.

II. FROM THE NINTH TO THE TWELFTH CENTURY

The Carolingian period saw the introduction of the Roman liturgy into Gaul; a Capitulary of 789 ordered bishops "ut secundum morem romanum baptizent."[14] The papal sacramentary that Pope Hadrian I sent to

10. See St. Caesarius, *Serm.* 229, 6 (CCL 104:910): "Bonum et legitimum est ut qui sani sunt in paschalem sollemnitatem serventur, et secundum ecclesiasticam regulam in diebus quadragesimae ieiunent et vigilent, et ad oleum et ad manus impositiones accedant."

11. Council of Mâcon, can. 3, ed. C. De Clercq, *Concilia Galliae* (CCL 148A), 240: ". . . a suis erroribus vel ignorantia revocati omnes omnino a die quadragesimo cum infantibus suis ad ecclesiam observare praecipimus, ut impositionem manus certis diebus adepti et sacri olei liquore peruncti legitimi diei festivitate fruantur et sacro baptismate regenerentur. . . ."

12. St. Caesarius of Arles, *Serm.* 130, 5 (CCL 103:537–38).

13. *Liber ordinum* 86 (Férotin 217–19).

14. *Duplex legislationis edictum* 23,. ed. A. Boretius, *Capitula regum francorum* 1 (Hannover, 1881), 64. — See C. De Clercq, *La legislation franque de Clovis à Charlemagne* (Receuil de travaux . . ., 2nd series, fasc. 38; Louvain, 1936), 171–72, 176–78.

Charlemagne was not adequate for the use of priests and had to be supplemented; this accounts for the *Aniane Supplement,* known under the
doubtless inaccurate name of *Alcuin's Supplement.*[15] The emperor himself promoted the reform and launched an inquiry among the metropolitans of his territory regarding the way baptisms were being celebrated.[16]
The answers were often influenced by a little work whose exact origin
is unknown but which was very popular in ecclesiastical circles; its opening words were "Primo paganus."[17] It was a short list of the various rites
of initiation, the meaning of each being summed up in a sentence; for example: "Finally, the candidate receives from the high priest, by an imposition of the hand, the sevenfold Spirit of grace, in order that having been
gifted by grace with eternal life in baptism, he or she may have the strength
from the Holy Spirit to proclaim it to others."

The new practices were organized into a ritual in a compilation known
as *Ordo antiquus romanus* (*Ordo* L in Andrieu), which incorporated the
old *Ordo* XI as enriched by some Gallican additions; *Ordo* L is part of
the Romano-German Pontifical which originated in Mainz around 950.
The Ottos then introduced this Rhenish book into Rome; it was there accepted and revised until the appearance of the texts that are grouped under
the title of the Twelfth-Century Pontifical.[18]

1. *The Structure of the Ritual*

The principle was still maintained of celebrating the initiation of children in a group on the major baptismal feasts. But the books also included
the practice widespread in Gaul of having a single gathering prior to baptism and even a single continuous baptismal rite. In addition to an *ordo*
retaining the discipline of the seven scrutinies,[19] the Romano-German Pontifical contained two rituals—one for children and one for adults—that
combined into a single ceremony the entrance into the catechumenate,
the exorcisms, the *catechizatio* (which here meant what was done on Holy
Saturday), and the sacraments proper;[20] the renunciation of Satan and

---

15. See J. Deshusses, *Le Sacramentaire grégorien* 1 (Spicilegium Friburgense 16; Fribourg,
1971), 63–70.

16. A. Wilmart, *Analecta Reginensia* (ST 59; Vatican City, 1933), 153–79, and the references given there; in addition, J. M. Hanssens (ed.), *Amalarii episcopi opera liturgica omnia* 1. *Introductio, Opera minora* (ST 13; Vatican City, 1948), 135–251.

17. Alcuin, *Ep.* 234 and 237, ed. E. Dümmler, *Epistolae karolini aevi* 2 (MGH; Berlin:
Weidemann, 1895), 202–3 and 214–15, reproduces the text, which has caused it to be attrib-
uted to him. The document seems to be an explanation of Roman practice for the use of
Frankish clerics.

18. *OR* L (Andrieu, *OR* 5:49–57, 129–60, 261–64, 275–92, 401–5); — *PRG*; — Andrieu,
PR 1.

19. *PRG* 2:24–40, 93–94, 102–10.

20. *PRG* 2:155–64. See *Sacramentarium Fuldense saeculi X*, ed. G. Richter and A. Schön-
felder (Quellen und Abhandlungen zur Geschichte . . . Fulda 9; Fulda, 1912), 343–53.

the profession of faith were placed at the beginning and the old rites marking entrance into the catechumenate came only afterwards.

2. *Rites connected with Baptism*

a) The blessing of chrism on Holy Thursday was revised. The Gelasian Sacramentary in its final redaction had confused the formulary for the blessing of chrism with that for the blessing of the oil of exorcism;[21] the mistake was partially corrected by the compiler of *Ordo L*.[22]

b) The blessing of baptismal water was accompanied by several rites at the risk of distracting attention from the prayer whose wealth of meaning I have already pointed out.[23] In some churches the two candles lowered into the font were replaced by the Easter candle: there was thus a shift from the symbolism of light to that of Christ represented as going down into the Jordan. This action is found in *Ordo L*, as is the gesture of signing the water in the form of a cross.[24] The Frankish liturgists added still other actions that are to be found in the Roman Pontifical of the Twelfth Century.[25]

c) After the baptismal immersion the white garment was given to the neophyte with an accompanying formula of Gallican origin that passed into the Roman liturgy via *Ordo L*: "Accipe vestem sanctam candidam et immaculatam, quam perferas ante tribunal Domini nostri Iesu Christi, ut habeas vitam aeternam."[26] The giving of a candle came a little later; it made its appearance in the eleventh century[27] and is attested at Rome in the Pontifical of the Twelfth Century.[28] It reached back to a traditional initiatory symbolism, namely, the nuptial aspect evoked by the reference to the parable of the ten virgins.

---

21. *Ge* nos. 383–90 (pp. 61–63). The prayer *Deus incrementorum*, which has to do with the oil of exorcism, is used for the chrism, and two prayers referring to the chrism are applied to the oil of exorcism.

22. *OR L*, 25, 95–96 (Andrieu, *OR* 5:224–25); *PRG* 2: 99, 278–79, (pp. 75–76). The prayer *Deus incrementorum* is here restored to its proper place, but with the formula *Exorcizo te*, which is a revised text meant to be used in the blessing of chrism.

23. See above, pp. 45–46.

24. This gesture is already found in *Ordo XXIV*, which attests the practice of a suburbicarian diocese: *OR XXIV*, 47 (Andrieu, *OR* 3:296).

25. Andrieu, *PR* 1:243–45. The chrismation of the water is already mentioned in *Ordo XI* and *Ordo XXX B* (Andrieu, *OR* 2:445 and 3:247). It occurs again in *Ordo L* (Andrieu, *OR* 5:281), in *PRG* 2:104, and Andrieu, *PR* 1:245. I mentioned earlier that it was first practiced in Gaul and Spain.

26. *Bobbio Missal*, ed. E. A. Lowe (HBS 58; London, 1920), no. 250 (p. 75); *Liber ordinum* (Férotin col. 31). — Andrieu, *OR* 5:288; *PRG* 2:107.

27. *Ordo* of Jumièges, in Martène, Lib. I, cap. 1, a. 18 (M 424).

28. Andrieu, *PR* 1, 32, 28 (p. 246).

3. *Confirmation*

Confirmation was celebrated as soon as the bishop's presence made this possible; if he presided at the baptism, confirmation followed immediately.[29] This practice persisted down to our own time in some dioceses of Spain and Latin America. But since this sacrament was often separated from the first stage of initiation, the old Roman *ordo* was filled out, before and after the imposition of the hand and the anointing, with biblical verses referring to the gift of the Holy Spirit.[30]

Especially to be noted is the formula that appeared in *Ordo* L: "Confirmo et consigno te in nomine Patris . . ."[31] and that became, in the Pontifical of the Twelfth Century: "Signo te signo crucis, et confirmo te chrismate salutis, in nomine Patris et Filii et Spiritus Sancti."[32] Everyone will recognize the words that were still in use down to the most recent reforms.

4. *First Communion*

The communion of the newly baptized concluded the celebration. I shall simply cite the rubric in the Pontifical of the Twelfth Century:

> If the bishop is not present, they are to receive communion from the priest. Children not yet capable of eating and drinking are to receive communion by means of a leaf or a finger dipped in the blood of the Lord and placed in their mouths, while the priest says: "Corpus cum sanguine Domini nostri Iesu Christi custodiat te in vitam aeternam. Amen." If they are older, they are to receive communion in the usual way.[33]

§2. The Evolution of Initiation in the West from the Twelfth and Thirteenth Centuries On

BIBLIOGRAPHY

> J. Catalani, *Rituale Romanum . . . perpetuis commentariis exornatum* 1 (Rome, 1937), 23–183.
> _____, *Pontificale Romanum . . . prolegomenis et commentariis illustratum* 1 (Rome, 1738; reprinted: Mequignon, 1850), 43–80.

---

29. Andrieu, *PR*, 1, 32, 29 (p. 246): "Si episcopus adest, statim oportet confirmari chrismate. . . ." The treatise *Primo paganus*, however, influenced no doubt by the frequency of confirmations separated from baptism, puts the imposition of the bishop's hand after communion.

30. *OR* L, 39, 71–78 (Andrieu, *OR* 5:288–92). It was also by way of *Ordo* L that the prayer *Deus qui apostolis tuis* entered the Roman liturgy.

31. *OR* L, 74 (Andrieu, *OR* 5:290).

32. Nos. 32–33 (Andrieu, *PR* 1:247).

33. No. 29 (*ibid.*, 246).

J. Ernst, *Die Zeit der ersten Kommunion und die "Jahre der Unterscheidung" seit dem IV. allgemeinen Konzil von Lateran (1215)* (Mainz, 1927).

D. Van Den Eynde, "Notes sur les rites postbaptismaux dans les Eglises d'Occident," *Antonianum* 14 (1939) 257–76.

B. Neunheuser, *Taufe und Firmung* (Handbuch der Dogmengeschichte IV, 2; Freiburg: Herder, 1956). ET: *Baptism and Confirmation*, trans. J. J. Hughes (New York: Herder and Herder, 1964).

D. Van Den Eynde, "Les rites liturgiques latins de la confirmation," *LMD* no. 54 (1958) 53–78.

E. Llopart, "Las fórmules de la confirmació en el Pontifical romà," *Liturgica* 2 (Scripta et documenta 10; Monserrat, 1958), 121–80.

R. Levet, "L'âge de la confirmation dans la législation des diocèses de France depuis le Concile de Trente," *LMD* no. 54 (1958) 118–42.

P. Romane-Musculus, "La confirmation dans les Eglises de la Réforme," *LMD* no. 54 (1958) 154–59.

X. Seumois, "La structure de la liturgie baptismale romaine et les problèmes du catéchumenat missionaire," *LMD* no. 58 (1959) 82–110.

J. Toussaert, *Le sentiment religieux en Flandre à la fin du moyen-âge* (Paris: Plon, 1963).

P. Adam, *La vie paroissiale en France au XIVe siècle* (Paris: Sirey, 1964).

B. Jordahn, "Der Taufgottesdienst im Mittelalter bis zur Gegenwart," in *Leitourgia* 5 (Kassel: Stauda, 1970), 349–640 (chiefly on the Lutheran Churches).

A. Duval, "Le Concile de Trente et le baptême des enfants," *LMD* no. 110 (1972) 16–24.

J. M. Gy, "Die Taufkommunion der kleinen Kinder in der lateinischen Kirche," in H. Auf Der Maur and B. Kleinheyer (eds.), *Zeichen des Glaubens* [Festschrift B. Fischer] (Cologne: Benziger, 1972), 485–91.

H. Vinck, "Sur l'âge de la confirmation, un projet de décret au Concile Vatican I," *LMD* no. 132 (1977) 136–40.

I. BAPTISM IMMEDIATELY AFTER BIRTH

In the course of the twelfth century, as the result of a very gradual change, it became the common practice to celebrate baptism during the days after birth. Here is a rather odd testimony to the change:

> The canons order that baptism be celebrated only on Holy Saturday or on Pentecost, except in case of necessity. But this precept has adults in view. In the early Church adults who were sick could say so, and then they were baptized. Moreover, the fact that many were baptized at the same time augmented the glory of the Christian name. But all this does not apply to little children, for who is more ill than an infant who cannot make it known that it is ill? The baptism of children should therefore not be put off, for they may die of the least ailment.[34]

At that time the infant mortality rate was very high, but this was nothing new. In a period when desires for reform were widespread in the

---

34. Anonymous writer of the School of Anselm of Laon, no. 359, ed. O. Lottin, *RTAM* 13 (1946) 271.

Church, the new discipline seems to have been part of an effort to bring about moral improvement, for it could only inspire greater respect for the lives of infants.[35] This refinement of moral conscience and growth in a sense of personal responsibility on the part of parents had its foundation in a renewal in theology, where theologians were concentrating especially on original sin and the doctrine of salvation. The synodal statutes of the French dioceses, especially beginning in the thirteenth century, contained many exhortations to ensure that newborn children received the grace of the sacrament as soon as possible (*quam primum*); priests were insistently called upon to teach laypeople to baptize in danger of death, and the statutes began to envisage cases of accidents occurring during labor.[36] Thus it was not primarily liturgical concerns that led to the change I have indicated; the rituals, however, did reflect them and would continue to change with changing mentalities in the centuries ahead.

II. DEVELOPMENT OF THE RITES OF INITIATION

1. *Baptism by Infusion*

To facilitate the application of the new discipline baptism by infusion—which consists in pouring water on the child's head instead of immersing the whole child in a basin—gradually became common because it was easier; it became the almost universal practice in the fourteenth century.[37] But although immersion fell into disuse it still had its place in the rubrics.[38]

2. *A Continuous Rite of Baptism*

The continuous rite now became the rule because a preparatory session would have involved a delay. The catechumenate was abolished, but most of its component parts remained, being compiled from several sources and awkwardly linked to form a single series. There was no longer any giving or giving back of the symbol and the *Pater*, but the Creed and the Our Father were said, as the thirteenth-century Pontifical of the Roman

---

35. The case of infants suffocated in their parents' beds concerned bishops and gave rise to synodal regulations; eg., *Concilium loci incerti*, in E. Martène, *Thesaurus novus anecdotorum* 4 (Paris, 1717), col. 154: "Feminae moneantur ut pueros suos . . . iuxta se de nocte non collocent teneros, ne opprimantur et cum eis ad baptismum festinent et ad confirmationem. . . . "

36. *Ibid., passim*.

37. St. Thomas Aquinas, *Summa theologiae* III, 66, 7, justifies the other forms of baptism, "although it is safer to baptize by immersion, because this is the more common practice." Immersion was therefore the most common way of baptizing in his time.

38. *Rituale Romanum* of Pope Paul V, tit. 2, cap. 2, n. 20, and cap. 45, no. 45.

Curia attests.[39] The *Liber sacerdotalis* of Alberto Castellani, which was the first attempt at a Roman ritual (1523), had two *ordines* for baptism that were organized in this way. Among the preparatory studies done for a new book after the Council of Trent, Cardinal Santori's draft provided for the restoration of the ancient discipline of the scrutinies, especially in mission countries,[40] but this suggestion was not retained in the Roman Ritual promulgated by Paul V in 1614. This contained an *Ordo baptismi parvulorum* followed by an *Ordo baptismi adultorum*; in both cases baptism was a single continuous rite, the stages being marked only by the bringing of the catechumen into the church after the next-to-last exorcism and by the changing of the priest's vestments from violet to white after the prebaptismal anointing.[41] For those baptized in case of necessity, there were two corresponding *Ordines supplendi*, which contained practically the whole of the regular ritual, except for the sacramental rite proper, despite the blatant inappropriateness of catechumenal formulas for persons who had already received the grace of rebirth.[42]

3. The Rites of Confirmation

It is significant that the thirteenth-century Pontifical of the Roman Curia does not give the rites of baptism. It contains only an *Ordo ad consignandos pueros sive infantes*.[43] The bishop's role is thus limited to confirming children already baptized by a priest. The same is true of the Pontifical of William Durandus, which dates from between 1292 and 1295.[44] The bishop of Mende, whose work was to have such a great influence on subsequent Roman books, made a few changes in the ceremonial of confirmation. It was he who replaced the kiss of peace at the end of the ceremony with the slap (*alapa*), which he undertook to justify by a rather questionable symbolism.[45] He also replaced the laying of the hand on each confirmand[46] with a collective laying on of both hands: "elevatis et super confirmandos extensis manibus." In the eighteenth century Bene-

---

39. *Ordo ad cathecuminum faciendum* 52, 53 (Andrieu, *PR* 2:517).

40. G. A. Santori, *Rituale sacramentorum romanum . . .* (Rome, 1584 [date incorrect]), 20–106; see 125–40.

41. *Rituale Romanum*, tit. II, cap. 2, nos. 10 and 17; cap. 4, nos. 29 and 37.

42. *Ibid.*, cap. 5 and 6. See P. Jounel, *LMD* no. 80 (1964) 91.

43. *Ordo ad consignandos . . .* 345 (Andrieu, *PR* 2:452–53). There is also, in no. 53, an *Ordo ad cathecuminum faciendum* (pp. 513–17), which was in all likelihood a relic.

44. *De crismandis in fronte pueris* I, 1 (Andrieu, *PR* 3:333–35). The *Ordo in sabbato sancto* 4, 18, says simply: "prosequitur formam solitam baptizandi" (*PR* 3:591). The rite of baptism was reintroduced into the *Pontificale Romanum* of 1595.

45. William Durandus. *Rationale divinorum officiorum* VI, 84, 6–8 (Lyons: A. Cellier, 1672), 368.

46. See the Pontificals of the Twelfth Century 32, 31, and the Pontifical of the Thirteenth Century 34, 1 (Andrieu, *PR* 2:247 and 3:452): "imposita manu super capita singulorum."

dict XIV decided to restore the ancient gesture at the moment of anointing; he ordered ministers to lay the hand flat on the head of the person being anointed.[47]

III. DEVELOPMENTS IN THE DISCIPLINE OF INITIATION

Initially, the discipline that caused baptism to be celebrated in close proximity to birth brought no changes to the other sacraments of initiation. Bernard, bishop of Saintes in the mid-twelfth century, still thought that "the baptized should receive Holy Communion at least in the form of the Blood, as soon as possible," and he ordered that those requiring confirmation be brought to him without delay, for "it is risky to die without confirmation."[48] Soon, however, changes began to occur in these areas.

1. *First Communion Delayed (Thirteenth Century)*

"We formally forbid priests to give even unconsecrated hosts to children": this synodal prescription from Paris, dating very probably from the very early years of the thirteenth century,[49] indicates the rise of a new practice that was to spread very quickly. The spread was due to the Lateran Council of 1215, which ordered the faithful to receive the Eucharist at least at Easter, once they had reached the "age of discretion" (*annos discretionis*).[50] From this point on, a delay in first communion was to be found almost everywhere. The words used by the Fathers of the Council were, however, interpreted in different ways: some thought that the age of discretion was seven years, but many others very quickly began to speak of eleven or twelve and sometimes even a later age.[51] Confirmation, mean-

---

47. The correction was in fact made only in the *ordo* for confirmation that was put in an appendix of the Pontifical and intended for cases when there was only one confirmand.

48. Bernard of Saintes, *Decret.* 1–2, ed. J. Leclercq in *Revue du moyen âge latin* 2 (1946) 167–70.

49. Synodal statutes of Eudes de Sully, 91, ed. O. Pontal, *Les statuts synodaux français du XIIIe siècle* 1 (Collection des documents inédits sur l'histoire de France, série in 8°, vol. 9; Paris: Bibliothèque nationale, 1971), 86: "districte praecipimus presbyteris ne hostias, licet non sacratas, dent pueris ullo modo."

50. Lateran Council IV, can. 21 (DS 812); see Hefele-Leclerq, *Histoire des Conciles* (Paris: Letouzey, 1913²) 5/2:1349-50.

51. The same phrase is used again by the Council of Trent, Session 21 (1562), can. 4 (DS 1734): "If anyone says that eucharistic communion is necessary for little children before they reach the use of reason (*ad annos discretionis*), *anathema sit*" (trans. in J. Neuner and J. Dupuis [eds.], *The Christian Faith in the Doctrinal Documents of the Catholic Church* [Staten Island, N.Y.: Alba House, 1982], no. 1544, p. 423).

while, was still celebrated on the first occasion of the bishop's presence, without regard to the age of the children.[52]

2. Confirmation Delayed (Fourteenth Century)

Dependence on a minister who was not always at hand prevented the setting of a fixed age for confirmation, and this sacrament was in fact conferred at quite different ages, depending on circumstances. Meanwhile the experiment with the Eucharist led, towards the fifteenth century, to a reluctance to celebrate confirmation at a very early age. In any event, the *Catechismus ad parochos* that appeared in 1566, right after the Council of Trent, had this to say:

> Everyone ought to be aware that the sacrament of confirmation can be administered after baptism. It is more appropriate, however, that it not be administered until children have reached the age of reason. Consequently, while it does not seem right to wait until the twelfth year, it is desirable that the sacrament be put off until the child is seven.[53]

Most of the diocesan documents determined from this that confirmation was not to be administered before the age of seven.[54] In fact, beginning with this age, the celebration of confirmation might be held at any time during adolescence and sometime even beyond it.

3. Organization of Catechisms and Initiation (Seventeenth Century)

Once the Christian instruction of children was given an organized form in the seventeenth century, in keeping with the spirit of Trent, there was a tendency to correlate years of catechetical instruction and the sacraments.[55] The teaching of Christian doctrine began at about the age of seven, the age when confirmation could be administered. Meanwhile, first communion, which since the Lateran Council had been the first Easter communion and was therefore received during the Easter season, came to be a special festive day that was celebrated with solemnity, at least in the dioceses of France, and was accompanied by a profession of faith. It concluded the cycle of Christian instruction and corresponded usually with the end of a child's schooling, at the age of about eleven or twelve. Perhaps the idea was to make it parallel to the parish missions, which were

---

52. Synodal statutes of Eudes de Sully, 13, in Pontal (n. 49), 56: "Laypeople must often be reminded that they are not to wait too long for a visit of the bishop for confirmation."

53. *Catechismus ad parochos* II, 4, 15, ed. Gagey (Lyons-Paris, 1886), 1:365.

54. Different interpretations are possible of the words "si duodecimus annus non expectandus videatur."

55. See J. C. Dhotel, *Les origines du catéchisme moderne d'après les premiers manuels imprimés en France* (Théologie 71; Paris: Aubier, 1967).

a kind of adult catechesis that likewise ended with confession and a solemn communion. This view of first communion was in any case to play an important role in pastoral practice down to our own time.

4. *Confirmation After First Communion (Eighteenth Century)*

The emphasis on instruction gave rise in the mid-eighteenth century to a new custom that is attested by, for example, the *Instructions du Rituel de Toulon* of 1748: "In order to be sure that children presented for confirmation in this diocese are adequately instructed, it has been decided that they are to be confirmed only after having received their first communion."[56] It is important that we realize how significant a shift this was: in the past, confirmation had often been celebrated after first communion, but only for the practical reason that the bishop was not available; in principle, the Eucharist was the high point of the rites of initiation as it is of the entire sacramental system, and it was thought that if individuals were ready to partake of the Body of Christ, they were all the more ready to receive the gift of the Spirit.

The practice at Toulon became widespread throughout France after the Revolution, but for practical purposes it was not adopted elsewhere, and it met with resistance from the Roman authorities.[57] It was actually declining in some dioceses when a decree of Pius X raised a new problem.

5. *First Communion at About the Age of Seven*

The Decree *Quam singulari* of 1910[58] was a timely reminder that communion belongs not at the end of a child's formation but at the point when he or she is capable of personal responsibility and able to prepare to receive it fruitfully, that is, at about the age of seven. From this point on, it was no longer in France alone that the order of the sacraments of initiation was reversed,[59] at least until 1917 when the Code of Canon Law spoke

---

56. Ritual of Toulon, published in 1747; see Ordonnances synodales de Saint-Paul-Trois-Châteaux, published at Avignon in 1751: R. Levet, "L'âge de la confirmation," *LMD* no. 54 (1958) 121–25.

57. The erection in 1850 of the new dioceses of Saint-Denis on Reunion Island, Saint-Pierre in Martinique, and Basse-Terre in Guadalupe required that Rome give its approval to the first synodal statutes; the Congregation of the Council took the occasion to change the decrees on the age of confirmation. The same happened in connection with the first council of the ecclesiastical province of Algiers in 1873. Bishop Robert of Marseilles was encouraged to act on the same lines by Leo XIII in 1897. See Levet (n. 56), 131–33.

58. *AAS* 1 (1910) 625ff.

59. In France a first "private" communion was celebrated at about the age of seven, while a "solemn communion," usually connected with confirmation, was celebrated at the end of the period of catechetical instruction.

of confirmation being suitably received at about the age of seven.[60] In the years after the publication of the Code we see the age required for this sacrament being pushed back.[61] This was the prevailing practice at the time when the Second Vatican Council was convoked.

§3. Development of Initiation in the East

BIBLIOGRAPHY

> A. Raes, *Introductio in liturgiam orientalem* (Rome: Pontificio Istituto Orientale, 1947), 120-43.
> G. Kretschmar, "Die Geschichte des Taufgottesdienstes in der alten Kirche," in *Leitourgia. Handbuch des evangelischen Gottesdienstes* 5 (Kassel: Stauda, 1970), 274-96.
> L. Ligier, *La Confirmation, sens et conjoncture oecuménique hier et aujourd'hui* (Théologie historique 23; Paris: Beauchesne, 1973), 51-94: "Le dossier des liturgies orientales."
> H. Brakmann, "Liturgieberichte: Zu den Liturgien des christlichen Ostens," *ALW* 24 (1962) 393-96.

In the East the initiation of infants underwent by and large the same development as in the West. In the beginning it was celebrated, like that of adults, in a collective manner, but the feasts of the Easter season were rivaled as a time of celebration by Epiphany, the day on which the Lord's baptism was commemorated and on which there was a solemn blessing of water in all the rites. Celebrations connected with birth were also established: blessing of the infant and bestowal of a name on the eighth day; on the fortieth day, a purification of the mother at which the priest, like Simeon of old, took the child in his arms and laid it down before the altar. When the practice of individual baptism arose, all these other practices were often placed at the beginning of a continuous ceremony that connected entrance into the world and entrance into the Church even more closely than in the Latin Church. In addition, confirmation was never reserved to the bishop and therefore in normal circumstances it followed upon baptism, even for infants, and before communion.

---

60. 1917 *Codex iuris canonici*, can. 788: "Licet sacramenti confirmationis administratio convenienter in Ecclesia latina differatur ad septimum circiter aetatis annum, nihilominus etiam antea conferri potest, si infans in mortis periculo sit constitutus. . . ."

61. See the *Directoire de la Pastorale des Sacrements* published by the French episcopate in 1951, nos. 31-33: "The Church wishes confirmation to be administered at about the age of reason (that is, at the time of "private" first communion). . . . It would be contrary to the Church's intention to delay confirmation. . . . Historically, confirmation has been the second stage of Christian initiation . . . and should therefore be received before the Eucharist."

I. THE BYZANTINE, WEST SYRIAN, AND MARONITE RITES

BIBLIOGRAPHY

E. Mercenier and F. Paris, *La prière des Eglises de rite byzantin* 1 (Chevetogne, 1948²), 323–56.

B. Botte, "Le baptême dans l'Eglise syrienne," *OS* 1 (1956) 137–57.

G. Khouri-Sarkis, "Prières et cérémonies du baptême selon le rite de l'Eglise syrienne d'Antioche," *ibid.*, 158–84.

E. Hambye, "Le baptême dans les Eglises syriennes de l'Inde," *ibid.*, 255–66.

P. Verghese, "Relation between Baptism, 'Confirmation,' and Eucharist in the Syrian Orthodox Church," *Studia liturgica* 4 (1965) 81–93.

A. Mouhanna, *Les rites de l'initiation dans l'Eglise maronite* (Christianismos 1; Rome: Pontificio Istituto Orientale, 1978).

_____, "Le symbolisme dans les rites de l'initiation de l'Eglise maronite," in *I simboli dell'iniziazione cristiana . . .* (Studia Anselmiana 87, Analecta liturgica 7; Rome, 1983), 105–21.

L. Ligier, "Quand la définition d'un rite sacramentel engage celle de son ministre," in *Mens concordet voci, pour Mgr A. G. Martimort* (Paris: Desclée, 1983), 577–84.

These rites contain an ancient substance that is common to them all. The earliest source available to us is Byzantine and dates from the eighth century.[62] The Syrian *ordo*, which James of Edessa (d. 708) translated from the Greek but doubtless also adapted, can be partially reconstructed on the basis of various collections.[63] Many changes, however, have been made over the centuries, and the Maronite tradition has been heavily Latinized. The celebration in its present-day form begins at the door of the baptistery and continues inside.

1. *Outside the Baptistery*

The Syrians begin with a service of song and prayer that contains two Scripture readings: Rom 6:1-8 and John 3:1-8. After a prayer over the catechumen, the priest writes the person's name in a register and then signs him or her on the forehead with a sign of the cross. This is followed by the exorcisms, the rejection of Satan (facing the West), the acceptance of Jesus Christ (facing the East), and a thanksgiving formula. The Maronite Rite follows almost the identical pattern.

The Byzantine liturgy is less solemn. After an exsufflation and an anointing on forehead and breast there is a prayer over the catechumen; this is followed by four exorcisms and the rejection of Satan and acceptance of Christ (again with the symbolism of West and East).

The meaning of these rites seems to be well expressed in this passage from the Syrian prayer over the catechumen:

---

62. Codex Barberini gr. 336, pp. 170–214; ed. F. C. Conybeare, *Rituale Armenorum* (Oxford: Clarendon, 1905), 390–406.

63. Denz 1:267–328.

Merciful Lord, with a holy call you have called your servant from the darkness of error to knowledge of the truth; now write his name in your book. Count him among those who fear you. Let the light of your face be sealed upon him. Let the cross of your Christ be engraved on his heart and on his thinking so that he may flee the emptiness of this world and all the malice of the Enemy and walk in the way of your holy commandments.[64]

2. *In the Baptistery: The Baptismal Rites*

Among the Syrians and Maronites the child is anointed with "the oil of gladness" after a prayer that still conveys the original meaning of this gesture: "Under the shadow of my feeble hands send your Holy Spirit. . . ." Then the water is consecrated, and there is a second anointing of eyes, ears, breast, and hands, while a hymn is sung that speaks of the priestly anointing of the "spiritual lambs." The priest then places the catechumen in the font and performs the baptism by taking water in his cupped hand and pouring it three times on the child's head: "N. is baptized in the name of the Father and of the Son and of the Holy Spirit for the life that lasts for ever."

Among the Byzantines, after a diaconal litany of intercession and the consecration of the water, the priest blesses the oil and anoints the entire body in a token fashion; he then baptizes with three immersions.

3. *The Postbaptismal Rites*

Among the Byzantines the neophyte is immediately clothed after the baptismal bath; then, after an appropriate prayer: "Bestow upon him the seal of your holy, almighty and adorable Spirit," the priest anoints the forehead and several parts of the body while repeating the same words: "Sphragis dōreas Pneumatos hagiou." Communion is then given.

The same prayer is used among the Syrians; so, too, is the same anointing, but with a different prayer: "With the holy *myron*, which is the sweet odor of Christ our God, and with the seal of true faith and with the gift of the Holy Spirit, N. is signed in the name of the Father. . . ."[65]

II. THE ARMENIAN RITE

BIBLIOGRAPHY

Ritus baptismi et confirmationis apud Armenos, in Denz 383–99.

F. C. Conybeare, *Rituale Armenorum* (Oxford: Clarendon, 1905), 86–107.

---

64. G. Khouri-Sarkis, "Prières et cérémonies du baptême selon le rite de l'Eglise syrienne d'Antioche," *OS* 1 (1956) 164–65.

65. *Ibid.*, 179–80. On the introduction of the postbaptismal anointing into a rite that originally did not have it, see above, pp. 57ff.

G. Winkler, *Das armenische Initiationsrituale* (OCA 217; Rome: Pontificio Istituto Orientale, 1981).

The substance of the Armenian baptismal *ordo* belongs to the oldest stratum of the ritual. The latter, known as *Mashtoç*, may go back to the end of the fifth century, when it was supposedly composed on the basis of borrowings from neighboring Churches; but additions were made to it in the ninth century and, beginning in the eleventh, it was even affected by Latin influences.[66]

1. *Outside the Baptistery*

Since the thirteenth century the rite has begun with an imposition of hands and a liturgy of the word that ends with a prayer over the catechumen. Then come the renunciation (facing the West) and the acceptance (facing the East) in the form of a profession of Trinitarian faith by means of a creed. A prayer for deliverance from the forces of evil takes the place of an exorcism.

2. *In the Baptistery: The Baptismal Rites*

In the books, a new liturgy of the Word is always followed by the blessing of the oil, but in practice this is reserved to the Catholicos of Etchmiazin or to the bishop of one of the other four principal sees. Then the priest consecrates the water and pours it with his hand over the head of the child whom he has placed in the font; he then immerses the child three times and, having seated it in the water, washes its entire body. The sacramental formula is an expanded one: "N. is baptized in the name of the Father and of the Son and of the Holy Spirit; redeemed by the blood of Christ from the slavery of sin he receives freedom through adoption as child of the heavenly Father and becomes a co-heir with Christ and a temple of the Holy Spirit, now and always and for endless ages." Finally the Our Father is said.

3. *The Postbaptismal Rites*

After a prayer, "Sanctify him with your truth, fill him with the grace of your Holy Spirit" (only Catholics accompany this with a laying on of hands), the child is anointed on the forehead and the entire body: "The salutary oil that is being poured over you in the name of Jesus Christ is the seal of heavenly gifts. . . ." The child is then reclothed and taken into the sanctuary where it is placed on the altar, which it is made to kiss.

---

66. See A. Renoux, "Le rite arménien," *Bulletin du comité des études* 14 (1963) 245–78; Armenian ritual, espec. 271–72.

By way of communion a host is touched to its tongue. Finally, it is given crown and belt.

There is thus no prebaptismal anointing. If it ever existed (and it probably did), it has disappeared.

III. THE EAST SYRIAN RITE

BIBLIOGRAPHY

G. P. Badger, *The Nestorians and Their Rituals . . .* 2 (London: Masters, 1852; reprinted: Gregg, 1969), 195–214.

Ritus baptismi et confirmationis apud Nestorianos, in Denz 364–83.

G. Dietrich, *Die nestorianische Taufliturgie ins Deutsche übersetzt und historisch-kritisch erforscht* (Giessen, 1903).

A. Raes, "Où se trouve la confirmation dans le rite syro-oriental?" *OS* 1 (1956) 239–54.

D. Webb, "Paroles et gestes dans la liturgie baptismale de l'Eglise nestorienne," in *XXIVe semaine de Saint-Serge, 1977* (Bibliotheca EL, Subsidia 14; Rome: Edizioni liturgiche), 329–52.

The baptismal ritual for children seems to have been composed for the first time under Catholicos Isho'yab III (647–58), but it was revised in subsequent centuries and now has only extracts from the *ordo* meant for adults; it no longer contains exorcisms or a renunciation or an acceptance or a profession of faith.

1. *The Baptismal Rites*

The remaining elements of the ancient catechumenal *ordo* have been made part of an entrance liturgy that includes the singing of psalms, a laying on of the hand, and a signing that has been altered into an anointing. The company then enters the baptistery to the singing of biblical antiphons that speak of entrance into the bridal chamber and into the spiritual fold that is reserved to those who have been chosen and called. A liturgy of the Word (1 Cor 10:1ff.; John 2:23–3:9) introduces the blessing of the oil and the water; the priest anoints the breast of the child, and other ministers continue with the anointing of the entire body; the child is then immediately baptized by three immersions.

2. *The Postbaptismal Rites*

Once reclothed, the child is taken to the door of the sanctuary. The postbaptismal rites include an imposition of the hand that may go back to Isho'yab III and is accompanied by a prayer: 'May the pledge of the Holy Spirit that you have received, the mysteries of Christ in which you have shared, the new life that you have obtained, and the armor of justice that you have put on keep you from evil. . . .'

The postbaptismal anointing with an oil containing no balsam made its appearance only in the eleventh century and became widespread only later on; it probably took the place of a simple signing to which a formula was added: "N. is baptized and made perfect."

The manuscript rituals speak next only of a rite of desacralization of the water. Today it usually comes after the baptism, crowning, and communion.

IV. THE COPTIC AND ETHIOPIAN RITES

BIBLIOGRAPHY

Ritus baptismi et confirmationis Ecclesiae Alexandrinae Jacobitarum, in Denz 191–235.

M. Chaine, "Le rite éthiopien de la confirmation et du mariage," *Bessarione* 24 (1913) 249–83.

S. Grébaut, "Ordre du baptême et de la confirmation dans l'Eglise éthiopienne," *Revue de l'Orient chrétien* 20 (1927–28) 105–89.

L. Villecourt, "Lettre de Macaire, évêque de Memphis, sur la liturgie antique du chrême et du baptême à Alexandrie," *Le Muséon* 36 (1923) 33–46.

_____, "Le livre du chrême (ms Paris arabe 100)," *Le Muséon* 41 (1928) 49–80.

O. H. E. Burmester, "The Baptismal Rite of the Coptic Church," *Bulletin de la Société d'archéologie copte* 11 (1945) 27–86.

J. C. Duffes and C. Geay, *Le baptême dans l'Eglise copte* (Liturgie et catéchèse 1–2; Cairo: Institut catéchétique, 1973).

E. Trumpp, *Das Taufbad der aethiopischen Kirche* (Munich, 1978).

Directives on initiation in the Coptic Church are assembled chiefly in the *Book of Chrism*, which was doubtless composed in 1299; it contains a letter of Macarius of Memphis that goes back to the first half of the tenth century. As for the Ethiopian liturgy, Rome had been familiar with it since 1549 thanks to the translation by Tesfa Sion.[67] This liturgy follows the same schema as the Egyptian, and I need only mention its most striking peculiarities.

1. *The Baptismal Rites*

Among the Copts the current ritual begins with a prayer of purification for the mother and blessing for the child. This is followed by the ancient catechumenal formulas that still speak of instruction received by those who are preparing for baptism; they accompany the blessing of the oil by the priest and a first anointing on forehead, heart, shoulders, and hands.

---

67. In 1549 Abba Tesfa Sion, of the monastery of San Stefano dei Mori, published at Rome the ritual of initiation that was used in the Ethiopian Church. His translation was reprinted in the *Magna bibliotheca veterum patrum* 6 (Paris, 1644) 58–76 and partially in Martène, M 401 and 436, and in PL 138:929–50.

Then come the prayers for the registration of the name; these are connected with petitions for the removal of the evil powers and with a laying on of the hand.

In Egyptian practice the child's clothing is removed before the renunciation, acceptance, and Creed; it is anointed in a token fashion over its whole body with the "oil of gladness," which is different from the oil already used. There follows a long drawn-out formulary for the blessing of the water; this is organized like the Mass, with readings, prayer of the faithful, kiss of peace, thanksgiving, *Sanctus*, epiclesis, and Our Father. The child is baptized by three immersions, each accompanied by a different formula: "I baptize you in the name of the Father. Amen"; "I baptize you in the name of the Son. Amen"; "I baptize you in the name of the Holy Spirit. Amen."

Among the Ethiopians a prayer removing the consecration from the water separates baptism from confirmation.

2. The Postbaptismal Rites

With holy chrism—which, like the oil of gladness, can be blessed only by the patriarch—the priest begins a chrismation that extends to many parts of the body (a fifteenth-century ritual lists twenty-six): "Pour out your Holy Spirit through the anointing with holy chrism; let it be a lifegiving mark, a source of strength for your servant, a confirmation by your Son. . . ." Among the Ethiopians this chrismation disappeared in the seventeenth century, perhaps because strained relations with Egypt prevented the acquisition of chrism. Next comes an imposition of the hand, accompanied by two prayers; when the celebrant reaches the words, "Receive the Holy Spirit," he breathes in the form of a cross on the face of the neophyte. Then, while the choir continues to repeat these words, the neophyte receives the white garments and the crown. The prayer of the priest before communion echoes the same theme; among the Ethiopians communion is accompanied still by a cup of milk and honey.

Article IV: The Celebration of Initiation
(After Vatican II)

BIBLIOGRAPHY

Paul VI, Apostolic Constitution *Divinae consortium naturae* on the Sacrament of Confirmation (August 15, 1971): *AAS* 63 (171) 657–64 (= *EDIL* 2591–2601 = *DOL* 303 nos. 2499–2508).

L. Ligier, "Le nouveau rituel du baptême des enfants," *LMD* no. 98 (1969) 7–31.

J. B. Molin and G. Becquet, "La célébration de la Parole dans le nouveau rituel du baptême des enfants," *ibid.*, 32–58.

A. Iniesta, *El bautismo. Introducció pastoral, Comentario al nuevo ritual español . . .* (Renovación litúrgica 5; Madrid: Ed. PPC, 1970).

R. Béraudy, "Recherches théologiques autour du rituel baptismal des adultes," *LMD* no. 110 (1972) 25–50.

B. Kleinheyer, "Le nouveau rituel de la confirmation," *ibid.*, 51–71.

P. Jounel, "La consécration du chrême et la bénédiction des saintes huiles," *LMD* no. 112 (1972) 70–83.

L. Ligier, *La confirmation, sens et conjoncture oecuménique hier et aujourd'hui* (Théologie historique 23; Paris: Beauchesne, 1973).

A. Kavanagh, "Christliche Initiation in der nachkonziliaren katholischen Kirche," *Liturgisches Jahrbuch* 28 (1978) 1–10.

F. Brovelli, "Linee teologico-pastorali a proposito di iniziazione cristiana: dall'analisi dei nuovi rituali," *La scuola cattolica* 107 (1979) 247–74.

A. Kavanagh, "Symbolic Implications of Christian Initiation in Roman Catholicism Since the Second Vatican Council," in *I simboli dell'iniziazione cristiana* (Studia Anselmiana 87, Analecta liturgica 7; Rome, 1983), 223–41.

The conciliar Constitution *Sacrosanctum Concilium* set in motion a rather thoroughgoing reform of the liturgy of Christian initiation.[1] Two essential characteristics of this reform may be emphasized.

The first is a novelty: for the first time in the history of the Church there was to be a ritual "suited to the fact that those to be baptized are infants"; in the past, a slightly revised abridgment of the ceremonial for adults had always been used for children. And in fact an *Ordo baptismi*

---

1. *VSC* 64–71.

parvulorum was published on May 15, 1969.[2] Since in the discipline of the Latin Church confirmation is delayed until later on, I must mention here also the *Ordo confirmationis*, which was dated August 22, 1971, and the Apostolic Constitution *Divinae consortium naturae* of Paul VI, which made the anointing the essential rite of this sacrament and changed the accompanying formula.[3]

The second characteristic was a return to ancient tradition for the baptism of adults: "The catechumenate for adults, divided into several stages, is to be restored." In 1962 the Congregation of Rites had already authorized a division of the content of the old ritual into seven sessions separated in time.[4] The new ritual was promulgated on January 6, 1972.[5] In addition to the *Ordo catechumenatus per gradus dispositus* it contains an *Ordo simplicior* which can be celebrated in its entirety on a single occasion or divided into two or three sessions, an *Ordo brevior* for cases of necessity, and, above all, an *Ordo initiationis puerorum qui aetatem catecheticam adepti sunt.*[6]

To these liturgical books must be added the Lectionary for ritual Masses[7] and the corresponding part of the Sacramentary.[8]

Although the rite of infant baptism is quite a bit different from the others and is a single continuous celebration, I shall study all three together.[9]

§1. The Period of Initial Preparation

I. ADULTS

The Introduction to the ritual for adults speaks first of the evangelization that makes possible the awakening of faith and the discovery of the

---

2. *Rituale Romanum, Ordo baptismi parvulorum*, ed. typica, 1969 (henceforth: *OBP*). English translation: see below, note 9.

3. *Pontificale Romanum, Ordo confirmationis*, ed. typica, 1972 (henceforth: *OCO*). English translation: see below, note 9.

4. *AAS* 54 (1962) 310–15. See P. M. Gy, "Le nouveau rituel du baptême des adultes," *LMD* no. 71 (1962) 15–27 (decree, additions, and changes: 7–14).

5. *Rituale Romanum, Ordo initiationis christianae adultorum*, ed. typica, 1972 (henceforth: *OICA*). English translation: see below, note 9.

6. This ritual is part of the *OICA*, nos. 306–69.

7. *Missale Romanum, Lectionarium* 3 (ed. typica, 1972): *Pro missis ritualibus*, 431–515. English: *Lectionary for Mass* (Collegeville: The Liturgical Press, 1970), 1635–1818.

8. *Missale Romanum*, ed. typica secunda, 1975. English: *The Sacramentary* (Collegeville: The Liturgical Press, 1985), 750–83.

9. The English rituals, translated by the International Committee on English in the Liturgy, are collected in *The Rites of the Catholic Church* 1 (New York: Pueblo, 1976) (henceforth: *Rites*). New translations of the introductions are in *DOL*.

gospel, as well as initial contacts with the Christian community.[10] "Sympathizers" (or "inquirers") are gradually led to the point of "entrance into the order of catechumens" (*ad catechumenos faciendos*).[11] This celebration is the person's first official encounter with the Church: the applicants are asked to say what it is they seek, and they are welcomed by the priest, who signs them with the sign of the cross[12] and brings them into the place of assembly. After the Liturgy of the Word[13] they are given the Book of the Gospels and, when the faithful have prayed for them, they are sent away before the celebration of the Eucharist.

II. CHILDREN OF SCHOOL AGE

It often happens nowadays that young people who have not been baptized discover the faith between the age of seven and adolescence, due to contact with schoolmates or children in the neighborhood, or to involvement in movements for children or in other Christian groups. They can then enter upon a process comparable to that followed by adults; for their entrance into the catechumenate the ritual[14] provides a celebration comparable to that for adults, and indeed very little different from it, but including as well a dialogue between the priest and the parents or sponsors who present the children.[15] The French ritual breaks the entrance down into two separate stages: the acceptance of the request for baptism and, only a little while later, the ceremony of signing, entrance into the church, and presentation of the gospels; this ceremony is accompanied by a first reciprocal commitment of the child and the ecclesial assembly to the continuation of the journey.

III. INFANTS

There can be no question of a catechumenate in the case of infants. However, among the criteria for determining the date of baptism, the rit-

---

10. *OICA* nos. 9–13 (*DOL* 301 nos. 2336–40).

11. *OICA* nos 68–97: *Primus gradus* (*DOL* 301 nos. 2395–99 and *Rites* pp. 40–51).

12. Signings on forehead, ears, eyes, lips, heart, shoulders, and whole body, accompanied by suitable formulas and concluded by a prayer.

13. Gen 12:1-4a; Ps 33; John 1:35-42.

14. *OICA* nos. 306–29 (*DOL* 301 nos. 2458–67 and *Rites* pp. 131–37).

15. The French ritual breaks the entrance down into two separate stages: the acceptance of the request for baptism and, not until a little later, the ceremony of signing, entrance into the church, and presentation of the gospels; this ceremony is accompanied by a first reciprocal commitment of the child and the ecclesial community to the continuation of the journey.

ual emphasizes first of all the welfare of the child, but it also lists the recovery of the mother who should if possible be present for the baptism, and "pastoral considerations, such as allowing sufficient time to prepare the parents and to plan the actual ceremony."[16] This last, which is a single continuous rite, begins with questions addressed to those who present the child: What do they ask of the Church? Are they aware of the responsibilities they are accepting, and are they ready to fulfill these? Then comes the act of signing, which parents and sponsors can be invited to perform after the priest. Finally, there is the entrance into the Church.[17]

§2. The Period of Purification

I. ADULTS

1. *The Catechumenate*

The period of the catechumenate now begins. Those who have asked for baptism prepare for it with already initiated brothers and sisters from whom they learn Christian doctrine and in whose company they gain experience of the Christian life. This period is punctuated by liturgies of the Word, prayers for deliverance from evil and sin, and blessings given by priest, deacon, or even catechist.[18]

During this period the presentation of the Creed and Lord's Prayer may be anticipated: "They should be celebrated when the catechumens seem to be mature; otherwise, they do not take place."[19] After the Scripture readings[20] the Apostles' Creed (unless the Nicene-Constantinopolitan Creed is chosen) is proclaimed by the priest or by all the faithful. The presentation of the Lord's Prayer has its place in the context of instruction on prayer: on that day the Liturgy of the Word ends with the gospel pericope in which Jesus teaches his disciples the Our Father.[21]

2. *The Lent of the "Elect"*

The catechumenate, which is longer or shorter as need requires, ends with the rite of the *electio* or "decisive call,"[22] which consists of the enrollment of the candidates' names and begins the final stage of prepara-

---

16. *OBP* no. 8 (*DOL* 295 no. 2292).

17. *OBP* nos. 32–43 (*Rites* pp. 197–99).

18. *OICA* nos. 98–132 (*DOL* 301 nos. 2400–7 and *Rites* pp. 53–61).

19. *OICA* nos. 125–30 (*Rites* p. 60). The presentations are in *OICA* nos. 181–92 (*Rites* pp. 83–89).

20. Deut 6:1-7; Ps 19; Rom 10:8-13 or 1 Cor 15:1-8; John 3:16; Matt 16:13-18 or John 12:44-50.

21. Hos 11:1, 3-4, 8-9; Ps 23 or 103; Rom 8:14-17, 26-27 or Gal 4:4-7; Matt 6:9-13.

22. *OICA* nos. 133–51: *secundus gradus* (*DOL* 301 nos. 2408–14 and *Rites* pp. 63–70).

tion; this stage is usually coextensive with the Lent preceding baptism, which will be celebrated at Easter. On the third, fourth, and fifth Sundays of this period (Sundays of the Samaritan Woman, the Man Born Blind, and Lazarus), the scrutinies are celebrated in keeping with ancient custom.[23] The Scripture readings on these Sundays are a source of instruction[24] that is accompanied by intercessions for the future initiates and by prayers of exorcism. The entire assembly thus associates itself with the candidates as they advance toward baptism. Unless already celebrated, the presentation of the Creed and the Lord's Prayer takes place during the third to fifth weeks of Lent.

3. *As Baptism Draws Near*

On the eve of Easter the "giving back" of the Creed, the *Ephphetha* rite, and an anointing take place.[25] The candidates recite the profession of faith for the first time before the assembly. Then the celebrant repeats the gesture used by Jesus in healing a deaf-mute: he touches their ears and lips and says: "Ephphetha: that is, be opened, that you may profess the faith you have heard, to the praise and glory of God." They then receive an anointing with the oil of catechumens on both hands or on the breast[26]: "We anoint you with the oil of salvation in the name of Christ the Savior. May he strengthen you with his power, who lives and reigns for ever and ever."[27]

II. CHILDREN OF SCHOOL AGE

All the rites of this second stage are here celebrated on a single occasion.[28] When the children have progressed far enough spiritually to un-

---

23. *OICA* nos. 152–59 (*DOL* 301 nos. 2415–22); and see above, pp. 28–29.

24. (1) Exod 17:3-7; Ps 95; Rom 5:1-2, 5-8; John 4:5-42; — (2) 1 Sam 16:1b, 6-7, 10-13a; Ps 23; Eph 5:8-14; John 9:1-41; — (3) Ezek 37:12-14; Ps 130; Rom 8:8-11; John 11:1-45.

25. *OICA* nos. 193–207 (*Rites* pp. 89–93). The ritual also proposes that a Christian name be chosen (*OICA* nos 203–5; *Rites* p. 92) according to principles set down in *OICA* no. 88 (*Rites* p. 47).

26. "Or even on other parts of the body, if this seems desirable" (*OICA* no. 207; *Rites* p. 93).

27. The oil of catechumens is blessed by the bishop during the chrismal Mass of Holy Thursday. At baptisms of adults, however, the priest can bless it himself before the anointing (Decree of the Congregation for Divine Worship, December 3, 1970: *EDIL* 2238 = *DOL* 459 no. 3867). The formula for the blessing has been revised: "Lord God, protector of all who believe in you, bless this oil and give the wisdom and strength which it signifies to all who are anointed with it in preparation for their baptism. Bring them to a deeper understanding of the Gospel, help them to accept the challenge of Christian living, and lead them to the joy of new birth in the family of your Church. We ask this through Christ our Lord" (*OICA* no. 207; *Rites* p. 93).

28. *OICA* nos. 330–42 (*DOL* 301 nos. 2468–71 and *Rites* pp. 138–42).

derstand the meaning of the struggle against evil in which they must engage, the time has come to introduce them to a penitential ritual. After a liturgy of the Word, the congregation commends the future initiate to the Lord; a prayer of exorcism leads into the rite of anointing. As determined by the episcopal conferences the anointing may be replaced by a laying on of the hand.[29]

III. INFANTS

After the children have been welcomed, the rite continues[30] with a liturgy of the Word and a litanic prayer that ends with an invocation of the saints, among them the saints whose names the children will bear. This is followed by a prayer of petition: ". . .We now pray for these children who will have to face the world with its temptations, and fight the devil in all his cunning. Your Son died and rose again to save us. By his victory over sin and death, bring these children out of the power of darkness. Strengthen them with the grace of Christ. . . ." This prayer introduces the anointing or laying on of the hand.[31]

§3. The Sacrament of Baptism

In this part of the rite there are no substantial differences between the three rituals; they may therefore be studied together, although attention will be called to the peculiarities in the baptism of infants.

I. THE BLESSING OF THE WATER

The baptismal liturgy begins with the blessing of the water; in the ritual for adults this is introduced by the singing of litanies.[32] The old Roman prayer has been shortened and unified so that the biblical images from

---

29. The English ritual allows for either; the anointing may also be postponed to the day of baptism.

30. *OBP* nos. 44–52 (*Rites* pp. 199–203).

31. Only anointing on the breast is mentioned. The difficulty of unfastening the child's garments had led to the laying on of the hand as an alternative. There are occasions, however, on which the use of oil would be more meaingful; it is regrettable therefore that the permission given in the other rituals for an anointing of the hands has not been extended to infant baptism.

32. Optional formularies are provided in which acclamations make it easier for the congregation to participate: *OICA* no. 389; *OBP* nos. 223–24 (*Rites* pp. 175, 268–70). During the Easter season water blessed during the Easter Vigil is used and the blessing is replaced by a thanksgiving (*OICA* nos. 216 and 350; *OBP* no. 92; *Rites* pp. 98, 109, 220).

the New Testament—including burial in death with Christ in order to rise with him—are more clearly seen as fulfillments of the old covenant.

II. RENUNCIATION OF SATAN AND PROFESSION OF FAITH

In accordance with traditional practice, the theme of the struggle against evil is repeated one last time, since acceptance of Christ requires of the candidates a forcible rejection of the world of sin: "Do you reject Satan and all his works and all his empty promises?" "I do," reply the candidates who meanwhile have approached the font with their godfathers and godmothers. They then make the profession of Trinitarian faith; their entrance into the community of the faithful is thus shown to be a conscious, active step that will in a moment be sealed by the sacramental rite.[33]

All this requires adaptation when the candidates are infants. The priest asks the same questions, but of the parents and godparents, after he has first reminded them of the responsibility they are accepting when they have the child baptized.[34] It must be acknowledged that this procedure is not without its problems, both pastoral and theological, since the responsibility of the parents and godparents cannot be regarded as fully the same as that which adult candidates take on themselves. Too often, unfortunately, the only words said here in a fully authentic way are those that the celebrant adds: "This is our faith. This is the faith of the Church. We are proud to profess it, in Christ Jesus our Lord," and the "Amen" of the faithful who represent the entire assembly of believers at the celebration.

III. THE RITE OF WATER

Baptism is administered by a triple infusion or triple immersion, with the formula: "N . . . , I baptize you in the name of the Father and of the Son and of the Holy Spirit." During this ceremony the godfather or godmother puts a hand on the right shoulder of the godchild; if the can-

---

33. *OICA* nos. 217–29 and 352–55 (*Rites* pp. 98–103 and 145–47). The ritual has an alternative formula for the renunciation: "Abrenuntiatis peccato, ut in libertate filiorum Dei vivatis? . . . Abrenuntiatis seductionibus iniquitatis, ne peccatum vobis dominetur? . . . Abrenuntiatis Satanae, qui est auctor et princeps peccati?" In English: "Do you reject sin so as to live in the freedom of God's children? . . . Do you reject the glamor of evil and refuse to be mastered by sin? . . . Do you reject Satan, father of sin and prince of darkness?" If the anointing has not been done earlier it can be placed between the renunciation and the profession of faith.

34. *OBP* nos. 56–59 (*Rites* pp. 205–7).

35. *OICA* nos. 220–21 and 356–57; *OBP* nos. 60–61 (*Rites* pp. 100–101, 147, 207–8).

didates are infants, it is appropriate that it be the mother (or father) who holds the child over the font or receives it when it comes from the water.[35]

IV. THE POSTBAPTISMAL RITES

1. *Infants*

Newly baptized infants are immediately anointed on the forehead with holy chrism: "God the Father of our Lord Jesus Christ has . . . welcomed you into his holy people. He now anoints you with the chrism of salvation. As Christ was anointed Priest, Prophet, and King, so may you live always as members of his body, sharing everlasting life." They are then clothed in white, and each family is given a candle that had been lighted from the Easter candle: ". . . This light is entrusted to you to be kept burning brightly. These children of yours have been enlightened by Christ. They are to walk always as children of the light. May they keep the flame of faith alive in their hearts. When the Lord comes, may they go out to meet him with all the saints in the heavenly kingdom."[36]

In accordance with the Latin tradition, the other two sacraments of initiation are put off to a later time. In the new ritual they are, however, announced in a short address of the celebrant, who points out their connection with baptism: ". . . In confirmation they will receive the fullness of God's Spirit. In holy communion they will share the banquet of Christ's sacrifice. . . ." The congregation then says the Our Father and the rite ends with a blessing of the mothers and fathers of the newly baptized infants and of all the faithful present.[37] This part of the celebration takes place at the altar.

2. *Adults and Children of School Age*

For these newly baptized persons, confirmation and the Eucharist are normally to follow upon baptism, even if the bishop is not present and a priest presides at the ceremony.[38] In this case, the postbaptismal anointing is omitted (a novelty in the Roman tradition). As soon as they have been baptized, the neophytes receive their white garments from the godparents, as the priest says: "N. and N., you have become a new creation and have clothed yourselves in Christ. Take this white garment and bring it unstained to the judgment seat of our Lord Jesus Christ so that you may

---

36. *OICA* nos. 224–26 and 358–60; *OBP* nos. 62–66 (*Rites* pp. 101–2, 147–49, 209–10).

37. *OBP* nos. 67–71 (*Rites* pp. 210–13).

38. *OICA* no. 46 (*DOL* 301 no. 2373): "The priest who baptizes an adult or a child of catechetical age should, when the bishop is absent, also confer confirmation, unless this sacrament is to be given at another time (see no. 56)."

have everlasting life." In like manner, the candle lit from the Easter candle is given to them: "Godparents, please come forward to give the newly baptized the light of Christ. . . . You have been enlightened by Christ. Walk always as children of the light and keep the flame of faith alive in your hearts. When the Lord comes, may you go out to meet him with all the saints in the heavenly kingdom." On this eschatological note this part of the celebration ends.[39]

§4. The Sacrament of Confirmation

When confirmation does not follow directly upon baptism, the one who presides at it is normally the bishop, the "primary minister" (or "original minister," *minister originarius*) as he is called by Vatican II and by the ritual;[40] this "shows the close bond that joins the confirmed to the Church." When a great many people are to receive this sacrament at the same time, priests can be called upon to concelebrate the sacrament with the president. It is during a Eucharist, after the Liturgy of the Word, that confirmands receive the gift of the Spirit, after first renewing their profession of baptismal faith, in accordance with the directive of the liturgical constitution of Vatican II.[41]

Whether separated from baptism or following immediately upon it, confirmation has two essential rites: the imposition of hands and chrismation.

I. THE IMPOSITION OF HANDS

The celebration of the sacrament requires first of all an imposition of hands on all the confirmands together. It is introduced by a short address and accompanied by a prayer:

> All-powerful God, Father of our Lord Jesus Christ, by water and the Holy Spirit you freed your sons and daughters from sin and gave them new life. Send your Holy Spirit upon them to be their Helper and Guide. Give

---

39. *OICA* nos. 223–26 and 357–60 (*Rites* pp. 101–2, 147–49).

40. See *Lumen gentium* 26 (*DOL* 4 no. 146) and *OCO* nos. 7–8 (*DOL* 305 nos. 2515–16). The expression "ordinary minister," which has unfortunately been kept in the new Code of Canon Law (can. 882), amounts to saying that the ministers of the rite in the Eastern Churches are ordinarily extraordinary. Situations are anticipated in which priests are allowed to preside at this sacrament whether by law or by indult.

41. *VSC* 71 (*DOL* 1 no. 71): "The rite of confirmation is also to be revised in order that the intimate connection of this sacrament with the whole of Christian initiation may stand out more clearly; for this reason it is fitting for candidates to renew their baptismal promises just before they are confirmed." — *OCO* no. 23 (*Rites* pp. 307–8).

them the spirit of wisdom and understanding, the spirit of right judgment and courage, the spirit of knowledge and reverence. Fill them with the spirit of wonder and awe in your presence. We ask this through Christ our Lord.[42]

According to the Apostolic Constitution *Divinae consortium naturae*, "the laying of hands on the elect . . . is still to be regarded as very important, even if it is not of the essence of the sacramental rite."[43] For ever since the Acts of the Apostles, Christians have regarded this gesture as a sign of the gift of the Spirit.

II. CHRISMATION

As determined by Paul VI, in the Latin Church the sacrament is administered through an anointing of the forehead with chrism.[44]

1. *Holy Chrism*

The tradition is almost unanimous in making the confection of chrism a prerogative of the bishop; as a result, he is symbolically present at confirmation, even when he does not preside in person. The new *Ordo conficiendi chrisma*,[45] which, like the old, is celebrated after communion in the chrismal Mass on Holy Thursday, offers a choice of two consecratory formulas: the old prayer of the Pontifical, which came from the ancient sacramentaries, and a recently composed text that gives greater attention to the New Testament and the mystery of the Church. Both recall the meaning of anointing under the old covenant, a meaning fulfilled in the very name of Christ, the Messiah or "Anointed of the Lord." The baptized share in the mission of Jesus when the Spirit is bestowed on them in order to make them members of his body according to the grace given to each and in order that the Church may grow until it reaches the fullness of Trinitarian life in "eternal glory." The verb *conficiendi* in the Latin title of the rite calls attention to the act of commingling that perfumes

---

42. *OCO* nos. 24–25; *OICA* nos. 269, 363–64 (*Rites* pp. 308–9, 115–16, 149). The imposition is done simultaneously by all the priests who are to take part in the anointing.

43. Apostolic Constitution *Divinae consortium naturae DOL* 303 no. 2507.

44. *Ibid.*: "Sacramentum confirmationis confertur per unctionem chrismatis in fronte, quae fit manu impositione, atque per verba: 'Accipe signaculum Doni Spiritus Sancti.'" What precisely is meant by the clause "quae fit . . ."? It can at least be said that the anointing has the same meaning as the laying on of hands in the Acts of the Apostles.

45. *Ordo benedicendi oleum catechumenorum et infirmorum et conficiendi chrisma*, promulgated on December 3, 1970; trans. in *Rites* pp. 515–27, with a new translation of the Introduction in *DOL* 459 nos. 3861–72. See P. Jounel, "La consécration du chrême et la bénédiction des saintes huiles," *LMD* no. 112 (1972) 70–83; see also J. Rogues, "La préface consécratoire du chrême," *LMD* no. 49 (1957) 35–49.

the oil and thereby reminds us that the disciple must spread abroad the fragrance of Christ.[46]

2. Anointing on the Forehead

The bishop dips his thumb in the chrism and makes the sign of the cross on each confirmand, saying: "N, accipe signaculum Doni Spiritus Sancti" ("N, be sealed with the Gift of the Holy Spirit").[47] This is the formula used by the Byzantines, but with the addition of a verb. It is not easy to translate, because the meaning is that the gift in question is the Spirit himself.[48] These words bring out the meaning of the mystery being celebrated far better than the formula they replaced; the image of a seal is part of the traditional theology of this sacrament and is inspired by St. Paul: "It is God who . . . has both anointed us and marked us with his seal, giving us as pledge the Spirit in our hearts" (2 Cor 1:21 JB).

If the confirmands are numerous, they are divided into groups and receive the anointing from one of the concelebrating priests.

III. CONCLUDING RITES

The slap that used to follow upon the anointing in the old Pontifical (from the thirteenth century on) has, of course, been dropped. Now, with the words "Peace be with you," the bishop wishes the peace of Christ to each confirmand, and the latter replies "And also with you."[49] If the sacrament is not being celebrated during a Eucharist it ends with General Intercessions, the Our Father, and a blessing.[50]

§5. First Communion

After being baptized and confirmed, adults and children of school age take part in the Mass and receive their first communion.[51] The neophytes

---

46. See 2 Cor 2:15; Exod 30:22-25.

47. *OCO* no. 365; *OICA* nos. 231 and 365 (*Rites* pp. 310, 104, 149).

48. The Byzantine formula (see above, p. 79) has no verb, but it follows a prayer in which the same expression is part of a complete sentence. The difficulty of translating it is shown by the diversity among the approved formulas: e.g., German: "Sei besiegelt durch die Gabe Gottes, den heiligen Geist"; Italian: "Ricevi il sigillo dello Spirito Santo, che ti è dato in dono"; Spanish: "Recibe por esta señal el Don del Espiritu Santo"; French: "Sois marqué de l'Esprit Saint, le Don de Dieu."

49. In the case of infants the French ritual suggests "a gesture of friendship" and various formulas: "May he preserve you in peace"; "Go, the Lord is with you"; "Go, the Spirit of Jesus is with you."

50. *OCO* nos. 47-49 (*Rites* pp. 320-22).

51. *OICA* nos. 232-34 and 366-68 (*Rites* pp. 104-5, 149).

are mentioned during the intercessions in the Eucharistic Prayer,[52] and they can be given the Body and Blood of the Lord under both species.

When confirmation is administered separately from baptism, those who have received it are remembered in the same way, and the celebration ends with a solemn blessing or a prayer over the people: "God our Father, complete the work you have begun and keep the gifts of your Holy Spirit alive in the hearts of your people. Make them ready to live his gospel and eager to do his will. May they never be ashamed to proclaim to all the world Christ crucified living and reigning for ever and ever."[53]

According to tradition and the current liturgical books, first communion normally comes after confirmation, since it is the climax of initiation and of the sacramental system. The order is frequently reversed for pastoral reasons; this should cause us to reexamine the situation and, in addition, to avoid seeking theological reasons for what can only be required by concrete situations. In any case, if it be judged right to continue the present discipline, let us do so with the same prudence that marked the diocesan regulations of earlier centuries. For when these determined a particular age for receiving the sacraments, they usually did so in some such terms as these: "Although confirmation or first communion can be received at any age, we have decided that, in view of the circumstances, among us. . . ."

§6. The Period of Postbaptismal Catechesis or Mystagogia

The ritual of adult baptism recommends that the neophytes continue their formation after their initiation, especially by strengthening their sacramental practice with the help of their sponsors. The fifty-day Easter period that follows their entrance into the Church is an especially opportune time for learning to participate actively and consciously in the liturgical life and mission of Christians. The same point is made in regard to children of school age.[54] In the case of children baptized soon after birth, the ecclesial community should be especially careful that when the right time comes they are given the instruction they need if grace is to bear its fruits in them.

---

52. *OICA* nos. 377 and 391 (*Rites* pp. 161–62, 180). Note that in Eucharistic Prayer I (the Roman Canon) the newly baptized are mentioned in the *Hanc igitur* ("Father, accept this offering . . ."), and the sponsors in the Commemoration of the living.

53. *OCO* nos. 32–33 (*Rites* pp. 313–14).

54. *OICA* nos. 37–40, 235–37, and 369 (*DOL* 301 nos. 2364–67, and *Rites* pp. 105–6, 150).

§7. Reception into the Community of a Child Who Has Received Emergency Baptism

Baptism means entrance into the Church; therefore, even though the sacrament be administered in a quasi-private way because of danger of death, it is important that if the neophyte is restored to health, its membership in the community be given external expression. For this reason the ritual provides a celebration that includes all the baptismal ceremonies compatible with the situation of the baptized: reception of the child and commitment of the parents and sponsors, signing, entrance into the church, and, after a liturgy of the word and a prayer for the child, the anointing with chrism, the giving of the white garment and the candle, the Our Father, and the blessing of the parents.[55]

---

55. *OBP* nos. 165–85 (*Rites* pp. 254–61).

Article V: Commemorations of Baptism

BIBLIOGRAPHY

R. Daeschler, "Baptême (Commémoration du)," *Dictionnaire de spiritualité* 1 (Paris: Beauchesne, 1937) 1230-40.
P, Borella, *Commemorazioni battesimali* (Milan: Daverio, 1947).
P. Jounel, "Les vêpres de Pâques," *LMD* no. 49 (1957) 96-111.
B. Fischer, "Formes de la commémoration du baptême en Occident," *LMD* no. 58 (1959) 111-34.
_____, "Formen der Tauferinnerung in der Geschichte des privaten christlichen Morgen- und Abendgebets," in *Mens concordet voci, pour Mgr A. G. Martimort* (Paris: Desclée, 1983), 569-75.

Baptism is a decisive event in the life of a Christian, and the Church has always urged the faithful not only to remember it but also to commemorate it in the liturgy.

I. THE EASTER SEASON

The annual celebration of the Lord's resurrection is a time of grace for the baptized. During Lent they have associated themselves with those who have been preparing for initiation; this is clear especially from the Masses for the scrutinies. By praying for them the faithful have helped them in their struggle against the forces of evil, and by sharing in their penitential exercises they have recouped their own strength for the struggles of Christian life. Even bishops in their catecheses (as Chrysostom shows[1]) could not but recall their own Christian journey and that of the other faithful, and feel moved thereby to a new conversion.

---

1. St. John Chrysostom, *Baptismal Instructions* II, 19; III, 7, V, 24, 26 (Harkins 50-51, 57-58, 90-91; SC 50:144, 154, 212, 213).

The Easter Vigil provides the members of the community with an opportunity to relive their own rebirth, as the celebrant urges them to do after the celebration of baptism and confirmation, or at least after the blessing of the water: "Now that we have completed our lenten observance, let us renew the promises we made in baptism when we rejected Satan and his works, and promised to serve God faithfully in his holy Catholic Church." The process is completed in the Eucharist. The words "Easter communion" have signified, since the Middle Ages, nothing more than a duty to be performed, for this was the only communion made obligatory in the entire year. Today we are fortunately giving the words a deeper meaning and turning the Easter season into a privileged time in the Eucharistic life of believers, a time when the Eucharist becomes truly a commemoration of their participation in the death and resurrection of their Lord.

For the newly baptized Easter evening and the following week can become once again what they were in the past. There used to be gatherings that prolonged the baptismal experience; at Rome these included especially a procession to the baptistery and *consignatorium* while Psalms 113 and 114 and the Magnificat were sung: "He raises the poor from the dust, to make them sit with princes. . . . When Israel went forth from Egypt, Judah became his sanctuary. . . . The Lord has done great things for me."[2] The formularies of the Masses for the octave of Easter are filled with the thought of the *infantes*, those who have just been reborn into the life of God: thanksgiving to the Father who "gives your Church constant growth by adding new members to your family," petition that "all who are reborn in baptism [may] be one in faith and love" and that God may "help us put into action in our lives the baptism we have received with faith" and thus "prepare [us] for eternal joy."

II. OTHER COMMEMORATIONS

The discipline of baptism "as soon as possible" after birth, and the separation of baptism in time from confirmation and first communion led to the celebration of initiation on other days besides Easter. This led to other commemorations of baptism, though these have always been inspired by the model described a moment ago.

---

2. *OR* XXVII, 67–94 (Andrieu, *OR* 3:362–72). This practice spread throughout Gaul under the influence of Amalarius; see J. M. Hanssens, *Amalarii episcopi opera liturgica omnia* 3 (ST 140; Vatican City, 1950), 82.

1. *The Anniversary of Baptism*

This is the *pascha annotina* of the old sacramentaries, which provided special formularies for this commemoration of baptism on the same day a year later.[3] Here is a sample prayer for this anniversary: "God, in your providence the moments of the past are not lost and no hope of the future is in vain. Grant that the past solemnity that we are commemorating may be permanently effective, so that what we relive in memory we may always put into action."

This ancient practice has led some Christian families to celebrate anniversaries of baptism as they do birthdays. The result is a kind of reflection in the private sphere of what the Easter commemoration is for the Church as a whole.

2. *Solemn Communions*

The Eucharist is the only one of the three sacraments of initiation that can be repeated; it is therefore the best means individuals have of immersing themselves once again in the grace of their baptism. On some of life's more outstanding days communion takes on a solemn aspect by being associated, as it is during the Easter Vigil, with a profession of faith that is taken over from the ritual of baptism; the last of these celebrations, and one that is uniquely meaningful, is viaticum. This is the model on which countries in the French tradition have based a ceremony, often popular in character, to mark the end of the years of catechetical instruction.[4]

3. *Sunday Asperges*

When we speak of the Eucharist we inevitably bring to mind the Christian assembly and especially the assembly on Sundays. Sunday is in fact the oldest day for commemorating Easter. The rite of the Asperges before Mass spread almost everywhere beginning in the ninth century. It was monastic in origin, being intended as a purification of the conventual premises, but its baptismal character showed in the antiphons *Asperges me* from Psalm 51 and especially *Vidi aquam*, which is based on Ezekiel 47:1-2 and Psalm 118. Like the sprinkling that concludes the profession of faith by the congregation during the Easter Vigil, the Sunday sprinkling is "to remind us of our baptism," as the priest says in his short address to the congregation in the new Sacramentary, which allows the Asperges to be substituted for the penitential rite.

---

3. *Ge* nos. 504–9 (pp. 81–82).

4. See J. Daniélou, "Baptême, Pâques, eucharistie," in *Communion solennelle et profession de foi* (LO 14; Paris: Cerf, 1952), 132–33.

4. *Pilgrimage to the Baptistery*

When the practice of solemn first communion began in France, a procession to the baptistery was often part of the ceremonial; there the children renewed their profession of faith. This custom, which recaptured the insight at work in the ancient Easter Vespers, spread to many countries at the end of the eighteenth century and even to Rome under Pius X. In some places it gave rise to the devotion, which cannot be too much recommended, of visiting the church where one received one's new birth, somewhat as one might go to recollect oneself at the tombs of the martyrs.

If a brief summary of all that the mystery of initiation means to the Church were desired by way of conclusion, we could not do better than to repeat these words from a prayer in the old Spanish liturgy:

Familia tua, Domine Iesu . . .	Your family, Lord Jesus . . .
tuo nomine signata,	marked with your name,
sacro liquore mundata,	purified by the holy water,
tuo Spiritu plena,	filled with your Spirit,
tuo corpore et sanguine satiata.[5]	nourished by your body and blood.

---

5. *Oratio super albas tollendas*, in *Liber Mozarabicus sacramentorum*, ed. M. Férotin (Monumenta Ecclesiae liturgica 6; Paris: Didot, 1912), col. 142.

Chapter II

Penance and Reconciliation

P. M. Gy

BIBLIOGRAPHY

J. Morin, *Commentarius historicus de disciplina in administratione sacramenti paenitentiae* (Paris, 1651; 2nd ed.: Antwerp: F. Metelen, 1682).

Martène, Lib. I, c. 6, M 557–620.

J. A. Jungmann, *Die lateinischen Bussriten in ihrer geschichtlichen Entwicklung* (Innsbruck: Rauch, 1932).

A. Fernández, "La disciplina penitencial en la España romano-visigoda desde el punto de vista pastoral," *Hispania sacra* 4 (1951) 243–311.

C. Vogel, *La discipline pénitentielle en Gaule des origines à la fin du VIIe siècle* (Paris: Letouzey, 1952), espec. 182–97.

—————, "La discipline pénitentielle en Gaule des origines au IXe siècle. Le dossier hagiographique," *RevSR* 30 (1956) 1–26, 157–87.

A. Raes, "Les formulaires grecs du rite de la pénitence," in *Mélanges en honneur de Mgr Andrieu* (Strasbourg: Presses universitaires, 1956), 365–72.

LMD nos. 55 and 56 (1958): *La pénitence dans la liturgie*.

B. Poschmann, *Busse und Letzte Ölung* (Freiburg: Herder, 1951). ET: *Penance and the Anointing of the Sick*, trans. and revised by F. Courtney (New York: Herder and Herder, 1964).

C. Vogel, *Le pécheur et la pénitence dans l'Eglise ancienne* (Paris: Cerf, 1966; reprinted, 1982).

LMD no. 90 (1967): *La pénitence* (espec. L. Ligier, "Dimension personnelle et dimension communautaire de la pénitence en Orient," 155–88).

C. Vogel, *Le pécheur et la pénitence au moyen âge* (Paris: Cerf, 1969; reprinted, 1982).

H. Karpp, *La Pénitence. Textes et commentaires des origines de l'ordre pénitentiel de l'Eglise ancienne* (Traditio christiana; Neuchâtel: Delachaux et Niestlé, 1970).

P. M. Gy, "Les bases de la pénitence moderne," *LMD* no. 117 (1974) 63–85.

Conférences Saint-Serge, XXe Semaine d'études liturgiques . . . 1973 (Bibliotheca EL, Subsidia 3; Rome: Edizioni liturgiche, 1975).

P. M. Gy, "Le sacrement de la pénitence d'après le rituel romain de la pénitence de 1974," *LMD* no. 139 (1979) 125–37.

H. Vorgrimler, *Busse und Krankensalbung*, in M. Schmaus, A. Grillmeier, L. Scheffczyk, and M. Seybold (eds.), *Handbuch der Dogmengeschichte*, IV/3 (Freiburg: Herder, 1978).

D. Borobio, *La penitencia en la Iglesia hispánica del siglo IV al VII* (Nueva biblioteca de teología 40; Bilbao: Desclée de Brouwer, 1978).

A. Nocent, La penitence dans les ordines locaux transcrits dans le *De antiquis ritibus* de Edmond Martène, in *Paschale mysterium* (Studia Anselmiana 91; Rome, 1986), 115–38.

Christian penance, which has been counted as one of the seven sacraments by theologians since the twelfth century and by official documents of the Catholic faith since the thirteenth (especially the Fourth Lateran Council of 1215, canon 1 [DS 802]), is based, according to the Catholic interpretation, on passages in the New Testament. The first elements of a penitential discipline known to us date from the second and third centuries; from then on, its liturgical organization becomes more and more well-defined. In the course of the Church's history this sacrament has been organized in quite different ways and has shown important variations in the placing of the emphasis. Historians distinguish, at least for the West, three historical forms of penance: the penitential discipline of antiquity; the so-called "tariff-penance" of the early Middle Ages; and the modern discipline that began in the twelfth and thirteenth centuries.

§1. Penance in Antiquity

I. THE EARLY PENITENTIAL DISCIPLINE (TO THE FIFTH CENTURY)

The practice of penance, or, more accurately, the possibility of a second, postbaptismal forgiveness of sins in the case of a serious fall, begins to appear toward the middle of the second century in *The Shepherd*, written by Hermas, a Roman, and devoted entirely to the subject of penance. Some Christians of that period (for example, Tertullian after he became a Montanist) held the view that some sins are so serious as to make reconciliation impossible, even if the sinner is repentant.

In the time of St. Augustine, pagan public opinion seems to have shared the view of Christian rigorists (or the other way around).[1] But in its general practice the Church refused to allow that any sin is unforgivable; it did however agree that forgiveness is granted only once after baptism and cannot be repeated. This once-only character, by which penance resem-

---

1. See St. Augustine, *Serm.* 352, 9 (PL 39:1559): "Pagans often reproach Christians because penance has become an organized institution in the Church . . .: 'You cause human beings to sin by promising them forgiveness if they do penance. That is laxism and not education!'"

bled baptism, dissuaded Christians from sin. It was also to be understood, at least in the second century, in light of the conviction that God's judgment was imminent.

Penance had to do with serious sins. The distinction between mortal and venial sins as defined in twelfth-century theology was still unknown, but the authors of the patristic period did distinguish degrees of seriousness among sins, which they divided into two or three categories. A triad—idolatry, murder, and adultery—is attested, but it is doubtful that it was universally regarded as fundamental.

The doing of penance required a more or less lengthy period of time, during which penitents were deprived of communion and had to engage in practices of mortification. The Fathers stressed the importance of the community's prayer for these persons. The bishop was the one who judged when a penitent was ready to be reconciled; he also served as the minister of God's forgiveness by reconciling penitents with the Church and readmitting them to Eucharistic communion.

The length of the penance varied from one historical period to another, from region to region, and according to the seriousness of the sin committed. It could last an entire lifetime, though with the restriction prescribed by the Council of Nicaea[2] that a penitent near death could be reconciled so as to receive viaticum. At the other end of the spectrum, the *Didascalia of the Apostles* (third-century Syria) gives examples of penances lasting only a few weeks.[3] In the case of a dying person, moreover, a penitent confession was immediately followed by reconciliation.

The fact that penance was reserved for serious sins and had severe consequences for those subjected to it explains several things: that clerics were not admitted to it and that their sins were the object of a special discipline; that in the fourth century the severity of the penitential discipline probably persuaded people to delay their baptism; finally and above all, that it was normal for the majority of Christians not to have to do penance in the strict sense of this word. On the other hand, the Christian liturgy, no less than Old Testament prayers, made it clear that all had to acknowledge their sins and ask forgiveness of them. This is probably what we find in the *Didache* (end of the first century): "On the dominical day of the Lord come together to break bread and give thanks, after having also confessed your sins so that your sacrifice may be pure."[4]

In a well-known sermon, St. Augustine speaks of this penitential behavior that is coextensive with Christian life; at the same time he speaks of baptismal conversion and of the penance reserved for serious sins:

---

2. Council of Nicaea, can. 13(12) (DS 129).

3. *Didascalia apostolorum* c. 6; trans. R. H. Connolly, *Didascalia Apostolorum. The Syriac Version Translated* (Oxford: Clarendon, 1929), 52–53.

4. *Didache* 14, 1 (SC 248:192–93).

I said that penance is viewed in three ways in Sacred Scripture. The first penance is that of catechumens who thirst for baptism. . . .

The second is daily penance. Where in Scripture can we show this kind of daily penance? I have no better evidence than the daily prayer in which the Lord taught us what to say to the Father. He put it thus: "Forgive us our debts as we forgive our debtors" (Matt 6:12). . . .

There remains the third kind of penance. . . . It is more severe and painful and gives the penitents of the Church their name; these persons are barred from participation in the sacrament of the altar, lest by receiving unworthily they eat and drink their own condemnation. This penance is painful. The wound that has been inflicted is serious: perhaps the person has committed adultery or homicide or some sacrilege. The matter is serious; the wound is serious, deadly, mortal. . . . Dear brothers and sisters, let none propose to do this kind of penance; let none prepare for it, although if it comes let none despair.[5]

II. THE *ORDO PAENITENTIUM*

Penitents formed a special class in the Church and could be compared with the catechumens. The distinguishing characteristic of the *Ordo paenitentium* was its relation to the Eucharist and the liturgical assembly. In the third and fourth century the East went further and subdivided penitents into four classes: those who asked for penance but were not yet allowed to enter churches; those called simply "hearers," who, like the catechumens, could attend the Liturgy of the Word (they could hear it but were dismissed with the catechumens before the celebration of the Eucharist proper); finally, those called "kneelers" and those called called "standers," who attended the Eucharist but were still deprived of their rights as baptized Christians, since they could not offer or receive communion. "Kneelers," it seems, received an imposition of hands at the end of Mass.

In the West, too, there are traces in the old documents of the practice of dismissing penitents before the Eucharistic celebration proper. The only attestation for Rome suggests rather a dismissal just before communion.[6]

III. ADMISSION INTO THE *ORDO PAENITENTIUM*

Two questions arise with regard to this admission. The first, which has to do rather with the history of penance and thereby with the theology of the sacrament, is how those who became penitents acknowledged their guilt and became known as guilty to the bishop or his representa-

5. St. Augustine, *Serm.* 352, 7 and 8 (PL 39:1556–58).
6. St. Gregory the Great, *Dialogi* II, 12 (PL 66:178–80; SC 260:206–9).

tive. This communication, which plays the same role as the sacramental confession of sins in more recent historical forms of penance, must have taken various forms in antiquity.[7]

The second and properly liturgical question has to do with the appearance, probably at a fairly late period in antiquity, of a public ceremony in which individuals collectively entered the penitential state or in which new penitents were dismissed from the assembly and sent for a penitential sojourn in a monastery. The Scripture readings of the old Roman liturgy for the Monday after the first Sunday of Lent indicate perhaps that the dismissal of penitents originally took place on that day. The readings were Matthew 25:31-46, in which Jesus announces that on the day of judgment the Son of man will separate the sheep from the goats, and its counterpart, Ezekiel 34:11-46, which depicts the Lord as the shepherd who is going to visit his flock: "I will seek the lost, and I will bring back the strayed, and I will bind up the crippled, and I will strengthen the weak" (v. 16). It is tempting to make a parallel between penance and this two-part picture of the Lord as the shepherd who continues looking for his lost sheep until the day when he must separate the sheep from the goats.[8]

Be that as it may, on the Wednesday before the first Sunday of Lent (our Ash Wednesday) the Old Gelasian Sacramentary has a short ritual for the dismissal of penitents;[9] this ritual already existed in the sixth century, in the oldest stratum of this sacramentary. At Rome, priests shared in the ministry of penance.[10]

IV. PRAYER *FOR* AND *WITH* THE PENITENTS

The *ecclesia* concerned itself in several ways with the group of penitents that was to be seen in the assembly. In some places, the bishops imposed hands on the penitents at each Mass and prayed over them; the entire community prayed for them in the prayer of the faithful; during Lent, the community united with them in penitential prayer and action.

In Churches where penitents were dismissed before the offertory, the bishops blessed them at that point and said a special prayer over them. Thus the prayer in the Spanish liturgy reminded the Lord that he had heard the prayer of the tax collector and had made Rahab a member of his

---

7. See H. Vorgrimler, *Busse und Krankensalbung* (in the bibliography), 74.

8. This is Jungmann's hypothesis in his *Die lateinischen Bussriten in ihrer geschichtlichen Entwicklung* (Innsbruck: Rauch, 1932), 48-51.

9. *Ge* I, 15-16 (Mohlberg, nos. 78-83, pp. 17-18).

10. See A. Chavasse, *Le Sacramentaire gélasien* (Tournai: Desclée, 1958), 149. On the role of priests see *ibid.*, 141-45.

people.[11] According to the Greek historian Sozomen, a comparable practice existed at Rome in the fifth century, but at the end of Mass rather than at the offertory.[12] If this was indeed the custom, there may be a reminiscence of it in the *oratio super populum* that was said in the Masses of Lent down to Vatican II.[13]

The General Intercessions or prayer of the faithful was the usual liturgical context for the intercession of the entire *ecclesia* in behalf of the penitents; the Fathers regarded this intercession as very important, perhaps more important even than the atonement for sins committed. St. Ambrose, for example, urges penitents "to seek the patronage and intercession of the holy people. . . . Let Mother Church weep for you and wash away your sin with her tears. . . . [Christ] wants to see the many praying for the one."[14]

And, in fact, the ancient formularies for the prayer of the faithful usually contained an invocation for penitents.[15] At Milan, for example, this practice has continued down to our own day on the first Sunday of Lent.[16] In Gaul and Spain the solemn intercessions that we find between the readings of the Easter Vigil in the sacramentaries always contained an invitatory and *Flectamus genua* for penitents.[17]

At Rome there was a similar intention in the litany of Pope Gelasius, but it was not to be found subsequently in the solemn prayers of Good Friday; the omission may be due to the fact that the penitents had been reconciled the day before. In any case, such a petition did exist in the first half of the fifth century, at the time when Prosper of Aquitaine appealed to the prayer of the faithful in formulating the great Catholic principle that the norm of prayer determines the norm of faith: *lex supplicandi lex credendi.*[18]

---

11. *Liber ordinum,* ed. M. Férotin (Monumenta Ecclesiae liturgica 5; Paris: Didot, 1904), col. 94.

12. Sozomen, *Historia ecclesiastica* 7, 16 (PG 67:1460).

13. This is Jungmann's thesis in his "*Oratio super populum* und altchristliche Büssersegnung," *EL* 52 (1938) 77–96; and in *The Mass of the Roman Rite: Its Origins and Development (Missarum Sollemnia),* trans. F. A. Brunner, 2 (New York: Benziger, 1955), 427–32.

14. St. Ambrose, *De paenitentia* II, 10, 19–22, ed. R. Gryson (SC 179; Paris: Cerf, 1971), 190. Other texts in P. M. Gy, "Histoire liturgique du sacrement de la pénitence," *LMD* no. 56 (1958) 10.

15. The Latin texts have been edited and studied by P. De Clerck, *La "prière universelle" dans les liturgies latines anciennes* (LQF 62; Münster: Aschendorff, 1977). For the East, see, e.g., *Constitutiones Apostolorum* VIII, 9 (Funk 1:484–89).

16. P. De Clerck, *ibid.,* 156–57; *Missale ambrosianum duplex,* ed. A. Ratti and M. Magistretti (Milan: Ghirlanda, 1913), 121.

17. *Missale gothicum,* ed. L. C. Mohlberg (REDMF 5; Rome: Herder, 1961), nos. 242–43 (p. 64); see *Missale gallicanum vetus,* ed. L. C. Mohlberg (REDMF 3; Rome: Herder, 1958), nos. 157–58 (p. 38); *Liber ordinum,* ed. Férotin, col. 222.

18. DS 246: "that the remedies of penance may be granted to those who have fallen (*ut lapsis paenitentiae remedia conferantur*)."

V. THE RECONCILIATION OF THE PENITENTS

Except in the case of dying persons, the Churches of the West had but a single annual celebration of reconciliation for penitents, and it came at Easter time. It may originally have taken place during the Easter Vigil itself. In any case, we soon find it located on Holy Thursday at Rome and Milan and on Good Friday in Spain, so that the reconciled sinners could take part in the Eucharist at Easter.

The rite must have included an exhortation by the bishop and an imposition of hands on each penitent, as well as one or more prayers of the bishop asking God's forgiveness for the penitents. The prayer of the congregation for the penitents was also undoubtedly part of the ceremony in one or other form.

St. Ambrose has left us a summary of two homilies which he delivered on Holy Thursday and in which he speaks of the reconciliation of penitents. In a letter to his sister he reports what he preached on Holy Thursday in 383, when he commented on the reading from Jonah for that day: Is not Jonah the prophet who preached the message of repentance and was at the same time a prefiguration of the Savior?[19] Ambrose's *Commentary on the Six Days of Creation* also contains a whole passage that had been preached on Holy Thursday.[20]

In Spain, penitents were reconciled on Good Friday at the hour of None, that is, at the moment when Christ had died. The Mozarabic *Liber ordinum* has preserved the text of a sermon that liturgical custom had made a set part of the ceremony.[21] It is followed by the *Miserere*, after each verse of which the prayer of the good thief is used as a refrain: "Remember me, Lord, when you come into your kingdom." After the psalm, the cry "Indulgentia [forgiveness! forgiveness!]" is repeated several hundred times by the people and serves in addition as the refrain for a litany. Even across the centuries we can sense the depth of popular feeling at this ceremony.

The Roman liturgy did not provide any comparable forms of popular participation. On the other hand, the bishop's sermon was preceded by a fine address in which a deacon expressed the sentiments of the penitents and asked the bishop to reconcile them: These were the most propitious of all days for forgiveness and renewal, both through baptism and through the reconciliation of the penitents; the latter had acknowledged their sins and done penance, they now asked for forgiveness; the deacon therefore urged the bishop to exercise his priestly intercession and reconcile the peni-

---

19. Ambrose, *Ep.* 20, 25 (PL 156:1001–2).
20. Ambrose, *Hexameron* V, 24, 91–92, ed. S. Schenkl (CSEL 32), 203.
21. *Liber ordinum*, ed. Férotin, cols. 200–202.

tents to God.[22] The *sacramentum reconciliationis* itself consisted in the imposition of hands by bishop or priest and an accompanying prayer or *supplicatio sacerdotalis*. The gesture of imposing the hand conveyed basically the idea of prayer for the person on whom the hand was imposed. In *Ordo* L (the Romano-German Pontifical) one of the formulas of reconciliation addresses God thus: "Place your compassionate hand on our hand (*manum pietatis tuae manui nostrae superpone*) so that through your cooperation the imposition of our hand may be a means of pouring out upon them the grace of the Holy Spirit."[23]

The oldest antiphonary known to us has as one of the antiphons for penitents 1 Peter 5:6-7: "Humble yourselves beneath the mighty hand of God so that he may lift you up."[24]

The purpose of the prayers was to draw down God's forgiveness on sinners whose penances had shown that their repentance was sincere. Inseparable from this divine forgiveness was reconciliation with the Church and a return to the altar and Eucharistic communion.[25]

§2. Penance in the Early Middle Ages

1. THE SUBSTITUTION OF "TARIFF-PENANCE" FOR THE ANCIENT PENITENTIAL SYSTEM

The shift from the ancient system of penance to new forms of penitential discipline and liturgy had three causes. The first was that the system of public penance had proved in the long run to be a failure: it was too severe, and sinners were unwilling to submit to it.

Secondly, even in antiquity the idea had developed, especially among the monks, that all Christians, even the best among them, not only have a responsibility to pray for bad Christians but are themselves sinners in some measure. They themselves, therefore, must practice works of pen-

---

22. The Roman Pontifical of 1596 retained the largest section of the diaconal petition "Adest o venerabilis pontifex," which comes from *Ge* I, 38 (Mohlberg, nos. 353–54, pp. 56–57). The second part has disappeared; the third, "Redintegra in eis," is located in the Pontifical after the re-entrance of the penitents into the church. Three other Roman diaconal petitions are known: ed. V. Bulhart, CCL 9 (1957), 363.

23. *PRG* XCIX, 243: "Alia" (2:63) (= *OR* L, 49; Andrieu, *OR* 5:201).

24. R. Hesbert, *Antiphonale missarum sextuplex* (Brussels: Vromant, 1935), no. 209 A (Antiphonary of Compiègne, ninth century).

25. See the prayer *Deus misericors, Deus clemens* of the *Ordo commendationis animae* (Roman Ritual of 1614, tit. 6, c. 7, no. 4), which originally served to reconcile a penitent in danger of death: *Ge* I, 39 (Mohlberg, no. 363, p. 58).

ance, engage in penitential prayer,[26] and, finally (this conviction coming as a later development), receive the sacrament of penance.

There was a third factor that profoundly influenced the evolution of penitential discipline: the appearance in the Celtic Churches (where public penance seems never to have existed) and the spread throughout the West of a new, private penitential practice that might be repeated. The historians, following A. Boudinhon,[27] have called this new form "tariff-penance"; it was an intermediate stage between the ancient system and the system that took shape during the twelfth century. This distinction, however, while accurate from the viewpoint of penitential discipline, is less so from the viewpoint of the ritual of penance. Beginning in the period when, first in Ireland and England and then on the European continent, use was made of lists of penances graded according to the seriousness of the sins, the ritual of confession and the prayers of absolution (though less well known to us than the penitential tariffs and attested only from a somewhat later time) differed clearly from the public penitential liturgy. On the other hand, this new ritual anticipated the ritual of private penance whose overall shape was not to change from the ninth century on, except in points of detail. One characteristic of the new form of penance was that it applied henceforth to everyone, including children, who were not yet able to meet the demands of the old public penance, and clerics, whose state in the Church had previously been incompatible with that of the penitents.

II. THE RITUAL IN TARIFF-PENANCE

The ritual almost always took place in the church, with only the priest and the penitent involved.[28]

It comprised an exhortation by the priest, a questioning of the penitent regarding his or her faith, and a confession of sins. The confession

---

26. See Possidius, *Vita Augustini* 31 (PL 32:63): "He often told us in intimate conversation that the reception of baptism did not absolve Christians, and especially priests, however estimable, from the duty of doing fitting and adequate penance before departing from this life. And he acted on this himself in his last and fatal illness. For he ordered those Psalms of David which are especially penitential to be copied out and, when he was very weak, used to lie in bed facing the wall where the sheets of paper were put up, gazing at them and reading them, and copiously and continuously weeping as he read" (trans. F. R. Hoare, *The Western Fathers* [New York: Sheed & Ward, 1954], 242).

27. A. Boudinhon, "Sur l'histoire de la pénitence," *Revue d'histoire et de littérature religieuse* 2 (1897) 306–44, 496–524.

28. But the short ritual for penance that was added to the Gelasian Sacramentary (nos. 1701–5) in the Frankish territories contains an invitatory that seems addressed to persons other than the penitent.

took the form either of a direct admission by the penitent of the sins committed or of answers by the penitent to questions asked by the priest (this
was probably the most common form in the Middle Ages) or (it seems)
of a lengthy confessional formula in which the penitent accused himself
or herself in a general way of all possible sins.[29] The exact function of
this last-named formula is not clear, for by itself it would not be a basis
for applying a list of penances, and yet the documents do not indicate
whether it was followed by one of the other two forms of confession.

After the confession (or at some other point in the rite) priest and penitent prostrated themselves before the altar and recited several penitential
psalms. The list of seven penitential psalms, which would be frequently
used from then on, seems to have made its appearance with Alcuin. On
the other hand, the prayer of Christian antiquity displayed a widespread
conviction that some of the psalms were especially appropriate for
metanoia and the confession of sins and especially effective in eliciting
and promoting the penitential attitude required of every Christian.[30]

The priest then pronounced the penitential judgment, which consisted
in determining, in light of the sins committed, the form and duration of
the penance to be done. He would usually then dismiss the penitent who
was to return later for reconciliation. But an immediate reconciliation was
also possible in cases when it was foreseen that the penitent's situation
would make it impossible to return for reconciliation or when it was seen
that the penitent could not understand the need of such a return. The priest
reconciled the penitent by means of a series of prayers; that is—to use
the categories employed in later theology—the reconciliation took a
deprecative form.

III. EVOLUTION AND SURVIVALS OF THE LITURGY OF PUBLIC PENANCE

Public penance seems to have fallen into complete disuse at the end
of antiquity, but it was revived in Frankish lands in the Carolingian period in order to deal with the most serious sins.

The original first imposition of hands on the penitents on the first day
of Lent underwent extensive liturgical development in the ninth and tenth

---

29. *PRG* XCIX, 50 A (2:16–17).

30. In his *Tituli psalmorum* (PG 23:68–72); see P. Salmon, *Les tituli psalmorum* [Paris:
Cerf, 1959], 121ff.). Eusebius of Caesarea calls Ps 6, 24, 37, 50, 103 [LXX numbering] "a
teaching on confession" and says that Ps 29 is "a eucharist for confession." See St. Athanasius,
Ep. ad Marcellinum 10 (Ps 27:21): "*Metanoein* means to stop sinning; and this book [the
psalter] shows us how we are to do penance and what words we are to use in our *metanoia*."

centuries and took on a new form with the imposition of hair shirt and ashes and the expulsion of the penitents from the church.

Penitents in the early Church, like those in the Bible, had doubtless often voluntarily worn hair shirts and covered their heads with ashes. Beginning in the tenth century, the bishops blessed both articles and required the penitent to wear them.

Above all, however, the address by the bishop, the formula "Memento quia pulvis es," the response "In sudore vultus tui,"[31] and the expulsion from the church represented a complete reinterpretation of the rite. Instead of an entrance into the *ordo paenitentium* there was now an expulsion of penitents from the Christian community as expressed typologically by God's expulsion of Adam from paradise to the accompaniment of the words: "In the sweat of your face (*in sudore vultus tui*) you shall eat bread till you return to the ground, for out of it you were taken; you are dust, and to dust you shall return" (Gen 3:19). After Adam had sinned God expelled him from paradise, which was a prefiguration of the Church, until he should have done penance. During Lent, the public penitent would not be allowed into the church.

The same symbolism of restoration to the Church was expressed in the most visual way possible in the liturgy of reconciliation on Holy Thursday. In this rite the bishop himself led the reconciled penitents into the church, holding the first by the hand, while each in turn held the hand of the next in line.

More importantly, the rite was expanded and lengthened by the incorporation of dramatic elements. Henceforth, in addition, the role of the Christian community in the liturgy both of expulsion and of reconciliation was to pray the penitential psalms for the penitents.

The solemn liturgy of expulsion and reconciliation of penitents that was already in use in the Rhineland of the tenth century[32] was incorporated almost without change into the Roman Pontifical at the end of the fifteenth century and remained there down to our own time. It seems, however, never to have succeeded in establishing itself in Roman practice; on the other hand, the Roman Church did accept the blessing and imposition of ashes not only on penitents but on the entire Christian community. And in the final centuries of the Middle Ages the imposition of ashes at the beginning of Lent became a sacramental of sorrow for sin. Few sacramentals left such a deep impression on the souls of the people,

---

31. This response was subsequently used in Matins on Monday of Septuagesima week: R. J. Hesbert, *Corpus antiphonalium officii* 4 (REDMF 10; Rome: Herder, 1970), no. 6937; see vols. 1 and 2, nos. 52–54.

32. *PRG* 2:14–21, 59–67 (= Andrieu, *OR* 5:108–24, 192–207).

and the name "Ash Wednesday" entered the liturgical books and all the languages of the West.[33]

Independently of the imposition of ashes, some French cathedrals and some religious orders retained the practice, on both Ash Wednesday and Holy Thursday, of reciting the penitential psalms, which were followed by prayers of absolution.[34]

Another practice that is attested was a developed form of collective penitential rite with a prayer of absolution during Mass on Easter or Holy Thursday.[35] Whatever the significance the faithful may have attached to them, these rites did not have (and doubtless had never had) sacramental value in the teaching of the Church. They did, however, serve as sacramentals that provided a framework and extension of the great common activity of annual confession as prescribed by Canon 21 of the Fourth Lateran Council (1215). This confession was connected, in fact, with the Easter communion,[36] just as, in keeping with universal practice, every communion was preceded by confession.

§3. Modern Penance (Thirteenth Century Onward)

I. THE RITUAL DOWN TO VATICAN II

In private penance of the modern period the sacramental rite has not only become a secret affair, being performed apart from the community; in a way, the Scholastic theologians even stripped it of all right to a liturgy when they claimed that, contrary to the practice of their own age, neither a prayer of absolution nor a laying on of hands could be essential to the sacrament. In their view, which followed the lead of St. Thomas Aquinas,[37] the gospel statement "Whatever you loose on earth shall be loosed in heaven" necessarily implied that the form of the sacrament must be words in the indicative mood: "Ego te absolvo." The Church made this view its own at the Council of Florence (DS 1323) and, above all, at Trent (DS 1673), but without passing any judgment either on the earlier practice of the Western Church, which had showed no trace of "Ego te absolvo," or on Eastern usage.

---

33. See *The Church at Prayer* 4:68–69.

34. Martène, M 975–76, 1003, 1005–5.

35. N. Lemaître, "Pratique et signification de la confession communautaire dans les paroisses au XVIᵉ siècle," in Groupe de La Bussière, *Pratiques de la confession* (Paris: Cerf, 1983), 139–60.

36. DS 812.

37. St. Thomas Aquinas, *Summa theologiae* III, 84, 3.

Apart from the sacramental words, the other gestures and prayers accompanying confession and absolution were determined by local custom.

The Ritual of 1614 tried to restore a degree of cultic publicity to penance and to make it a more solemn affair: to this end it prescribed that as far as possible the priest should wear surplice and stole and should hear confessions in a church and in a confessional. Once the penitent had knelt and made the sign of the cross, the confessor was to ask, if necessary, what the penitent's state of life and occupation were and how long it had been since the previous confession. If the penitent was ignorant of the rudiments of the faith, the confessor was, time allowing, to give a very brief instruction or try to awaken the penitent's sense of responsibility in this area. Then came the confession proper, followed by the sacramental exhortation called for by the Council of Trent. This admonition, however brief, had the same function as the *correptio* for which St. Augustine and the Fathers had made provision; it was a Word of God that urged conversion and intense sorrow for sin.

The Ritual of 1614 was the first to prescribe that the priest be separated from the penitent by a grill. It also prescribed that after the *Misereatur*, when the priest was beginning the strictly priestly prayer, the *Indulgentiam*, he should raise his right hand toward the penitent ("dextra versus penitentem elevata"[38]). At the same time, however, the Ritual made it clear that only the "Ego te absolvo" was essential. The Ritual thus intended to keep and even restore the ancient gesture used in reconciling penitents.

On the other hand, the absolution from censures that immediately preceded the "Ego te absolvo" was not originally meant as a precautionary absolution. In an age when the ecclesiastical and the strictly sacramental spheres were not yet clearly distinguished, the prayer of absolution not only brought forgiveness of sins but at the same time restored the penitent to communion with the faithful and the sacraments of the Church: "Et restituo te unitati et communioni fidelium et sanctis Ecclesiae sacramentis."[39]

Finally, the prayer *Passio Domini*, while applying the merits of Christ and the saints to the penitent, was also an act of that priestly intercession that the Fathers had regarded as so important. For the priest, while loosing sins in the name of God, is also a minister of the Christ who intercedes with the Father.

---

38. The two main sources of the Ritual of 1614 contained nothing similar, but the imposition of hands is found in the Milanese Ritual of St. Charles Borromeo (text in A. Ratti, *Acta Ecclesiae Mediolanensis* 2 [Milan, 1902], col. 1323).

39. Thus in the Ritual of Cardinal Giulio Antonio Santori: *Rituale sacramentorum Romanum* (Rome, 1584–1602), 288.

II. THE *ORDO PAENITENTIAE* OF 1974

A new Roman Ritual of penance was published in 1974,[40] in keeping with the Council's decision that "the rites and formularies for the sacrament of penance are to be revised so that they more clearly express both the nature and effect of the sacrament."[41] But the new ritual is also based, especially in its doctrinal introduction, on the teaching of *Lumen gentium* (8 and 11) on the ecclesial dimension of the sacrament of penance, namely, that in the act of obtaining God's forgiveness the penitent is also reconciled to the Church.

The ritual also gives liturgical embodiment to the *Normae pastorales* published by the Congregation for the Doctrine of the Faith with regard to general absolution.[42] These norms, as well as Vatican II's call for a communal celebration of the sacraments whenever feasible (*VSC* 27), require that three rites of penance be distinguished: the individual rite; the communal rite with individual confession and absolution; and the communal rite "with general confession and absolution." It must be noted, however (the Ritual of 1974 emphasizes this point and the new Code does so even more strongly), that there is no question of three possibilities freely available and to be regarded as complementary. The use of general absolution is authorized but subject to strict disciplinary regulations. On the other hand, there is no such restriction on use of the second of the three rites; the only two conditions here are that there be a sufficiently large number of confessors and that each penitent not take a long time in the confessional.

The rite for individual confession is almost identical in its structure with the earlier rite, but it is quite different in the proposed manner of its celebration. The likeness of structure perhaps explains why the new manner of celebrating the sacrament has caught on only slowly.

The liturgical regulations make it clear that the sacrament should be truly celebrated and that here, as in other areas of the liturgy, an effort to get through it expeditiously does not promote, and is not without an

---

40. *Rituale Romanum . . . Ordo paenitentiae*, ed. typica (Vatican Polyglot Press, 1974). Translated in *The Rites of the Catholic Church* 1 (New York: Pueblo, 1976), 339–445, with new translation of the Introduction in *DOL* 368 nos. 3066–3109.

41. *VSC* 72 (*DOL* 1 no. 72).

42. Sacred Congregation for the Doctrine of the Faith, *Normae pastorales circa absolutionem sacramentalem generali modo impertiendam: AAS* 64 (1972) 510–14 (= *EDIL* 2828–31 = *DOL* 361 nos. 3038–51). — Changes were later introduced into these norms by canons 960-63 of the Code of 1983 and incorporated in turn in the Ritual: see *Emendations in the Liturgical Books Following upon the New Code of Canon Law*, trans. International Commission on English in the Liturgy (Washington, D.C., 1984), 17–20 (Latin original: Vatican Polyglot Press, 1983, and see *Notitiae* 20 [1983]).

impact on, the fruitfulness of the sacramental action. It is suggested that the celebration include the reading of a passage from Scripture (which, if need be, the priest may recite from memory) and that the exhortation after the confession of sins should both encourage the penitent to contrition and shed light on the connection between the sacrament of penance and the paschal mystery. Once the penitent has been told what penitential work is to be performed, he or she expresses contrition in one of the formulas suggested or in the penitent's own words. The priest then raises his hands (or hand) and pronounces the formula of absolution:

> God, the Father of mercies,
> through the death and resurrection of his Son
> has reconciled the world to himself
> and sent the Holy Spirit among us
> for the forgiveness of sins;
> through the ministry of the Church
> may God give you pardon and peace,
> and I absolve you from your sins
> in the name of the Father, and of the Son,
> and of the Holy Spirit. — Amen.[43]

Here, as in other sacraments, a distinction must be made between the sacramental formula (that is, the entire formula) and the essential words, "I absolve . . . Spirit" (in use since the thirteenth century), which suffice in danger of imminent death. Considered in its entirety,

> the form of absolution indicates that the reconciliation of the penitent comes from the mercy of the Father; it shows the connection between the reconciliation of the sinner and the paschal mystery of Christ; it stresses the role of the Holy Spirit in the forgiveness of sins; finally, it underlines the ecclesial aspect of the sacrament, because reconciliation with God is asked for and given through the ministry of the Church."[44]

The celebration ends with a verse of praise from the psalms and words of peace for the penitent.

The two communal rites resemble one another except in one important point: the second of them does not include an individual confession of sins. In both, there is a true liturgy of the Word with a homily, an examination of conscience, and, for example, a penitential litany. When there is individual confession, this is followed by individual absolution, and the rite ends with a prayer of thanksgiving for God's mercy. When individual confession is not possible, the prayer of general absolution takes a more solemn form.

---

43. *Rites* 1:263.
44. *Ordo paenitentiae* 19 (*DOL* 368 no. 3084).

Chapter III

Prayer for the Sick
and
Sacramental Anointing

A. G. Martimort[1]

GENERAL BIBLIOGRAPHY

J. de Launoy, *De sacramento unctionis infirmorum liber* (Paris: Typis viduae E. Martini, 1673).

Martène, M 621–53.

J. C. Trombelli, *Tractatus de sacramentis per polemicas et liturgicas dissertationes distributi. De extrema unctione* (3 vols.; Bologna, 1776–78).

A. Chavasse, *Etude sur l'onction des infirmes dans l'Eglise latine du IIIe au XIe siècle 1. Du IIIe siècle à la réforme carolingienne* (Lyons: Librairie du Sacré-Coeur, 1942. (Only volume 1 was published; volume 2 exists only in the typewritten copy of the 1938 dissertation that is deposited in the library of the Facultés catholiques of Lyons.)

B. Botte, "L'onction des malades," *LMD* no. 15 (1948) 91–107.

C. Ortemann, *Le sacrement des malades, histoire et signification* (Lyons: Ed. du Chalet, 1971).

La maladie et la mort du chrétien dans la liturgie. Conférences Saint-Serge, XXIe Semaine d'études liturgiques 1974 (Bibliotheca EL, Subsidia 1; Rome: Edizioni liturgiche, 1974). ET: *Temple of the Holy Spirit. Sickness and Death of the Christian in the Liturgy*, trans. M. J. O'Connell (New York: Pueblo, 1983) (does not include the essays of M. Arranz and A. M. Triacca).

R. Béraudy. "Le sacrement des malades. Etude historique et théologique," *Nouvelle revue théologique* 106 (1974) 600–34.

---

1. Canon A. Chavasse was unable, for reasons of health, to revise the very authoritative chapter he had contributed to earlier editions of *The Church at Prayer*. In the circumstances, I thought it better to compose a new chapter that would take into account the works published in the interval and that would, above all, explain the new Roman Ritual of 1972 in the light of the tradition.

E. J. Lengeling, " 'Per istam sanctam unctionem . . . adiuvet te Dominus gratia Spiritus Sancti': Der heilige Geist und die Krankensalbung," in *Lex orandi, lex credendi. Miscellanea . . . Cipriano Vagaggini* (Studia Anselmiana 79, Sacramentum 6; Rome, 1980), 235–94.

Jesus' action of healing the sick was a sign of the kingdom and one that he often connected with the forgiveness of sins. He gave his apostles in turn the power to heal through signs: anointing with oil (Mark 6:12), laying on of hands (Mark 16:18). This mission was not limited to the time of the Church's beginnings: the Letter of James gives instructions that apply to all times (5:13-16): "Is any among you sick? Let him call for the elders (*tous presbyterous*) of the church, and let them pray over him (*ep' auton*), anointing him with oil (*aleipsantes elaiō*) in the name of the Lord; and the prayer of faith will save the sick man, and the Lord will raise him up (*egerei*); and if he has committed sins, he will be forgiven. Therefore confess your sins to one another, and pray for one another, that you may be healed."[2]

Throughout the history of the Church, these various New Testament ideas, and especially the instructions in the Letter of James, were to remain the norm governing the liturgy of the sick and the theology of anointing, even where explicit reference was not made to these sources.[3] The New Testament data explain in particular the ambivalence the tradition has found in this sacrament, which is meant both for healing and for the forgiveness of sins.

§1. Prayer for the Sick and Anointing During the First Seven Centuries

I. BLESSING OF OIL FOR THE SICK

a) *The Earliest Formularies*

The ancient collections of canons deal especially with the blessing of oil for the sick and provide formularies for this action. The earliest, as far as we know at present, is the one in the *Apostolic Tradition*, which dates from the beginning of the third century. After citing the Eucharistic Prayer, Hippolytus goes on to say:

---

2. See the excellent commentary that E. Cothenet gives of this passage in his essay, "Healing as a Sign of the Kingdom, and the Anointing of the Sick," in *Temple of the Holy Spirit. Sickness and Death of the Christian in the Liturgy*, trans. M. J. O'Connell (New York: Pueblo, 1983), 33–53. — On the passage in James see also B. Reicke, "L'onction des malades d'apres saint Jacques," *LMD* no. 113 (1973) 50–56, and the bibliographies given by each of these two commentators.

3. A. Chavasse, *Etude sur l'onction des infirmes dans l'Eglise latine du IIIe au XIe siècle* 1 (Lyons: Librairie du Sacré-Coeur, 1942), 201–2.

> If anyone offers oil, let him [the bishop] give thanks in the same way as for the offering of bread and wine (not using the same words but expressing the same idea) and say: "Lord, just as by sanctifying this oil, with which you anointed kings, priests, and prophets, you give holiness to those who are anointed with it and receive it, so let it bring comfort to those who taste of it (*gustantibus*) and health to those who use it (*utentibus*)."[4]

As a result of the wide distribution of Hippolytus' book, this prayer was to influence the later formularies; Rome would also continue to use it for blessing oil at the end of the Canon of the Mass. Nonetheless, only the Ethiopic version of the *Apostolic Tradition* kept the formula as such.[5] The *Testament of the Lord*, which originated in Syria (fifth century), gives a different formula, and one that already displays a confusion, later frequent in the East, between the oil of the sick and the oil used for the exorcism of catechumens:

> Lord God, who have given us the Spirit Paraclete; Lord, saving name that is steadfast and hidden from the foolish but revealed to the prudent; Christ, who have sanctified us and in your mercy have instructed these servants [= the priests] whom you have chosen in your wisdom; you who sent knowledge of your Spirit into us sinners by your holiness when you gave us the gift of the Spirit; you who cure every illness and suffering and have given the gift of healing to those whom you judged worthy of it: send the fullness of your compassion upon this oil, which is an image of your gentleness, so that it may set free those who are suffering, restore the sick to health, and sanctify those who are being converted and coming to faith in you, for you are mighty and to be praised for ever and ever. *The people are to respond:* Amen. *The same prayer is to be said over the water.*[6]

---

4. *La Tradition apostolique de saint Hippolyte. Essai de reconstitution*, ed. B. Botte (LQF 39; Münster: Aschendorff, 1963), 18–19. In a note Botte explains why he disagrees on one or two points with the interpretation given in Chavasse 29–39. — See E. Segelberg, "The *Benedictio olei* in the *Apostolic Tradition* of Hippolytus," *OC* 48 (1964) 268–81.

5. H. Duensing, *Der aethiopische Text der Kirchenordnung des Hippolyt* (Abhandlungen der Akademie der Wissenschaften in Göttingen, phil.-hist. Klasse. 3. Folge, 32; Göttingen: Vandenhoeck & Ruprecht, 1946), 24–25. — The Sahidic and Arab versions, which omit the prayers of ordination and the anaphora, say nothing of the blessings that followed the latter. Only the *Canons of Hippolytus*, can. 3, have kept the rubric: "If there is oil, let him [the bishop] pray over it in this way, not using the same words but expressing the same idea" (ed. R. Coquin, PO 31 [Paris, 1966], 354–55).

6. I, 24–25, ed. I. Rahmani (Mainz: Kirchheim, 1899; reprinted: Hildesheim: Olms, 1968), 48–49; French trans. by F. Nau in P. Cipriotti, *La version syriaque de l'Octateuque de Clément* (Paris: Letheilleux, 1967), 39–40. — A baptismal ritual interpolated in the Ethiopic recension of the *Traditio apostolica*, XXII P, contains a formula for "the oil of anointing which the bishop prepares for those who are going to receive the bath and for the sick faithful" (Duensing [n. 5], 118 [text] and 121 [translation]). The interpolation is not as old as thought by A. Salles, *Trois antiques rituels du baptême* (SC 59; Paris: Cerf, 1958).

The compiler of the *Apostolic Constitutions* (end of the fourth or beginning of the fifth century) also includes a blessing of water and of oil among a group of canons of unknown origin. The bishop or, in his absence, a priest is to pray in the name of the person who has offered this water and this oil and is to ask the Lord to make these elements "efficacious in producing health, driving out sicknesses, putting demons to flight, and foiling ambushes."[7]

The Egyptian prayerbook known as the Euchologion of Serapion, which dates from the fifth or perhaps the fourth century, likewise contains a blessing for water and for oil that can be compared with that in the *Apostolic Constitutions* and is perhaps from a related source.[8] But a few pages further on, the Euchologion offers another, much more developed formula for the oil of the sick. In addition to the effects already listed, this prayer also asks for the forgiveness of sins, and for "soundness of soul, body, and spirit" (1 Thess 5:23), so that "his name may have glory who was crucified for us, who rose again, who took our diseases and infirmities upon himself (Isa 53:4): Jesus Christ, who will also come to judge the living and the dead."[9]

It is hard to determine what use may have been made of the various texts of which I have been speaking. At least they testify that all the Churches of the early centuries were careful to have a formulary with which a bishop or his priests could bless the oil intended for use in the healing, at once bodily and spiritual, of the sick. The Nestorian synod of 554, at which Catholicos Joseph presided, gave evidence of the same concern when in its canon 19 it laid down the following rule for "those who deliberately give themselves to devilish works," that is, to superstitions: "When one of those who have fallen into this serious illness is converted, let them offer him as a means of healing the oil of prayer that has been blessed by the priests, along with the water of prayer, just as they would to those who are sick in body."[10]

b) *Latin Formularies*

Among the Latin formularies for the blessing of oil for the sick, at least one predates the eighth century, namely, the Roman prayer which, amid

---

7. *Constitutiones Apostolorum* (Funk 1:532). — Text reproduced in the *Octateuch of Clement* and translated by F. Nau in Cipriotti (n. 6), 93.

8. No. 17 (Funk 2:178–80). — See the translation in A. Hamman, *Prières des premiers chrétiens* (Paris: Desclée De Brouwer, 1981²), 134; ET: *Early Christian Prayers*, trans. W. Mitchell (Chicago: Regnery, 1961), no. 195 (pp. 125–26).

9. No. 29 (Funk 2:190–92; Hamman 139; Mitchell no. 207, p. 130).

10. J. B. Chabot, *Synodicon orientale*, in *Notices et extraits des manuscrits de la Bibliothèque Nationale* 36 (1902) 106 (text) and 363–64 (translation).

various alterations of its text, has remained in use down to our time and is still used in somewhat revised form in the *Ordo benedicendi oleum . . .* of 1971 and the *Ordo unctionis . . .* of 1972. It was to be found in both the Gelasian[11] and Gregorian[12] sacramentaries; the latter seems to give the original text. A. Chavasse believes it can be dated as early as the fifth or end of the fourth century.

> From highest heaven, Lord, send the Holy Spirit, the Paraclete, on this fat (*pinguedinem*) of the olive tree, which you have deigned to draw from this sturdy tree in order to relieve our bodies. Let your holy blessing make it be, for any who anoint themselves with it . . .[13] or apply it to themselves, a bodily remedy that rids the body of all pain, all weakness, all sickness. It is the oil with which you anointed priests, kings, prophets, and martyrs,[14] your good oil that you have blessed, Lord, and that remains in our vitals, in the name of our Lord Jesus Christ.[15]

It is easy to spot the echoes of Hippolytus in this text. Also from Hippolytus, as we have seen, is the Roman practice of placing this blessing at the end of the Canon of the Mass. The papal liturgy in the Gregorian Sacramentary, which supposes that the Mass is being concelebrated, has the pope and his priests pronounce this blessing.[16] Where the Gregorian mentions only the body, however, the Gelasian twice adds the spirit: "mentis et corporis"; and where the Gregorian says "tutamentum mentis et corporis," the Gelasian has a fuller text: "tutamentum corporis, animae et spiritus." Does the difference reflect a doctrinal development? In fact, the two versions are likely to have been more or less contemporary and, in any case, only the bodily effects are listed in detail in the course of the blessing in both sources.[17]

Other Latin formularies may be earlier than the seventh century, even though they have been transmitted in relatively late manuscripts. They represent traditions proper to Spain, the Narbonnaise, and Gaul.[18] Most

---

11. *Ge* 382.

12. *Gr* 334.

13. *Ge* adds: *gustandi.* "(that it may be) absorbed." A. Chavasse thinks the word was part of the original text.

14. On this "anointing of the martyrs" see W. Dürig, "Die 'Salbung der Märtyrer.' Ein Beitrag zur Märtyrertheologie der Liturgie," *SE* 6 (1954) 14–47; E. Lanne, "L'onction des martyrs et la bénédiction de l'huile," *Irénikon* 31 (1958) 138–55.

15. From the French translation of A. Chavasse, who comments on the text, 40–51.

16. *Gr* 333: "Antequam dicatur *Per quem haec omnia Domine semper bona creas*, levantur de ampullis quas offerunt populi et benedicat tam domnus papa quam omnes presbyteri."

17. The nuanced presentation of this textual problem by A. Chavasse, 44–45, does not deserve the reproaches directed at it here and there; see B. Seeboüé, *L'onction des malades* (Lyons: Publications Profac, 1972), 24, note 16.

18. There is a Visigothic formula that may be very old: the one in ms. Silos 3, ed. J. Janini, *Liber ordinum sacerdotal* (Studia Silensia 7; Silos, 1981), 77–78: "Domine Iesu Christe

of them invoke the action of the Holy Spirit on the oil; several invoke Christ the physician or Christ who bore our sicknesses and sufferings. At times, too, there is a citation of the passage in James or an allusion to it; in addition to asking for the cure of bodily ills,[19] two of these prayers expressly ask for the forgiveness of sins.

II. THE APPLICATION OF THE OIL AND THE VISITATION OF THE SICK

As we read the prayers for the blessing of the oil and the Roman prayer in particular, it becomes clear that once blessed by the bishop or his priests the oil could be given to the sick who would use it themselves as a medicine or to whom it could be applied by those caring for them; it was a liniment, an unguent, but it could also be drunk.[20] This was likely the case in the various Churches of antiquity; for the West, A. Chavasse has collected a good number of witnesses that leave no doubt on this point.[21] In his letter of 416 to Decentius of Gubbio, Pope Innocent I cites the Letter of James and comments: "This must undoubtedly be understood as referring to the faithful who are sick and can be anointed with the holy oil of chrism which the bishop has prepared and which is to be used for anointing not only by priests but by all Christians in their own need or that of their families."

At the same time, however, Innocent I regards this practice by lay Christians as a temporary makeshift ("in sua aut in suorum necessitate"), for he immediately goes on to express surprise that Decentius has interpreted the passage in James in a way that would exclude the bishop:

> But I regard as unwarranted your hesitation about whether a bishop can do what presbyters can certainly do. If the text speaks of presbyters, it is because bishops are prevented by other occupations from visiting all of the sick. In fact, if the bishop is able, or thinks it right, to visit someone, then

---

qui per Apostolum . . ." (also ed. M. Férotin, *Liber ordinum* [Paris: Didot, 1904], col. 23–24, note). Chavasse comments on it, 71–73, and also studies (64–70) the formula *In tuo nomine* (Férotin, col. 8–11), which is doubtless much later (Férotin, pp. xxi–xxii). — The prayer "Omnipotens Deus qui creaturam olei" (Férotin, col. 22–23) was doubtless originally also a blessing of the oil for the sick (Chavasse 82). — For the blessing of the oil of the sick, the Bobbio Missal, which probably reflects practice in the Narbonnaise, has a group of three formulas, one of them an exorcism (ed. E. Lowe, HBS 58, nos. 574–76), which Chavasse analyzes, 76–79. The Milanese texts (Chavasse 51–57) are difficult to date.

19. There is a long list of these ills in the prayer *In tuo nomine* (see the preceding note).

20. In the formula of the Gelasian Sacramentary (above, note 13); also the words "potionis admixtum" of the prayer *In tuo nomine* (Chavasse 69, note 4); and the words "omnes qui ex eo ungendi sunt aut sumpti accipiunt" of the Bobbio Missal (Chavasse 79).

21. Chavasse 78–149, 168–75.

he to whom the preparation of chrism is reserved can unhesitatingly bless and anoint with the chrism.[22]

In fact, visitation of the sick by the bishop or his priests was a ministry already urged upon them by St. Polycarp of Smyrna back in the second century.[23] Hippolytus in his turn advised that the bishop be told who is sick "so that if it seems good to him he may visit them, for it is a great source of strength to the sick when the high priest is mindful of them."[24] In commenting on this text the *Canons of Hippolytus* add: "They find relief in their sickness when the bishop comes to them and especially when he prays over them, for the shadow of Peter healed the sick—unless they have reached the end of their lives."[25] This is doubtless the first witness to a liturgy for visitation of the sick. The expression "he prays over them" recalls the Letter of James and suggests a laying on of hands.[26] But the *Canons of Hippolytus* also envisage the case of sick persons whose state is not serious or close to death: it will be "a remedy for them to go to the church and receive the water of prayer and the oil of prayer."[27] A testimony that agrees with the *Canons* is given by the Egyptian Euchologion attributed to Serapion. This contains a "Prayer for the Sick" and a "Blessing (*cheirothesia*) of the Sick" that implies an imposition of hands: "Extend your hand, O Lord. . . ."[28] In Africa, in the first decades of the fifth century, St. Augustine's biographer tells us of him that "if he were specially asked by people who were ill to pray to the Lord for them in their presence and lay his hands on them, he would go at once."[29]

Anointing by bishop or priests is attested both in the East and in the

22. See text and French translation in R. Cabié, *La lettre du pape Innocent Ier à Décentius de Gubbio* (Bibliothèque de la RHE 58; Louvain, 1973), 31; commentary 59–61; see Chavasse 89–99.

23. St. Polycarp, *Ep. ad Philippenses* VI, 1 (SC 10:210–11): "Presbyters . . . must be compassionate and merciful to all; let them bring back the straying, let them visit the sick. . . ."

24. *Traditio apostolica* 34 (Botte 80–81). The Sahidic version and the *Canons of Hippolytus* leave no doubt that it is the bishop, and not the deacons, who will visit the sick. — The *Didascalia apostolorum* 16 (Connolly 148) also emphasizes visitation of the sick, but assigns this task rather to deacons.

25. Canon 24, ed. and trans. R. Coquin, PO 31 (1966), 390–91.

26. See A. Malvy, "Extrême-onction et imposition des mains," *RechSR* 7 (1917) 519–23; idem, "L'onction des malades dans les Canons d'Hippolyte et les documents apparentés," *ibid.*, 9 (1919) 222–29.

27. Canon 21 (Coquin 388–89); compare the *Euchologion of Serapion*, no. 17 (above, note 8). In the East the oil for the sick is always called *euchelaion*.

28. *Euchologion of Serapion* VII–VIII (Funk 2:164–67).

29. Possidius, *Vita Augustini* 27 (PL 32:56), trans. F. R. Hoare, *The Western Fathers* (New York: Sheed & Ward, 1954), 226.

West,[30] but apart from the Euchologion of Serapion we have no descriptions of the ritual from before the second half of the seventh century.

§2. The Anointing of the Sick in the Eastern Churches Since the Eighth Century

BIBLIOGRAPHY

Denz 2:483–525, 551–52.
C. De Clercq, *Ordre, mariage, extrême-onction* (Bibliothèque catholique des sciences religieuses; Paris: Bloud et Gay, 1939).
J. Dauvillier, "Extrême-onction dans les Eglises orientales," *Dictionnaire de droit canonique* 5 (Paris: Letouzey, 1953), 725–89.

The continuation of anointing of the sick among the Nestorians after the synod of 554 is problematic.[31] It seems, however, some early pontificals contained a blessing of oil for the sick under the title "Oil of health."[32] The Nestorians subsequently used an odd mixture of oil and dust from the sanctuaries, blessing it "for the purpose of healing and as a remedy for body and soul."[33] The modern pontificals of the Uniat Chaldeans have a blessing of oil for the sick that has doubtless been influenced by Latin practice.[34]

The other Eastern Churches have a ritual that is more or less dependent on the Byzantine. The latter, as found in the earliest known euchologia[35] and particularly in the euchologion of the collection Barberini gr. 336 (eighth century),[36] already contained some prayers for the sick

---

30. For the West see Chavasse 150–62; for the Syrian East, J. Dauvillier, "Extrême-onction dans les Eglises orientales," *Dictionnaire de droit canonique* 5 (Paris: Letouzey, 1953), 758.

31. W. de Vries, *Sakramententheologie bei den Nestorianern* (OCA 133; Rome, 1947), 281–83.

32. I. Vosté, *Pontificale iuxta ritum Ecclesiae Syrorum orientalium id est Chaldaeorum. Versio latina* (Vatican Polyglot Press, 1937–38), 274–75, cites a letter from a Chaldean bishop assuring him on this point, but without giving any reference or details regarding these "ancient manuscripts"; see also *ibid.*, 271–72, and Dauvillier 750–53.

33. Vosté 399; Denz 517–18. The mixture is called "Hnana."

34. Vosté 268–69.

35. M. Arranz, "Christologie et ecclésiologie des prières pour les malades de l'Euchologe slave du Sinaï," in *L'Eglise dans la liturgie. Conférences Saint-Serge, XXVIᵉ Semaine d'études liturgiques, Paris 1979* (Bibliotheca EL, Subsidia 18; Rome: Edizioni liturgiche, 1980), 19–66, gives references (19–23) to the oldest euchologia as edited by A. Dmitrievskij, *Opisanie liturgitcheskikh rukopisej . . .* 2 (Kiev, 1901). — See also M. Arranz, "Les sacrements de l'ancien Euchologe constantinopolitain. 1. Etudes préliminaire des sources," *OCP* 48 (1982) 284–335 (see 329).

36. A. Strittmatter, "The Barberinium S. Marci of Jacques Goar," *EL* 47 (1933), nos. 223–27 (p. 358).

and one or two prayers for blessing the oil. Two formulas have been in almost continuous use down to our own day. The first is for the blessing of the oil:

> Lord, in your compassionate mercy you heal the sufferings of our souls and our bodies. Master, do you yourself sanctify this oil and let it become a remedy for those anointed with it; let it do away with all suffering, every defilement of flesh or spirit, and every evil, so that in this, too, your most holy name may be glorified, Father, Son, and Holy Spirit, now and always and ages without end. Amen.[37]

In the earliest euchologia the second prayer is described only as "Prayer over the sick," without any rubric indicating that it is for use in anointing. In later books, however, this prayer, in a revised version, is given as an accompaniment to anointings:

> Holy Father, physician of souls and bodies, you sent your only Son, our Lord and our God, to cure every sickness and preserve from death. By the grace of your Christ deliver, too, this servant of yours from the bodily illness that torments him (her); give him (her) life according to your good pleasure so that he (she) may through good works offer you fitting thanksgiving.[38]

From the eleventh century on[39] the sacrament became part of an extensive liturgical whole that is to be celebrated (theoretically in the church) either during Mass on seven days or in one ceremony by seven priests as part of a Mass or of orthros or vespers.[40] After the blessing of the oil, each priest in turn presides over a liturgy of the word (including a *prokimenon*, epistle, alleluia, gospel, and litany) and anoints the sick person with the formula "Holy Father, physician of souls and bodies. . . ." The practice has grown of doing the anointing with a brush on forehead, chin, nostrils, mouth, breast, hands, and so on.[41] At the end, the priests lay the Book of the Gospels on the head of the sick person. There is, of course, a "Short Service of Holy Oil," but it always includes concelebration.[42]

---

37. Strittmatter no. 226; J. Goar, *Euchologium sive Rituale Graecorum* (Venice: Javarina, 1730²), 335; French trans. in E. Mercenier and F. Paris, *La prière des Eglises de rite byzantin* 1 (Chevetogne, 1948²), 428; Arranz, "Christologie et ecclesiologie . . ." (note 35), 51.

38. Strittmatter, no. 223; Dmitrievskij (note 356), 5; French trans. by A. Chavasse in the earlier editions of *L'Eglise en prière*; modern text in Goar 338; French trans. in Mercenier and Paris 433. — On the evolution of this text see Arranz, "Christologie et ecclésiologie . . .," 26–27.

39. Bibl. nat. ms. Coislin 213, ff. 107–9; see Dmitrievskij 1017–20; Arranz 23.

40. Goar 332–48; Mercenier and Paris 420–26.

41. Goar 356, note 38; Mercenier and Paris 433. — Euchologion Coislin 213 prescribes that the anointing be done "in the form of a cross on face, ears, breast, and hands" (Dmitrievskij 1019).

42. Mercenier and Paris 446–47, following the Slavic *Trebnik* published in Rome.

Among the Armenians,[43] Copts,[44] and Western Syrians,[45] the rite is called "Ritual of the Lamp": each priest in succession (seven among the Armenians and Copts, five among the Syrians) lights a lamp[46] and presides, as among the Byzantines, over a liturgy of the Word. The anointings are administered with oil from the lamp; the laying on of the gospel is preceded by a laying on of hands. A comparative study of the formulas is still needed in order to establish the reciprocal influences exercised by the various rites. The passage from the Letter of James is read everywhere; literal fidelity to the apostle's words is probably what has led to the requirement that several priests participate.

The history of the sacrament of anointing in the East is nonetheless rather confused: rites preserved in the books have often disappeared from practice; a distinction is not always made between the oil of the catechumens and the oil of the sick,[47] nor between the anointing of the sick and penance; the anointing itself is not always reserved to the sick or even to the living.[48]

§3. The Anointing of the Sick in the Latin Church from the End of the Seventh to the Twentieth Century

BIBLIOGRAPHY

Add to the general bibliography:
C. De Clercq, "*Ordines unctionis infirmi* des IXe et Xe siècles," *EL* 44 (1930) 100–22.

---

43. Denz 519–23.

44. Ritual of Gabriel V (1409–27), ed. with Italian trans. by A. Abdallah (Studia orientalia christiana aegyptiaca; Cairo, 1962), 345–47; Latin trans. in Denz 483–84; French trans. in *Perpetuite de la foi . . .*, ed. J. P. Migne, 3 (1841) 921–22. — Pontifical of Tuki and ms. Vatic. copt. 78 and 55 (Denz 484–506). — M. Chaine, "Le rituel éthiopien 'Liber lampadis,' " *Bessarione* 29 (1913) 420–51; 30 (1914) 12–41, 212–31.

45. Denz 506–23. The Pontifical of Michael the Great (thirteenth century) also contains a blessing of the oil of catechumens and of the sick by the bishop and concelebrating priests, then another blessing of the oil by a simple priest; see I. Vosté, *Pontificale iuxta ritum Syrorum occidentalium. Versio latina* (Vatican Polyglot Press, 1941), 59–63. — See W. de Vries, *Sakramententheologie bei den Syrischen Monophysiten* (OCA 125; Rome, 1940), 211–13.

46. This rite is also contained at times in Byzantine euchologia, for example, Coislin 213 (Dmitrievskij 1018). — St. John Chrysostom, *In Matthaei evangelium homiliae* 32, 6 (PG 57:384), seems to be already familiar with the use of lamp oil: "For this table [the altar] is much more respectworthy and pleasing [than yours], and this lamp than [your] lamp; this is well known to all those who have been anointed in a timely way with the oil of faith and have been delivered from their illnesses."

47. This is true of the Syrian Jacobites; see Vosté (note 45) 59, note.

48. Dauvillier (note 30) provides extensive documentation for all these vagaries.

P. Browe, "Die letzte Ölung in der abendländischen Kirche des Mittelalters,"
ZKT 55 (1931) 515–61.

P. Borella, "Materia e forma dell'estrema unzione nell'antico rito ambrosiano,"
Ambrosius 20 (1944) 13–18; "L'orazione ed imposizione delle mani nell'estrema
unzione," *ibid.*, 49–57.

H. B. Porter, "The Origin of the Medieval Rite for Anointing the Sick or Dying,"
JTS 7 (1956) 211–25.

P. Borella, "L'estrema unzione nell'antico rito ambrosiano," *Ambrosius* 38 (1962)
89–95, 153–61.

A. Duval, "L'extrême-onction au Concile de Trente, sacrement des mourants ou sacrement des malades?" *LMD* no. 101 (1970) 127–72.

A. M. Triacca, "*Impositio manuum super infirmos.* L'unzione degli ammalati
nell'antica liturgia ambrosiana," in *Eulogia . . . Miscellanea . . . Burkhard
Neunheuser* (Studia Anselmiana 68, Analecta liturgica 1; Rome, 1968), 509–90.

——————, "Le rite de l'*impositio manuum super infirmum* dans l'ancienne
liturgie ambrosienne," in *La maladie et la mort du chrétien dans la liturgie* (see
General Bibliography), 339–60.

An important inventory and analysis of about 250 medieval *ordines* for the anointing
of the sick has been made by R. Dalla Mutta and, it is to be hoped, will soon be
published; see for now his contribution to *Mens concordet voci, pour Mgr Martimort*
(Paris: Desclée, 1983), 608–18.

I. FORMATION AND DEVELOPMENT OF THE RITUAL FOR VISITATION OF THE SICK

It was the second half of the seventh century that saw the beginning
in the Latin Church of a comparable organization of rituals for the care
of the sick. The first Roman sacramentaries actually mentioned neither
imposition of hands nor anointing,[49] while the supplements added to them
at the time in question contained only a collection of prayers, the grouping of which was to have an influence on later developments. Thus the
Sacramentary of Hadrian had two prayers *Ad visitandum infirmum* before an *Oratio super paenitentem*;[50] the Old Gelasian had four prayers:
Super infirmum in domo, followed by prayers *Ad missam pro infirmo*,
an *Oratio pro reddita sanitate*, and prayers *Intrantibus in domo sive
benedictio*.[51] The Eighth-century Gelasians incorporated this ritual into
a larger collection of prayers: it followed upon the purification of con-

---

49. The Spanish *Liber ordinum* has an *Ordo ad visitandum vel perungendum infirmum*
that begins with the rubric: "Ingrediens sacerdos ad infirmum facit ei signum crucis in capite de oleo benedicto" (Janini [note 18], 58–60; Férotin, col. 71–73).

50. *Gr* 987–88. In the view of J. Deshusses, *Le sacramentaire grégorien* 1:54, this appendix to the Gregorian must date from the pontificate of Leo II (682–83).

51. *Ge* 1535–47. According to A. Chavasse, *Le sacramentaire gélasien* 518, 521, 686,
these formulas must have entered the sacramentary during the second half of the seventh
century.

ventual premises and preceded the *Reconciliatio paenitentis ad mortem*, the *Commendatio animae*, and the various rites of burial.[52]

From here the ritual passed into the Carolingian supplement to the Sacramentary of Hadrian, where it was located after the reconciliation of penitents on Holy Thursday and was again followed by the *Reconciliatio paenitentis ad mortem* and the liturgy of death.[53] But the Carolingian reform did not allow the faithful themselves any longer to apply the oil of the sick. In addition, the ninth-century sacramentaries inserted the sacramental anointing and, often, an imposition of hands, into the midst of these texts; they also incorporated a whole anthology of new prayers, especially "Domine Deus qui per apostolum tuum locutus es: infirmatur quis in vobis. . . ." The monastic books in particular added antiphons, psalms (especially the group already known as the *Septem psalmi paenitentiales*), litanies, and hymns, thus establishing an office to be celebrated either in the church or at the bedside of the sick person, and requiring a full ceremonial and sometimes the presence of several priests.[54] The rite usually began with the sprinkling of holy water and included confession, sometimes the prayers for reconciliation *ad mortem*, communion, and a blessing of the sick person.

In the Celtic Church visitation of the sick and anointing gave rise to a *missa sicca* that included prayers, a reading, a profession of faith, and prayers before and after communion.[55]

The pontifical that was compiled about 950 at Saint Alban's Abbey in Mainz, and would quickly spread throughout the entire Latin Church, had two lengthy rituals of the sick. One of these, the *Ordo ad visitandum et unguendum infirmum*, did not, despite its title, include an anointing; it consisted, after the greeting of the priests, of a sprinkling and incensation, the singing of the penitential psalms, a litany, *capitella* of psalm

---

52. *Gell* 2878-87. Note that the *Liber ordinum* also has the *Ordo* for the sick followed by that for penance *ad mortem* and the liturgy of death.

53. *Gr* 1386-95. The Supplement adds two prayers from the Gregorian before those from the Gelasian.

54. See especially the Sacramentary of Essen (Düsseldorf D 1), a sacramentary from Sens (Stockholm, Bibl. roy. A 136), and one from Saint-Martin in Tours (Tours, Bibl. munic., ms. 184). The texts and a description of all the rituals for the sick in the ninth-century sacramentaries are given in J. Deshusses, *Le sacramentaire grégorien* 3 (Spicilegium Friburgense 28; Fribourg, 1982), 126-54. — For the capitularies and synods that passed laws regarding the anointing of the sick in the Carolingian period see B. Poschmann, *Penance and the Anointing of the Sick*, trans. and revised F. Courtney (New York: Herder and Herder, 1964), 244-49.

55. *Book of Dimna* (middle of the seventh century) and *Book of Mulling* (ninth century), in P. E. Warren, *The Liturgy and Ritual of the Celtic Church* (Oxford: Clarendon, 1981), 167-73; *Stowe Missal*, ed. G. Warner, 2 (HBS 32; 1915), 33-36. — An almost identical structure in ms. Vatic. Palat. lat. 485 (ninth century) from the Abbey of Lorsch: C. De Clercq, "Ordines unctionis infirmi des IXe et Xe siècles," *EL* 44 (1930) 102-4.

verses, four prayers, and another psalm (Ps 143), followed always by *capitella* and fourteen formulas of blessing for the sick.[56] The other *Ordo ad unguendum infirmum* encased the sacramental rites in a less prolix celebration: the sick person was supposed to have already made confession; the ceremony began with a sprinkling and the prayer "Deus qui per apostolum"; two psalms, 6 and 50, were then sung with antiphons; all the priests imposed hands on the sick person; Psalm 120 was sung with its antiphon and was followed by two prayers; next came the anointings ("perunguant singuli sacerdotes . . ."); the hymn "Christe, caelestis medicina Patris" was then sung, and finally the ritual proposed five prayers. At this point the sick person received communion under both species. Without any break in continuity the pontifical then added formulas for absolution and other prayers intended for after confession; then four formulas for the blessing of the sick person by the bishop, if he were present, or the priests.[57]

It was chiefly in monastic circles that the rites for the sick in the ninth and tenth centuries reached a length almost comparable to that of the rites in the Eastern euchologia. The principal effort in the following centuries would be to prune this luxuriant growth and put some order into the sequence of rites.

II. THE RITES OF ANOINTING

Unlike the other Churches, Rome reserved the blessing of the oil of the sick to the solemn chrismal Mass of Holy Thursday, at which the bishop presided. This Roman discipline was gradually extended to the entire West.

The first rituals for the visitation of the sick that mention anointing were perhaps those of Spanish or Irish provenance. The Spanish ritual was satisfied to announce the anointing in a rubric;[58] the Irish *ordines* supplied a formula, "Ungo te de oleo sanctificato in nomine Trinitatis ut salveris in saecula saeculorum,"[59] which is also found elsewhere.[60] For two centuries a great diversity was to be the rule both in the number of anointings and in the formulas accompanying these (a diversity sometimes attested by the rubrics in ninth-century manuscripts.

---

56. *PRG*, Ordo CXXXIX (2:246–56).

57. *PRG*, Ordo CXLII (2:257–70).

58. Above, n. 49.

59. Above, n. 55.

60. Ritual of Lorsch (above, n. 55) and Sacramentary of Saint Remi in Rheims (now lost) (PL 78:539).

The part or parts of the body to be anointed were not always speci-fied. Then a new rubric appeared: "Et sic perungat infirmum de oleo sanc-tificato, crucem faciendo in collo, in gutture et inter scapulas, et in pectore seu in loco ubi dolor imminet amplius perungatur."[61] At almost the very same time a new practice was introduced: "Multi enim sacerdotes infir-mos perungunt insuper in quinque sensibus corporis, id est in superciliis oculorum, et in auribus deintus, et in narium summitate sive interius, et in manibus exterius, id est de foris. In omnibus ergo eius membris crucem faciant, ut si in quinque sensibus mentis et corporis aliqua macula inhaesit, hac medicina sanetur."[62]

From the standpoint of the formulas used, A. Chavasse distinguishes three types of ritual. Rituals of the first type "agree in having all the anoint-ings be administered during the recitation of one or more formulas, with-out having a specific formula correspond to each anointing."[63] Rituals of the second type "have each anointing accompanied by a special formula" that is phrased in the indicative mood, as, for example: "Ungo oculos tuos de oleo sanctificato, ut quidquid inlicito [visu] deliquisti, huius olei unc-tione expietur";[64] in these formulas the penitential nature of the anointing is emphasized while the medicinal aspect is blurred. Rituals of the third type

> almost always limit the anointings to the five senses, and have each anoint-ing accompanied by a deprecative formula; there are two main forms of this: either "Per istam sacri olei unctionem et Dei benedictionem remittat tibi Dominus quidquid deliquisiti [per visum . . .],"[65] or the one that would become classic: "Per istam unctionem et suam piissimam misericordiam in-dulgeat tibi Dominus quidquid per [visum . . .] deliquisti."[66]

It is to be noted that the rituals almost always prescribed not only an anointing but an imposition of hands, which was highlighted by the prayer

61. E.g., the Sacramentary of Corbie (Bib. Nat. lat. 12050) and the Sacramentary of Essen (Düsseldorf D 1): J. Deshusses, *Le sacramentaire grégorien* 3:146 and 150.

62. Same two sacramentaries (Deshusses 3:146 and 151).

63. Sacramentaries of Saint-Amand (Bibl. Nat. lat. 2291; Deshusses 3:147), Saint-Denis (Bibl. Nat. lat. 2290; Deshusses 3:147), etc. Examples of these formulas in the ninth cen-tury: Deshusses nos. 4001–3 (3:130–31).

64. Most of the *ordines* assembled by Martène, which were in use between the tenth and twelfth centuries or even in the thirteenth: 1, 3, 12, 15, 16, 17, 18, 19, 20, 22, 23, etc. (M 621, 623, 635, 636, 637, 638, 639, 640, 642, 643). — The Sacramentary of Figeac-Moissac (Bibl. Nat. lat. 2293, eleventh century) gives a prayer for each anointing: Martène, *Ordo* 21 (M 631).

65. Pontifical of Sens (Bibl. Nat. lat. 934): Martène, *Ordo* 18 (M 638).

66. Already, "iuxta consuetudinem quorundam," in the Pontifical of Apamea (Andrieu, *PR* 1:276), then universally in the thirteenth-century Pontifical of the Roman Curia (An-drieu, *PR* 2:491–92). — Other formulas: Rheims, Bibl. munic. 340 (Martène, *Ordo* 10 [M 630]), Narbonne, Pontifical of Canon Pech (Martène, *Ordo* 13 [M 633]).

accompanying it. The imposition of hands was especially important in the Ambrosian liturgy.

III. FROM THE ANOINTING OF THE SICK TO "LAST ANOINTING"

For various reasons the sacrament of anointing gradually came to be administered not in order that the sick might be healed but to prepare Christians for death. A first reason was doubtless the mere fact that in the liturgical books, even as early as the eighth-century Gelasians, the ritual of anointing was set alongside the ritual for penance *ad mortem* and the ritual of the *Commendatio animae*. Another cause was the heavier emphasis, which we have just seen, on the penitential effect of the anointing. Penance *ad mortem* was regulated by the discipline used in the public penance of antiquity; that is, even after being reconciled, the penitent had to observe until death the strict measures imposed, especially abstention from sexual relations and from meat. When penance *ad mortem* lost this character and was replaced by private penance, the anointing took over the prayers and disciplinary regulations of private penance. That is why we find the following dialogue appearing in the rituals and especially in a Roman pontifical of the twelfth century: "The priest says to the sick man: 'Why have you summoned me, brother?' 'That you may anoint me.' Then the priest says: 'May our Lord Jesus Christ bestow on you a genuine and easy anointing; but if the Lord looks upon you and heals you, will you preserve the anointing?' 'I will preserve it.' "[67]

The priest then blessed a hair shirt and ashes; he mixed the ashes with holy water and sprinkled the sick person with them, and then gave the hair shirt. Meanwhile, however, the formulas accompanying these rites always asked for healing. Eucharistic communion, which had always been part of the ritual of prayer for the sick, was clearly turning into viaticum.[68]

It is to be noted that the terms *extrema unctio* or *unctio exeuntium*, which theologians and canonists used from the twelfth century on, were rarely to be found in the rituals before the fifteenth century.[69]

---

67. London, British Library, ms. Add. 17005 (Andrieu, *PR* 1:267). — Same rites, with almost identical formulas, in almost all the copies of the thirteenth-century Pontifical of the Roman Curia (Andrieu, *PR* 2:488).

68. This change appears explicitly only in the thirteenth-century Pontifical of the Roman Curia (Andrieu, *PR* 2:493), but at that time communion was the subject of a distinct ritual.

69. V. Leroquais, *Les Pontificaux manuscrits des bibliothèques publiques de France* (Mâcon: Protat, 1937), finds the term "extreme unction" in only two pontificals from the second half of the fourteenth century: 2:54 and 3:324.

IV. THE SHORT RITUAL FROM THE THIRTEENTH
TO THE TWENTIETH CENTURY

While the churches were still using the lengthy *ordo* of the sick that had been made popular by the Romano-German Pontifical, the *Consuetudines Cluniacenses* (eleventh-twelfth century) already contained a very abbreviated and more logical ritual. The sick monk had confessed in advance; after the greeting "Pax huic domui" and the incensation and sprinkling, the priest said the prayer "Omnipotens sempiterne Deus qui per beatum apostolum. . . ." Then, while the community sang psalms with antiphons, the priest anointed the five senses. He next went to the church for the Eucharist in order to give communion to the sick man.[70] This Cluniac ritual, which was carried throughout Europe in the Cluniac customaries, exerted an influence on the Pontifical of the Roman Curia, especially in the "long" recension from the middle of the thirteenth century.[71]

It was in this last form that the Franciscans adopted it and popularized it while shortening still further the *ordo* for the anointing of the sick.[72] With a few variants this new *ordo* made its way down the centuries: having been accepted in the sixteenth century into the Rituals of Alberto Castellani (1523)[73] and Cardinal J. A. Santori (end of the sixteenth century),[74] it entered the Ritual of Paul V (1614) and subsequently underwent only one noteworthy modification in the edition of 1925. The main variants had to do with the location of the sprinkling, confession, and, above all, communion, as well as with some of the prayers. After the greeting, the priest said three prayers that came from the Pontifical of the Roman Curia: "Introeat Domine," "Oremus et deprecemur," and "Exaudi nos Domine." While the priest was performing the anointings, those present were asked to say the seven penitential psalms. The anointings were seven in number and included one on the loins (this disappeared for good in 1917: canon

---

70. *Liber tramitis aevi Odilonis abbatis* nos. 193–94, ed. P. Dinter (Corpus consuetudinum monasticarum 10; Sieberg: Schmitt, 1980), 269–72; Martène, *De antiquis monachorum ritibus*, Lib. 5, c. 8, nn. 16–17 (M 1140–41). — See G. Hürlimann, *Das Rheinauer Rituale* . . . (Spicilegium Friburgense 5; Fribourg, 1959), 29–31, 45–49, 147–52.

71. Andrieu, *PR* 2:486–95.

72. L. Bracaloni, "Il primo rituale francescano nel Breviario di S. Chiara," *Archivum Franciscanum Historicum* 16 (1923) 76–77. — See S. J. P. Van Dijk and J. Hazelden Walker, *The Origins of the Modern Roman Liturgy* (Westminster, Md.: Newman, 1960), 341–45; S. J. P. Van Dijk, *Sources of the Modern Roman Liturgy* (Leiden: Brill, 1963), 1:231–40; 2:385–90.

73. *Liber sacerdotalis* (Venice, 1523), ff. 114v–122.

74. *Rituale sacramentorum Romanum Gregorii papae XIII . . . iussu editum* (Rome, 1584, according to the—incorrect—date on the title page), 301–39.

947 §2) and one on the feet (which ceased to be obligatory at the same time: canon 947 §3). The anointings were preceded by a formula, "In nomine Patris et Filii et Spiritus Sancti extinguatur in te omnis virtus diaboli . . .," which was evidently meant to accompany an imposition of hands ("per impositionem manuum mearum"), but the medieval rubrics often omitted the gesture[75] and were followed in this respect by the Ritual of 1614; the gesture was restored in the Ritual of 1925. After the anointing, the Our Father and *capitella* of psalm verses led into three prayers: "Domine Deus, qui per apostolum," which, as we saw, was already part of the ninth-century sacramentaries,[76] then "Respice quaesumus Domine," from the Sacramentary of Hadrian,[77] and "Domine sancte Pater . . . qui benedictionis tuae gratiam," from the Gelasian.[78] A blessing, "Dominus Iesus Christus apud te sit," which was probably of Visigothic origin, was not retained.[79] The Franciscan ritual had dropped all echoes of penance *ad mortem*. The *Ordo ad communicandum infirmum* remained distinct from the ritual for anointing and for a while was placed after it; then, without discernible reason it began to precede it in some manscripts from the end of the fourteenth century on.[80] At the end of the sixteenth century, Santori judged the custom of giving communion first and extreme unction second to be now universal in the Latin Church, even though it was contrary to ancient practice;[81] the anomaly would be eliminated only after Vatican II.

The Ritual of 1614 also introduced an *ordo* for the visitation of the sick that was completely distinct from the *ordo* for anointing; in the judgment of A. Chavasse it was "an original grouping of psalms, readings, and prayers that has no equivalent in the ancient liturgical books." It contained four units, each with a gospel passage, a prayer, and a psalm. This *ordo* made use of the traditional lists of psalms and prayers to be found in the sacramentaries and the Romano-German Pontifical, but it could only have been composed at Rome, for the choice of gospel readings seems to have been inspired by the Roman votive office *pro infirmis*.[82]

---

75. Or they used the formula for an anointing *ad caput*, as was still done in the short recension of the Pontifical of the Roman Curia.

76. J. Deshusses, *Le sacramentaire grégorien* 3, no. 3988.

77. *Gr 988*.

78. *Oratio pro reddita sanitate: Ge* 1543; *Gell* 2887; Phillipps 1905.

79. It had been transmitted in *PRG* LIII (2:269).

80. Pontifical of John of Cardailhac, Archbishop of Toulouse (Leroquais [n. 69, above] 1:174); Pontifical of John Barozi, Bishop of Bergamo (1449–65) (Andrieu, *PR* 3:234).

81. Santori, *Rituale sacramentorum . . .* (n. 74, above), 323.

82. A. Chavasse made a detailed study of this *ordo* in earlier editions of *L'Eglise en prière* (pp. 609–11 of the third edition, 1965).

§4. Vatican II and the Ritual of Paul VI

BIBLIOGRAPHY

P. M. Gy, "Le nouveau rituel romain des malades," *LMD* no. 113 (1973) 29–39.
J. Stefanski, "Von der letzten Ölung zur Krankensalbung: Schwerpunkte bei der Redaktion der neuen Ordnung für die Krankensakramente," in *Liturgia opera divina et umana (Miscellanea A. Bugnini)* (Bibliotheca EL, Subsidia 26; Rome: Edizioni liturgiche, 1982), 429–52.

I. "ANOINTING OF THE SICK" INSTEAD OF "LAST ANOINTING"

The history of the discussions at the Council of Trent shows that the teaching of the fourteenth session on the sacrament of extreme unction reflected the desire of the Fathers to move away from the medieval theology of this sacrament and a refusal to think of extreme unction as the sacrament only of those facing death.[83] Since that time, patristic and liturgical studies have revealed much more about the tradition behind this sacrament, and Vatican II was able on that basis to take a further step. Without rejecting the medieval name "extreme unction" it made clear its preference for "anointing of the sick."[84] It twice suggested that more was at issue than a difference in terminology: "As soon as any one of the faithful begins to be in danger of death from sickness or old age, the fitting time for that person to receive this sacrament has certainly already arrived."[85]

II. THE SACRAMENTAL SIGN

The Latin ritual as a whole had certainly remained faithful to the teaching of the Letter of James, which in fact it always cited. On the other hand, the formula accompanying each anointing expressed only one effect of the sacrament, namely, the forgiveness of sins; moreover the anointings given to the sense organs had taken on a primarily penitential cast: "quidquid per (visum, etc.) deliquisti." The first and most important reform introduced by the Constitution *Sacram unctionem* (November 30, 1972) in which Paul VI applied the teaching of the Council[86] consisted precisely in altering the sacramental formula by introducing into it expressions suggesting the text both of James and the Council of Trent: "Per istam sanc-

---

83. A. Duval, "L'extrême-onction au Concile de Trente, sacrement des mourants ou sacrement des malades?" *LMD* no. 101 (1970) 127–72.
84. *VSC* 73 (*DOL* 1 no. 72).
85. *Ibid.*; *Lumen gentium* 11 (*DOL* 4 no. 141).
86. *AAS* 65 (1973) 5–9 (*EDIL* 2918–23; *DOL* 408 nos. 3315–19).

tam unctionem et suam piissimam misericordiam adiuvet te Dominus gratia Spiritus Sancti, ut a peccatis liberatum te salvet atque propitius allevet." The new formula echoes two noteworthy traditional perspectives on this sacrament. The first is that the grace bestowed is the work of the Holy Spirit, as the formulas in the ancient liturgies always made clear;[87] this had been true especially of the Roman prayer for the blessing of the oil. The second is that the sacrament of anointing is a remedy for both soul and body, for while it has a penitential effect, even to the point of supplying for the sacrament of penance if the latter is not possible, it brings above all a grace of health, strength, alleviation of suffering, and even at times of healing.

The text of the prayer *Emitte* for the blessing of the oil was also improved and enriched in the ritual for the holy oils that was published on December 3, 1970:

> Lord God, loving Father,
> you bring healing to the sick
> through your Son Jesus Christ.
> Hear us as we pray to you in faith,
> and send the Holy Spirit, man's Helper and Friend,
> upon this oil, which nature has provided
> to serve the needs of men.
> May your blessing
> come upon all who are anointed with this oil,
> that they may be freed from pain and illness
> and made well again in body, mind, and soul.
> Father, may this oil be blessed for our use
> in the name of our Lord Jesus Christ
> (who lives and reigns with you for ever and ever.
> — Amen).[88]

The change in the formula for the anointings is accompanied by two other decrees with regard to the sacramental sign. One has to do with the number of the anointings. Vatican II had expressed its wish that "the number of the anointings . . . be adapted to the circumstances."[89] A mid-

---

87. E. J. Lengeling (general bibliography for this chapter) cites numerous texts (248–83).

88. *Ordo benedicendi oleum infirmorum* (*Rites* 1:522–23). The chief addition is of everything that precedes the word "emitte" ("send"), while the clauses "unde unxisti sacerdotes, reges, prophetas et martyres" and the phrase "permanens in visceribus nostris" have been omitted.

89. *VSC* 75 (*DOL* 1 no. 75). — J. C. Didier, "Sur le ministre de l'onction des malades," *Esprit et vie* 74 (1964) 488–92, raised the question of the minister of this sacrament in light of its history in the early centuries and expressed a wish for greater flexibility in the present discipline. See also P. Rouillard, "Le ministre du sacrement de l'onction des malades," *Nouvelle revue théologique* 101 (1979) 395–402. The new *Code of Canon Law* (1983), can. 1003 § 1, leaves no room for flexibility: "Every priest, and only a priest, validly administers the anointing of the sick."

dle way has therefore been sought between the multiplied anointings allowed in the ritual inherited from the Middle Ages and the single anointing that served as sign in cases of necessity; henceforth the rite is to consist of two anointings, one on the forehead and one on the hands, but with a single formula covering the two. Particular rituals, however, can keep or introduce more numerous anointings or anointings applied to other parts of the body, depending on the culture and traditions of the various peoples.[90]

The other decision of Paul VI was in response to a concern of the episcopal conferences of the Third World countries: although olive oil has traditionally been required as the matter used in the anointing of the sick because it corresponds to the biblical image that gives anointing its sacramental symbolism as liniment and medication, it is henceforth permissible to use another oil, if need be, provided it be vegetable ("quod tamen a plantis sit expressum").[91]

III. THE NEW RITUAL

To these changes, which required the personal intervention of the pope, the new ritual promulgated on December 7, 1972, added important liturgical adjustments.

We saw earlier that in the East and sometimes in the West the sacrament of the sick was concelebrated. The new ritual provides that should two or more priests be present, only one does the anointings and says the formula but each of the others may lay his hand on the sick person, and they may take turns saying the opening and concluding prayers.[92]

Since the blessing of the oil of the sick has never been as strictly reserved to the bishop as has the confection of chrism, the new ritual allows that "in a case of true necessity" any priest can bless the oil during the ceremony of anointing; in principle, however, a priest is to use oil blessed by the bishop at the chrismal Mass.[93] If the priest is using oil already blessed, a prayer of thanksgiving said over it before performing the anointings will serve to bring out the sacramental symbolism.

---

90. *Rituale Romanum, Ordo unctionis infirmorum eorumque pastoralis curae*, ed. typica (Vatican Polyglot Press, 1972), no. 24. The rite is in *The Rites of the Catholic Church* 1:582–642; there is a new translation of the Introduction in *DOL* 410 nos. 3321–61; see no. 3344.

91. *Ordo unctionis*, no. 20 (*DOL* 410 no. 3340).

92. *Ordo unctionis*, no. 19 (*DOL* 410 no. 3339).

93. *Ordo unctionis*, no. 21 (*DOL* 410 no. 3341); *Ordo benedicendi oleum infirmorum*, no. 8 (*DOL* 459 no. 3868); *Code of Canon Law* (1983), can. 999 §2. — For this blessing the priest uses the one from the chrismal Mass; but the ritual also gives an alternative formula: *Ordo unctionis* no. 242 (*Rites* 1:639).

The traditional gesture of imposing the hand, which was restored in 1925, receives greater emphasis in the new ritual. It is done in silence; while not essential, it is an integral part of the rite,[94] in keeping with the model given us in the Letter of James.

The Ritual of 1972 urges that whenever possible the sacrament be made part of a more complete liturgical celebration: greeting by the priest, sprinkling, catechetical address—or, better, the traditional (but shortened) prayer, "Lord God, you have told us through your apostle James . . ."[95]—penitential act (or sacramental confession of the sick person), reading from Sacred Scripture (for which the ritual offers an abundant selection of passages), and litanic prayer; after the laying on of hands and the anointings, a concluding prayer, Our Father, and blessing.

The ritual also provides that the whole rite may be celebrated during Mass; above all, it describes and encourages the "celebration of anointing in a large congregation."[96] This situation may occur, for example, at places of pilgrimage or during a day's meeting of sick people. Such a celebration of the sacrament has obvious spiritual value, for it allows seriously ill or aged persons to consecrate their state, to unite themselves with the sufferings of Christ, and to receive the graces they need in their time of trial. Those present, moreover, gain an understanding of the true nature of this sacrament.

Finally, as called for by Vatican II,[97] the Ritual of 1972 offers for cases of necessity a "continuous rite of penance, anointing, and viaticum," in which the logical sequence is restored and repetitions are avoided.

The Introduction to this ritual should be reread frequently, since it begins with a doctrinal summary of the meaning of illness in the economy of salvation. It also gives a short catechetical instruction on the sacrament and locates its administration in the broader framework of pastoral care of the sick, for which the entire Christian community is responsible along with the priest.[98]

---

94. *Ordo unctionis*, no. 5 (*DOL* 410 no. 3325).

95. *Ordo unctionis*, no. 239 (*Rites* 1:637).

96. *Ordo unctionis*, nos. 83–92 (*Rites* 1:606).

97. *VSC* 74 (*DOL* 1 no. 74).

98. *Ordo unctionis*, nos. 1–7, 32–37, and Section I of Chapter I, 'Visitation and Communion of the Sick" (nos. 42–45) (*DOL* 410 nos. 3321–27, 3352–57, and *Rites* 1:593–94).

Chapter IV

Ordinations

P. Jounel

Introduction: *Ordo* and *Ordinatio*

BIBLIOGRAPHY

B. Botte, "Collegiate Character of the Presbyterate and Episcopate," in *The Sacrament of Holy Orders* (Collegeville: The Liturgical Press, 1962), 75–97.

G. Dix, "The Ministry in the Early Church," in K. E. Kirk (ed.), *The Apostolic Ministry. Essays on the History and the Doctrine of Episcopacy* (London: Hodder & Stoughton, 1946), 183–303; see 193–96 ("The Meaning of Ordination").

P. M. Gy, "Notes on the Early Terminology of Christian Priesthood," in *The Sacrament of Holy Orders*, 98–115.

P. Van Beneden, *Aux origines d'une terminologie sacramentelle: Ordo, ordinare, ordinatio dans la littérature chrétienne avant 313* (Spicilegium sacrum Lovaniense 38; Louvain, 1974).

In approaching the study of the liturgy of ordinations as this has developed in the tradition of the Church, it is important to know in advance what precise meaning the patristic period gave to the words *ordo*, *ordinatio*, and *ordinare* and their Greek equivalents. For, whatever the further development these terms underwent down the centuries, it is their original meaning that must be kept in mind if we wish to understand the liturgical formularies.

1. *Ordo*

The word *ordo* had its place not in the religious vocabulary of Roman antiquity but in the vocabulary of its civic institutions. The term there signified a well-defined social body that was distinct from the people: the senatorial order (*ordo clarissimus*), then the order of knights. In the life of the city an *ordo* was a body of those who governed. This explains the recurring phrase *ordo populusque*, "the 'order' and the people."

Because the word *ordo* had no pagan connotations, Christians were not averse to using it to describe the situation of the clergy within the people of God. At the beginning of the third century Tertullian could write: "Differentiam inter ordinem et plebem constituit Ecclesiae auctoritas."[1] In the fourth century the distinction was sanctioned by imperial law, which recognized the existence of an *ordo ecclesiasticus*.[2]

In the beginning, the word *ordo* was used of the clergy as a whole, but it soon came to designate the various hierarchic strata into which the clergy was divided: the order of deacons or of subdeacons, the order of the presbytery (*ordo presbyterii*), the episcopal order (*ordo episcoporum*).[3] In Christian antiquity the word always referred to a collectivity; it was therefore a matter not so much of receiving an order as of entering an order, of being received into it. That is why St. Jerome, a priest, and St. Avitus, a bishop, could use the expression *homo ordinis mei* to signify a priest and a bishop respectively.

After falling into practical disuse among theologians and canonists, *ordo* in the collective sense was brought back into use by Pius XII in several of the Apostolic Constitutions whereby he established the Catholic hierarchy in mission countries and, even more so, by the Second Vatican Council in its Dogmatic Constitution *Lumen gentium* on the Church (no. 22).

2. *Ordinatio*

At Rome *ordinatio* was the technical term for the appointment of officials. It could therefore be taken over unchanged by Christians to signify the choice made of someone to carry out an ecclesiastical function.[4] The highest ecclesiastical functions, however, are liturgical in nature; they require a previous consecration or blessing. The term *ordinatio* came therefore to signify also the rite of consecration or blessing. As early as the opening years of the fifth century, St. Jerome applied it to the imposition of hands on clerics.[5] It passed immediately into current use, although the sacramentaries gave the more specific title *consecratio* to the long prayer

---

1. Tertullian, *De exhortatione castitatis* 7, 3 (CCL 2:1024–25).

2. *Codex Theodosianus* 16, 26.

3. B. Botte, "Collegiate Character of the Presbyterate and Episcopate," in *The Sacrament of Holy Orders* (Collegeville: The Liturgical Press, 1962), 83–92.

4. J. Gaudemet, "Holy Orders in Early Conciliar Legislation," in *The Sacrament of Holy Orders*, 185.

5. St. Jerome, *Commentarius in Isaiam* XV, 58, 10 (PL 24:591): "Plerique nostrorum *cheirotonian*, id est ordinationem clericorum. . . ."

that accompanied the imposition of hands in the ordination of bishops, priests, and deacons.[6]

3. *Greek Terminology*

The *Apostolic Tradition* of Hippolytus is witness to an effort at establishing a technical terminology in Greek. In secular Greek an official was said to be "instituted" or "established" in his office (*kathistatai*); he could also be said to be "designated" (*cheirotoneitai*).[7] Hippolytus applies both terms to ecclesiastical offices, but limits the use of the second to ordinations in the strict sense, that is, to offices that make the chosen person a member of one of the three levels in the hierarchic structure and for which a consecration is required. The ritual gesture used in this consecration was the imposition of hands (*cheirothetein*); it was of Jewish origin[8] and is attested in the Acts of the Apostles. Hippolytus' intention in his choice of words is to bring out the fact that an ordination (*cheirotonia, cheirotonein*) necessarily implies an imposition of hands. This important distinction sheds light on what is meant when the *Apostolic Tradition* says of the lector (for example): "The lector is instituted (*kathistatai*) when the bishop gives him the book, for he does not receive an imposition of hands (*oude gar cheirotheteitai*)."[9]

§1. Ordinations in the Early Church

BIBLIOGRAPHY

Documents

Hippolytus of Rome, *La Tradition Apostolique. Essai de reconstitution*, ed. B. Botte (LQF 39; Münster: Aschendorff, 1963).

Didascalia et Constitutiones Apostolorum, ed. F. X. Funk (2 vols.; Paderborn: Schöningh, 1905; reprinted: Turin: Bottega d'Erasmo, 1959).

"Prières d'ordination de l'Eglise ancienne," *LMD* no. 138 (1979) 143–49.

Studies

J. Lécuyer, "Episcopat et presbyterat dans les écrits d'Hippolyte de Rome," *RechSR* 41 (1953) 30–50.

G. Dix, "The Ministry in the Early Church," in K. E. Kirk (ed.), *The Apostolic Ministry* (London: Hodder & Stoughton, 1946), 196–201, 216–27.

B. Botte, "Holy Orders in the Ordination Prayers," in *The Sacrament of Holy Orders* (Collegeville: The Liturgical Press, 1962), 5–29.

---

6. *Le* 942 and 952 (titles); — *Gr* 23, 29, 32.

7. The word means to vote by raising the hand, as opposed to *klēroun* or election by drawing lots.

8. E. J. Kilmartin, "Ministère et ordination dans l'Eglise chrétienne primitive. Leur arrière-plan juif," *LMD* no. 138 (1979) 49–51 and 91.

9. Hippolytus of Rome, *Traditio apostolica* 2 (Botte 30–31).

J. M. Hanssen, *La liturgie d'Hippolyte . . .* (OCA 155; Rome: Pontificio Istituto Orientale, 1959).

A. Rose, "La prière de consécration pour l'ordination épiscopale," *LMD* no. 98 (1969) 127–42.

C. Vogel, "L'imposition des mains dans les rites d'ordination en Orient et en Occident," *LMD* no. 102 (1970) 57–72.

A. Lemaire, "Les ministères dans la recherche neo-testamentaire," *LMD* no. 115 (1973) 30–60.

E. J. Kilmartin, "Ministère et ordination dans l'Eglise chrétienne primitive. Leur arrière-plan juif," *LMD* no. 138 (1979) 49–92.

L. Lecuyer, *Le sacrement de l'ordination* (Théologie historique 65; Paris: Beauchesne, 1983).

The ordination ritual that Hippolytus gives in his *Apostolic Tradition* allows us to be present in a measure at an ordination in the early years of the third century, for he both prescribes the rites to be performed and gives the prayers to be said. More importantly, however, he presents us with a vision of the Church's hierarchic order that would be given the supreme stamp of approval, seventeen centuries later, in the Apostolic Constitution *Sacramentum ordinis* of Pius XII (1947) and the Constitution on the Church of Vatican Council II.

I. THE RITES OF ORDINATION OF BISHOP, PRIEST, AND DEACON

1. *Ordination of a Bishop*[10]

The election of a bishop by the entire people must precede his ordination. The rites themselves take place on a Sunday in the presence of the people, the college of priests, and the neighboring bishops. The bishops begin by imposing hands on the candidate, while "all keep silent, praying in their hearts for the descent of the Spirit." Then one of the bishops, "at the request of all," says the prayer of blessing "while laying his hand on the one who is being made a bishop." In this prayer he asks God to pour out on the candidate the sovereign Spirit whom he gave through Jesus Christ to his apostles. He then lists the functions of a bishop: to feed the holy flock, to exercise the high priesthood by serving God night and day, to propitiate him and offer the gifts of the holy Church, to forgive sins, distribute offices, and exercise the power of loosing that was given to the apostles. After the ordination prayer the new bishop receives the kiss of peace and greetings from the entire congregation. Next, the deacons present him with the offering, on which he lays his hands "together with the entire *presbyterium*," and he then says the Eucharistic Prayer.

---

10. *Ibid.*, 2–3 (Botte 4–11).

2. *Ordination of Priests*[11]

In speaking of the ordination of a priest, the *Apostolic Tradition* does not mention a prior popular ratification of the choice of candidate. Other contemporary documents, however, do attest to this approval. Ordination consists in an imposition of the bishop's hand on the head of the candidate, "while the priests likewise touch him," and in a prayer of the bishop. The latter asks that the ordinand be given the Spirit of grace and counsel proper to the presbyterate "so that he may be a helper and may govern the people," as the elders once helped Moses. The *Apostolic Tradition* explains that if the priests impose hands along with the bishop in the ordination of a priest, this is "because of the common and like Spirit of their office." A priest does not ordain: "He makes the gesture, while the bishop ordains."

3. *Ordination of Deacons*[12]

A deacon, like a bishop and a priest, must be chosen by the people. "The bishop alone imposes hands on him" because a deacon "is ordained not to the priesthood but to the service of the bishop, to do the latter's bidding. He is not a member of the council of the clergy but administers and lets the bishop know what is needed. . . . This is why the bishop alone ordains a deacon." In the ordination prayer the bishop invokes the Spirit of grace and zeal on this servant whom God has chosen to serve the Church and bring the gifts to the altar, in order that after having served well, he may attain to a higher degree.

II. APPOINTMENT TO LESSER ORDERS[13]

Between the members of the hierarchy and the body of the faithful there are several categories of persons who stand apart: widows, readers, virgins, subdeacons, and healers. Access to three of these groups requires an official appointment: a widow must be "instituted [appointed] by word only; she is not to receive an imposition of the hand because she does not offer the oblation and has no liturgical function"; a reader "is instituted when the bishop gives him the book, for he does not receive an imposition of hands"; "a subdeacon does not receive an imposition of the hand, but is appointed to follow the deacon."

Such is the organization of the Church that is shown to us by the ordination ritual of the *Apostolic Tradition*: at the summit is the three-leveled

---

11. *Ibid.*, 7 (Botte 20–23).
12. *Ibid.*, 8 (Botte 22–27).
13. *Ibid.*, 10–13 (Botte 30–33).

hierarchy whose members are consecrated through an imposition of hands by a bishop; then come the lesser degrees where there is no imposition of hands. Although the prayers accompanying the rites of ordination are carefully composed, Hippolytus does not claim for them the same importance as for the gesture of imposing hands, which has come down from the apostles. Therefore he says specifically: "It is not at all necessary for the bishop to use the same words that I have given . . . but let each one pray according to his ability."[14]

All ordination rituals that have been used in the Church flow from that given by Hippolytus. The patriarchate of Alexandria is the only one that has kept substantially the same formularies as in Hippolytus; on the other hand, only the Roman liturgy has always prescribed the rites to which the *Apostolic Tradition* assigns normative value: the imposition of hands by several bishops for the ordination of a new bishop; the imposition of hands by the entire presbyterate in the ordination of a priest; advancement to lesser orders by a simple presentation of the relevant instruments, without any imposition of hands. When the liturgy of ordinations was revised in 1968, the Roman liturgy also adopted Hippolytus' prayer for the consecration of a bishop; in 1972 it was inspired by his terminology when it replaced "minor orders" with "instituted ministries."

§2. Ordinations in the Eastern Churches

I. THE EARLY FORMULARIES OF ORDINATION

At the end of the fourth century and during the fifth, the *Apostolic Tradition* was expanded and had glosses added to it; it also found a place in the liturgico-canonical compilations, thus showing how successful it had been. Some of these compilations—the Syrian *Apostolic Constitutions*, for example—are important for any liturgical study of ordinations in the East, because they are the direct source of the various rituals, both Alexandrian and Antiochene.[15] One document of lesser importance also deserves our attention because of its antiquity and doctrinal wealth; I am referring to the ritual of ordination in the *Euchologion of Serapion*, an Egyptian formulary that may go back to the fourth century.

---

14. *Ibid.*, 9 (Botte 28–29).

15. See J. M. Hanssens, *La liturgie d'Hippolyte* [vol. 1] (OCA 155; Rome: Pontificio Istituto Orientale, 1959), 116–20, for a synoptic presentation of the texts (in Latin) of episcopal ordination according to the *Epitome*, the *Testamentum Domini*, the *Canones Hippolyti*, and the *Constitutiones Apostolorum*. — On all these collections see *The Church at Prayer* I: pp. 25–26.

1. *The Ordination Ritual of the Apostolic Constitutions*[16]

The rite for the ordination of a bishop is identical with that of Hippolytus. I note only that in addition to the election of the bishop by the people, a triple ratification of this choice is required before the ordination; that among the bishops present there is a distinct group of three consecrators, which was the minimum number required by the Council of Nicaea;[17] and that a new rite makes its appearance, namely, the imposition of the Book of the Gospels on the head of the candidate. "When all have fallen silent, one of the most worthy among the bishops stands beside the altar with two others, while the rest of the bishops and the priests pray silently, and the deacons hold the divine gospels open on the head of the one being ordained."[18]

The prayer of consecration follows; here the prayer from the *Apostolic Tradition* is framed in a lengthy development that calls to mind all the major figures of the old Law, from Abel, via Noah, Abraham, Moses, and Aaron, to Samuel.

The ordinations of priest and deacon still have their early simplicity. In presbyteral ordination, however, the imposition of hands by the entire presbyterate has been dropped, while on the other hand the prayer refers to the candidate having been chosen by his peers: "He has been co-opted into the presbyterium by the choice and judgment of all of the clergy." The prayer for the ordination of a deacon calls to mind the example of St. Stephen and ends, as in the *Apostolic Tradition*, with a wish to see the new deacon advance later on to a higher degree.

The principal innovation in the ritual of the *Apostolic Constitutions* has to do with the ordination of subdeacons and readers: these, too, are now ordained by an imposition of hands. The prayers accompanying the rites call to mind, in the case of a subdeacon, the guardians of the sacred vessels belonging to the tabernacle of the old covenant and, in the case of a reader, the memory of Ezra: "You trained Ezra your servant to read your laws to the entire people; at our prayer equip now your servant."

2. *The Ordination Prayers in the Euchologion of Serapion*[19]

Although there are problems with attributing to Bishop Serapion of Thmuis the collection of prayers published under his name, "it is proba-

---

16. See the passages giving the ritual of ordinations in Book VIII of the *Constitutiones Apostolorum*: ordination of a bishop, 4, 2–5, 12 (Funk 472–77); ordination of a priest, 16, 2–5 (Funk 520–23); ordination of a deacon, 18, 2–3 (Funk 522–25); ordination of subdeacons, 21, 2–4 (Funk 524–27); ordination of readers, 22, 2–4 (Funk 526–27).

17. H. Bruns, *Canones apostolorum et conciliorum* 1 (Berlin: Reimer, 1839), 15. See J. Gaudemet, *L'Eglise dans l'Empire romain (4ᵉ–5ᵉ siècles)* (Paris: Sirey, 1959), 338–39.

18. The rite is attested for around 400 by Palladius (PG 47:53) and Severian of Gabala (PG 25:533). See J. Lécuyer, "Note sur la liturgie du sacre des évêques," *EL* 66 (1952) 369–72.

19. F. X. Funk, *Didascalia et Constitutiones apostolorum* 2:188–91.

ble that these prayers represent a very early usage in one of the Egyptian Churches."[20] The title given to each of the three prayers is interesting because it links the two technical terms for "institution" and "ordination by imposition of hands": *Cheirothesia katastaseōs episkopou.*

While imposing hands on a deacon, the bishop asks the Lord, who has "chosen bishops, priests, and deacons for the worship of the catholic Church," to establish (or institute: *katastēson*) his servant "as a deacon of his catholic Church and to give him the spirit of knowledge and discernment so that in the midst of the holy people he may be able to minister in worship with purity and without reproach."

The prayer over a priest is formulated in the plural: "We stretch out our hand, O Lord, . . . upon this man, and we ask that the Spirit of truth descend upon him." Perhaps we are to see in this plural a reference to the joint imposition of hands by the presbyterium together with the bishop. The latter continues by asking God, who gave Moses power to communicate his own spirit to those whom he chose, that he would give his priest "prudence and the knowledge that springs from a good heart": "May he have the divine Spirit within him and so be able to govern your people, dispense your divine oracles, and reconcile your people with you, the uncreated God."

In the prayer of episcopal ordination, the bishop is seen as successor of the apostles and, by way of the Lord Jesus who has chosen him, as successor also of the prophets and patriarchs: "Lord, make this man a living (= zealous) bishop, a holy bishop in successsion to your holy apostles, and give him the grace you gave to all your true servants, the prophets and patriarchs."

II. THE CELEBRATION OF ORDINATIONS IN THE PRESENT-DAY EASTERN RITES

BIBLIOGRAPHY

Documents
    J. Goar, *Euchologion sive Rituale Graecorum* (Paris, 1647; Venice, 1730²; photographic reprint: Graz, 1960), 194–261.
    J. Morin, *Commentarius de sacris Ecclesiae ordinationibus* (Antwerp-Amsterdam: H. Desbordes, 1695²), 15–208, 310–448.
    E. Martène, *De antiquis Ecclesiae ritibus* Lib. I, c. 8, art. 11: *Ordo* 19 (Byzantine rite); *Ordo* 20 (Maronite rite); *Ordo* 21 (East Syrian rite); *Ordo* 22 (West Syrian rite); *Ordo* 23 (Coptic rite): M 685–89.

---

20. B. Botte, "Holy Orders in the Ordination Prayers," in *The Sacrament of Holy Orders* (see note 3, above), 19. The author also gives a translation of the three prayers from the *Euchologion* (18–19).

J. Assemani, *Codex liturgicus Ecclesiae universalis*, vols. 9–13 (Rome, 1756–66; photographic reprint: Paris, 1902).

Denzinger 2:1–363.

M. Blondeel, *Les ordinations chez les Melkites* (Harissa: Imp. Saint-Paul, 1946).

E. Mercenier and F. Paris, *La prière des Eglises de rite byzantin* 1 (Chevetogne, 1948²), 367–96.

A. Raes, "Les ordinations dans le Pontifical chaldéen," *OS* 5 (1960) 63–81.

I. H. Dalmais, "Formules les plus caractéristiques des ordinations orientales," *Bulletin du Comité des études* no. 38–39 (1962) 384–93.

G. Khouri-Sarkis, "Le rituel du sacre des évêques et des patriarches dans l'Eglise syrienne," *OS* 8 (1963) 137–212 (translation of the rite by B. de Smedt, 165–212).

O.H.E. Burmester, *Ordination Rites of the Coptic Church*, text of Ms. 253 Lit., Coptic Museum, trans. and annot. (Publications de la Societe d'archeologie Copte, Textes et documents; Cairo, 1985).

Studies

J. Hanssens, "Les oraisons sacramentelles des ordinations orientales," *OCP* 18 (1952) 297–318.

B. Botte, "La formule d'ordination 'La grace divine . . .' dans les rites orientaux," *OS* 2 (1957) 285–96.

I. H. Dalmais, *Les liturgies d'Orient* (Je sais, je crois 111; Paris: Fayard, 1959), 88–97.

E. Lanne, "Les ordinations dans le rite copte, leurs relations avec les *Constitutions apostoliques* et la *Tradition* de saint Hippolyte," *OS* 5 (1960) 81–106.

B. Botte, "Les ordinations dans les rites orientaux," *Bulletin du Comité des études*, no. 36 (1962) 13–18.

I. H. Dalmais, "Ordinations et ministères dans les Eglises orientales," *LMD* no. 102 (1970) 73–81.

It is not possible here to study the ritual of ordination in each of the Eastern rites; I shall therefore point out the elements found in all and then give a more detailed presentation of the Byzantine ritual.

1. *The Constants*

For their ritual of ordinations all of the Eastern rites depend more or less directly on the ritual in the *Apostolic Constitutions*; this is true not only of the rites that originated in the patriarchate of Antioch (West Syrian, East Syrian, Byzantine, Armenian, Maronite), but also of the Coptic rite of the patriarchate of Alexandria.[21] That is why, despite noteworthy differences, they are fundamentally the same in the number of orders, the rite of ordination, and the sacramental formula itself.

---

21. E. Lanne, "Les ordinations dans le rite copte, leurs relations avec les *Constitutions apostoliques* et la *Tradition* de saint Hippolyte," *OS* 5 (1960) 81–106. — There is a Latin translation of the Coptic ordination ritual in Denz 2:1–64, that is reproduced in part in J. M. Hanssens, *La liturgie d'Hippolyte* (n. 15), 384–91. — English translation in O.H.E. Burmester, *Ordination Rites of the Coptic Church* (Publications de la Société d'archéologie copte; Cairo, 1985).

In addition to, and below, the major orders of episcopate, presbyterate, and diaconate, the Eastern Churches have only two minor orders: that of the subdeacon and that of the reader or cantor (psalmist). The subdeacons of the Eastern Churches are in fact quite the same as the acolytes of the Roman tradition. Readers, cantors, and psalmists belong to one and the same order, and their respective functions are quite similar: to read the Scriptures except for the gospel (and sometimes the reading from the Apostle) or sing the psalms. Only the Syrian Church has a special blessing for cantors or psalmists. The East has no rite of tonsure separate from the rite for the reception of the first minor order; tonsure is ordinarily given as part of the ordination of a reader.

For the rite of ordination, all the rituals follow the one in the *Apostolic Constitutions*: imposition of hands by the celebrating bishop alone, to the exclusion of the other two consecrators at the ordination of a bishop and of the presbyterium at the ordination of a priest; ordination to the minor orders is by imposition of the hand prior to the giving of the instruments. There is, however, one collective gesture: in the ordination of the Catholicos of Seleucia-Ctesiphon "while the first among the metropolitans places his right hand on the head of the Catholicos, the other metropolitans place their right hands on his body, and the bishops extend their hands."[22] Finally, there is one rite in the *Apostolic Constitutions* that became universal in the East and eventually entered the Roman liturgy: the placing of the Book of the Gospels on the head of the one being consecrated a bishop. The meaning is that the power of the gospel must permeate the candidate.[23]

A final trait common to all the Eastern rites is the use of a declarative formula that was perhaps the formula of ordination in the Church of Antioch in the time of St. John Chrysostom and St. Gregory of Nazianzus, even though the *Apostolic Constitutions* do not refer to it. The Byzantine Rite has it in the same form for the ordination of bishop, priest, and deacon: "Divine grace, which always heals what is disabled and makes up for what is lacking chooses N. as bishop (priest, deacon) of. . . . Let us therefore pray for him that the grace of the Holy Spirit may come upon him."[24]

It would doubtless be an exaggeration to say that this prayer is the form of the sacrament in the Eastern Churches (the Chaldeans have turned it into a simple preparatory prayer of the consecrating bishop).[25] But at

---

22. A. Raes, "Les ordinations dans le Pontifical chaldéen," *OS* 5 (1960) 78–79.

23. B. Botte, "Holy Orders in the Ordination Prayers" (n. 20), 15.

24. B. Botte, "La formule d'ordination 'La grâce divine' dans les rites orientaux," *OS* 2 (1957) 285.

25. A. Raes (n. 22), 68.

least the reader will realize the theological importance of the formula. It is in agreement with the beginning of the Roman consecratory prayers inasmuch as it says that God himself is the one who calls a baptized Christian to serve him in holy orders ("Divine grace"), because it is he who gives his Church its hierarchic organization and distributes the orders for the growth of the body of Christ (Roman prayers of ordination). To be noted also is that in the Eastern Churches the declarative mood of the formulas is preferred in other sacraments as well: "The servant of God, N., is baptized" (Byzantine baptism); "The servant of God, N. [the groom], receives as a crown the servant of God, N. [the bride]" (Byzantine marriage).

2. Ordinations in the Byzantine Rite[26]

The ordination of a reader or a cantor corresponds in fact to the three Latin ordinations of acolyte, cleric, and reader (lector). During a first imposition of his hand the bishop asks God to array in spotless garments his servant N. "who has decided to go before his holy mysteries in the role of candle-bearer." He then cuts the candidate's hair in the form of a cross, clothes him in the *phelonion* or *sticharion*, and once again puts his hand on the candidate's head while saying the prayer of ordination to the lectorate. After this prayer the bishop opens the Book of the Epistles on the reader's head. Subdeacons then lead the new reader to the center of the church, and he there does a short reading from the Book. If the ordinand is a cantor, he sings a *prokimenon*. The rite concludes with an address from the bishop, who ends by presenting the new reader to the congregation: "See, the servant of God, N., has become a reader for the holy Church of N., in the name of the Father . . .," and giving him a candlestick with a lighted candle.

The ordination of a subdeacon is a simpler affair. The bishop begins by giving the candidate the cincture proper to subdeacons; he then places his hands on the candidate's head and asks the Lord to enable his chosen one "to love the splendor of his house, take his place before the door of his holy temple, and light the lamp in the tabernacle of his glory." The new subdeacon then receives a basin, pitcher, and towel, and goes to the bishop so that the latter may wash his hands.

The ordination of a deacon takes place during the liturgy, at the end of the anaphora. Two deacons present the candidate to the bishop; the ordinand then genuflects on his right knee and touches his forehead to the altar table. The bishop imposes his hand on the man's head and says

---

26. J. Goar, *Euchologion sive Rituale Graecorum* (Paris, 1647), 233–316. French translation in E. Mercenier and F. Paris, *La prière des Eglises de rite byzantin* 1 (Chevetogne, 1948²), 367–96.

aloud the formula "Divine grace," to which the congregation responds with *Kyrie eleisons.* Placing his hand on the candidate's head once again, the bishops says in a low voice two prayers in which he asks the Lord to send the Holy Spirit on his servant, "for it is not through the laying on of my hands but through the visitation of your rich mercies that grace is given to those who are worthy of you." Finally, the bishop vests the deacon in the *orarion* and the liturgical garments proper to his order; as he gives each vestment he says "*Axios* (He is worthy)."

The ordination of a priest takes place during the liturgy at the beginning of the offertory, at the time of the Great Entrance. It follows the same format as the ordination of a deacon. Two priests present to the bishop the man now being called to the presbyterate; the ordinand then kneels on both knees and touches his forehead to the altar table. The bishop covers him with his own *omophorion* and lays his hand on the man's head while saying aloud the formula "Divine grace" and then, in a low voice, two further prayers. In the first of these the bishop asks the Lord to enable his priest "to conduct himself in a manner worthy of the great grace of priesthood that he has received." In the second, he lists a priest's functions: to stand at the altar, to proclaim the gospel of the kingdom and exercise the sacred ministry of the Word, to offer spiritual gifts and sacrifices and renew the people in the bath of rebirth. Finally, the bishop crosses the *orarion* over the chest of the new priest and gives him the priestly cincture and the *phelonion*, saying at each of these actions "*Axios* (He is worthy)." The priest next exchanges the kiss of peace with the other priests and then takes part in the concelebration as first after the bishop.

The ordination of a bishop takes place during the liturgy after the Little Entrance. It has two parts. First, the clergy present the candidate to the consecrating bishop, who is accompanied by several other bishops (at least two) wearing their episcopal vestments. The candidate is asked to make a threefold confession of faith, after which he receives the *hypogonation* and the episcopal staff. After the singing of the troparia and Trisagion comes the second part of the ordination, which closely resembles the ordination of a priest. The candidate is led to the altar by his consecrators; there he kneels, puts both arms on the altar, and leans his head against it. The primary consecrator places the open Book of the Gospels on the man's head, and the other bishops hold it there; the consecrator then says aloud for all to hear: "By way of the election and approval of the beloved priests and clerics of the city of N., divine grace. . . ." He then places his hand on the head of the new bishop and recites two prayers in a low voice. In the first he asks God to make his servant "an irreproachable high priest and to adorn him with every dignity": "Make him holy so that he may pray worthily for the salvation of the people and be heard by you." In the second prayer he recalls that the bishop occupies the very throne of God in the Church and must offer sacrifice for the entire people; he then asks for the newly ordained bishop the virtues that will make him a true shepherd, an imitator of him who gave his life for his flock: may he be "a guide for the blind, a light for those in darkness, a tutor to the ignorant, a teacher for children, a torch in the world." At the end of this prayer the other bishops remove the Book of the Gospels which has remained open on the head of the new bishop. The later is then vested in the *omophorion* while the clergy acclaim him as "*Axios*." "After this, the consecrating bishop and the other bishops embrace the newly ordained. After the ritual acclamation they mount to their thrones. The new bishop is seated first and gives the peace for the reading of the Apostle. He is also the first to receive the precious Body and Blood of Christ. He then distributes these to the bishop who consecrated him and to the others."[27]

§3. The Ancient Roman Ritual of Ordinations

BIBLIOGRAPHY

Documents
  Liber diurnus Romanorum pontificum, ed. H. Foerster (Bern: Francke, 1958).
  Sacramentarium Veronense, ed. L. C. Mohlberg, L. Eizenhöfer, and P. Siffrin (REDMF 1; Rome: Herder, 1956).
  Sacramentarium Gregorianum, ed. J. Deshusses (Spicilegium Friburgense 16; Fribourg, 1971).
  Ordines Romani XXXIV, XXXV, XXXVI, XXXIX, XL (Andrieu, *OR* 3:535–613; 4:3–205, 273–308).

Studies
  B. Botte, "*Secundi meriti munus,*" *QL* 21 (1936) 84–88.
  _____, "Le sacre épiscopal dans le rite romain," *QL* 25 (1940) 22–32.
  M. Andrieu, *OR* 3 and 4 (introductions to the *Ordines* listed above).
  M. Righetti, *Manuale di storia liturgica* 4 (Milan: Ancora, 1959²).
  R. Béraudy, "Les effets de l'ordre d'après les préfaces d'ordination du Sacramentaire leonien," in *La tradition sacerdotale* (Lyons: Mappus, 1959), 81–107.
  B. Kleinheyer, *Die Priesterweihe im römischen Ritus. Eine liturgiehistorische Studie* (Trierer theologische Studien 12; Trier: Paulinus-Verlag, 1962), 26–84.
  A. Santantoni, *L'Ordinazione episcopale. Storia e teologia dei riti dell'ordinazione nelle antiche liturgie dell'Occidente* (Studia Anselmiana 69, Analecta liturgica 2; Rome, 1976).

The Roman rite of ordinations that was in use from the fifteenth to the twentieth century had two easily distinguishable strata: the first consisted of the ancient Roman ritual of ordinations that had reached its full development by the time of St. Gregory the Great (d. 604); the second

---

27. Mercenier and Paris 389.

consisted of a set of additions of Frankish origin, most of them dating from the Carolingian period. I shall therefore treat the two rituals separately, with the intention less of following historical chronology than of bringing out more clearly the essential rites.

The Day for Ordinations

As early as the first half of the third century, the *Apostolic Tradition* appointed Sunday as the day for the consecration of a bishop. Sunday must soon have become the day for priestly and diaconal ordinations as well, since two centuries later we find St. Leo the Great taking vigorous steps to see that this rule is followed everywhere in the Church in the name of the sacred canons and the tradition of the Fathers: "Non passim sed die legitimo ordinatio celebretur."[28] The only legitimate day is Sunday, which begins at nightfall on Saturday evening. Ordination is therefore to take place at the beginning or end of the nocturnal vigil, provided those who receive it and those who give it have been fasting. The fast before ordination is to some extent assimilated to the fast before Easter, while the weekly Easter is celebrated during the vigil of ordination: "Solum enim maiores nostri resurrectionis dominicae diem hoc honore dignum iudicaverunt."[29] The connection between priesthood and the paschal mystery was so clear that a century later Pope Pelagius I (555–560) would ask a bishop to send his deacon for episcopal consecration during the Easter Vigil: "ut sabbato ipso noctis magnae post baptismum cum Dei gratia valeat ordinari."[30]

The Roman Church long remained faithful to the rule of ordaining a bishop only on a Sunday. The only exception was that from the tenth century on, the *natalicia apostolorum* were considered the equivalents of Sundays. At the end of the fifth century the Roman Church adopted a much more restrictive discipline for the ordination of priests and deacons. In a *Constitutum* that took the form of a letter to be given to bishops after their consecration Pope Gelasius (492–96) stated: "Let him be aware that the ordinations of priests and deacons are to be celebrated only on Saturday evening at the end of the fast of the fourth, seventh, or tenth months [June, September, or December], or at the beginning of Lent and of the middle week of Lent."[31]

---

28. St. Leo the Great, *Ep. 10 ad episcopos provinciae Viennensis* 6 (PL 54:634). — See also his *Ep. 9 ad Dioscorum Alexandrinum episcopum* (PL 54:635–36); *Ep. 6 ad Anastasium Thessalonicen. episcopum* 6 (PL 54:620); Andrieu, *OR* 3:582 and 555.

29. St. Leo the Great, *Ep. 10* (PL 54:634).

30. Pelagius, *Ep. Tulliano episcopo Grumentino*, ed. P. Ewald in *Neues Archiv* 5 (1880) 552 (PL 161:472), cited in Andrieu, *OR* 3:583.

31. Gelasius, *Ep. 15*, in A. Thiel, *Epistolae Romanorum pontificum . . .* (Braunsberg: Peter, 1868), 380. — See Andrieu, *OR* 3:556.

On the other hand, no set day was appointed for conferring the lesser orders. It was the Frankish sacramentaries of the tenth and eleventh centuries that located them in the Mass of Ember Saturdays after each reading.

I. THE ORDINATION OF BISHOP, PRIESTS, AND DEACONS

In studying the Roman ritual of ordinations from the sixth to the eighth century, we must make use of two series of documents: the sacramentaries, which give the text of the prayers said by the ordaining bishop, and the *Ordines*, which describe the rites.

1. *The Ordination Formularies*

Two ancient sacramentaries provide the formularies for the consecration of a bishop and the ordination of priests and deacons: the Verona Sacramentary[32] and the Gregorian Sacramentary.[33] The former was compiled around 560–80, and the second was composed a half-century later, but the ordination formularies that they transmit are earlier and may go back to the time or even the very person of St. Leo the Great. With variants due simply to the negligence of copyists, these formularies remained the three ordination prayers of the Roman Pontifical down to our own time. The prayer for the consecration of a bishop was replaced in 1968 by the prayer from the *Apostolic Tradition*; the other two, however, are still in use.

All three prayers, which were given the form of prefaces in the tenth century, follow the same pattern. The consecrating bishop first contemplates the mystery of the sacred hierarchy as found in God and celebrates its embodiment in the Church. He then calls down upon the ordinand the grace that makes men bishops, priests, or deacons. Finally, he prays that the new minister of the Lord may be granted the virtues required by his role.

a) *The mystery of the hierarchy*. — The sacred hierarchy is a gift that God the Father has given in Christ. Orders, functions, honors, dignities all come from the Father: "Deus honorum omnium, Deus omnium dignitatum" (B[ishop]); "Deus honorum dator et distributor omnium dignitatum" (P[riest]); "Deus honorum dator, ordinumque distributor, officiorumque dispositor" (D[eacon]). The mystery of the hierarchy, which proceeds from the Father, is organized by "his word, his power, and his

---

32. *Le* 942–47: *Consecratio episcoporum;* 948–51: *Benedictio super diaconos;* 952–54: *Consecratio presbyteri.*

33. *Gr* 21–26: *Benedictio episcoporum;* 27–29: *Oratio ad ordinandum presbyterum;* 30–32: *Orationes ad ordinandum diaconum.*

wisdom: Jesus Christ, his Son and our Lord" (D) for the sake of the growth
and spread of the Church, which is the body of Christ (D). It finds visible
expression in holy orders. These, which are primarily for service, have
three degrees: "sacri muneris servitutem trinis gradibus ministrorum" (D),
namely the "sacerdotales gradus atque officia levitarum" (P).

b) *The three sacred orders.* — The three sacred orders have each a
special function to carry out for God's glory in the Church. Though established by the Lord (priesthood) or the apostles (diaconate), they have
their roots in the history of the people of the former covenant, and this
history sheds light on their nature.

The *episcopate* is the order of high priesthood: "cum pontifices sum-
mos regendis populis praefecisses" (P), "quem ad summi sacerdotii
ministerium elegisti" (B). The bishop is above all else the priest to whom
the Lord has entrusted the fullness of his own mystery: "Comple in sacerdote tuo mysterii tui summam" (B). He is therefore essentially one who
is consecrated. The prayer of ordination develops this point at length with
the aid of the typology of Aaron: like the Hebrew high priest, the bishop
receives the mystical anointing, the outpouring of the Spirit; the garments
in which Moses clad Aaron at God's command are a symbol of the holiness that shines in the soul of the bishop: "Pontificalem gloriam non iam
nobis honor commendat vestium sed splendor animarum" (B). But the
bishop's activity in the Church is not limited to the performance of rites.
Like the priests of the Aaronic line, the bishops of the new covenant have
inherited the authority of Moses and the mission of the apostles: like Moses
they are appointed "regendis populis" and must govern "innumeras mul-
titudines"; like the apostles, they are "doctores fidei" and must teach "to-
tum orbem" (P). Such is the responsibility that the Lord entrusts to each
of them when he assigns them their episcopal chair for the purpose chiefly
of governing his Church throughout the world: "ad regendam Ecclesiam
suam et plebem universam" (B). The bishops exercise this responsibility
collectively, for together they form a college, an *ordo* (P).

The *presbyterate* is the order of helpers of the *ordo episcoporum*: "Sint
probi cooperatores ordinis nostri," says the ordaining bishop (P). He
bestows the second of the "sacerdotales gradus," the responsibility proper
to the second rank, "secundi meriti munus." Alongside the bishops he sets
honored men of the second rank, "sequentis ordinis viros et secundae dig-
nitatis," so that they may share the daily lives and priestly activity of the
bishops, "ad eorum societatis et operis adiumentum." Priests are fellow
workers of the episcopal order in the three areas of cultic priesthood, gover-
nance, and teaching, just as Eleazar and Ithamar were for Aaron, the council of seventy elders (*presbyteroi*) for Moses, and the disciples for the
apostles. The close relation of episcopate and presbyterate has its basis
in the innermost depths of the mystery of the sacred hierarchy, because

both share in one and the same spirit: Just as the spirit of Moses passed into the council of elders and Aaron's fullness of consecration into his sons, and as the apostles communicated their faith to preachers of second rank, "secundis praedicatoribus," whom they had taken as associates, "fidei comites," so the spirit of the bishop animates the entire presbyterium (P).

The *diaconate* is the order of service, in the unqualified sense of the term. A deacon is ordained "in opus ministerii" (D). Although the name of St. Stephen is not spoken, the memory of him hovers over the entire prayer of diaconal ordination: it is Stephen who establishes a special link between the order of the deaconate and the outpouring of the "sevenfold" Spirit; it is the virtues of Stephen that are presented as the virtues specific to the deacon. However, in the period when the Roman prayer of ordination was composed, the activity of the deacon was already limited to liturgical ministry. Therefore the formula calls to mind above all the typology of the sons of Levi, who were the guardians first of the Ark and then of the temple, and the bishop says that he dedicates these chosen men to the service of God's house: "quos tuis sacrariis servituros in officium diaconii suppliciter dedicamus" (D).

c) *The prayer of ordination.* — The prayer might almost be called an epiclesis: the "sevenfold" Spirit is called down upon the deacon and the spirit of holiness upon the priest, while the anointing which is to sanctify the bishop is simply the outpouring of the Spirit (1 John 2:20): "ut tui Spiritus virtus et interiora eius repleat et exteriora circumtegat" (B). Here are the essential parts of the three ordination prayers:

> Comple in sacerdote tuo ministerii [mysterii *in the sacramentaries*] tui summam, et ornamentis totius glorificationis instructum caelestis unguenti rore [fluore *in the sacramentaries*] sanctifica. (Episcopate)

> Da, quaesumus, omnipotens Pater, in hunc famulum tuum presbyterii dignitatem; innova in visceribus eius spiritum sanctitatis, ut acceptum a te, Deus, secundi meriti munus obtineat censuramque morum exemplo suae conversationis insinuet. (Presbyterate)

> Emitte in eum, quaesumus, Domine, Spiritum Sanctum, quo in opus ministerii tui fideliter exsequendi septiformis gratiae tuae munere roboretur. (Diaconate)[34]

---

34. Translation: "Complete in your priest the fullness of your ministry (or: mystery) and, having enriched him with all the adornments of thy glory, sanctify him with the dew (or: stream) of heavenly unction" (episcopate). — "Grant, we beseech you, almighty Father, the dignity of priest to this servant of yours; renew in his inmost heart the spirit of holiness so that he may obtain and receive from you, O God, the office of second dignity and may by the example of his own behavior commend a strict way of life" (priesthood). — "Send upon him, we beseech you, O Lord, the Holy Spirit who will strengthen him with the gift of your sevenfold grace to carry out faithfully the work of your ministry" (diaconate).

d) *The prayer for the ordained.* — After pronouncing the formula of ordination the bishop asks the Lord to grant his servants the virtues they need in their new state.

If we prescind from the lengthy Gallican expansion that became part of the Pontifical in the tenth century ("Sint speciosi munere tuo pedes . . . ut fructum de profectu omnium consequatur"), the Roman prayer for the bishop is extremely terse. The consecrating bishop has already asked that the candidate be wholly permeated by the Spirit and has called down upon him the Glory of the Lord. What more can he wish for? He is satisfied, therefore, to recall the bishop's mission as a mediator appointed between God and his people "ad exorandam misericordiam" and to ask that he be always faithful to this duty. As a man in the service of his people, "abundet in eo constantia fidei, puritas dilectionis, sinceritas pacis"; as a man of God, may he derive his authority and strength from God alone: "sis ei auctoritas, sis ei firmitas, sis ei potestas" (B).

For priests and deacons the Church asks the spirit of holiness (P): "eluceat in eis totius forma iustitiae" (P); "abundet in eo totius forma virtutis" (D). The prayer of diaconal ordination dwells briefly on the virtues required for the exercise of holy orders: "auctoritas modesta, pudor constans, innocentiae puritas et spiritualis observatio disciplinae" (D). Priests and deacons owe this tribute to the Lord whom they serve. They owe it as well to the people whom it is their responsibility to lead to goodness: the teachings of God are to be resplendent in their lives so that the Christian community may follow their example and especially the example of their chastity: "ut suae castitatis exemplo imitationem sancta plebs acquirat" (D). Such a program can be carried out only by men whose perseverance has its solid ground in Christ (D).

2. *The Rites*

The essential rite of ordination is the imposition of hands by the bishop on the head of the ordinand. In the ancient Roman ritual this gesture expressing the gift of the Spirit was not overshadowed, as it was to be later on, by a multiplicity of secondary rites.

a) *The rites of episcopal ordination.* — At Rome an episcopal ordination had somewhat different resonances depending on whether it was the ordination of a Roman pontiff by the suburbicarian bishops or the ordination of a bishop of central Italy by the pope in his role as metropolitan. *Ordines* XL A and XL B describe the former, and *Ordines* XXXIV (nos. 14–45), XXXV (nos. 38–74), and XXXVI (nos. 29–39) the latter.

The ordination of a pope took place in St. Peter's.[35] After the litany,

---

35. *OR* XXXVI, 41 (Andrieu, *OR* 4:203). *OR* XL A, whose description I am following, may go back to the sixth century (Andrieu, *OR* 4:294). The text is also to be found in *Liber diurnus Romanorum pontificum*, ed. H. Foerster (Bern: Francke, 1958), 111.

the Bishop of Albano said the first prayer (the collect "Adesto") and the Bishop of Porto the second ("Propitiare"). The Book of the Gospels was then brought, opened, and held on the head of the candidate by deacons. The Bishop of Ostia then said the prayer of consecration, and the archdeacon gave the pallium to the new pope. The latter finally ascended to his chair, gave the peace to all the priests, and intoned the *Gloria in excelsis Deo*.

When the pope consecrated a bishop he enjoyed the privilege of bestowing the episcopate by himself, without the assistance of two other bishops.[36] Whenever the clergy and people of a Church presented to the pope a priest or deacon whom they had elected their bishop, the pope first had the man examined by his archdeacon; then on Saturday, the eve of the ordination, he had him appear before him for questioning in the presence of all the clergy.[37] The consecration took place on Sunday. The *Kyrie* was not sung at the beginning of this Mass. After the Gradual the archdeacon went to the *secretarium* with the acolytes and subdeacons to vest the candidate in dalmatic and chasuble and to put his sandals on him. The retinue then brought him into the church, and the pope, after presenting him to the people, urged the congregation to pray: "Oremus pro eodem viro, ut Deus et dominus noster Iesus Christus tribuat ei cathedram episcopalem ad regendam ecclesiam suam et plebem universam."[38] The choir then intoned the litany while the pope, priests, and candidate prostrated themselves before the altar. "Completa vero laetania, surgent et tunc benedicet eum."[39] *Ordo* XXXVI tells us the form the blessing took: "Pontifex vero ponet manum super caput ejus et dicit unam orationem in modum collectae, alteram eo modulamine quo solet contestata cantari."[40] It is easy to see here a reference to the prayer 'Propitiare" and the great prayer which in the time of *Ordo* XXXVI followed Gallican usage and took the form of a preface. The Lord Pope then gave the kiss of peace to the new bishop, who in turn gave it to the other bishops and the priests. The pope then had the newly consecrated take his seat in the first row of bishops. At the time of communion he himself gave him the *formata*[41] and the holy Eucharist.

---

36. *OR* XXXV, 65–66 (Andrieu, *OR* 4:44). The early *ordines* for ordination date from the middle or end of the eighth century (*OR* XXXIV and XXXIX), the end of the ninth (*OR* XXXVI), or the beginning of the tenth (*OR* XXXV).

37. The substance of these rites entered the *PR*, Lib. III: "De scrutinio serotino, quo antiqui utebantur antequam electus in episcopum consecraretur."

38. *OR* XXXIV, 38 (Andrieu, *OR* 3:612).

39. *Ibid.*, no. 40 (613).

40. *OR* XXXVI, 37 (Andrieu, *OR* 4:202).

41. The *formata* was a kind of directory given to a new bishop to guide him in his functions. There is an example of such a directory in an appendix to *OR* XXXV (Andrieu, *OR* 4:47–57).

The bishop took part of the consecrated bread and communicated himself at the altar; the remainder he set aside in order that for forty days he might receive communion from the Eucharistic offering at the Mass of his consecration. Then, at the pope's bidding he gave communion to the entire congregation.

b) *The rites of presbyteral and diaconal ordination* — The rites of ordination to the diaconate and presbyterate are described in *Ordo* XXXIV (nos. 4–13) and, in a form already contaminated by Gallican usages, in *Ordines* XXXVI (nos. 4–28) and XXXIX (nos. 1–31). Priests and deacons could be ordained only at a public ordination that took place during Ember week.

On Monday of that week the candidates were called together by the pope; in his presence they took an oath on the relics of the saints that they had committed none of the serious sins that barred access to orders. On Wednesday, during a Mass celebrated by the pope in St. Mary Major's, the candidates for orders took their place in the presbyterium in the presence of all; a lector went to the ambo to read out their names to the people, along with the order to which they were to be raised; the lector then added: "Si quiş habet contra hos viros aliquam querellam, exeat confidenter propter Deum et secundum Deum et dicat. Memor sit tamen omnino communionis suae."[42] The same proclamation was made on Friday during the station at Holy Apostles. The ordination began on Saturday afternoon at St. Peter's.[43] The ordinands stood beneath the ambo until the end of the Gradual. The pope in a loud voice then called each of them to his chair and specified the titular church to which the new priest or deacon would henceforth be assigned: "Talis presbyter, regionis tertiae, titulo tale, Ille."[44]

Those to be ordained deacons now came forward, vested in the dalmatic, and stood with bowed heads. The pope then asked the congregation to pray: "Oremus, fratres dilectissimi," and the choir intoned the litany, while the celebrant and ordinands prostrated themselves.[45] When the litany was finished, "stat pontifex in sede sua, singillatim imponens manus capiti-

---

42. OR XXXVI, 9 (Andrieu, OR 4:196).

43. Although all public ordinations were celebrated in St. Peter's, the pope alone was consecrated a bishop at the altar of the Confession. Other bishops were consecrated in the oratory of the monastery of St. Martin, which lay very close to the Vatican basilica; priests and deacons were ordained in the rotunda of St. Andrew. See Andrieu, OR 4:127–28 and 147–48. Ordo XXXIX, 12, says that Mass is to begin at the seventh hour (Andrieu, OR 4:284). Anticipation of the Sunday vigil in Ember week, like anticipation of the Easter Vigil, was already habitual in the ninth century.

44. OR XXXIX, 19 (Andrieu, OR 4:284).

45. OR XXXIV, 7–10 (3:605–6).

bus eorum et benedicet eos."[46] The blessing that followed the imposition of hands on the head of each candidate consisted of the prayer "Exaudi, Domine" and the ordination prayer "Deus honorum dator."[47] The pope then gave them the kiss of peace, and they in turn gave it to the other deacons; they then went back to their place near the pope.

The *Ordines Romani* sum up in one sentence the rite of priestly ordination: "Archidiaconus induit planitas ad presbyteros, stans ante altare, et iterum ducit eos ante pontificem and accipiunt orationem presbyterii ab ipso."[48] A Frankish *ordo* says more specifically that the pope "dat benedictionem consecrationis solus per se" but adds that this is a privilege reserved to the Roman pontiff, for when other bishops ordain a priest, the other priests present, or at least two or three dignitaries, "manus super caput ipsius qui consecratur imponunt."[49] After reciting the two prayers of ordination the pope gives the kiss of peace to the new priests, who in turn give it to the bishops and the other priests and then take their place in the front row of priests. The Mass continues with the reading of the gospel by one of the new deacons. At communion the newly ordained priests are the first to receive the Eucharist. They are to reserve as much of the consecrated offering as they need for communion during the next eight days.[50]

An examination of the Roman ritual of ordinations shows a strict parallelism between the rites by which the three sacred orders are conferred: choice of the candidate by the clergy and ratification of this choice by the people; collective prayer of petition; imposition of hands by the bishops (for episcopal consecration), by bishop and priests (presbyterate), and by the bishop alone (diaconate); episcopal prayer of ordination; kiss of peace given by the ordainer and exchanged by the ordinand with the members of the order to which he now belongs; participation in the Eucharist according to rank. The ordination rite is thus a true manifestation of the mystery of the hierarchy in the Church.

II. ORDINATION TO THE LESSER ORDERS

The letter that Pope Cornelius wrote to Fabius of Antioch in 251 informs us that at that time the bishop of the Church of Rome had forty-six

---

46. OR XXXVI, 18 (4:198).

47. OR XXXV, 24–25 (4:37).

48. OR XXXIX, 23 (4:285).

49. OR XXXV, 27–28. The same *ordo*, nos. 29–30, gives the two prayers for priestly ordination (Andrieu, OR 4:38–39).

50. OR XXXVI, 23 (4:199); OR XXXIX, 25 (4:285). — On this practice see Andrieu, OR 3:586–91 and 4:277–78.

priests, seven deacons, seven subdeacons, forty-two acolytes, and fifty-two exorcists, lectors, and doorkeepers.[51] This is exactly the same list of offices, with the same hierarchy among them, that we find in the invitatory of the third of the solemn prayers on Good Friday (fourth century). From the fourth to the ninth century the letters of the popes and the chronicles often repeat the same list, which seems to have constituted a *cursus honorum* in that period.[52]

The liturgical documents show only three lesser orders: lector, acolyte, and subdeacon. Although *Ordines* XXXIV and XXXV, which describe the rites of ordination, do not predate the eighth century, they transmit practices that are much older; corroboration of this is given by a sixth-century document.[53] They may take us, back, therefore, to the time of St. Gregory the Great.

1. Ordination of Lectors

If we are to understand the ritual for the ordination of lectors, we must realize that those who filled this office were usually adolescents.[54] *Ordo* XXXV explains that if the father of a family intends one of his sons for the lectorate, he begins by having him adequately instructed and then lets the pope know that he wants to offer this boy to his service. The Apostolic Lord appoints a day on which the candidate is to read in public at a nocturnal vigil so that his abilities may be judged. If the test is conclusive and positive in its result, the pontiff blesses the young cleric: "Intercedente beato Petro principem [!] apostolorum et sancto Paulo vas electionis, salvet et protegat et eruditam linguam tribuat ei Dominis" (Through the intercession of Blessed Peter, prince of the apostles, and of Saint Paul, vessel of election, may the Lord save and protect him and grant him an instructed tongue"). The *Ordo* ends by saying: "Et respondent omnes: Amen. Et deinceps fiet in ecclesia lector" ("And all answer: Amen. And henceforth he shall be a lector in the church").[55]

---

51. Eusebius of Caesarea, *Historia ecclesiastica* VI, 43, 11 , ed. G. Bardy 2 (SC 41; Paris: Cerf, 1953), 156. See B. Fischer, "Esquisse historique sur les ordres mineurs," *LMD* no. 61 (1960) 58–69; P. Jounel, "Les ministres dans l'assemblée," *LMD* no. 60 (1959) 35–69. The substance of M. Andrieu's study, "Les ordres mineurs dans l'ancien rit romain," *RevSR* 5 (1925) 232–74, is repeated in his introductions to *OR* XXXV and XXXVI.

52. M. Andrieu, "La carrière ecclésiastique des papes et les documents liturgiques du moyen âge," *RevSR* 27 (1947) 90–120.

53. John the Deacon, *Epistola ad Senarium*, ed. A. Wilmart, *Analecta Reginensia* (ST 59; Vatican City, 1933), 170.

54. See Andrieu, *OR* 4:3–11.

55. *OR* XXXV, 4. Note that after giving the Roman ritual for the ordination of a lector (nos. 1–4) *Ordo* XXXV, which was composed in Frankish territory, goes on to give the Gallican ritual for the same ordination (nos. 5–6).

2. *Ordination of Acolytes and Subdeacons*

The ordination of acolytes and subdeacons is described in *Ordines* XXXIV (nos. 1–3) and XXXV (nos. 7–9 and 11–14). It takes place during Mass while the bishops and priests are distributing communion to the people. After the future acolyte has donned the chasuble, he is presented to the Apostolic Lord, who gives him the *sacculum* or linen bag. The ordinand receives this in hands covered by the chasuble and then prostrates himself while the pontiff pronounces the following blessing: "Intercedente beata et gloriosa semperque sola virgine Maria et beato Petro apostolo, salvet et custodiat et protegat te Dominus" ("Through the intercession of the blessed and glorious and ever virgin Mary and blessed Peter the apostle, may the Lord save and guard and protect you"). [56] "Et ex illa die fiet acolytus" ("And from that day on he shall be an acolyte"). [57] To understand this rite of ordination we need to know that in the sixth century the function of the acolyte was to take the Eucharist to those who were absent and to present the *sancta* to priests at the breaking of the bread: "Acolithi vero sacramentorum portanda vasa suscipiunt et ministrandi sacerdotibus ordinem gerunt" ("Acolytes receive the vessels for carrying the sacrament, and they have the office of ministering to the priests"), says John the Deacon. [58]

John the Deacon (sixth century) describes as follows the ordination and function of subdeacons: "Cuius hic apud nos ordo est ut, accepto sacratissimo calice, in quo consuevit pontifex sanguinis immolare mysterium, subdiaconus iam dicitur" ("Among us the ordination of a subdeacon is as follows: Having received the sacred chalice in which the high priest is accustomed to offer the mystery of the blood, he is now called a subdeacon"). This is precisely the ritual described in the two *Ordines*. The ordination of subdeacons follows immediately on that of acolytes, while the communion of the people is still going on. After the candidates have sworn that they have not committed any of the crimes that bar access to orders, the archdeacon or the pope gives them the chalice; the ordinands then prostrate themselves and the pope recites over them the same blessing that he has already said over the acolytes. [59]

---

56. *OR* XXXIV, 2 (Andrieu, *OR* 3:603). On the order of acolytes at Rome see Andrieu 3:543–47. The *sacculum* was the linen bag in which the acolytes received the consecrated bread to be presented to the priests at the moment of the fraction (*OR* I, 101). Although Pope Innocent does not specifically say so in his letter to Decentius of Gubbio, it was in a *sacculum* that acolytes used to carry the *fermentum* to the priests of the urban titles at the end of the papal Mass (PL 55:516).

57. *OR* XXXV, 8 (Andrieu, *OR* 4:34).

58. John the Deacon, *Ep. ad Senarium* 10 (Wilmart 176).

59. *OR* XXXIV, 3 (Andrieu, *OR* 3:604); *OR* XXXV, 11. — See Andrieu 3:547–54).

3. Clerical Tonsure

Ordo XXXVI refers in summary fashion to the blessing that young boys assigned to serve the pope as *cubicularii* had received from the archdeacon when they entered upon their office (nos. 1–2). Is this "prima benedictio" to be identified with the giving of clerical tonsure? Very probably, if we look at contemporary *Ordines* that distinguish between *cubicularii laici* and *cubicularii tonsorati*.[60] In 595 St. Gregory the Great had decreed at a synod that henceforth young laymen would no longer be admitted to the immediate service of the pope and that this office should instead be reserved to clerics or monks.[61] It seems a rather likely development that the tonsure worn by *cubicularii* who were monks should have come to be given to clerics of the pontifical household and then to individuals whom it was desirable to include among the clergy without having them pass through the stage of lector or acolyte. That is how a number of popes could pass from the clerical state to the subdeaconate and then to the deaconate and episcopate.

Although the Gregorian Sacramentary has no formula for minor orders,[62] it does have a prayer *ad clericum faciendum*[63] that explicitly refers to the removal of hair.

§4. The Romano-Frankish Ordination Ritual

BIBLIOGRAPHY

a) *Ancient Sources*
   Liber sacramentorum Romanae Aeclesiae ordinis anni circuli . . . (Sacramentarium Gelasianum), ed. L. C. Mohlberg, L. Eizenhöfer, and P. Siffrin (REDMF 4; Rome: Herder 1960), nos. 140–62 and 736–86.
   Missale Francorum . . ., ed. L. C. Mohlberg, L. Eizenhöfer, and P. Siffrin (REDMF 2; Rome: Herder, 1957), nos. 1–44.

---

60. *OR* I, 33 (Andrieu, *OR* 2:78) see 3:545–47.

61. See St. Gregory the Great, *Registrum epistolarum* V, 57, ed. Ewald-Hartmann 1:363. See Andrieu, *OR* 2:40.

62. The failure of the papal sacramentary to contain the ritual for minor orders may seem surprising, but, as I noted earlier, the formularies for blessing lectors, acolytes, and subdeacons amounted to very little. The Frankish redactor of *OR* XXXVI must have been thinking of one of the sacramentaries of his own country when he remarked, after speaking of the first blessing given to young *cubicularii*: "Deinde, sicut Sacramentorum codex continet, quando et ubi libitum fuerit, usque in subdiaconatus officium ordinantur" (Andrieu, *OR* 4:195).

63. *Gr* 1246–50. — The *Liber ordinum* of Toledo (the text of which goes back to the seventh century) likewise has an *Ordo ad ordinandum clericum* (Férotin, cols. 40–42) that includes vesting (with *tunica* and *alba*) and tonsure. The antiphon and prayer in this *ordo* show that the subjects are young children.

Liber sacramentorum Gellonensis, ed. A. Dumas (CCL 159; Turnhout: Brepols, 1981), nos. 373–85.

Statuta ecclesiae antiqua, ed. C. Munier (Bibliothèque de l'Institut de droit canonique de l'Université de Strasbourg 5; Paris: Presses Universitaires de France, 1960).

b) *Medieval Texts*

M. Metzger, *Zwei karolingische Pontifikalien vom Oberrhein* (Freiburg: Herder, 1914).

A. Martini, *Il cosidetto Pontificale di Poitiers* (Paris: Bibl. de l'Arsenal, cod. 227) (REDMF 14: Rome: Herder, 1979), 1–12.

PRG, nos. 1–19, 56–67, and 71.

Roman Pontifical of the Twelfth Century, nos. 1–11 (Andrieu, *PR* 1:123–54).

Pontifical of the Roman Curia in the Thirteenth Century, nos. 1–14 (Andrieu, *PR* 2:327–82).

Pontifical of William Durandus, nos. 2–17 (Andrieu, *PR* 3:335–96).

c) *Modern Practice*

Pontificalis ordinis liber, ed. A. Patrizi Piccolomini and John Burkard (Rome, 1485) (= Paris, Bibl. Nat., Res. B. 92 fol.).

Pontificale Romanum (first typical ed. promulgated by Clement VIII on February 10, 1596; last typical ed., February 28, 1962).

d) *Studies*

J. Catalani, *Pontificale Romanum . . . nunc primum prolegomenis et commentariis illustratum* 1 (Rome, 1738; reprint in three volumes: Paris: Leroux et Jouby, 1850).

B. Botte, "Le rituel des ordinations des *Statuta ecclesiae antiquae*," *RTAM* 11 (1939) 223–41.

A. Chavasse, *Le Sacramentaire gélasien* (Tournai: Desclée, 1958), 5–27.

M. Andrieu, "Le sacre épiscopal d'après Hincmar de Reims," *RHE* 48 (1953) 22–74.

B. Kleinheyer, *Die Priesterweihe im römischen Ritus. Eine liturgiehistorische Studie* (Trierer theologische Studien 12; Trier: Paulinus-Verlag, 1962), 85–247.

A. Chavasse, P. M. Gy, P. Jounel, and A. G. Martimort, "Les ordinations," *Bulletin du Comité des études* 36 (1962) 19–92.

A. Santantoni, *L'ordinazione episcopale. Storia e teologia dei riti dell'ordinazione nelle antiche liturgie dell'Occidente* (Studia Anselmiana 69, Analecta liturgica 2; Rome, 1976). Many formularies for the rites of episcopal ordination in the West are given on pp. 232–302.

It is not possible to pass from the early Roman ritual of ordinations to the ritual in the Pontifical of Clement VIII without noticing a fundamental change. True enough, one still finds in the celebration of major orders the rite of the imposition of hands, performed according to the prescriptions of the *Apostolic Tradition*, and the three ordination prayers from the fifth century. But, on the one hand, in the ordinations of bishop and deacon, an interruption breaks the unity of the prayers and, on the other, the traditional rites are followed by new and much more eye-catching rites that attract more of the attention of the faithful. The ordination liturgy familiar to a St. Leo or a St. Gregory showed a functional sobriety and had only the minimum number of extremely clear signs that St. Augustine saw as the mark of Christian liturgy.[64] Romano-Frankish usage replaced a liturgy that combined simplicity and depth with a set of rites whose purpose was to show what effects grace and sacramental power have on those who receive them. Thus the mystical anointing of a bishop is concretized in the chrismal anointing of his head; his authority as shepherd in the bestowal of the crozier and ring and in his enthronement; his sublime dignity as pontiff in the donning of miter and gloves. The Eucharistic power of the priest is expressed in the anointing of his hands and the bestowal of chalice, bread, and wine; his power to forgive sins in a second imposition of hands. The deacon's responsibility for proclaiming the gospel is shown by the giving of the Book of the Gospels to him. In short, the sacramental sign has developed into a profusion of symbols that bring the liturgy to the threshold of sacred drama. The danger that the secondary would take precedence over the essential was very great, and the Church succumbed to it. Not until 1950 would the Pontifical drop the following words: "Episcopus moneat ordinandos quod instrumenta, in quorum traditione character imprimitur, tangant."[65]

I. THE ORDINATION RITUAL AT ROME IN ABOUT THE YEAR ONE THOUSAND

As the year 1000 drew near, the Roman ritual of ordinations was that of the Romano-German Pontifical, which had been composed at Mainz in about 950.

The very plan followed in this new book points to a new conception of orders. The three major orders of episcopate, presbyterate, and diaconate no longer form a homogeneous whole: ordinations run from tonsure to presbyterate and the sequence has as its crown the *Ordo qualiter in Romana ecclesia presbyteri, diaconi vel subdiaconi eligendi sunt* (no. 16), while episcopal ordination is joined with the crowning of king and emperor (nos. 56–70). The successor of the apostles is thus turned into a feudal lord.

1. *The Romano-Frankish Ritual for the Three Major Orders*

a) *Consecration of a bishop.* — In the period between *Ordo XXXIV* and the Romano-German Pontifical, the rite of episcopal consecration had undergone important developments, both in the formularies and in the rites.

---

64. St. Augustine, *De doctrina christiana* III, 9, 13 (CCL 32:86).

65. SCR, Decree *Variationes in rubricis Pontificalis Romani* (February 20, 1950): *AAS* 42 (1950) 448.

Two new formularies call for attention: the examination to which the candidate, vested in a cope, is subjected after the collect, and the addition within the prayer of consecration. The examination shows its origin in the title that it still has in the book: *Incipit examinatio in ordinatione episcopi secundum Gallos* (no. 63a). The section added to the Roman prayer of consecration ("Sint speciosi munere tuo pedes . . . de profectu omnium consequatur") is not without grandeur: "non ponat lucem tenebras, nec tenebras lucem; non dicat malum bonum nec bonum malum."

But it is the new rites that constitute the principal innovation. The chief ones are the rites of anointing. After having implored the Lord on behalf of his chosen one: "Caelestis unguenti rore sanctifica" ("Sanctify him with the dew of heavenly anointing"), the pontiff stops and gives material symbolization to his prayer by pouring sacred chrism over the head of the new bishop: "Ungatur et consecretur caput tuum caelesti benedictione in ordine pontificali" ("May your head be anointed and consecrated with heavenly blessing in the order of bishops"). At the end of the prayer of ordination he also anoints the new bishop's hands and then the thumb separately with sacred chrism.[66] The rites of anointing are followed by others that bring out the dignity and functions of the bishop: the blessing and bestowal of ring and crozier.

b) *Ordination of a priest.* — The ritual for the ordination of priests in the Romano-German Pontifical shows expansions that parallel those in the consecration of a bishop. The ordaining bishop begins by ascertaining the fitness of the candidate; to this end he asks the priests who are presenting the candidate whether he is worthy, and then he asks the candidate himself some questions: Is he resolved to receive the priesthood? To remain in it? To obey his bishop? To each question the ordinand answers, "Volo." The most notable of the formularies added to the ancient ones is the prayer "Deus sanctificationum." It is given under the title *Item consecratio* that it already had in the *Missale Francorum* (no. 32) and the Gelasian Sacramentary (no. 148). The ordination prayer is followed by the vesting of the new priest, then the consecration of his hands with holy oil, and finally the bestowal, with appropriate prayers, of a chalice and paten containing wine, water, and host. Thus, while the Roman prayer

---

66. Initially a bishop's hands were consecrated only if he were passing directly from diaconate to episcopate. If he were already a priest, this rite, which had been performed at his priestly ordination, was not repeated. See M. Andrieu, "L'onction des mains dans le sacre épiscopal," *RHE* 36 (1930) 343–47; G. Ellard, *Ordination Anointings in the Western Church before 1000 A.D.* (Monographs of the Mediaeval Academy of America 8; Cambridge, Mass., 1933); A. Malvy, "Unctio pollicis," *Bulletin de littérature ecclésiastique* 38 (1937) 213–32.

presents the priest as member of the presbyterium and collaborator of the bishop, the new ritual shows him also as celebrant of Mass. He is robed in liturgical vestments and has his hands consecrated so that he may take the chalice: "Accipe potestatem offerre sacrificium Deo tam pro vivis quam pro defunctis." The ordination ends with the blessing *in consummatione presbyterorum:* ". . . ut sitis benedicti in ordine sacerdotali et offeratis placabiles hostias," which was given at the end of Mass.

c) *Ordination of a deacon.* — In the ordination of a deacon the innovations consist in the emphasis on the diaconal vestments and the giving of the Book of the Gospels. Like the prayer "Deus sanctificationum" in priestly ordination, the prayer "Domine sanctae spei," which marks the climax of the deaconal ceremony, is already to be found in the *Missale Francorum* (no. 26) and the Gelasian Sacramentary (no. 156). These two formularies may have been the prayers of ordination in the old Gallican ritual.

d) *The sources of this ritual.* — The new formularies just discussed were taken from an ancient ritual of Gaul that dated at least from the seventh century[67] and had already been drawn upon by the Old Gelasian Sacramentary and the *Missale Francorum*. It is to be noted that for the ordinations of priest and deacon these two sacramentaries give, in succession, the Roman *ordo* and the Gallican *ordo* without allowing them to intermingle. After the Roman formularies of ordination the Gallican formularies are given under the title *Consummacio presbyterii* ("Sit nobis, fratres . . . Item benedictio: Sanctificationum omnium auctor") and *Ad consummandum diaconatus officia* ("Commune votum communis oratio prosequatur. . . . Sequitur benedictio: Domine sanctae spei").

An examination of these formularies brings to light a conception of major orders that differs a bit from the Roman conception. Here the bishop is seen as the successor of the apostles more than as the heir of Moses and Aaron: the head of a local Church is transformed into a missionary bishop who is always on the road "ad evangelizandum pacem, evangelizandum bona." We think of St. Martin or St. Amand when the consecrator asks that the man on whom he imposes hands may have the grace to carry out his ministry of reconciliation "in verbo et in factis et in virtute signorum et prodigiorum."

A priest is no longer a member of an urban presbyterium but the head of a small community. His title *presbyter* calls to mind not so much the counsel of elders as the gravity that becomes an old man. Attention is focused less on the figures of the old covenant than on the pastoral directives that St. Paul gave to Titus and Timothy. The collaborator of the

---

67. A. Chavasse, *Le Sacramentaire gélasien* (Tournai: Desclée, 1958), 5–27.

ordo episcoporum, who, as befitted his rank, played only a modest part in Eucharistic concelebration, is now the president of the liturgical assembly, the celebrant of the mysteries of the Lord's Body and Blood. The deacon, for his part, is "sanctis altaribus minister" and performs a service that assimilates him to the angels ("angelorum ministeriis") and at the same time makes him the successor of the seven deacons of the apostolic community; the twofold reference makes clear an indisputable need of holiness.

The rites of anointing, vesting, and bestowal of cult objects and sacral insignia, which appeared in Rome for the first time at the end of the tenth century, had become part of the usage of the Frankish Churches during the ninth. The anointing of the priest's hands is even much older, since it is attested at the beginning of the eighth century by the *Missale Francorum* (nos. 33–34).[68] As for the rites of episcopal consecration, we find a description of them in the letter that Hincmar of Rheims wrote to Adventius of Metz in 869–70 in order to supply him with a detailed guide to the ceremony to be followed in the ordination of a metropolitan.[69] In this document Hincmar refers to his own consecration that took place at Rheims in 845. His witness is all the more important since the rites he regards as traditional were to appear in the Frankish sacramentaries or pontificals only at the beginning of the tenth century. He is thus the first witness to the chrismal anointing of a bishop's head in the middle of the ordination preface, to the giving of ring and crozier, and to the enthronement of the new bishop (none of which appear in the Romano-German Pontifical). Here is what he wrote:

> When he reaches the point where crosses are indicated, the consecrator is to take the container of chrism in his left hand. While singing the words contained [in the *Ordo*], at each indication he uses the chrism to make a cross with his right thumb on the head of the one being consecrated. . . . Then he puts the ring on the next-to-last finger of his hand, while saying why the ring is being given. . . . Then he gives him the staff of holy governance.

The anointing of the bishop's hands makes its appearance around the year 900 in a pontifical from Cahors, which also gives the formulas for the two rites of anointing as well as for the bestowal of ring and crozier.[70]

---

68. *Ge* 147–48 and 155–56; *Missale Francorum* 25–26 and 31–32.

69. *Hincmari archiepiscopi Remensis epist. 29 ad Adventium episcopum Metensem* (PL 126:186–88); critical text and commentary in M. Andrieu, "Le sacre épiscopal d'après Hincmar de Reims," *RHE* 48 (1953) 22–73.

70. The bestowal of crozier and ring is attested in Spain at the beginning of the eighth century by Isidore of Seville, *De ecclesiasticis officiis*, Lib. II, c. 5, no. 12 (PL 83:783–84): "Huic autem dum consecratur datur baculus . . . datur et annulus." The Fourth Council of Toledo (633), can. 28, attests to the same practice: H. Bruns, *Canones apostolorum et conciliorum* (n. 17), 1:231–32.

In about 823–25 Amalarius appealed to an already firmly established Gallican usage for the anointing of a priest's hands, which he connected with Numbers 3:3: "Hunc morem tenent episcopi nostri; manus presbyterorum ungunt de oleo."[71] He made no reference, however, to the giving of chalice and paten, which was a rite of recent origin when the monk of Mainz incorporated it in his pontifical in 950. It was likewise in the tenth century that the practice of giving the Book of the Gospels to the deacon was introduced, as well as the formulas for the vesting of priest and deacon that became part of the Mainz Pontifical.

2. *The Romano-Frankish Ritual of Minor Orders*

The old Roman liturgy had conferred the orders of lector, acolyte, and subdeacon by giving book, linen bag, and chalice, respectively, and accompanying the action with a simple blessing. The Roman-German Pontifical, however, has a new ritual for minor orders. It contains five similar *ordines* for the conferring of the orders of porter, lector, exorcist, acolyte, and subdeacon. To the porter the bishop entrusts the keys of the church; to the reader the Lectionary; to the exorcist the book of exorcisms. To the acolyte he now gives not the linen bag for carrying the *sancta* for the Eucharistic fraction but a processional torch and an empty cruet for presenting the wine at Mass. The subdeacon receives the empty chalice and paten, the cruets, the basin and towel. These same rites would be followed in the Roman liturgy until 1972.

The introduction into Rome of the ritual for minor orders that was followed in the Frankish lands represented a double innovation: it revived orders that had long since fallen into disuse (porter and exorcist), and it provided a detailed and relatively developed formulary for each of the five minor orders.

But that which was an innovation in Rome at the end of the tenth century had been traditional in the Frankish territories ever since the seventh. We find this ritual in the *Missale Francorum* and, minus the order of acolyte, in the Old Gelasian Sacramentary.[72] The seventh-century Frankish sacramentaries in turn drew upon a still older source, the famous apocryphon entitled *Statuta ecclesiae antiqua*,[73] for the rite and formula

---

71. Amalarius, *Liber officialis* II, 13 (Hanssens 2:227).

72. Here are the sources of the ritual for minor orders as found in *PRG*. Porter: *Ge* 748–49; *Missale Francorum* 9–10. Lector: *Ge* 751 (prayer); *Missale Francorum* 13 (prayer). Exorcist: *Ge* 752–53; *Missale Francorum* 14–15. Acolyte: Sacramentary of Angoulême, ed. Cagin, 2069 (first prayer); *Missale Francorum* 11 (second prayer); Sacramentary of Corbie: PL 78:219 (third prayer). Subdiaconate: *Ge* 754–55; *Missale Francorum* 19–20. —On ordination as acolyte see A. Snijders, "Acolytus cum ordinatur, eine historische Studie," *SE* 9 (1957) 163–98.

73. *Statuta ecclesiae antiqua*, ed. C. Munier (Paris: Presses Universitaires de France, 1960), 96–99. See B. Botte, "Le rituel des ordinations des *Statuta ecclesiae antiqua*," *RTAM* 11 (1939), 223–41.

used in conferring each of the orders. The *Statuta* was attributed to the fourth Council of Carthage (398), but must have come into existence in Southern Gaul at the end of the fifth century. Whatever the nature and value of its sources, the *Statuta* as such was a purely archaizing creation, since at that period some of the orders did not exist everywhere or were no longer in use.

It must be noted, however, that neither the *Statuta* nor the Frankish sacramentaries required the successive reception of each of the minor orders by candidates for the diaconate. The Gelasian Sacramentary reproduces a letter of Pope Zosimus (417–18) in which he says:

> If a person has been enrolled from childhood among the ministers of the Church, he must remain a lector until he is twenty; if an adult desires to enter the divine service, he is to remain a lector or an exorcist for five years; then he is to be ordained either an acolyte or a subdeacon; he is to remain in this order for four years and then, if he is worthy, he is to receive the blessing for the diaconate.[74]

The obligation to receive all the orders in succession does not predate the eleventh century.

3. *The Ritual for Clerical Tonsure*

The *Ordo ad faciendum clericum* (no. 3) had undergone extensive development since the Gregorian Sacramentary; the one prayer of the latter has now become an invitatory (*prefatio*) at the beginning of the new ritual. The latter has two parts: the vesting, which is followed by the prayer "Omnipotens sempiterne Deus," and the tonsure, which is accompanied by the verse "Dominus pars" and the antiphon "Tu es qui restitues." This is followed by the recitation of the entire psalm "Domini est terra" and the antiphon "Hic accipiet." The prayer "Praesta quaesumus" concludes the rite.[75]

The ritual for clerical tonsure in the Romano-German Pontifical is dependent on the Supplement that was added to the Gregorian Sacramentary in about 800. This means that by the end of the eighth century in the Frankish territories the old Gregorian prayer *Ad clericum faciendum* had already become an invitatory and that the recitation of the "Dominus pars" and the singing of Psalm 24, "Domini est terra," was already traditional.

---

74. Zosimus, *Epist. 9 ad Hesychium Salonen.* (PL 56:572–73). — See A. Chavasse, *Le Sacramentaire gélasien* (n. 67), 13.

75. *Gr* 1246–50.

II. THE RITUAL OF ORDINATION FROM THE THIRTEENTH TO THE TWENTIETH CENTURY

Between the introduction of the Romano-Frankish liturgy into Rome and the recasting of the ritual of ordinations in 1968, this ritual underwent only secondary developments. The first printed edition of the Roman Pontifical (1485) simply put its seal of approval on the final additions that William Durandus had made to the ritual used from the tenth to the twelfth century. Here are the changes introduced at that time.

1. Concelebration

The Mass of concelebration at an episcopal consecration is attested for around 1200 by the Pontifical of Apamea and by Innocent III; the practice may already have been a longstanding one in Rome. The pontifical of the second half of the thirteenth century says explicitly: "When the pontiff comes to the altar after the offertory, the bishop who has just been consecrated and is to concelebrate with the consecrating celebrant draws near to the corner of the altar."[76] In the case of new priests the rubric is less assertive: "The priests come to the altar and take their places, standing at the right and left of the altar with their Missals, and they all read in a low voice as if they were celebrating."[77] The new bishop and the new priests receive the Body of the Lord from the hands of their consecrator, and the chalice from the deacon.[78]

2. Elevation of the Subdiaconate to the Rank of a Major Order

It was toward the end of the twelfth century that the subdiaconate began to be regarded as a major order; Peter Cantor (d. 1179) says: "De novo, institutum est subdiaconatum esse ordinem sacrum."[79] The ritual for the subdiaconate nonetheless always remained the ritual for a minor order, since it was conferred by the giving of the chalice and not by an imposition of hands. Certain secondary rites, however, gradually began to give special emphasis to the subdiaconate: first, the bestowal of maniple and alb,[80] then the singing of the litanies,[81] and finally the opening address "Filii dilectissimi, ad sacrum subdiaconatus ordinem promovendi . . . huc accedite," which appeared for the first time in the Roman Pontifical of 1485.

---

76. Andrieu, *PR* 2:365.

77. *Ibid.,* 2:349.

78. *Ibid.,* 2:350 and 366.

79. PL 205:184.

80. Andrieu, *PR* 1 (Roman Pontifical of the Twelfth Century), 129. — The formulas of the PR of Clement VIII had appeared in the Pontifical of the Roman Curia (Andrieu, *PR* 2:335–36).

3. *The Innovations of Durandus of Mende*

There is no need to explain here how the pontifical that William Durandus (d. 1298) composed for his diocese of Mende became the basis for the Pontifical of the Roman Church. It is appropriate, however, to point out the decisive role that the bishop of Mende played in the form taken by the ritual of ordinations from his time forward. In this area, except for the addition made to the ritual of the subdiaconate in the fifteenth century, the Roman Church until 1968 followed the Pontifical of William Durandus almost word for word.[82]

A first innovation was the addresses given by the bishop before conferring each of the orders from ostiariate to presbyterate. Until that time the pontificals had simply specified the functions of each order, and the bishop had improvised an instruction thereon, based on the Pseudo-Isidorean treatise *De officiis septem graduum*. A propos of the lector, for example, this treatise said: "The lector is to read in behalf of him who preaches, and to proclaim the readings and bless bread and all the new fruits."[83] In these addresses William Durandus showed a keen sense of the tradition as he made skillful use of various sources. His other interventions were not all as fortunate. The new priests who concelebrated the Mass of their ordination no longer received communion from the chalice. Furthermore, the bishop of Mende showed little liking for silence: thus he prescribed words to accompany the imposition of hands in the ordination of deacons and the consecration of bishops and prescribed the *Veni Sancte Spiritus*[84] to be sung during the anointings of priests and bishops. Finally, he multiplied complementary rites; at the end of the consecration of a bishop came the blessing and bestowal of miter and gloves, the enthronement of the new bishop, even outside his own cathedral, and the *Te Deum*; at the end of a presbyteral ordination the singing of the response "Iam non dicam," the profession of faith using the Apostles' Creed, a second imposition of hands giving the power to forgive sins, the unfolding of the chasuble, the promise of obedience to the bishop and his successors, and a final admonition "Quia res."[85] This profusion of gestures and

---

81. Andrieu, *PR* 3 (Pontifical of William Durandus), 349.

82. *Ibid.* For the additions—which are clearly set off typographically—see especially 388–89 (bishop) and 371–73 (priest).

83. This treatise is reproduced in *PRG*, no. 14; see E. Dekkers, *Clavis patrum latinorum* (SE 3; Steenbrugge: St.-Pietersabdij, 1961²), no. 1222.

84. In the PR this was replaced by the *Veni creator,* which was already used for the ordination of priests, but at a different point, in the Pontifical of the Roman Curia; see Andrieu, *PR* 3:346.

85. Note further that it was William Durandus who introduced clerical tonsure among the ordinations and prescribed that it be celebrated after the singing of the *Kyrie* (Andrieu, *PR* 3:336). The giving of the surplice as clerical vestment had appeared some years earlier in the long version of the Pontifical of the Roman Curia (Andrieu, *PR* 2:327).

formulas, sometimes displaying an artificial symbolism (like that of the chasuble that was at first left folded up in the back), further weighed down the Romano-German Pontifical, which itself had already overloaded the ancient Roman ritual.

§5. The New Ritual for Ordinations

BIBLIOGRAPHY

Text
De Ordinatione diaconi, presbyteri et episcopi, editio typica (Vatican Polyglot Press, 1968).
Ordination of Deacons, Priests, and Bishops in The Rites of the Catholic Church (New York: Pueblo, 1980).

Studies
P. Jounel, "Le nouveau rituel d'ordination," *LMD* no. 98 (1969) 63–72.
M. Cnudde, "L'ordination des diacres," *ibid.*, 73–94.
B. Kleinheyer, "L'ordination des prêtres," *ibid.*, 95–112.
B. Botte, "L'ordination de l'évêque," *ibid.*, 113–26.
W. J. Grisbrooke, "Les réformes récentes des rites d'ordination dans les Eglises," *LMD* no. 139 (1979) 7–30.
G. Wainwright, "Prières récentes d'ordination dans quelques Eglises chrétiennes," *ibid.*, 73–100.
"De ordinatione diaconi, presbyteri et episcopi. Commento al nuovo rito delle Ordinazioni," *EL* 83 (1969) 5–98.

The conception of the sacrament of orders that the Church had in the early centuries has been restored in our own twentieth century. This restoration was undertaken by Pius XII. He began by making it clear that the two bishops who accompany a bishop as he consecrates a new member of that order are themselves consecrators and not simple assistants, as the terminology of the Roman Pontifical implied.[86] He went on to decide that the imposition of hands and the prayer accompanying it are the essential rites in the sacred orders of diaconate, presbyterate, and episcopate.[87] Finally, he reminded the bishops that in addition to their responsibility for their respective dioceses, they are collegially responsible for the evangelization of the world.[88]

---

86. Pius XII, Apostolic Constitution *Episcopalis consecrationis* (1944): *AAS* 36 (1944) 131.
87. Pius XII, Apostolic Constitution *Sacramentum Ordinis* (1947): *AAS* 40 (1948) 5.
88. Pius XII, Encyclical *Fidei donum* (1957): *AAS* 49 (1957) 237: "While each bishop is pastor in the full sense only of the part of the flock that is entrusted to his care, his position as legitimate successor of the apostles by divine institution gives him a share of the responsibility for the apostolic mission of the entire Church."

The Second Vatican Council would subsequently integrate this vision of sacred orders into its own vision of the mystery of the Church and of the ministries carried on therein in the service of the people of God. The episcopate, whose sacramental nature is affirmed, makes the man who receives it a member of the college of the successors of the apostles, while the presbyterate introduces its recipients into the college of co-workers of the bishop, that is, the presbyterium. Episcopate and presbyterate are the two degrees of priesthood. Deacons are specifically the servants of the bishop and the Christian community. The diaconate is not by its nature a stage in a journey to priesthood but can be exercised as a permanent ministry. For this reason it can be conferred on married men.[89] Nonetheless, the *cursus* established in the Middle Ages remains: one must be a deacon in order to receive presbyteral ordination and a presbyter in order to become a bishop.

Pope Paul VI completed the restoration of the sacrament of orders by suppressing the subdiaconate and minor orders.[90] He replaced them with ministries bestowed not by "ordination" but by "institution," in keeping with the terminology of the *Apostolic Tradition* of Hippolytus; these ministries are in the service of the Word (lectors) and of the Eucharist (acolytes). A man becomes a member of the clergy only when he receives the diaconate.[91] Tonsure, which used to make men clerics, has in effect been suppressed; it has been replaced by a simple rite of admission for candidates to the diaconate and presbyterate.

These principles, which controlled the revision of ordinations at the juridical level, also guided the revision of their rites.

I. THE REVISED ORDINATION RITES

1. *Change of Terminology*

The revised rites of ordination were promulgated by Paul VI in his Apostolic Constitution *Pontificalis Romani* of June 18, 1968.[92] The first point to be noted is a change of terminology. In the past the Roman Pontifical spoke of priests and deacons being ordained but of bishops being consecrated; now the term "ordination" is applied to all three degrees of the sacrament in order to bring out its unity. The old sacramentaries for

---

89. Paul VI, Motu Proprio *Ad pascendum* (August 15, 1972): *AAS* 64 (1972) 534 (*EDIL* 2894–2912 = *DOL* 319 nos. 2576–91).

90. Paul VI, Motu Proprio *Ministeria quaedam* (August 15, 1972): *AAS* 64 (1972) 529–34 (*EDIL* 2877–93 = *DOL* 340 nos. 2922–38).

91. Motu Proprio *Ad pascendum* (n. 89).

92. *AAS* 60 (1968) 369–73 (*EDIL* 1080–88 = *DOL* 324 nos. 2606–12).

their part made no distinction, but spoke indifferently of *benedictio, ordinatio* or *consecratio* in their titles and then always used *consecratio* for the essential rite of each order.[93]

2. *Structure of the Rites*

The three ordinations of bishop, priest, and deacon are identical in structure. They are celebrated between the Liturgy of the Word and the Liturgy of the Eucharist. In France, however, the presentation and election of the ordinand can take place at the beginning, before the singing of the *Gloria in excelsis*. A wide selection of readings prepares the congregation for celebrating the sacrament in light of the Word of God.

The opening rites consist in the presentation and election of the ordinand, the bishop's homily, which is addressed first to the people and then to the ordinand, and finally the questions addressed to the latter. The text proposed as a model for these three addresses is based on the conciliar Constitution on the Church. In the past, only the consecration of a bishop began with an examination. Now a similar examination marks the beginning of each of the three ordinations. After the examination, the litany of the saints is sung while the ordinand prostrates himself on the floor.

The consecratory rites consist of an imposition of hands, which is done in silence, and of an immediately following prayer, the two forming an organic whole. The prayer, which is no longer in the form of a preface, can be sung in its entirety by the bishop. It is not interrupted by any other rite.

The explanatory rites have been simplified, and the formulas accompanying them have been either eliminated or radically altered so as to do away with a medieval allegorism that has become unintelligible today. The vesting in particular is no longer performed by the bishop, and it is done in silence, for while the wearing of liturgical vestments undeniably has a general symbolism, it would be stretching things to assign a particular meaning to each vestment of the three sacred ministers. The kiss of peace concludes the ordination.

The Eucharist is normally celebrated by all the bishops and priests present. They are assisted by the deacons.

II. THE ORDINATIONS OF BISHOP, PRIEST, AND DEACON

Sunday is the preferred day for the ordinations of bishop, priest, and deacon, since they call for the largest possible attendance of the faithful.

---

93. *Le* 942, 948, 952; 21, 27, 35; *Ge* 757, 761, 766; *Gr* 21, 27, 30.

It is appropriate that a bishop be ordained in a church of the diocese for which he will henceforth be responsible.

1. *Ordination of a Bishop*

When the principal consecrator and the other consecrating bishops have taken their place, the ordinand is presented by two priests in the name of the local Church, if in fact it is to a residential see that he has been appointed. The papal letter of appointment is then read and the entire assembly gives its consent to it. The homily of the principal consecrator calls attention to the function of a bishop, which is to preach, intercede for the people, and lead the flock, but also, since he is a member of the episcopal college, to be solicitous for all the Churches. In the examination to which he then turns, the consecrator repeats the essential points made in his homily, while adding an explicit call for obedience to the pope.

After the litanies of the saints, which are sung over the prostrate ordinand, all the bishops present impose hands on him; the principal consecrator then places the open Book of the Gospels on the candidate's head, and two deacons hold it in place there during the prayer of consecration. The prayer that had been used in the Roman Church ever since the fifth century has now been replaced by the prayer from the *Apostolic Tradition*. This prayer, which has always been used in the Eastern rites of Syria and Egypt, expresses better than the old one the theology of the episcopate that is formulated in Chapter III of the Constitution *Lumen gentium*.[94] The essential part of the prayer, which is said by all of the bishops, reads thus:

> So now pour out upon this chosen one
> that power which is from you,
> the governing Spirit
> whom you gave to your beloved Son, Jesus Christ,
> the Spirit given by him to the holy apostles,
> who founded the Church in every place to be your temple,
> for the unceasing glory and praise of your name.

"The language and teaching" of this prayer "have their roots in the entire early Christian tradition."[95] Christ, the supreme pastor and priest, chose the apostles and strengthened them for their mission by giving them the power of the same Holy Spirit with which he himself was filled; their

---

94. English translation of the Coptic text in O.H.E. Burmester (n. 21), 110–14. French translation of the Syriac text, which is used only for the consecration of the patriarch in the Syrian Church of Antioch, in *OS* 8 (1963) 202–4. In the Coptic and Syriac versions the original text in the *Traditio apostolica* has undergone extensive development.

95. A. Rose, "La prière de consécration pour l'ordination épiscopale," *LMD* no. 98 (1969) 128. Rose's article shows how this text is in close touch with the sources of revelation.

mission and grace have been passed down from century to century through episcopal consecration, which is a "true sign and cause, that is, a sacrament, of the supreme ministry and priesthood."[96]

The anointing of the new bishop's head with sacred chrism begins the explanatory rites. May God "pour out on you the oil of mystical anointing and enrich you with spiritual blessings."

The anointing is followed by the presentation of the Book of the Gospels to the new bishop: "Receive the Gospel and preach the Word of God with unfailing patience and sound teaching."

The principal consecrator then puts the ring on the ring finger of the new bishop's right hand: "Take this ring, the seal of your fidelity. With faith and love protect the bride of God, his holy Church."

In silence he then puts the miter on the head of the new bishop. Lastly he gives him his staff, saying: "Take this staff as a sign of your pastoral office: keep watch over the whole flock in which the Holy Spirit has appointed you to shepherd the Church of God."

If the new bishop has been ordained in his own diocese, he is now led by his consecrator to the cathedral, where, after exchanging the kiss of peace with all the bishops present, he presides over the concelebration. If the ordination takes place in another diocese, the principal consecrator invites the new bishop to take the first place among the concelebrating bishops; during the Eucharistic concelebration he likewise takes first place after the principal consecrator, who presides.

When the prayer after communion has been said, the new bishop, accompanied by his consecrators, walks through the church and blesses the people; then, if he has been presiding at the concelebration, he gives the final blessing.

2. *Ordination of a Priest*

The ordination begins with the summoning of the ordinand and his presentation to the bishop by a priest appointed to this task. The bishop asks this priest whether the candidate has the requisite qualifications. On receiving an affirmative answer and then the consent of the assembly, the bishop says: "We rely on the help of the Lord God and our Savior Jesus Christ, and we choose this man, our brother, for priesthood in the presbyteral order."

In his homily the bishop tells the people of the functions proper to a presbyter in the Church of Christ, and then speaks to the ordinand himself of the spirit in which he must carry out his functions, "united with the bishop and subject to him." The examination emphasizes the point

---

96. J. Lecuyer, "La prière d'ordination de l'évêque," *Nouvelle revue theologique* 89 (1967) 605.

that the presbyter's role is to be "with the help of the Holy Spirit . . . a conscientious fellow worker with the bishops in caring for the Lord's flock." His service consists in the ministry of the Word, the celebration of the mysteries, and union with the person of the high priest, Jesus Christ. It must be carried out in communion with the bishop and his successors and with "respect and obedience" to them.

After the litanies of the saints have been sung over the prostrate ordinand, the bishop imposes hands on his head, and then all the priests present do the same. These other priests then group themselves around the bishop until the end of the ordination prayer. For this prayer the old formulary has been kept, using the text as given in the ancient sacramentaries. The only important change in it comes at the end. The essential part has no variants:

> Almighty Father,
> grant to this servant of yours
> the dignity of the priesthood (*presbyterii dignitatem*).
> Renew within him the Spirit of holiness.
> As a co-worker with the order of bishops
> may he be faithful to the ministry (*secundi meriti munus*)
> that he receives from you, Lord God,
> and be to others a model of right conduct.

The conclusion makes it clear that the presbyteral ministry is both ecclesial and missionary: "May he be faithful in working with the order of bishops, so that the words of the Gospel may reach the ends of the earth, and the family of nations, made one in Christ, may become God's one, holy people."

All the rites that follow are simply explanatory, their purpose being "to render explicit in gestures and symbols what is implicitly contained in the essential rite."[97] First, then, some priests help the new priest to don stole and chasuble. The man then returns to the bishop so that the bishop may consecrate his hands with sacred chrism and pray that Jesus would preserve him "to sanctify the Christian people and to offer sacrifice to God."

The deacon who will assist at the altar now brings the paten, containing bread, and the cup, into which he has poured wine and water. He presents these to the bishop, who in turn gives them to the newly ordained priest with the words: "Accept from the holy people of God the gifts to be offered to him. Know what you are doing, and imitate the mystery you celebrate: model your life on the mystery of the Lord's cross."

The bishop then gives him the kiss of peace, and if circumstances permit, the other priests do the same.

---

97. B. Botte, "L'ordination de l'évêque," *LMD* no. 98 (1969) 114.

In the concelebration of the Eucharist the new priest takes first place among the priests.

3. *Ordination of a Deacon*

Whether the man being ordained will be a permanent deacon or move on to the priesthood, and whether he is a married man or a celibate, the rite of ordination is the same except for a variant in the introductory section. After the homily, one who is a celibate is asked by the bishop to make a commitment to lifelong celibacy "for the sake of the kingdom and in lifelong service to God and mankind." If the ordinand is married, the French ritual calls for the bishop to ask the ordinand's wife whether she accepts "what this ordination will entail for her conjugal and familial life."

After the summoning of the ordinand and his presentation to the bishop, the bishop proceeds to the election: "We rely on the help of the Lord God and our Savior Jesus Christ, and we choose this man, our brother, for the order of deacons."

In his homily the bishop explains to the people the mission of a deacon, which is to "help the bishop and his body of priests as a minister of the Word, of the altar, and of charity. He will make himself a servant of all." He then lists the functions specific to a deacon. He reminds the ordinand himself that, in accordance with the etymological meaning of the order he is receiving, he is to "serve Jesus Christ, who was known among his disciples as the one who served others." In the examination that follows, the bishop asks the ordinand whether he is truly willing to carry out this ministry and proclaim the faith "in word and action." He asks, among other things, whether the candidate is "resolved to maintain and deepen a spirit of prayer appropriate to your way of life and, in keeping with what is required of you, to celebrate faithfully the liturgy of the hours for the Church and for the whole world."

After the litanies of the saints have been sung over the prostrate ordinand, the bishop imposes his hands on his head and then says the prayer of consecration. The old formulary has been retained in its substance, but "the extent and importance of the Levitical typology have been reduced, and mention of the seven co-workers of the apostles has been inserted; the list of virtues has been revised, and reference to Christ the servant has replaced the final allusion to promotion to a higher order."[98] The central invocation has remained unchanged:

> Lord,
> send forth upon him the Holy Spirit,
> that he may be strengthened

---

98. M. Cnudde, "L'ordination des diacres," *ibid.*, 88–89.

by the gift of your sevenfold grace
to carry out faithfully the work of the ministry.

When the ordination prayer has been said, the deacons or priests help the new deacon to put on a stole and then a dalmatic. He then receives the Book of the Gospels from the bishop, who says: "Receive the Gospel of Christ, whose herald you now are. Believe what you read, teach what you believe, and practice what you teach."

Finally, the bishop gives the kiss of peace to the newly ordained, who exchanges it with the other deacons.

During the Eucharistic liturgy the new deacon exercises his ministry: he brings the bread and wine to the bishop and serves him at the altar; he helps him in distributing communion after having himself first received under both species.

4. *Admission to Candidacy for Ordination as Deacons and Priests*

The rite of admission to candidacy for ordination as deacons and priests is celebrated when the candidates have reached a maturity of purpose and are shown to have the necessary qualifications.

Those professed in clerical religious institutes are not bound to the celebration of this rite.

The intention of receiving orders is to be expressed publicly by the candidates. The bishop or the major superior of a clerical religious institute accepts their intention publicly.[99]

The rite of admission is celebrated in a church or in some other place, during a liturgy of the Word that may or may not be followed by the Eucharist.

In his homily the bishop explains the meaning of the rite that he is performing. At the end of it he tells the candidates to come forward when their names are called and to manifest their intention before the Church. He asks them if they are resolved "in response to the Lord's call . . . to complete [their] preparation so that in due time [they] will be ready to be ordained for the ministry of the Church" and if they are resolved "to prepare yourselves in mind and spirit to give faithful service to Christ the Lord and his body, the Church." On receiving their positive answers, he declares that the Church welcomes their intention with joy. He then urges the congregation to pray. A series of intentions concerning the candidates are proposed, and the bishop concludes by calling down the Lord's blessing on these individuals.

---

99. *Ordination of Deacons, Priests, and Bishops*, chapter 1 (*Rites* 2:39).

Chapter V

Instituted Ministries

P. Jounel

BIBLIOGRAPHY

Documents
> *De Institutione Lectorum et Acolythorum*, editio typica (Vatican Polyglot Press, 1972).
> *Institution of Readers and Acolytes*, in *The Rites of the Catholic Church* 2 (New York: Pueblo, 1980), 3–22. New translation of the introductions to the several chapters in *DOL* 343 nos. 2940–48.

Studies
> R. Béraudy, "Les ministres institués dans *Ministeria quaedam* et *Ad pascendum*," *LMD* no. 115 (1973) 86–96.
> P. Jounel, "Les ministères non ordonnés dans l'Eglise," *Notitiae* 18 (1982) 144–55; reprinted in *LMD* no. 149 (1982) 91–106.
> G. P[asqualetti], "Commentarium de nova disciplina et ritibus circa ministeria," *Notitiae* 9 (1973) 18–33.

In his Motu Proprio *Ministeria quaedam* of August 15, 1972, Pope Paul VI suppressed the minor orders and subdiaconate, as well as tonsure, in the Latin Church,[1] but he kept the offices attached to these orders. The fundamental novelty in all this is that these offices are conferred no longer by an ordination but by institution in, or appointment to, an ongoing function or ministry, in accordance with the practice attested at Rome in the third century by the *Apostolic Tradition*.[2] The papal document thus makes a clear distinction between ministries for which a person is ordained by an imposition of the bishop's hands and all other

---

1. Motu Proprio *Ministeria quaedam*: *AAS* 64 (1972) 529 (*EDIL* 162 = *DOL* 340 no. 2923.
2. Hippolytus of Rome, *Traditio apostolica* 10–11 (Botte 30).

ministries, whether liturgical or nonliturgical, in the people of God. Among the latter ministries, two are the object of an institution: those of the lector and the acolyte. In addition to these two instituted ministries, which are universal in the Latin Church, episcopal conferences can consider applying to the Apostolic See for permission to establish others—that of catechist, for example—in their own territories.

1. *Institution*

Institution, which takes place during a liturgical celebration, bestows a permanent function on the layperson who receives it. It is given not for a limited period but for good, even if circumstances prevent the person from exercising it any longer. In addition, it brings responsibilities apart from liturgical service. Thus a reader is called upon (according to the papal document) to "take care of preparing other faithful who by a temporary appointment are to read the Scriptures in liturgical celebrations." According to the rite, he also receives a catechetical mission to prepare his brothers and sisters for the reception of the sacraments; he can therefore be entrusted with preparing parents for their child's baptism or engaged couples for their marriage. He can also be given responsibility for instructing the faithful of a parish or group in the understanding of the Scriptures. In like manner, an acolyte can be given, in addition to his liturgical functions, the duty of "instructing other people who by temporary appointment assist the priest or deacon in liturgical celebrations." The ministry of lector may therefore be fittingly described as "the service of the Word" and the ministry of acolyte as "the service of the Eucharist."

Finally, institution in a ministry demands of the person that his manner of life be consistent with the service he has accepted.

2. *The Two Instituted Ministries*

The ministries of the Word and the altar, which in the past were the responsibility of lector, acolyte, and subdeacon, are two important functions that must be continued. As a matter of fact, the tradition had already turned the subdeacon into the principal reader (he read the epistle) and the principal acolyte (he brought the bread and wine to the altar at the offertory). Since this order had no specific responsibility of its own, its suppression has made the functions of lector and acolyte respectively stand out more clearly.

a) *Institution in the Service of the Word*

Institution in the service of the Word is accomplished by the bishop (or major superior of religious) during a Mass or a liturgy of the Word. A selection of readings is proposed for this celebration. Institution always includes a brief presentation of the candidates. In the homily that precedes the institution proper, the bishop explains the nature of the mission about to be given and brings out its spirit. In the homily offered to the bishop as a model we read:

> As readers and bearers of God's word, you will assist in this mission [of preaching the Gospel to the whole world], and so take on a special office within the Christian community; you will be given a responsibility in the service of the faith, which is rooted in the word of God. You will proclaim that word in the liturgical assembly, instruct children and adults in the faith, and prepare them to receive the sacraments worthily. You will bring the message of salvation to those who have not yet received it. Thus with your help men and women will come to know God our Father and his Son Jesus Christ, whom he sent, and so be able to reach eternal life.

The bishop then calls upon them "to accept it [God's Word] yourselves" and to "meditate on it constantly." Finally, after a prayer over those he is instituting, he gives each a Bible while saying: "Take this book of holy Scripture and be faithful in handing on the word of God, so that it may grow strong in the hearts of his people."

b) *Institution in the Service of the Eucharist*

Institution in the service of the Eucharist takes place during the celebration of the Mass, after the reading of the gospel. A selection of readings is given for this service of the word. After the candidates have been presented, the bishop explains in his homily that an acolyte serves the body of Christ both in the Eucharist and in the life of the Church. According to the model homily proposed, the bishop says, for example:

> Dear sons in Christ, as people chosen for the ministry of acolyte, you will have a special role in the Church's ministry. The summit and source of the Church's life is the eucharist, which builds up the Christian community and makes it grow. It is your responsibility to assist priests and deacons in carrying out their ministry, and as special ministers to give holy communion to the faithful at the liturgy and to the sick.

The bishop then urges the candidates to make their lives a spiritual sacrifice in union with the sacrifice of Christ and to show true love for the body of Christ, which is the Church, and in particular for the weak and the sick.

After praying over those whom he is instituting, the bishop gives each a vessel containing bread or wine for the Eucharist and says: "Take this vessel with bread (wine) for the celebration of the eucharist. Make your life worthy of your service at the table of the Lord and of his Church."

The new acolytes then present the bread and wine at the altar for the offertory.

3. Noninstituted Ministries

In addition to the instituted ministries there are some others, liturgical or caritative, that laypersons exercise. The liturgical ministries are described in the *General Instruction of the Roman Missal.*[3] One among them has been the object of a special set of regulations: that of the extraordinary minister of the Eucharist. According to the Instruction *Immensae caritatis,*[4] this ministry requires a delegation: the bishop can appoint some of the faithful by name to serve as extraordinary ministers of the Eucharist; these individuals can give communion to themselves, distribute communion to others, and bring it to the sick in their homes, if no priest, deacon, or acolyte is available to do so or if, during Mass, there is a large number of communicants. In addition, the bishop can allow any priest exercising his sacred functions to appoint some fit person to distribute communion in a particular case, if this seems truly necessary. If time allows, the person chosen should receive a delegation according to a ritual established for this purpose.[5]

---

3. *GIRM* 67–68 (*DOL* 208 nos. 1457–58).

4. Instruction *Immensae caritatis* (January 29, 1973): *AAS* 65 (1973) 264 (*EDIL* 2967–82 = *DOL* nos. 2073–88).

5. *Rite of Commissioning Special Ministers of Holy Communion* in *Rites* 2:165–67, with new translation of Introductions in *DOL* 343 nos. 2949–52.

Chapter VI

Marriage

J. Evenou

BIBLIOGRAPHY

Sources
   Le 1105–10.
   Ge 1443–55.
   Gr 833–39.
   Martène: M 690–706.
   Denz 2:364–82.
   A. Raes, *Le mariage. Sa célébration et sa spiritualité dans les Eglises d'Orient* (Irénikon
      collection; Chevetogne, 1959).

Studies
   R. Metz, *La consécration des vierges dans l'Eglise romaine* (Bibliothèque de l'Institut
      de Droit canonique de l'Université de Strasbourg 4; Paris: Presses Universitaires
      de France, 1954), Appendix: "Le rituel du mariage" (367–410).
   K. Ritzer, *Formen, Riten und religiöses Brauchtum der Eheschliessung in den christ-
      lichen Kirchen des ersten Jahrtausends* (LQF 38; Münster: Aschendorff, 1962,
      1982²). French translation: *Le mariage dans les Eglises chrétiennes du Ier au XIe
      siècle* (LO 45; Paris: Cerf, 1970).
   J. B. Molin and P. Mutembe, *Le Rituel du mariage en France du XIIe au XVIe siècle*
      (Théologie historique 26; Paris: Beauchesne, 1974).
   "*L'Ordo matrimonii*," *EL* 93 (1979) 245–514.
   A. Nocent, "Contribution à l'étude du rituel du mariage," in *Eulogia. Miscellanea
      liturgica . . . Neunheuser* (Studia Anselmiana 68; Rome, 1979), 243–66.
   K. Stevenson, *Nuptial Blessing. A Study of Christian Marriage Rites* (Alcuin Club
      Collections 64; London: S.P.C.K., 1982).
   La celebrazione cristiana del matrimonio. Simboli e testi (Studia Anselmiana 93,
      Analecta liturgica 11; Rome, 1986).

The sacrament of marriage is a complex matter, since it brings into
play interpersonal, familial, social, and ecclesial relationships. Moreover,

185

its celebration had been characterized from the beginning by an extraordinary variety of juridical and canonical arrangements and of usages and rites, a variety that the Church acknowledged and accepted even though it sought unity in the other areas of its cult.[1] This attitude is really not surprising, since the celebration of marriage is so closely bound up with the social practices that accompany the establishment of home and hearth in the various countries.

§1. The First Three Centuries

The Christians of the first generations looked at marriage in the light of the teaching of Christ and the apostles. In the celebration of it they conformed to the practices of their respective countries, to the extent that these practices were not opposed to the Christian faith. "Christians do not differ from other men and women in country or language or customs. . . . They marry like everyone else."[2] The anonymous author of the *Letter to Diognetus* may not expressly intend to refer to the ceremonial of marriage, but he nonetheless describes the de facto situation in the second century.

1. *Marriage in the Roman World*

Whatever the differences in detail from region to region, the people throughout the Mediterranean basin in the first three centuries of the Christian era had fundamentally the same conception of marriage and of how it was to be celebrated.

According to Roman law[3] of the imperial age, marriage consisted essentially in a mutual consent (*consensus*): "It is consent that makes a marriage valid."[4] A legally recognized exchange of consents required only a few conditions: age, permission from parents, and absence of impediments created by kinship, affinity, or civil law. The same was true of the promise of marriage (*sponsalia*). The traditional ceremonial of marriage was thus optional.

The definitions given by jurists should not, however, make us under-

---

1. The Council of Trent expressly sanctioned this diversity in a passage that is cited by the Second Vatican Council (*VSC* 77 = *DOL* 1 no. 77).

2. *Ad Diognetum* 5, 6, ed. H. I. Marrou, SC 33bis (Paris: Cerf, 1965), 62–63.

3. J. Gaudemet, *Sociétés et mariage* (Strasbourg: Cerdic-Publications, 1980).

4. Ulpian (d. 228), cited in the *Digest* of Justinian: "Nuptiae consensu contrahentium fiunt" (35, 1, 15); "Nuptias non concubitus sed consensus facit" (50, 17, 30). In the view of the Roman jurists it was not the fact of cohabitation but the resolve to live together that gave rise to a marriage.

value the usages and custom of Roman society, for these showed the place occupied by the family cell in the life of the city.

A betrothal, which was clearly distinct from marriage in the third century, was celebrated at a family meal: after the exchange of promises,[5] the fiancé gave the young girl an iron ring, which she wore on the fourth finger of her left hand, and some presents (*arrhae sponsaliciae*) as a pledge of their future union. In the following century, a kiss—added perhaps in the third century—gave juridical value to the promise of marriage.

The marriage ceremony itself had three stages. The first was the dressing of the bride, who was given a crown made from myrtle or orange branches and a yellow veil with red highlights (*flammeum*), which was the distinctive mark of married women. The donning of the veil was so important that *nubere*, "to don the veil," became a synonym for "to marry." The second stage of the ceremony likewise took place in the home of the young girl: the presentation of the bride by a married woman (the *pronuba* who acted as a kind of maid of honor), the consultation (always favorable) of the soothsayers, and, above all, the reading of the contract (*tabulae nuptiales*) in the presence of witnesses who signed it. After the exchange of consents,[6] the *pronuba* delivered the young girl to her husband by having them join hands (*dextrarum iunctio*).[7] A sacrifice to the family gods then preceded the wedding feast. The third stage of the celebration took place in the evening: a procession accompanied the bride to her husband's house; the latter led her into the house in accordance with a detailed ceremonial and then offered her water and fire; the pair were then conducted to the bridal chamber, where the husband removed the bride's cloak, and everyone else withdrew.

2. Marriage Between Christians

Until the Peace of Constantine, the only celebration of marriage that Christians experienced were these rites performed within the family. In a society in which Christians were very much a minority, they did not regard themselves as obliged to depart from the customs of the city in this matter; in fact, they undoubtedly did not even think of doing so. They were content simply to avoid any idolatrous elements in the ceremony (such as the consultation of the soothsayers and the sacrifice[8]) and the licentious aspects of the wedding feast and the procession.

---

5. "Spondesne? — Spondeo" ("Do you promise?" — "I promise").

6. The traditional form at Rome was: "Ubi tu Gaius, ego Gaia."

7. Originally it was the father or guardian of the young girl who did this.

8. Sometimes the crowning was also eliminated because of its use in pagan worship; see Tertullian, *De corona* 13, 4, and 14, 2 (CCL 1:1061 and 1063).

The Church was comfortable with the Roman juridical conception of marriage as effected by consent. Echoing the great jurists of the third century, St. Ambrose stated: "The contract entered into by the spouses constitutes a marriage."[9] It was within this legal framework that the Church would specify its own requirements, the chief of which was the prohibition of divorce, which Roman law allowed. The Church also had to assert its control over the moral conditions for marriages between the faithful. As early as the beginning of the second century we find St. Ignatius of Antioch writing: "It behooves men and women entering into marriage to contract this union with the advice of the bishop, so that their marriage may be in accordance with the Lord and not motivated by passion."[10]

The chief purpose of this recommendation was to dissuade Christians from marrying non-Christians. The permission of the bishop was also to be asked for marriages of clerics and of orphans entrusted to the bishop's care and for marriages not recognized by the law, such as that of a patrician woman with a freedman or a slave. The taking of such steps did not of itself imply any liturgical act. It is not possible to extend to the entire Catholic Church the *professio matrimonii* (announcement of a planned marriage to the community and authorization of it by the community) that Tertullian attests for the Montanist church.[11]

3. Marriage in Christ

There is no evidence before the fourth century of the existence of a liturgical blessing or any participation of a priest in the marriage rites. The faithful were not unaware, however, that the act they were accomplishing according to the customs of the city was transformed from within by their baptism. They knew that they were entering into a union *in Christ* and that, according to the teaching of St. Paul, their union was the sign of a higher union, that of Christ and the Church (Eph 5:32). Evidence of this conviction is Tertullian's treatise *Ad uxorem*[12] and, in iconography, a sarcophagus and a cup (depiction on the bottom of the interior) showing Christ himself crowning two spouses and presiding at the joining of their hands, which are placed on the Book of the Gospels.[13] Thus while

---

9. St. Ambrose, *De institutione virginum* 6 (PL 16:330): "Facit coniugium pactio coniugalis."

10. St. Ignatius of Antioch, *Ad Polycarpum* 5, 2, ed. P. Th. Camelot, SC 10 (Paris: Cerf, 1969), 150–51.

11. Tertullian, *De pudicitia* 4, 4 (CCL 2:1287); *De monogamia* 11, 1–2 (CCL 2:1244).

12. Tertullian, *Ad uxorem* (CCL 1:371–94). On Tertullian's thought see R. Uglione, "Il matrimonio in Tertulliano tra esaltazione e disprezzo," EL 93 (1979) 479–94.

13. See *DACL* 10/2 (1932) 1095 and 1924.

the human gestures remained the same, they were lifted to another plane: "They are but one in the flesh, they are but one in the spirit. . . . Christ sends them his peace. Where the two of them are, Christ is also there."[14]

§2. The Fourth to the Seventh Centuries

BIBLIOGRAPHY

> *Il matrimonio nella società altomedioevale* (2 vols.; Spoleto: Centro italiano di studi sull'alto medioevo, 1977). See especially C. Vogel, "Les rites de la célébration du mariage: leur signification dans la formation du lien durant le haut moyen âge" (1:397–465).

The entire history of Christian marriage prior to the establishment of a nuptial liturgy makes it clear that when such a liturgy did develop after the Peace of Constantine, it was bound to develop on the basis of secular customs. It was inevitable that the blessing of Christ should find visible expression in the blessing that the father of the family or the bishop or a priest invited to the wedding gave, either when the veil was put on the young woman (Rome and Milan), or when she was crowned (in the East) or at the moment of the *dextrarum iunctio* or the moment when the spouses entered the bridal chamber (Gaul, Spain, and the Celtic countries). The Bible, of course, provided examples of prayer and blessings for marriage.

1. Rome and Milan: The "Velatio Nuptialis"

At the end of the fourth century St. Ambrose[15] and Pope Siricius[16] refer to a ceremony that is subsequently described by St. Paulinus of Nola in about 403 in an epithalamium he composed for the marriage of Julian, a lector (and future bishop of Eclanum), son of the bishop of Benevento, and the daughter of the bishop of Capua. Here Julian's father leads the betrothed couple to the altar, and the father of the young girl gives the nuptial blessing to the spouses, whose heads are covered during the entire prayer by a veil (*velum* or *velamen*) that is separate from the *flammeum*.[17]

---

14. Tertullian, *Ad uxorem* II, 8, 7 and 9 (CCL 1:393–94). He also speaks of "this union which the Church arranges, the sacrifice confirms, the blessing consecrates, and the angels celebrate, and which gives the Father joy" (8, 6). Is this to be interpreted as the first witness to a ritual blessing? See H. Crouzel, "Deux textes de Tertullien concernant la procédure et les rites de mariage," *Bulletin de littérature ecclésiastique* 74 (1973) 3–13.

15. St. Ambrose, *Ep.* 19, to Vigilius, Bishop of Trent (PL 16:984): "Cum ipsum coniugium velamine sacerdotali et benedictione sanctificare oporteat."

16. Pope Siricius, *Ep.* 7, to various bishops concerning Jovinian, in the year 390 (PL 13:117): "Nos sane nuptiarum vota non aspernantes accepimus, quibus velamine intersumus."

17. St. Paulinus, *Carmen* 25 (CSEL 30:244–45; Latin text given in Ritzer [see bibliography] 399 [French 419–20]).

As late as the fifth century the blessing seems not to have had a set text. The Verona Sacramentary gives the title *Velatio nuptialis* to this blessing and provides a formulary for it that may go back to the fifth century, though it cannot be attributed to St. Leo, any more than can the formulary for the *velatio virginis*, which is parallel to it.[18]

The nuptial blessing, which used to be sung in the mode of a preface,[19] is, in its form, one of the solemn prayers of the Roman liturgy: it is a consecratory preface, like the ordination prayers, the prayers for the consecration of baptismal water and sacred chrism, and the Eucharistic Prayer itself. It speaks only of the wife, even though at a later time the veil was extended to cover the husband's shoulders as well.[20]

From among all the customs in the marriage ceremony, it was to this one, the veiling, that Rome decided to give liturgical status: like the virgin who is betrothed to Christ, her only spouse, a Christian woman who is being joined to a Christian man in marriage receives a veil from the hands of the Church as a sign of her new state. Using language resembling that found in Roman epigraphy, the blessing paints a picture of a Christian wife; it sets the holy women of the Old Testament before her as models, while at the same time it sees the marriage in the perspective both of Genesis and of the marriage of Christ and the Church; it also asks the grace of fruitfulness for the new wife.

The nuptial blessing was traditionally given during Mass[21] before the celebrant's *Pax Domini* and the kiss of peace, which he gave to the husband and the husband to the wife. The sacramentaries have a special formulary for this Mass; it includes a special preface ("Qui foedera") and *Hanc igitur*. The ancient lectionaries display a fairly wide variety of texts. As a first reading they have 1 Corinthians 6:15-20 ("Glorify God in your bodies"); 1 Corinthians 7:32-35 (marriage and virginity), which was the passage most widely used in the Middle Ages; and Ephesians 5:22-33, which was used much more rarely, although it was to be the only one kept in the Missal of St. Pius V. The gospel most widely used in the lec-

---

18. *Le* 1110 (a reconstruction of the original text is proposed by Ritzer 342–43 [French 421–24]); from the Verona Sacramentary the text passed to the Gelasian (*Ge* 1451). The text in the Gregorian Sacramentary (*Gr* 838) is different in part but the structure is the same.

19. The singing of the blessing was kept in French Missals until the middle of the nineteenth century.

20. This was already being done in the fourth century—at least outside of Rome—according to the testimony of Paulinus of Nola: "Ille iugans capita amborum sub pace iugali velat eos dextra" (*Carmen* 25, 227–28). The final alteration of the text ("videant ambo" instead of "videat") had not yet made its appearance in the tenth century (*PRG* 2:417).

21. The first mention is in the so-called *Praedestinatus* (between 432 and 440): "Sacerdotes, nuptiarum initia benedicentes, consecrantes et in Dei mysteria sociantes" (PL 53:670). Location of the blessing: *Ge* 1449, 1453; *Gr* 837.

tionaries is Matthew 19:1-6,[22] but John 2:1-11 (wedding feast of Cana), John 3:27-29 ("He who has the bride is the bridegroom"), and Matthew 22:1-14 (parable of the wedding feast) also occur. In France, however, the votive Mass of the Trinity was often used for marriages. A second blessing brings the Mass to an end.[23]

The nuptial blessing, which was for centuries the only liturgical rite of marriage at Rome, was prescribed for clerics in minor orders,[24] offered to laypersons, but refused to Christians guilty of fornication[25] and to those entering upon second marriages.[26] The Church also recognized the family rites of betrothal but played no part in them. From Rome and Milan the nuptial blessing passed into Southern Gaul, thanks to St. Caesarius of Arles,[27] and subsequently made its way elsewhere as the Roman rite was adopted.

2. Gaul, Spain, and the Celtic Countries: The "Benedictio in Thalamo"

The most widespread form of marriage liturgy in Gaul and the Celtic countries consisted in a blessing of the spouses in the bridal chamber. St. Avitus of Vienne (ca. 494–518) draws a parallel between the consecration of virgins, which took place in the sanctuary ("in sancti altaris thalamo") and the blessing that the bride received in the bridal chamber ("in thalamo").[28] In reporting the marriage of St. Amator, future bishop of Auxerre (d. 418), Stephen Afer describes the ceremony as it existed in the sixth century: the priest or bishop was invited to give the blessing to the spouses in the bridal chamber.[29] This custom recalls the story in the Acts of Thomas,[30] but it also had a basis in the biblical story of the nuptials of Tobias

---

22. The Roman Missal of 1570 would keep Matt 19:3-6.

23. Ge 1454.

24. Pope Siricius, Ep. ad Himerium Tarracon. (ca. 384), IX, 3 (PL 13:1142).

25. See St. Caesarius of Arles, Serm. 42, 5 (CCL 103:1880).

26. See Ambrosiaster, Comm. in Ep. I ad Cor., 7, 40 (PL 17:225-26); Comm. in Ep. I ad Tim. 3, 12 (PL 17:470); Pope Nicholas I, Responsa ad Bulgarorum consulta (886), c. 3 (MGH Epist. 4:568ff.).

27. Vita S. Caesarii I, 59 (MGH, Script. rerum. Merov. III, 481). But the blessing in the church was to be given three days before the wedding.

28. St. Avitus, Ep. 49 (PL 59:266–67).

29. Stephen Afer, Vita Amatoris Antissiodorensis, in Acta Sanctorum, Maii I (1860) cols. 52–53.

30. This apocryphon from the beginning of the third century was originally in Syriac and of Gnostic origin, but it is also known in Latin. It contains a blessing in thalamo which the king of Andropolis asks the apostle to give his daughter: Lipsius and Bonnet, Acta apostolorum apocrypha II, 2 (Leipzig, 1903), 114–15; English translation in E. Hennecke and W. Schneemelcher, New Testament Apocrypha 2 (Philadelphia: Westminster, 1965), 447ff. See Ritzer 54–57 (French 107–10).

and Sarah (Tob 8:4-10), which is mentioned in the text of the nuptial blessing preserved in the Bobbio Missal.[31]

The blessing in the bridal chamber was eliminated in Gaul when the Roman rite was received, but it persisted in England[32] and returned to the continent in the eleventh century via Normandy.

The Visigothic liturgy of Spain was also familiar with this blessing, but in addition it contained a very rich development of the marriage ritual: blessing of the bridal chamber, votive office for the eve and morning of the wedding, blessing given in the church to the spouses, and again to the wife alone, during a Mass at which they received communion, and finally a last blessing of both together.[33]

Spain was also familiar with two gestures that would be taken over into the medieval rituals: the giving of the bride to the groom (*traditio puellae*) by the priest in the place and name of the father, and an *Ordo arrarum*, which was a result of the importance attached to the betrothal. As the first stage in the process by which a young girl passed from her father's clan to her husband's clan, the betrothal included the giving of pledges to the girl's family and was the occasion for a blessing. The engaged couple brought two rings to the priest; the prayer that followed was both a blessing of the ring and an invocation of God's favor on the couple. The exchange of a kiss sealed the betrothal.

This blessing added a degree of strict obligation to the betrothal. It is understandable, therefore, that the betrothal should have been celebrated closer and closer in time to the marriage, until finally, at the beginning of the eleventh century, it came immediately before the wedding Mass.

As in Gaul, the liturgy indigenous to Spain was gradually replaced by the Roman liturgy, especially as regards the Mass, and was finally suppressed entirely under Gregory VII.

3. The East: The Rite of Crowning

BIBLIOGRAPHY

I. H. Dalmais, "La liturgie du mariage dans les Eglises orientales," *LMD* no. 50 (1957) 58–69.

---

31. E. A. Lowe, *The Bobbio Missal* (HBS 58; London, 1920), nos. 550–51. The *benedictio thalami super nubentes* is of Visigothic rather than Gallican origin.

32. See, e. g., the Pontifical attributed to Egbert (eleventh century), ed. G. Greenwell (Publications of the Surtees Society 27; London, 1853), 125–26.

33. *Liber ordinum* (Férotin, cols. 433–40); *El Sacramentario de Vich*, ed. A. Olivar (Monumenta Hispaniae sacra, ser. liturg. 4; Barcelona, 1953), 209–15; *El Sacramentari, Ritual i Pontifical de Roda (c. 1000)*, ed. J. R. Barriga Planas (Fundació Salvador Vives Casajuana; Barcelona, 1975), 329–40. The blessing of the spouses in the bridal chamber (see the Bobbio Missal) has here become a blessing of the chamber prior to the marriage.

Mariage [Byzantine rite], traduit par Denis Guillaume (Rome: Diaconie apostolique, 1979).

G. Baldanza, "Il rito del matrimonio nell'Eucologio Barberini 336. Analisi della sua visione teologica," *EL* 93 (1979) 316–51.

G. Passarelli, "La cerimonia dello stefanoma (incoronazione) nei riti matrimoniali bizantini secondo il codice Cryptense G. b. VII (X° sec.)," *EL* 93 (1979) 381–91.

G. Baldanza, "Il rito matrimoniale dell'Eucologio Sinaitico Greco 958 ed il significato della coronazione nella *Doxa kai time*. Proposte per una ricerca teologica," *EL* 95 (1981) 289–315.

While the Roman Church of the fourth century was giving liturgical status to the familial rite of the *velatio* of the bride, the Eastern Churches were adopting a different ancient practice as the specific rite of marriage: the crowning of the spouses. The Latin verb for "to marry" was *nubere* (to veil); the Greek was *stephanoun* (to crown), and even today the Byzantine rite of marriage is entitled "The Office of Crowning" (*Akolouthia tou stephanōmatos*).[34]

a) *The Office of Crowning*

In classical Greek antiquity the crowning of the spouses was one of the customs at a marriage: it followed upon the giving (*ekdosis*) of the young girl by her father to her husband. According to St. Gregory of Nazianzus, the ceremony took place in the home: psalms were sung (including, certainly, Psalm 128), and a bishop or priest who was present was asked to give his blessing to the new spouses and even to put the crowns on their heads.[35] This rite seems to have acquired its importance first in Armenia. The use of crowns, permeated as it was by superstition and magic, was rejected by Christians of the second century (see Tertullian), but it was adopted without reserve from the fourth century on, and St. John Chrysostom even attached an ascetical meaning to it: "Crowns are placed on the heads of the spouses as a symbol of their victory, for they have reached the port of marriage unconquered by pleasure."[36]

It was quite natural that the church rather than the home should be regarded as the appropriate place for the priest's blessing, which from the

---

34. J. Goar, *Euchologion sive Rituale Graecorum* (Venice: B. Javarina, 1730;[2] reprinted, 1960), 314. At Rome too the spouses were still wearing crowns in the ninth century (see Pope Nicholas I, *Responsa ad Bulgarorum consulta* [n. 26]); crowns continued in nonliturgical use in the West down to the twentieth century, at least in rural areas (see A. Van Gennep, *Manuel du folklore français contemporain* [Paris: Picard, 1946], 1/2:397–403).

35. St. Gregory of Nazianzus, *Ep.* 231: "Let the father put crowns on them if he so wishes. That was the decision I came to when I had occasion to be present at weddings, namely, that it is for the fathers to put crowns on the couple and for us to say the prayers" (text and translation in P. Gallay, *Grégoire de Nazianze. Textes choisis* [Collection des Universités de France: Paris: Les Belles Lettres, 1941], 2:122–23).

36. St. John Chrysostom, *Homiliae in I Tim.*, 9, 2 (PG 62:546).

fourth century on was given on the eve at Constantinople and was increasingly understood to be a liturgical act. Other customary gestures, such as the joining of the couple's hands and the giving of the bride to the groom, were likewise increasingly regarded as the prerogative of the priest.[37]

The blessing and imposition of the crowns was accompanied by a formulary that developed at length the biblical symbolism of this rite. The Coptic ritual has this prayer:

> Holy God, who give your saints imperishable crowns and unite heaven to earth, bless now these crowns made ready for me to put on the heads of your servants.
> May they be for them:
>> Crowns of glory and honor. — Amen.
>> Crowns of salvation and blessing. — Amen.
>> Crowns of joy and unanimity. — Amen.
>> Crowns of rejoicing and gladness. — Amen.
>> Crowns of virtue and uprightness. — Amen.
>> Crowns of wisdom and understanding. — Amen.
>> Crowns of courage and steadfastness. — Amen.
> The Father blesses, the Son crowns, and the Holy Spirit sanctifies and makes perfect.[38]

The Syrian ritual speaks in analogous terms of "crowns sealed with the sign of the life-giving cross."[39] The crowning is accompanied in the Byzantine Rite by two formulas: "N., the servant of God, receives as his crown, N., the servant of God" (and conversely for the bride). Since the eleventh century this rite has gradually acquired lengthy prayers that are real centones of biblical references; they recall the patriarchs and call down upon the couple all the temporal blessings of the old covenant.

The crowning, which took place in church, was celebrated during the Eucharistic liturgy, a practice still observed among the Ethiopians. Among the Armenians it takes place before the Eucharist, but the newlyweds are expected to receive communion. At Byzantium and in the other rites, the Eucharist was first replaced by communion in the presanctified gifts when the spouses met the conditions for communicating, and then in the fifteenth century all reference to communion disappeared. The only echo of it that remains is the presentation to the spouses, after the Our Father,

---

37. This was true in Egypt from the fourth century on; see Timothy of Alexandria, *Responsa canonica* 11 (Pitra, *Jus Graec.* 1:631).

38. See A. Raes, *Le mariage. Sa célébration et sa spiritualité dans les Eglises d'Orient* (Chevetogne, 1959), 40–41.

39. *Ibid.*, 123.

of a cup of wine in remembrance of the wedding at Cana and the Eucharistic cup.[40]

In the Byzantine Rite the crowning of the couple is followed by an outburst of joy that finds expression in a kind of sacred dance performed by the priest and the new spouses around the gospel. The Chaldean Rite keeps the celebration going until the house of the groom is reached:

> The new bride is led in procession and brought with great solemnity into the house of her husband amid cries of joy; she is dressed in all her finery and covered with a precious veil. The members of her new family come to meet her at the door and, as a pledge of abundance and prosperity, pelt her with raisins, fruits, grain, and small coins.[41]

The laying aside of the crowns has also been given ritual form.

The priest's blessing, which was initially reserved exclusively for first marriages, was made obligatory during the eighth and ninth centuries; Byzantine law refused to recognize a marriage that had not been blessed.[42]

b) *The Office of Betrothal*

In addition to the classic informal betrothal, which left the parties free to break off the engagement, there was a betrothal that included pledges, an exchange of rings, the kiss of peace, and the joining of the hands of the couple; to this kind of betrothal the Code of Justinian assigned juridical value. The blessing of the engaged couple, which was still a recent phenomenon in the eighth century, resembled that of marriage so closely that from the tenth century on, the two rites were performed one after the other, despite the purely formal distinction between them. The ritual included an exchange of consents, the blessing of the rings that had been previously placed on the altar, and a lengthy prayer of blessing for the couple. The Syrian Churches used to add—and the Armenian Church still does—a gift to the bride-to-be of a cross, which she was to wear around her neck.

---

40. Among the Armenians the blessing of the cup reserved for the newlyweds (*ibid.*, 96) makes this reference explicit: "Lord, our God, who created all things wisely and who established the universe and beautified the wedding at Cana in Galilee and blessed the cup in the upper room: bless this cup, Lord, through this sign of the holy cross, that it may serve the union of these your servants and the healing of their bodies and souls, so that they may become worthy to glorify the Father and the Son and the Holy Spirit, now and always and for endless ages. Amen."

41. *Ibid.*, 191.

42. *Novelle* 89 of Emperor Leo VI the Wise (886–912). See J. Dauvillier and C. De Clercq, *Le mariage en droit canonique oriental* (Paris: Sirey, 1936).

c) *The Liturgical Formularies*

Due to their selection of biblical readings, the lyricism of their songs, and the amplitude of their priestly prayers, the Eastern rites vie with one another in depth of thought and beauty of expression. There is no richer source available for a solidly grounded theology of marriage.

i. *The Readings*

In the Greek Church Ephesians 5:20-33 and John 2:1-11 are read at a marriage. The Armenian Church has the longest list, with readings assigned to each stage of the celebration: for the betrothal, Proverbs 9:12-17; Song of Solomon 8:14; Hosea 14:6-10; Isaiah 27:11-13; Galatians 4:2-7 and 4:13; Luke 1:26-28; for the blessing of the bride's dress, Isaiah 61:10—62:3; 1 Peter 3:1-9; John 2:1-11; for the crowning, Genesis 1:26-28; Genesis 2:21-24; Isaiah 61:9—62:6; Ephesians 5:11-23; Matthew 19:2-9; for the setting aside of the crowns, Hosea 14:6-8; 1 Timothy 2:9-15; John 2:1-11.[43]

ii. *The Songs*

In addition to the marriage psalms (19:5; 45; 128) and Psalm 21, which is a coronation psalm (see v. 3), some rites use nonbiblical compositions whose theology is on a par with their lyricism. Here is how the Church of Antioch celebrates marriage as a figure of the wedding of Christ and the Church:

> To the heavenly bridegroom who out of love betrothed himself to the Church that had been defiled by the nations and who by his crucifixion purified and washed her and made of her a glorious bride, and invited the prophets, apostles, and martyrs to his wedding feast: to him be glory.[44]
>
> There has never been a bride like the one the First Born married. He acquired her before all else and by his death set up a wedding feast for her. He mounted the wood and she was near him; he opened his side and she was washed by his blood; she raised her voice and said: Holy, holy, holy is the Son, and in all things like his Father.[45]

The Chaldean liturgy has chants that are not inferior to those:

> The Son of God crowned with beauty and glory the Church whom he made his bride. He invited the armies of heaven and the inhabitants of earth to his wedding that they might serve at his feast. He wove crowns for her from the blazing rays of light that stream from his inaccessible Father. He adorned her head with them as with jewels. He sent his orders out to the

---

43. Raes (n. 38), 77–101 (Denz 2:451–82).
44. *Ibid.*, 117.
45. *Ibid.*, 118–19.

crossroads, inviting all generations. He calls them that they may come with their gifts to the wedding banquet of the Church, the royal bride to whom the Son of the Most High has betrothed himself in love.[46]

Do such songs as these make the participants forget the spouses who stand before the priest and cause them to think only of Christ marrying the Church? No, for in fact the man and woman on their wedding day are eminent signs of Christ and the Church, according to Ephesians 5:25-32.

iii. *The Prayers*

The prayers, whether of petition (in litanic form) or of blessing, are inspired primarily by the Bible. Thus the Church of Antioch, which is always alert to the mystery of the union of Christ and the Church, addresses the couple as follows: "May Christ, the faithful bridegroom, seal your marriage with his true love. As he finds his joy in the Church, so may you find your happiness in each other."[47]

But the Church also sees human marriage as a foretaste of the happiness that awaits all who will share in the wedding feast of the Lamb. Here is a prayer from the Chaldean Rite:

> Heavenly bridegroom, who on the day of your Parousia will lead your invited guests into the spiritual bridal chamber of heaven: we pray you, have mercy on us.
>
> Heavenly bridegroom, whose wedding feast will last throughout eternity, grant unanimity to this man and woman who worship you and put their hope in you and are united in accordance with your law.[48]

The Chaldean ritual also has a lengthy blessing to be spoken over each of the spouses; they are attributed to St. Ephraem and are reminiscent of the blessings that the patriarchs gave to their children. Here are some passages from the blessing of the husband:

> May Christ the Lord lift up your head and grant you success in this world as in the next. . . . May Christ rule your life. May he bless your undertakings. . . . May your harvest be as abundant as the flooding of the Tigris. May you grow and bear fruit in every way, as the Euphrates does among the peoples. . . . May the shadow of the radiant cross protect you night and day. May your household prosper and give you unending joy. . . . May your sleep be untroubled. May you wake in the morning rejoicing; may you experience happiness at noon; may you find rest at all times. Proceed from virtue to virtue; advance from glory to glory; climb from level to level; progress from good to good. . . . May the Holy Trinity grant you every blessing and may God be glorified in you. Amen.[49]

---

46. *Ibid.*, 178.
47. *Ibid.*, 129.
48. See *ibid.*, 183.
49. See *ibid.*, 186–88.

§3. Marriage at the Door of the Church in the Middle Ages

The rite of marriage remained unchanged in the East after the tenth century, but the same was not true in the West. The eleventh century saw the secular marriage ceremony turned into a liturgical action that was celebrated immediately before Mass, but outside the Church, *in facie ecclesiae.*

In the ninth and tenth centuries, which were a time of violence and social anarchy, priests had to deal with the civil formalities of marriage. Synods and capitularies demanded that marriage be celebrated publicly in order to ensure the woman's free consent; they insisted that the spouses must receive the nuptial blessing and that priests must make a prior investigation. The influence of the collection of Pseudo-Isidorean decrees, which date from 845, played a large part in shifting the civil formalities of marriage to the ecclesiastical forum. Theologians and canonists began to count marriage as one of the sacraments and, while they followed Roman law in maintaining that marriage consists solely in the consent of the couple, so that it is valid even without formalities or publicity, they also deemed it necessary for Christians to follow Church custom and marry "sub sacerdotali benedictione."[50]

In order to ensure the public character of marriage, the old rite of the blessing *in thalamo,* which had been kept in England, was revived in Normandy and spread from there throughout France. On the evening of the marriage, the priest blessed the spouses themselves as well as the bridal chamber and the wedding ring, even if the couple had not received a blessing in the church earlier that day. But a blessing of the couple under these conditions soon began to appear inappropriate and insufficiently public. The Synod of Rouen in 1012 forbade the practice;[51] this did not prevent the blessing *in thalamo* from being continued, but it now lacked any juridical or sacramental value.[52]

---

50. See, e.g., G. Le Bras, "La doctrine du mariage chez les théologiens et les canonistes depuis l'an mille," *DTC* 9 (1926) 2123–2214.

51. Canon 13, cited in Ritzer 311 (French 390–91).

52. Despite the new strictness of the post-Tridentine period, many dioceses retained the custom of a more or less solemn blessing *in thalamo* until the nineteenth century. For example: the Ritual of Perigueux, 1827: "Having donned surplice and stole, the parish priest . . . first sprinkles the married couple, who stand modestly near the marriage bed, then the bed and those present." But the blessing in this case was to take place between the marriage ceremony in the church and the wedding feast. On the rite and its formulary see J. B. Molin and P. Mutembe, *Le Rituel du mariage en France du XIIᵉ au XVIᵉ siècle* (Théologie historique 26; Paris: Beauchesne, 1974), 255–70. An eighteenth-century engraving depicting the ceremony is reproduced in M. Segalen, *Amours et mariage de l'ancienne France* (Paris: Berger-Levrault, 1981), 120.

In order to give maximum publicity to the exchange of consents, it was decided that it should no longer take place in the home of the bride but at the door of the church, *in facie ecclesiae*. The phrase is to be understood in the material sense.[53] The two earliest *ordines* for marriage *in facie ecclesiae* are from a Missal of the Abbey of St. Melanius in Rennes and a pontifical used in the Norman abbey of Lyre.[54] Here is the text from the Rennes Missal (beginning of the twelfth century):

> *Ritual for blessing the husband and wife:*
> The priest, vested in alb and stole and carrying holy water, is to take his place in front of the church door. After sprinkling the couple he is to question them in a prudent manner to find out whether they are resolved to marry in accordance with the law; he will make sure that they are not related, and he will instruct them on how they are to live together in the Lord.
> Next, following custom, he tells the parents to give their daughter to the groom, and tells the groom to give her her dowry, the record of which he then reads out in the presence of all those attending. The priest has her marry him with a ring that is blessed in the name of the Holy Trinity and that he puts on her right hand; the man is also to give her a gift of some gold or silver coins according to his means. The priest then gives the blessing as set down in the book; after this they enter the church and he begins the Mass. The bride and groom are to carry lighted candles during the Mass and are to make their offering; before the priest says the *Pax Domini* he places the couple beneath a veil, as is customary, and there gives them the nuptial blessing. Finally, the husband receives the gesture of peace and gives it to his wife.[55]

The rites that here precede the wedding Mass—exchange of consents, giving of ring and coins, transfer of the dowry before witnesses—are simply the traditional rites of betrothal, *sponsalia de futuro*, which have now been turned into the rite of marriage itself, *sponsalia de praesenti*.[56] Only the *dextrarum iunctio* had belonged specifically to the ancient ceremonies of marriage proper, but this gesture is no longer understood here as the giving of the young girl to the bridegroom; it is seen rather as a symbol of the reciprocal giving of the spouses to each other, a giving that also finds expression in the words they speak.

The expression of consent could be reduced to a "Yes" in response to

---

53. We also find the expression "ante valvas ecclesiae." The ceremony sometime took place in a porch, called "the marriage porch." Artists always showed the marriage of the Blessed Virgin or that of St. Anne being celebrated *in front of* the Jerusalem temple, in keeping with the practice familiar to the artists themselves.

54. Martène (M 692 for Rennes, 693 for Lyre); see Molin and Mutembe (n. 52), 284–86 (Rennes), 286–87 (Lyre).

55. French translation following C. Chardon, *Histoire des sacrements* (1745), 1026.

56. As a result of the Crusades this new approach also entered the Armenian and Maronite rituals; see Raes (n. 38), 73–74, 137–38.

questions asked by the priest, or it could be significantly expanded, as in the Ritual of Châlons: "I, N., take N. here as my wife and spouse, and I promise her good faith and fidelity; I shall keep her in health and sickness, and I shall not exchange her for another as long as she lives." In the same Ritual, when the husband puts the ring on his wife's finger he says: "N., with this ring I marry you, and with my goods I endow you, and with my body I honor you."[57]

As thus expanded in the eleventh century, the part played by the spouses caused the original role of the priest to be forgotten. His function had been to supervise the *traditio puellae* in the place and name of the girl's father, that is, to ensure the husband's freedom of consent in cases of a marriage being forced by the parents. Such was the original meaning of the words "Ego coniungo vos" and equivalent formulas;[58] more simply, it was the meaning of the priest's action of joining the couple's hands.

§4. Marriage in the West After the Council of Trent

The Council of Trent in 1563 was the first to require canonical form for validity; in practice, this meant the appearance of the couple before their own parish priest (decree *Tametsi*).[59] The "Ego coniungo vos" formula became widespread and tended to be looked upon as the sacramental formula, comparable to "Ego te baptizo." The Roman Ritual published in 1614 emphasized the role of the priest at the expense of that of the couple. In addition, the rite, which was to take place in the church (with the couple kneeling before the altar), reduced the formulary to a minimum: expression of consent in the form of a "Yes" to the question asked by the priest; joining of their hands, followed by the "Ego coniungo vos" and a sprinkling with holy water; blessing of the ring, which the husband then placed on his wife's finger, but with accompanying words from the priest; some psalm verses and a short concluding prayer. The wedding Mass[60] followed, with the nuptial blessing after the Our Father[61] and a

---

57. Martène, *Ordo* 11 (M 701), which represents the usage of Chalons at the beginning of the sixteenth century.

58. In the marriage ritual for Switzerland (*Collectio rituum,* 1955) the formula was still: "May the Lord deign to confirm the union upon which you have just entered. For my part, in virtue of the authority conferred upon me, I ackowledge it as valid and legitimate in the eyes of the Church. In the name of the Father . . ." (180).

59. DS 1813–16. See A. Duval, "La formule 'Ego vos in matrimonium coniungo . . .' au Concile de Trente," *LMD* no. 99 (1969) 144–53.

60. The wedding Mass had lost its special preface (reinstated in France beginning with the Paris Missal of 1738) and *Hanc igitur.*

61. On the location of the blessing within the Mass see Molin and Mutembe (n. 52) 223–28; on the manner of receiving it, 228–32. The ceremonial of the marriage veil or canopy con-

final blessing that developed the one given in Scripture for the marriage of Tobias and Sarah (Tob 7:15).[62]

The Council of Trent did not intend to suppress particular rituals: "If any regions follow other praiseworthy customs and ceremonies when celebrating the sacrament of marriage, the Council earnestly desires that by all means these be retained."[63]

And in fact the diocesan rituals, at least in France, long kept a certain number of practices, such as the betrothal blessing, the canopy for the nuptial blessing, and the blessing of the marriage bed. But beginning in the seventeenth century the rituals also displayed a decorum, and even an austerity, that henceforth found a place in all aspects of worship and caused the excision of everything that was regarded as an abuse:

> Parish priests are exhorted to display a great deal of seriousness in all ceremonies connected with marriage, to keep those present within the bounds of modesty, and, above all, to prevent anything secular and contrary to the holiness of the place and the sacrament of marriage from being done in the church; for example, presents and gifts are not to be given to the newlyweds there, nor are traveling entertainers, fiddlers, and other such folk to be brought in on the excuse of providing joyous music.[64]

But the universal and increasingly strict implementation of the Roman Ritual gave an impression of aridity and impoverishment, a fact recognized by Vatican II.[65]

---

tinued in France until the middle of the nineteenth century, at least in rural areas. On the usage of the canopy and the popular names given to it see A. Van Gennep (n. 34), 1/2:453–55. From the twelfth century on, children born before the marriage were also placed under the canopy; the effect of this was to legitimize them: "If the man and woman being married have had children before their marriage, they too are to be put under the canopy and blessed along with their father and mother" (*Rituel de la province de Reims* [1677], 228). In the eighteenth century the practice still continued, but in separation from the blessing and accompanied by a prayer that gave it a penitential cast; this change contributed to the disappearance of the custom (*Rituel de Paris* [1701], 384).

62. This blessing already existed in the Visigothic liturgy: *Liber ordinum* (Férotin, col. 438; ms. A = Silos 3); *El Sacramentario de Vich* (ed. A. Olivar), no. 1425.

63. Session XXIV, *De matrimonio*, Decree *De reformatione*, cap. 1; text in J. Alberigo, et al. (eds.), *Conciliorum oecumenicorum decreta* (Bologna: Istituto per le scienze religiose, 1963³), 756. This passage is repeated in *VSC* 77 (*DOL* 1 no. 77 [which is cited here. — Tr.]).

64. *Rituel de la province de Reims* (1677), 228. On liturgical and extraliturgical customs in France see A. Van Gennep (n. 34), 373–480. The white veil of the married woman seems to have made its appearance in France only in the second part of the nineteenth century, probably as the veil used in the Marian sodality.

65. *VSC* 77 (*DOL* 1 no. 77). The Reformation did not bring any break with the rites of marriage, which continued to be those of the Middle Ages, even though the Reformers in their theology did not accept marriage as a sacrament. The main lines of the evolution of the rituals in the various confessions down to our day, especially in the Anglo-Saxon world, are traced in K. Stevenson, *Nuptial Blessing. A Study of Christian Marriage Rites* (Alcuin Club Collections 64; London: S.P.C.K., 1982), 123–68 and 189–214.

§5. The Celebration of Marriage After Vatican II

BIBLIOGRAPHY

P. M. Gy, "Le nouveau rituel romain du mariage," *LMD* no. 99 (1969) 124–43.
S. Mazzarello, "De novo ordine celebrandi matrimonium," *EL* 83 (1969) 251–77.
C. Braga, "La genesi dell'*Ordo matrimonii*," *EL* 93 (1979) 247–57.

> The marriage rite now found in the Roman Ritual is to be revised and enriched in such a way that it more clearly signifies the grace of the sacrament and imparts a knowledge of the obligations of the spouses. . . .
>
> Marriage is normally to be celebrated within Mass, after the reading of the gospel and the homily and before "the prayer of the faithful." The prayer for the bride, duly emended to remind both spouses of their equal obligation to remain faithful to each other, may be said in the vernacular.
>
> But if the sacrament of marriage is celebrated apart from Mass, the epistle and gospel of the nuptial Mass are to be read at the beginning of the rite and the blessing is always to be given to the spouses.[66]

Citing the very words of the Council of Trent, the Constitution on the Liturgy of Vatican II acknowledges the legitimacy of other customs in the celebration of marriage and urges the episcopal conferences to develop their own rites that are suited to the usages of place and people.

The new *Ordo celebrandi matrimonium*, which was promulgated on March 19, 1969, is offered as a model on which the episcopal conferences are to develop particular rituals for their territories (Introduction, 12–16); they may also, however, prepare a completely new rite (Introduction, 17–18).[67]

1. *The Teaching Contained in God's Word*

Whether or not a marriage is celebrated with a Eucharist, it is always preceded by a liturgy of the Word. This liturgy is a very important occasion for proclaiming to an often disparate assembly the meaning of a marriage that is contracted "in Christ." The lectionary for marriage, now considerably expanded by comparison with the past, contains thirty-five biblical passages: eight Old Testament readings and seven psalms; ten readings from the apostolic letters and ten from the gospels. The two accounts of creation (Gen 1:16-31 and 2:18-24) show marriage as God willed it at

---

66. *VSC* 77–78 (*Dol* 1 nos. 77–78).
67. The English language *Rite of Marriage* is in *Rites* 1:531–70. Adaptation for France: *Rituel pour la célébration du mariage a l'usage des diocèses de France* (Turnhout: Brepols, 1970) (approval and confirmation, April 14 and June 2, 1969). For Poland, see W. Nowak, "De novo ritu celebrandi matrimonium usui diocesium Poloniae accomodato," *EL* 93 (1979) 392–97. For an essay in adapting the rite to Black Africa see L. Mpongo, *Pour une anthropologie chrétienne du mariage au Congo* (Kinshasa: Limete, 1968).

the beginning; Jesus would later refer to these passages when reminding his hearers of the fundamental law of deep and definitive union that the creator willed for human marriage (Matt 19:36 and Mark 10:6-9). The stories of the marriage of Isaac and Rebekah and the marriage of Tobias and Sarah show how those couples long ago lived out their love under the gaze of the Lord. The mystery of which marriage is a sign is suggested in the account of the wedding at Cana (John 2:1-11) and then expounded by St. Paul, who sees marriage as symbolizing the union of Christ and the Church (Eph 5:2, 21-33). The prophet Jeremiah (31:31-33) and the Song of Solomon (2:8-10, 14, 16a, and 8:6-7a) prepared the way for understanding of this mystery. The plan of life that a Christian family should follow is developed in a final series of passages: either explicitly, as in St. Peter (1 Pet 3:1-9) or implicitly in reminders of how solid a house built on rock is and of the requirements of mutual love, respect for one's own body, tenderness, and kindness that should guide the development of all shared life in Christ.

The couple will have had the opportunity to reflect on the readings they choose; along with the message of the Church they will be transmitting something of their own message to their relatives and friends. In his homily the priest helps the assembly to understand the mystery of marriage better and prepares the couple for their commitment.

2. *The Course of the Rite*

The structure of the rite and its integration into a Mass or at least into a liturgy of the Word were determined by the conciliar Constitution. It is easy to find in that document the elements that, greatly enriched, ultimately found a place in the Ritual of 1969. A first stage corresponds to the old rite of marriage *in facie ecclesiae*: the questions that precede the giving of consent, the reception of the couple's consent by the priest, the blessing and giving of the rings; a second stage corresponds to the oldest Roman rite: the nuptial blessing proper; and, finally, a closing blessing.

The priest normally welcomes the future spouses at the church door; the latter is no longer the site of the celebration itself, but has become the place for a sympathetic human welcome.

The opening prayer (a selection of four is provided) calls to mind one or another aspect of marriage: unity, fidelity, mutual love, sacrament of the covenant between Christ and the Church, joy, procreation.[68]

The rite of marriage takes place after the Liturgy of the Word: after three questions regarding the freedom with which they are marrying, the

---

68. *Ordo celebrandi matrimonium*, Opening Prayers (nos. 106–9). No. 106 is based on a sentence in the old Roman nuptial blessing; nos. 107 and 108 are new compositions; no. 109 is taken, with alterations, from the Sacramentary of Fulda.

fidelity they intend, and their acceptance of responsibility for children, the couple join their right hands. This gesture, which henceforth precedes the giving of consent, is part of the oldest Roman tradition on marriage (the *dextrarum iunctio*) and of marriage in the Bible (Tob 7:13 Vg), but it has lost all reference to its original meaning, the *traditio puellae*. With hands joined, the couple express their own consent in a formula which is substantially that used in England since the Middle Ages and formerly used in many dioceses of France.[69] The priest receives their consent in a deprecative statement that emphasizes the action of God rather than the role of the minister: "You have declared your consent before the Church. May the Lord in his goodness strengthen your consent and fill you both with his blessings. What God has joined, men must not divide" (no. 46).

At the end of a lengthy evolution, the Roman Ritual now accepts the custom of having two rings and not just one. After a short prayer of blessing (three forms are given), the spouses place the rings on each other's fingers, while emphasizing the gesture with a short sentence that sees the wedding ring as a symbol of love and mutual fidelity. The couple is invited to take an active part in the Eucharist by bringing the bread and wine to the altar and, even more, by receiving the Body of Christ and drinking from the cup of the covenant.

A rich variety of formularies characterizes the Eucharistic liturgy for marriage. There are two new prayers over the gifts in addition to the old one. The old Gelasian preface "Qui foedera" is given, along with two others; each of them takes a different approach to the meaning of the covenant struck between the spouses: it is "an unbreakable bond of love and peace" that by its fruitfulness enriches both the human race and the Church" (Preface I); it symbolizes the new covenant between God and his people (II); it reveals the love of God and sanctifies human love (III).

The Missal has taken over the *Hanc igitur* of the old sacramentaries but has notably altered it and applied it to the two spouses.[70]

The nuptial blessing—the former *Oratio super sponsam*—is once again in the place assigned it in the Gelasian Sacramentary: between the Our Father and the greeting of peace, the prayer "Deliver us, O Lord" being omitted. In accordance with the bidding of the council, the old Roman formulary for the nuptial blessing has been emended so as express the duties of husband as well as wife, although it has not lost its basic character as a blessing of the wife.[71] On the other hand, the references to the women of the Bible have been reduced to a general statement.

---

69. P. M. Gy, "Le nouveau rituel du mariage," *LMD* no. 99 (1969) 132, n. 19.

70. The Canadian episcopal conference won approval (February 10, 1982) of a special Eucharistic Prayer for the wedding Mass.

71. There is a comparison of the old and new versions in S. Mazzarello, "De novo ordine celebrandi matrimonium," *EL* 83 (1969) 264–66.

The Ritual provides two new formularies along with the old one. Each of them brings out in its own way the meaning of marriage and the part it plays in God's plan; it goes on to call down the blessing of the Lord on the wife, then on the husband, and finally on both together. The reference to the Eucharist is, of course, to be omitted if the couple are not to receive communion; in this case a marriage ceremony without a Mass would be preferable.

During the blessing the priest keeps his hands extended over the couple, as in other prayers for the consecration of persons. Since the ceremony of veiling has long since fallen into disuse, its revival would be artificial and probably not understood.

The celebration concludes with a final blessing. This is no longer the old blessing of Tobit, *Deus Abraham* (Tob 7:15 Vg), but a threefold blessing modeled on the Gallican and Hispanic blessings. The first of the three formularies (nos. 125–27) is based on the ancient Spanish blessing;[72] the second is Trinitarian; the third harks back to the wedding feast at Cana. The English Ritual adds a fourth (no. 37).

In the form of a wish these blessings sketch briefly the ideal of Christian marriage and remind the newlyweds of what their home should be in time to come:

> God the eternal Father keep you in love with each other, so that the peace of Christ may stay with you and be always in your home. — May your children bless you, your friends console you and all men live in peace with you. — May you always bear witness to the Love of God in this world so that the afflicted and the needy will find in you generous friends, and welcome you into the joy of heaven (no. 125).

3. *Adaptations*

The liturgy of marriage has always been open to the use of local customs. The present Roman Ritual provides an abundant selection of readings, prayers, and songs, thus making it possible to adapt the celebration as much as possible to the spouses and the congregation attending the liturgy. The Ritual is also open to ancient customs that have continued in use here and there, for example, the kiss of the spouses in the Canadian Ritual or the blessing of thirteen silver coins in some dioceses, as well as to customs borrowed from other rites that are practiced in the same part of the world (the crowning, for example, has been introduced into the ritual of the Latin patriarchate of Jerusalem), or to gestures that have made their appearance here and there in more recent times, for example, the placing of the wife's bouquet on the altar, the presenting of a Bible, or the signing of the registers before the Eucharistic liturgy. Finally, though

---

72. See *Liber ordinum* (Férotin, col. 437).

the Ritual cannot anticipate all possible situations, it does provide a celebration adapted to cases when one of the spouses is not baptized (Chapter III).[73]

§6. The Mystery of Marriage

BIBLIOGRAPHY

P. Evdokimov, *Le sacrement de l'amour* (Paris: Ed. de l'Epi, 1962).
Le mariage dans l'Eglise ancienne, texts chosen and edited by F. Quéré-Jaulmes (Lettres chrétiennes; Paris: Ed. du Centurion, 1969).
A.G. Martimort, "Contribution de l'histoire liturgique à la théologie du mariage," *Esprit et vie* 88 (1978) 129-37.
A.M. Triacca, " 'Celebrare' il matrimonio, suo significato teologico-liturgico (Anamnesis-Methexis-Epiclesis)," *EL* 93 (1979) 407-56.

In their rituals for marriage the Churches use passages from the Bible, gestures, prayers, and songs to express and glorify marriage; the Roman Church does so in a restrained way, the Eastern Churches exuberantly. What they express is more than simply an ideal; it is the mystery contained in Christian marriage. In the eyes of Christians, marriage looks beyond the purely familial or social spheres and calls for the action of God: "The witness to these words [of consent] is the God who is enthroned invisibly above this altar."[74]

Marriage is already holy as a human reality because it plays a part in the plan of God the creator, who has made man and woman in his own image: "Father, by your plan man and woman are united, and married life has been established as the one blessing that was not forfeited by original sin or washed away in the flood."[75]

Marriage, which Christ sanctified at Cana, receives its blessing from him, along with the demands made of it by the new law; involving as it does the difference and complementarity of man and woman, it becomes a permanent, indissoluble sign of the new covenant: "To reveal the plan of your love, you made the union of husband and wife an image of the covenant between you and your people. In the fulfillment of this sacra-

---

73. There is the distressing case of a marriage in which one party is baptized but not a Catholic; see Paul VI, Motu Proprio *Matrimonia mixta* (March 31, 1970): *AAS* 62 (1970) 257-63 (*EDIL* 2076-79 = *DOL* 354 nos. 2999-3012). See also the new regulations for the dioceses of France (October, 1970): *Documentation catholique* 67 (1970) 1123-32. There is also a paradoxical case: the marriage of non-Christians in the Church; see J. Lopez-Gay, "Un rito christiano para matrimonios no christianos. Una experiencia de la Iglesia del Japon," *EL* 93 (1979) 505-14.

74. Armenian ritual; see Raes (n. 38), 88.

75. *Rite of Marriage*, no. 33 (*Rites* 1:544).

ment, the marriage of Christian man and woman is a sign of the marriage between Christ and the Church."[76]

The Eastern rituals never weary of hymning this mystery of marriage by linking the incarnation, Cana, and the cross, as in this canticle that the Maronite Church attributes to St. Ephraem:

> Christ, son of Mary and of the race of David your servant, you who donned the flesh of our humanity and thus sprang from us and became one of us; Christ, the bridegroom who married the holy and faithful Church and in the upper room gave her your body and your holy blood . . . extend your right hand, O God, and bless this husband and wife . . . who have come to holy Church for her priests' blessing.[77]

While being a sacrament that consecrates a state of life—the shared life of man and woman—marriage is also, despite its inevitable limitations, a prefiguration of the marriage of heaven: "Grant that as they come together to your table on earth, so they may one day have the joy of sharing your feast in heaven."[78]

The Syrian Rite puts the same idea much more expressively:

> Make us worthy, O God, to share the joy of your endless feast, the unfailing gladness of your bridal chamber, the happiness of your banquet that is not limited by time. May we live in joy with all who are invited to share it and in gladness with all the guests who rejoice in it. . . . And we shall sing to you canticles of glory and thanksgiving.[79]

This dimension of Christian marriage is doubtless often beyond the ken of those who come asking for the Church's blessing on their marriage. Christian communities, and first and foremost the priest, have a duty therefore to take advantage of the pastoral instructions for which the Ritual makes provision, and do all they can to open up to the future spouses perspectives revealing the mystery of marriage insofar as it refers to Christ and the Church (see Eph 5:21-32).

---

76. *Ibid.*, no. 120 (p. 566).
77. Raes 150.
78. *Rite of Marriage*, no. 120 (*Rites* 1:567).
79. Raes 121.

Chapter VII

The Consecration of Virgins

A. Nocent

BIBLIOGRAPHY

L. Duchesne, *Origines du culte chrétien* (Paris: de Boccard, 1920[5]), 440–48.

P. de Puniet, *Le Pontifical romain, histoire et commentaire* 2 (Paris: Desclée de Brouwer, 1931), 142–78. ET: *The Roman Pontifical: A History and Commentary*, trans. M. V. Harcourt (New York: Longmans, Green, 1932f.).

P. Oppenheim, *Die Consecratio virginum als geistesgeschichtliches Problem* (Rome: Officium libri catholici, 1943).

O. Harrisson, "The formulas *Ad virgines sacras*. A Study of the Sources," *EL* 66 (1952) 252–69, 352–66.

H. Leclercq, "Vierge et virginité," *DACL* 15 (1953) 3094–3113.

R. Metz, *La consécration des vierges dans l'Eglise romaine* (Paris: Presses Universitaires de France, 1954).

C. Coebergh, "Saint Léon le Grand, auteur de la grande formule *Ad virgines sacras* du Sacramentaire Léonien," *SE* 6 (1954) 282–326.

L. Brou, "Le fragment liturgique Colmar 144, reste d'un Pontifical irlandais du VIIIe siècle," *Bulletin de littérature ecclésiastique* 56 (1955) 64–71.

R. Metz, "L'ordo de la consécration des vierges dans le Pontifical dit de Saint-Aubin d'Angers (IXe–Xe siècle)," in *Mélanges en honneur de Mgr Michel Andrieu* (Strasbourg: Palais universitaire, 1956), 327–37.

R. Schilling, "Le voile de consecration dans l'ancien rite romain," *ibid.*, 403–14.

R. Metz, "La consécration des vierges en Gaule, des origines à l'apparition des livres liturgiques," *Revue du droit canonique* 6 (1956) 321–39.

_____, "La consécration des vierges dans l'Eglise franque, du VIIe au XIe siècle," *RevSR* 31 (1957) 105–21.

J. Magne, "La prière de consécration des vierges *Deus castorum corporum*. Etude du texte," *EL* 72 (1958) 245–67.

M. Righetti, *Manuale di storia liturgica* 4 (Milan: Ancora, 1959[4]), 484–92.

R. Metz, "Benedictio seu consecratio virginum," *EL* 80 (1966) 265–93.

A. Nocent, "Il mistero di Cristo nella *Velatio sponsae* e nella *Velatio virginum*," *Rivista Liturgica* 55 (1968) 368–77.

R. Metz, "La consécration des vierges," *Vie consacrée* 41/1 (1969) 5–25.

Pontifical Romanum . . . Ordo consecrationis virginum, editio typica (Vatican Polyglot Press, 1970). Translation: *Consecration to a Life of Virginity* in *The*

Rites of the Catholic Church 2 (New York: Pueblo, 1980), 132–64, with new translation of the Introduction in *DOL* 395 nos. 3253–62.

"Documenta, explanatio circa Ordinem consecrationis virginum," *Notitiae* 7 (1971) 107–10 (*DOL* 395 no. 3262, note).

R. Metz, "Le nouveau rituel de la consécration des vierges, sa place dans l'histoire," *LMD* no. 110 (1972) 88–115.

M. M. Croiset, "Virginité et vie chretienne au regard du ritual de la consécration des vierges," *LMD* no. 110 (1972) 116–28.

A. M. Triacca, "Fondamenti liturgico-sacramentali delle forme di 'vita di consacrazione,'" *Rivista Liturgica* 60 (1973) 287–320.

M. Auge, "I riti della professione religiosa e della consacrazione delle vergini. Struttura e contenuto teologico," *Rivista Liturgica* 60 (1973) 326–40.

In the pre-Vatican II Pontifical the consecration of virgins was seen as a specifically monastic celebration; in addition, its use was reserved by law to nuns taking solemn vows. In fact, the ritual for this consecration had even fallen into complete disuse when in 1868 Dom Guéranger happily undertook to restore it to favor among the Benedictine nuns of Sainte-Cecile de Solesmes. And yet this is a liturgical action that has meaning for the entire Church, for it underscores the role and meaning of virginity in the Christian economy, while at the same time it is an important theological locus for the theology of marriage.[1] It is to the liturgy of the *Velatio virginum*, along with the Masses for the Common of Virgins[2] and the legends of the holy virgin martyrs of antiquity, that we must go for the ideal of the Christian virgin that has been admired and practiced in the tradition of the Church. This is why the conciliar Constitution on the Liturgy decided (no. 80) that the rite for the consecration of virgins should be revised; use of this rite, moreover, has been extended to secular institutes and to women living a life of virginity in the world.

§1. Meaning of the Rite: The Christian Virgin as Bride of Christ

Early Christian literature makes it clear that some Christian women practiced complete continence while continuing to live in the world. Even after groups living a common life had been established, some women continued to observe continence and virginity in the world without choosing to adopt any form of monastic life. This was still the case even once the Church had provided a rite as its seal of approval on the mature decision of a woman to vow herself to continence.

---

1. It is not possible to construct a theology either of marriage or virginity without taking into account the theology of the other state.

2. E. Loehr, "La vierge chrétienne d'après les messes du commun des vierges," *Vie spirituelle* 73 (1945) 166–77.

The earliest explicit references to a special celebration for the consecration of a virgin date from the fourth century, between 350 and 400. Pope Liberius consecrated Marcellina, sister of St. Ambrose, in the Basilica of St. Peter in Rome.[3] A letter of Pope Siricius to a virgin specified that the *velatio* should take place on Christmas, Epiphany, or Easter; in this ceremony the bishop addressed some words to the virgin and put on her a veil like that of married women.[4]

Beginning with this first hint of a ritual, the bishop reserved to himself the right to preside at the consecration of virgins. He was in the place of Christ, and the consecration of a virgin was looked upon as a marriage between Christ and this woman who was vowing herself to virginity. The words "betrothal" and "nuptials" come often from the pen of the Fathers when they are discussing consecrated virgins; this is the case as early as the third century. In the fourth century the title *Sponsa Christi* was a current one for such women. The ritual of consecration showed that this was not a mere comparison, for it borrowed its usages from the ritual of marriage.

As everyone knows, the liturgy of marriage gave Christian status to the practices of the ancient city and consisted essentially in the *velatio* of the wife to the accompaniment of a prayer of blessing during the Eucharist. The ritual for the consecration of virgins followed the very same pattern, as we can already see from the letter of Pope Siricius.

This scheme was the basis for the development of the celebration. The formularies would henceforth never weary of repeating nuptial themes, not always in the most felicitous way, especially beginning with the tenth century and the Romano-German Pontifical. The introduction of the giving of a ring and then the persistent allusions in the Pontifical of William Durandus at the end of the thirteenth century would turn the ritual for the consecration of virgins into a real, and lavish, marriage ceremony.

The consecration must be distinguished from the vow of virginity. The old Roman Pontifical and the new *Ordo* alike suppose that the vow of virginity has already been taken. The *velatio* is therefore regarded as a completion, a seal upon the vow of virginity. It might be said that there is the same difference between the vow of virginity and the consecration as between the commitment made by the promises of marriage and the blessing later given to the spouses during the Mass. But this is not necessarily the way things have to be. It is quite possible to think that a consecration can take place anywhere and in any circumstances of life, and that religious profession subsequently determines how one intends to live out this virginal consecration.

---

3. St. Ambrose of Milan, *De virginibus* 3, 1, ed. O. Faller (CSEL), 57–58.
4. PL 13:1182.

The origin of the ritual for the consecration of virgins and its later development allow us to be as realistic as possible in the theology of mystical marriage that permeates this ritual.

§2. The Consecration of Virgins in the Roman Sacramentaries

The first liturgical formulary for this consecration occurs in the Verona Sacramentary. When virgins are here consecrated on the feast of Sts. Peter and Paul, there is a special *Hanc igitur* for the Canon of the Mass of consecration.[5] Among the Masses for September, under the title *Ad virgines sacras*, there is a prayer, "Respice, Domine, propitius," and a lengthy prayer of blessing, "Deus castorum corporum benignus habitator."[6]

This last-named formulary was to persist down the centuries. Its teaching is very rich: the incarnation, which has restored human beings to divine favor, also makes it possible for them to live angelic lives. The encounter of a virgin with the Son of God is a far greater thing than conjugal union, sacred though the latter is. But God alone can preserve this kind of greatness.

The Gelasian Sacramentary repeats the formulas of the Verona Sacramentary, but at the end of the prayer of blessing it introduces a reference to the wise and foolish virgins. In addition, the Gelasian has three formularies for Mass on the day of consecration; the first and third each have their own special *Hanc igitur*.[7]

The fifth-century witnesses show that the virgins received a veil.[8] The Gelasian Sacramentary has a formulary, probably of Frankish origin, for blessing some distinctive articles of clothing but not specifically the veil.[9]

Except for prayers for the blessing of the garments the other sacramentaries contribute nothing new.[10]

§3. The Nuptial Ceremonial of the Romano-German Pontifical

The Rhenish Pontifical of the tenth century has a very fully developed ceremonial that is inspired by various marriage rituals of the time and includes songs that give the entire celebration a very lyrical character. These sung texts, which are antiphons or responses, are taken either from

---

5. *Le* 283 (p.37): "Coniunctio oblationis virginum sacratarum."

6. *Le* 1103–4 (pp. 138–39).

7. *Ge* I, 103–7 (nos. 787–803; pp. 124–28).

8. To the letter of Pope Siricius, mentioned above, add: Innocent I, *Ep. ad Victricem Rotomagensem* (PL 20:478–79): "velari a sacerdote meruerunt . . ."; Gelasius, *Ep. ad universos episcopos* 12, ed. A. Thiel, *Epist. Rom. pontif.* 1:139: "velamen imponere."

9. A. Chavasse, *Le sacramentaire gélasien* (Paris: Desclée, 1958), 32–33.

10. *Gr* 995 (p. 341). — *Gell* 2604–10 (pp, 405–8).

the Common of Virgins or from special offices and are based on the New Testament or the Passions of the virgin martyrs.

The Romano-German Pontifical offers two distinct, though very similar celebrations, which take into account the two different states now traditional: one supposes a virgin living in a monastery, the other a virgin living in the world.[11]

In the case of a nun, the young girl is presented to the bishop by her parents before the Mass. The bishop takes her hand, which she has previously covered with an altar cloth. An antiphon is sung: "Ipsi sum desponsata cui angeli serviunt, cuius pulchritudinem sol et luna mirantur."[12]

After the singing of the Gradual,[13] the virgin comes forward to the altar with her *Adstipulator* who must give assent to the consecration.[14] The bishop blesses the veil and garments with three prayers.[15] After donning her new garments, except for the veil, the virgin returns carrying a lighted candle in each hand.[16] She sings the verse "Suscipe me, Domine" (Ps 119:116), which chapter 58 of the Rule of St. Benedict prescribes for the profession of a monk.

Next comes the singing of the litanies and the formula of blessing.[17] The latter, which includes a prayer and a preface, is taken from the Verona Sacramentary. After having asked the virgin whether she is ready to take on the responsibilities inherent in her commitments, the bishop places the veil on her, to the accompaniment of a Frankish formula: "Accipe velamen sacrum, puella, quod perferas sine macula ante tribunal Domini nostri Iesu Christi, cui flectitur omne genu coelestium, terrestrium et infernorum. . . ."

The virgin then sings: "Induit me Dominus cyclade auro texta et immensis monilibus ornavit me."[18] The prayer "Famulam tuam, Domine," from the Gregorian Sacramentary, ends this part of the celebration.[19]

---

11. *PRG* 1:38–46, 51–54.

12. *Ibid.*, 39. — The text is from the *Passio* of St. Agnes (PL 17:813).

13. But some groups of manuscripts have a rubric that locates the consecration of virgins after the gospel: "Virgines autem et viduae post perfectum evangelium debent velari, quia decet eas et per evangelium praedicari" (*PRG* 1:38–39).

14. In the Roman practice of the *traditio puellae* the girl was presented by her parents. The most important manuscripts bring in at this point the *adstipulator*, who makes known the consent of the parents (*PRG* 1:39).

15. The first is from *Ge* 791 (p. 126); the second is from *Gell* 2605 (p. 406); the third may have been based on *Gr* 1252 (p. 419).

16. *PRG* 1:41. The allusion here is to the parable of the prudent virgins. Many marriage rituals, however, contain a similar custom. The Byzantine ritual of marriage, for example, has the married couple carrying candles.

17. *PRG* 1:42–43.

18. *Passio* of St. Agnes (PL 17:814).

19. *Gr* 995 (modified).

The nun now sings two other antiphons, each followed by a prayer of the bishop.[20] The latter then gives the virgin a ring, with the formula: "Accipe anulum fidei,"[21] and puts the crown on her head with the words "Accipe signum Christi."[22] The virgin next sings the antiphon, "Anulo suo subarrhavit me Dominus Iesus Christus, et tamquam sponsam decoravit me corona."[23] The bishop then commends her to the faithful and threatens with canonical penalties anyone who tries to turn her from her commitments.

At the offertory the virgin offers candles. At communion some of the sacred species are reserved so that she may communicate from them for eight days.[24] After the Mass the nun is restored to the care of the abbess.[25]

In the case of a virgin living in the world,[26] there is no presentation to the bishop during Mass, no giving of a ring, no placing of a crown on her head. These elements of the celebration were in fact innovations of the Romano-German Pontifical in its ritual for the consecration of nuns. To be noted are two short formulas for the blessing of the virgin.

§4. Local Adaptations of the Ritual for the Consecration of Virgins

1. In his *De antiquis ritibus Ecclesiae* Dom Edmond Martène's transcription of manuscripts dating from the late ninth to the fifteenth century acquaints us with the usages of various Churches.[27] The oldest, his

---

20. The first antiphon is a repetition of the "Ipsi sum desponsata," which has already been sung; it is followed by the prayer "Da quaesumus omnipotens Deus ut haec famula tua,' which is from the Sacramentary of Gellone, no. 2616 (p. 409). The second antiphon is "Posuit signum in faciem meam, ut nullum praeter eum amatorem admittam," from the *Passio* of St. Agnes (PL 17:814); it is followed by the prayer "Deus plasmator corporum . . .," which probably had its origin in a legendary *Passio Matthaei*. See R. Metz, *La consécration des vierges dans l'Eglise romaine* (Paris: Presses Universitaires de France, 1954), 205–6, and *PRG* 1:44-46.

21. "Accipe anulum fidei, signaculum Spiritus sancti, ut sponsa Dei voceris, si ei fideliter servieris" (*PRG* 1:45).

22. "Accipe signum Christi in capite, ut uxor eius efficiaris et, si in eo permanseris, in perpetuum coroneris" (*PRG* 1:45).

23. The substance of this text originates in the *Passio* of St. Agnes (PL 17:813).

24. *PRG* 1:46. — A forty-day supply of consecrated bread was set aside for a bishop at his consecration (*OR* XXXV), an eight-day supply for a priest (*Ordo* XXXVI). See above, pp. 158, 159.

25. "Vide quomodo istam Deo sacratam repraesentes immaculatam ante tribunal Domini nostri Iesu Christi" (*PRG* 1:46).

26. *PRG* 1:51-54.

27. Martène transcribes thirteen *Ordines*. A. G. Martimort's work, *La documentation liturgique de Dom Edmond Martène* (= M), has made it possible to date these *Ordines* quite precisely. In nos. 742-54 M lists the various editions of Martène and gives information on the dates of the *Ordines*, studies of them, if they exist, and so on.

Ordo 3, which is a manuscript of the last quarter of the ninth century[28] from Saint-Gatien in Tours, gives a description and texts that do not contain the innovations in the Romano-German Pontifical (which is later than the Saint-Gatien manuscript); there is thus no giving of ring or crown. Nor does Martène's *Ordo* 1, a ninth-century manuscript from Jumièges,[29] mention these innovations. His *Ordo* 5, which is from Apamea,[30] is for practical purposes identical with the Roman Pontifical of the twelfth century. The fourteenth-century *Ordines* show the influence of the Pontifical of William Durandus, whose ritual I shall describe below. Martène's *Ordo* 13, from the fourteenth century, is interesting because it deals with the consecration of Carthusian nuns;[31] the user is referred to the Roman Pontifical, but the following special features are noted: the bishop puts a maniple on the nun's right arm, with the formula: "Exspecta Dominum, viriliter age, et confortetur cor tuum et sustine Dominum." He likewise puts a stole on her with the words: "Tolle iugum Domini super te, et disce ab eo quia mitis est et humilis corde." He then gives the nun the cross by placing it on her right shoulder with the words: "Abnega temetipsum et tolle crucem tuam quotidie et sequere Dominum." The nun then sings while kneeling: "Dexteram meam et collum meum cinxit lapidibius pretiosis, tradidit manibus meis inaestimabiles margaritas."

2. J. Deshusses, in his edition of the Gregorian Sacramentary, describes the special features of various ninth-century manuscripts with their organization and their prayer formulas.[32] With his aid the reader can become acquainted with the *Ordines* of Paris,[33] Cambrai,[34] Sainte-Geneviève of Paris,[35] Modena,[36] and Padua.[37]

3. The Pontifical of William Durandus, from the end of the thirteenth century, would be taken over almost unchanged by subsequent Pontificals and especially by the modern Roman Pontifical. The Romano-German Pontifical served William as a foundation, but he revised it in significant ways. The title he adopted for the ritual we are discussing was *De benedictione et consecratione virginum.*[38] The entire redaction of this Pontifical

---

28. M 744.

29. M 743.

30. M 746.

31. M 754.

32. J. Deshusses, *Le Sacramentaire grégorien* 3 (Spicilegium Friburgense 28; Fribourg: Editions universitaires, 1982).

33. *Ibid.*, no. 479 (p. 226).

34. *Ibid.*, no. 480 (p. 226).

35. *Ibid.*, no. 481 (p. 226).

36. *Ibid.*, no. 482 (p. 227).

37. *Ibid.*, no. 483 (p. 228).

38. Andrieu, *PR* 3:411.

reflects its author's juridical outlook as well as his love of spacious and dramatic celebrations. In his ritual of the consecration of virgins he was heavily influenced by the ritual of ordinations.

On the preceding evening or on the morning of the consecration itself the bishop questions the young woman with regard to her age (she must be twenty-five), her intentions, and her virginity ("et carnis integritate").[39]

The consecration takes place after the Gradual. In this ceremony the bishop represents Christ; in his name the archpriest summons the virgins: "Prudentes virgines, aptate lampades vestras, ecce sponsus venit, exite obviam ei." Carrying a lighted candle in each hand, the virgins come forward and the archpriest presents them to the bishop while emphasizing the element of mystical marriage in the consecration of a virgin. The bishop addresses them three times: "Venite," and they answer: "Et nunc sequimur."[40] They then sing the "Suscipe me, Domine."[41]

Next, escorted by the *paranymphes*,[42] they come forward to the bishop and stand in a half-circle around him to hear his address. After this he questions them very specifically about their resolve; then, as in the ritual of ordination, each virgin places her hands in those of the bishop and kisses his hand. The litanies are then sung, again as in the ritual of ordination.[43] The bishop then blesses the garments and sprinkles them with holy water;[44] he does the same for the veil.[45] As in the Romano-German Pontifical, the bishop bestows the ring and the crown, but the Pontifical of Durandus adds formulas of blessing.[46] The virgins then go off to don their new garments, except for the veil; they then return and sing the antiphon "Regnum mundi."[47] The prayer and preface are taken from the Verona

---

39. *Ibid.*

40. The third time, the bishop sings "Venite, filiae, audite me, timorem Domini docebo vos." These antiphons were from various local rituals and cite Ps 34:11.

41. The second part is not "et non confundas me ab expectatione mea," but "ut non dominetur omnis iniustitia."

42. This person and function recall the marriage customs of antiquity, where the woman attending the wife was called *pronuba* or *nympheutria*.

43. This practice was taken from the Roman Pontifical of the thirteenth century, with some additions; but it is also found in most manuscripts of the Romano-German Pontifical (*PRG* 1:41).

44. Three prayers taken from the Roman Pontifical of the thirteenth century (Andrieu, *PR* 2:414–15).

45. The two prayers for this blessing were taken from the Roman Pontifical of the twelfth century (Andrieu, *PR* 1:156 or *PRG* 1:40–41).

46. The formula for the blessing of the ring was taken from the marriage ritual and slightly modified: "Creator humani generis . . . ut que eos gestaverint . . . in castitate perseverent." Durandus may have composed the prayer for the blessing of the crown: "Benedic, Domine, ornamenta ista."

47. This was a response in the Office of Virgins; in the Breviary of St. Pius V it became the eighth response in the Roman Office of Non-virgins. The singing of it was an innovation of the ritual for the consecration of virgins.

Sacramentary, but with the ending slightly changed.[48] The bestowals of veil, ring, and crown have been given a new emphasis and take place according to a symmetrical pattern: call by the bishop, giving of the insigne, antiphon sung by the virgin, concluding prayer by the bishop.[49] Finally, the bishop pronounces the anathema against those who influence virgins to fall short of the perfection of their state.

At the offertory the virgins offer their candles and, if they wish, other gifts as well. Hosts are prepared for their communion on this day and the three succeeding days. Before communion, the bishop sings a blessing over the virgins. At the end of Mass the virgins are entrusted to the care of the abbess.

The Roman Pontifical subsequently introduced only slight changes into this celebration. Thus the Mass of the day had to be celebrated, the prayer proper to the consecration being said *sub unica conclusione* with the prayer of the day. The *Veni Creator* was sung after the litanies. The virgins now carried only one candle. Until 1965 they no longer received from the chalice,[50] nor were consecrated hosts laid aside for them for the following days. After the blessing the bishop commissioned them to celebrate the Hours; this was an important change as far as the history of the role of nuns in the Church was concerned. The *Te Deum* was sung and then the bishop led the nuns to the door of the enclosure, where he handed them over to the abbess with the traditional exhortation "Vide quomodo."

§5. The Consecration of Virgins in the Ritual of 1970

The Second Vatican Council ordered that the rite of the consecration of virgins be revised.[51] This will to renewal was in response to the desires of some bishops and religious circles. The intention was to preserve the solemnity of the celebration but to strip away its lavish display while at the same time not overly reducing its scale. Repetitions were to be avoided and elements not adapted to our times were to be excised. In the process,

48. This blessing was, in modified form, from the Supplement to the Gregorian Sacramentary: *Gr* 1254 (p. 420).

49. To the antiphons that the *PRG* already offered for the use of the virgins there were added two others: "Ancilla Christi sum . . .," from the Office of St. Agnes (Roman Pontifical of the thirteenth century; Andrieu, *PR* 2:415), and "Ecce quod concupivi iam video," from the same source (see the *Passio* of St. Agnes: PL 17:819–20). The bishop for his part sang "Veni electa mea" and 'Veni sponsa Christi," which were antiphons in the Common of Virgins. — The virgins wore the ring on the right hand.

50. This traditional custom was still followed in the Roman Pontifical of 1485. It was restored, in accordance with *VSC* 55, by the new *Rite of Communion under Both Kinds* (March 7, 1965), no. 1, 4 (*DOL* 268 no. 2105).

51. *VSC* 80 (*DOL* 1 no. 80).

the ritual has been scripturally enriched, and some euchological texts that had become corrupt in the course of time have been restored to their original form. But while organizing the rite in a way that is clear and easy to understand, the reformers were concerned also to keep its authentic meaning as the celebration of a marriage between Christ and the woman who is consecrating her virginity to him. Certain formulas of a nuptial kind have indeed had to be suppressed because they made our contemporaries uneasy, but the fundamental theme of betrothal to Christ has not been diminished.

At the same time, however, the ritual harks back to a situation that existed long ago, and restores the outlook in terms of which the rite can be properly celebrated. As everyone knows, in the early Church consecrated virgins lived in the world, independently of any religious institution. This same choice is now available again. In fact, Section A of the new ritual is concerned with women who live in the world or are members of secular institutes; Section B then turns to women in monastic life. The Introduction (no. 4) thus restores an original situation and considerably widens the range of uses for this ritual. Some may be surprised, however, that this consecration is reserved to women living in the world, members of secular institutes, and nuns, and not extended to other religious women. This is indeed the present situation, but it could change in the future.

The ritual for the consecration of virgins is innovative in that it allows this consecration as long as there has been no marriage and the women who desire consecration have not publicly lived a disordered life. The ritual thus requires a formal and juridical virginity but not the physical integrity that the Pontifical of William Durandus seemed to demand. At the same time, however, the Introduction (no. 5) also recalls the qualities of perseverance, constancy, character, wisdom, and prudence women need if they are to be admitted to this consecration.

The ritual can be adapted in the local Churches, various religious communities, or secular institutes. It is intended as a means of sanctification and of service to the Church and can therefore be adjusted to fit varying circumstances, in accordance with the principles set down in the Constitution on the Liturgy.[52]

The new ritual has thus departed from the decisions taken in 1951 in the Apostolic Constitution *Sponsa Christi*, which reserved this consecration to cloistered nuns.[53]

---

52. *VSC* 37–40 (*DOL* 1 nos. 37–40).

53. *AAS* 43 (1951) 16: "Solemnes antiquae formulae consecrationis virginum, quae in Pontificali Romano habentur, monialibus reservantur."

The two rituals of consecration—for women living in the world and for women in monastic life—have the same overall structure. The celebration takes place between the Liturgy of the Word and the Liturgy of the Eucharist and no longer after the Gradual, as in the old Pontifical.

The celebration opens with the bishop's call to the candidate, followed by his homily. A text has been composed that develops the theology of consecration; it is offered for the bishop's use, but only as an example. The bishop then questions the candidate about her resolve to persevere in virginity and receive the consecration. The examination is followed by a litany that replaces the General Intercessions. At this point the virgin renews her intention of virginity or makes her religious profession. The old Pontifical did not include this renewal; however, it was contained, in dialogue form, in the examination that the bishop conducted at the beginning of the ceremony. The new ritual seems to have wanted to juxtapose in a more expressive way the virgin's self-giving to the Lord and the Lord's consecration of this gift to him.

The prayer of consecration is now said or sung. The text, which we saw appearing first in the Verona Sacramentary,[54] has been restored to its original purity; some passages of it may be omitted, depending on circumstances. The symbols of the woman's consecration are then presented to her: the ritual limits itself to the veil and the ring and to a single formula that covers the giving of both. If it be desirable, the bishop can also give the consecrated virgin the Book of Hours. He does this, however, not at the end of Mass, as formerly, but at the end of the consecration and before the offertory. At the end of Mass the bishop pronounces a solemn blessing over the virgin. The singing of the *Te Deum* is optional.

In its revised form the *Ordo* has gained in clarity while retaining its dignity. Of the many former antiphons, some of them from the Passion of St. Agnes, only one has been kept as an optional chant by the schola: "Ipsi sum desponsata . . .," "I am espoused to him whom the angels serve; sun and moon stand in wonder at his glory." During the Eucharistic Prayer the consecrated virgin is mentioned in a special intercession.

When the virgin being consecrated is living a monastic life, the rite has the same structure but with some additions. For example, at the beginning the schola sings the antiphon "Prudentes virgines" ("Be wise: make ready . . ."). The bishop calls the nun by singing, once, the words "Venite, filiae, audite me . . ." ("Come, listen to me, my children . . ."). To this the candidate replies: "Et nunc sequimur in toto corde . . ." ("Now with all our hearts we follow you . . ."). (The ritual also offers a different form

---

54. See above, note 5. The text attributed to St. Leo, as well as its primitive form, have been studied in two articles of O. Harrisson and J. Magne (see the bibliography for this chapter), while its origin has been studied by C. Coebregh (see the bibliography).

of the call and response: nos. 52–53 [= 138–39].) After making her profession the nun sings: "Suscipe me, Domine . . ." ("Uphold me, Lord . . .").

The ritual of profession may be separated from that of consecration; in this case any repetition of formulas or symbols is to be avoided. The ritual also has the profession precede the consecration. The reason for this is clear, and I have already emphasized it: religious profession is the virgin's gift of herself to God, while the consecration is, as it were, the response of God who consecrates this virgin as his spouse.

In its theological content the ritual not only retains the riches of the past but adds to them. This is especially true from the viewpoint of use of the Bible. The Lectionary of 1969 (nos. 784–88) had already provided a lengthy selection of readings; the ritual for the consecration of virgins has the same list but adds two further Old Testament pericopes: Isaiah 44:1-5 and Jeremiah 31:31-37. The latter emphasizes in particular the prophetic value of virginity: God will raise up a new Israel, whose members will not be limited to Israelites according to the flesh, for this will be an Israel according to the Spirit. In addition, the celibacy of Jeremiah himself (the only known case in the Old Testament) is a sign and announces the end of transmission of the promises through carnal generation. There are thus ten Old Testament passages for use in the first reading (nos. 81–90 in the Latin *Ordo*). For the second there are sixteen passages, from Acts, the letters of Paul or John, and the Apocalypse (nos. 91–106). For the gospel there are fifteen possible pericopes (nos. 123–37).

Despite the revisions made in this ritual it still provides, especially in the prayer of consecration, a fine synthesis of the relations between virginity and marriage. The virgin renounces the sexual element in marriage (the *sacramentum*) but still seeks to achieve what marriage signifies (the *res*), namely, union with Christ. Thus virginity effects what marriage signifies.[55] Given this approach, it is natural that the virgin be seen from two points of view: that of her self-gift to Christ and that of her self-gift to the Church. The formula accompanying the presentation of the insignia is the best expression of this theology.[56]

---

55. See A. Nocent, "Il mistero di Cristo nella *Velatio sponsae* et nella *Velatio virginum*," *Rivista Liturgica* 55 (1968) 368–77.

56. *Ordo consecrationis virginum*, no. 25: "Accipite, filiae carissimae, velamen et anulum, vestrae consecrationis insignia; et fidem Sponso vestro intactam servate; nec umquam obliviscamini vos Christi servitio mancipari et Corporis eius, quod est Ecclesia." *Consecration to a Life of Virginity*, no. 25: "Dearest daughters, receive the veil and the ring that are the insignia of your consecration. Keep unstained your fidelity to your Bridegroom, and never forget that you are bound to the service of Christ and of his body, the Church" (*Rites* 2:145).

Chapter VIII

Christian Death

D. Sicard

GENERAL BIBLIOGRAPHY

Martène, Lib. 3, cap. 11–15; M 913–38.

E. Bishop, *Liturgica Historica* (Oxford: Clarendon, 1918), 182–92: "Burial Services of the Eighth Century."

B. Capelle, "L'antienne *In Paradisum*," *QL* 8 (1923) 161–76.

L. Gougaud, "Etude sur les *Ordines commendationis animae*," *EL* 44 (1935) 3–27.

A. C. Rush, *Death and Burial in Christian Antiquity* (Studies in Christian Antiquity 1; Washington, D.C.: The Catholic University of America, 1941).

Le mystère de la mort et sa célébration (LO 12; Paris: Cerf, 1951).

A. G. Martimort, "Comment meurt un chrétien," *LMD* no. 44 (1955) 5–28.

P. M. Gy, "Les funérailles d'après le rituel de 1614," *LMD* no. 44 (1955) 70–82.

Andrieu, *OR* 4:523–26.

A. Chavasse, *Le Sacramentaire gélasien* (Paris: Desclée, 1958), 57–61: "Le rituel des funérailles."

Reforming the Rites of Death = *Concilium* no. 32 (1968).

Le nouveau Rituel des funérailles = *LMD* no. 101 (1970).

J. Ntedika, *L'évocation de l'au-delà dans la prière pour les morts* (Recherches africaines de théologie 2; Louvain, 1971).

Le nouveau Rituel des malades = *LMD* no. 113 (1973).

La maladie et la mort du chrétien dans la liturgie. Conférences Saint-Serge XXI, 1974 (Bibliotheca EL, Subsidia 1; Rome: Edizioni liturgiche, 1975). ET: *Temple of the Holy Spirit. Sickness and Death of the Christian in the Liturgy*, trans. M. J. O'Connell (New York: Pueblo, 1983).

D. Sicard, *La liturgie de la mort dans les Eglises latines, des origines à la réforme carolingienne* (LQF 63; Münster: Aschendorff, 1978).

En face de la mort = *LMD* no. 144 (1980); see also *LMD* no. 145 (1981) 127–69.

For all human beings and for the groups to which they are bound by ties of blood, friendship, leisure interests, or proximity, death—a rendezvous all flesh must keep—is a unique and decisive event. It is a challenge and a source of anxiety to Christians no less than to other human beings. Men and women are afraid to die, and they avoid thinking of their "final hour" or at least avoid speaking of it. Death has been called the "taboo" subject of the twentieth century.

Christ experienced death, and the gospel narratives tell us that he foresaw it long in advance, predicted its coming, and prepared himself for it. He changed the meaning of death by turning it into a passage to the glory of the resurrection. He led the human race and every individual human being into a new history: the history of the world of the resurrection.

> Christ won this victory when he rose to life, for by his death he freed man from death. Faith, therefore, with its solidly based teaching, provides every thoughtful man with an answer to his anxious queries about his future lot. At the same time it makes him able to be united in Christ with his loved ones who have already died, and gives hope that they have found true life with God.[1]

The death of Christians can be defined as their encounter with Christ in the mystery of his passion and death. This encounter alone allows them to experience their own passage. The Roman Ritual says, in speaking of the liturgy for celebrating the death of a Christian, that its component elements are meant to help "the dying person, if still conscious," to "imitate Christ in the face of the anxiety about death that is common to all men" and to "accept suffering and death in the hope of heavenly life and resurrection, for Christ, by his power, destroyed our death by his own dying."[2]

§1. The Celebration of Death as a "Passover"

BIBLIOGRAPHY ON VIATICUM

M. Andrieu, *Immixtio et consecratio* (Paris: Picard, 1924).
L. Beauduin, "Le Viatique," *LMD* no. 15 (1948) 117–34.
A. Bride, "Viatique," *DTC* 15 (1950) 2842–58.
J. Hannon, *Holy Viaticum* (Canon Law Studies 314; Washington, D.C.: The Catholic University of America, 1951).

---

1. Vatican Council II, Pastoral Constitution *Gaudium et spes* on the Church in the Modern World 18 (Flannery 918).

2. *Rite for the Commendation of the Dying*, no. 139 = Chapter VI of the *Rite of Anointing and Pastoral Care of the Sick*, in *The Rites of the Catholic Church* 1 (New York: Pueblo, 1976), 573–642 (no. 139 is on p. 622). The Introduction to the *Rite of Anointing* is newly translated in *DOL* 410 nos. 3321–61.

The entire liturgical pedagogy of the Church down the centuries has been guided by the desire to make dying Christians aware that they should join themselves to Christ in the paschal mystery of his victorious death and resurrection. Thus the Instruction *Eucharisticum mysterium* of May 25, 1967 (no. 39), which is cited in the Introduction to the new *Rite of Anointing* (no. 26), said that "communion received as viaticum should be considered a special sign of participation in the mystery that is celebrated in the Eucharist: the mystery of the death of the Lord and his passage to the Father." The Instruction was simply repeating a most constant liturgical tradition and the most ordinary disciplinary prescriptions. To help dying Christians accept their death, the Church urges them to celebrate it as a passage to the Father, to make of it a "Passover" in the full sense.

The Ritual links the practice of receiving communion as viaticum with the gospel: "Those who eat my flesh and drink my blood have eternal life, and I will raise them up on the last day" (John 6:54). When the faithful are strengthened by the Body of Christ in their passage from this life, they take with them a pledge of the resurrection.[3] The rite of communion given as viaticum is in fact something that predated the ritual prescriptions known to us from the texts of the early liturgy. A judicious scholar has written: "The precept of viaticum is undoubtedly more than an ecclesiastical law; it expresses a divine command."[4] The corresponding ecclesiastical law found expression as early as 325 in canon 13 of the first ecumenical council of Nicaea. The council was not creating a new obligation or reminding Christians of a forgotten precept; it was concerned rather to provide penitents with both reconciliation and participation in the Eucharist and thus give to all, even those faithful who had been excommunicated for apostasy during persecution, the opportunity to profit by the mercy of God and to participate by their death in the passage of Christ, who on the last day will raise up those who eat his Body and drink his Blood: "The old canonical law is likewise to be followed in the case of those who are departing from this life: Those about to die should not be deprived of the ultimate and most necessary viaticum."[5]

---

3. See the Instruction *Eucharisticum mysterium*, no. 39, cited in the *Rite of Anointing*, no. 26 (*DOL* 410 no. 3346).

4. A. G. Martimort, "Comment meurt un chrétien," *LMD* no. 44 (1955) 5. According to the author, the idea of the reception of viaticum as a divine precept is a common opinion of the theologians; he refers the reader to M. de la Taile, *Mysterium fidei* (Paris: Beauchesne, 1921), *Elucidatio* 49. See also A. Bride, "Viatique," *DTC* 15 (1950) 2853–56.

5. DS 129. To the urging of Nicaea may be added that of Innocent I, *Lettre à Decentius de Gubbio* (416), ed. R. Cabié (Louvain, 1973), 28–30, and the Council of Orange (441), can. 3, ed. C. Munier (CCL 148), 78–79. Also to be mentioned are the testimonies regarding the deaths of St. Basil (PG 29:315), St. Ambrose (PL 14:43), St. Benedict (PL 56:202), and St. Paulinus (PL 53:860).

The reception of communion as viaticum is a practice attested universally by the patristic, canonical, and hagiographical documents of the fourth, fifth, and sixth centuries.

I. THE FIRST RITUALS OF VIATICUM

The first liturgical traditions have come down to us in two main forms: the one transmitted by the Roman *ordo* for funerals that is contained in the Berlin Sacramentary of the eighth century, and the one transmitted by Andrieu's *Ordo* XLIX, the ritual most often reproduced.

The eighth-century Gelasian Sacramentary that is classified as Phillipps 1667 in the State Library at Berlin contains (fol. 173^v–174^r) a Roman ritual for death. Its description of viaticum has no exact parallel elsewhere but is not without interest:

> As soon as the hour of death approaches, they begin to read the passion of the Lord in the Gospel of John.
>
> Next, they begin to sing the psalm "Quemadmodum" with the antiphon "Tu iussisti nascere mi domine." After that the litany "Christe audi nos."
>
> When the litany is ended, the priest says the prayer for the commendation of the soul.
>
> Then, before the soul leaves the body, the priest gives the person communion with the body and blood, those present being careful to see that the person does not die without viaticum, which is the body of the Lord.[6]

Unlike the better known tradition in *Ordo* XLIX, the Phillipps ritual places the viaticum communion after the reading of the passion from St. John and after the singing of a psalm, antiphon, and litany and a priest's prayer of recommendation. Preparation for death is here structured by a liturgy of the Word (the Passion According to St. John) and a liturgy of bread (viaticum), the two being linked by a penitential section consisting essentially of Psalm 42, its antiphon "Tu iussisti," and a litany (the content of which is not further specified). All this amounts to a real celebration of a "passover," the eyes of all being fixed on the passage that Christ experienced when "his hour had come to depart out of this world to the Father" (John 13:1).

---

6. *Liber sacramentorum Augustodunenis,* ed. O. Heiming (CCL 159 B), no. 1914 (pp. 241–42). Latin text: "Primitus enim ut adpropinquaret hora exitus, incipiunt legi evangelium Johannis de passione Domini. Deinde incipiunt canere ps. Quemadmodum cum ant. Tu iussisti nascere mi domine. Postea laetania: Christe audi nos. Ipsa expleta, dicit sacerdos orationem anime commemorationis. Inde vero antequam egrediatur a corpore, communicet eum sacerdos corpus et sanguinem illum praevidentes ut sine viaticum non exeat, hoc est corpus domini."

The tradition represented by *Ordo* XLIX is reported by a large number of witnesses.[7] Here is the text:

> As soon as you see death approaching, the person is to receive communion from the holy sacrifice, even if he or she has already eaten that day, because communion will defend the person and help in attaining to the resurrection of the just. For it is communion that will raise him or her up.
>
> After the reception of communion the narratives of the Lord's passion are to be read by priests or deacons in the presence of the sick person's body until the soul departs from it.[8]

The importance of viaticum for the resurrection of the just is so great that the law of Eucharistic fast is suspended, as well as the law forbidding communion more than once a day. Disciplinary prescriptions earlier than or contemporary with *Ordo* XLIX were so aware of the "necessity" of viaticum that they gave it priority over all ecclesiastical laws. On this point the 1983 Code of Canon Law repeats the Code of 1917, which itself had summed up all earlier legislation: "Even if they have received Communion in the same day, those who are in danger of death are strongly urged to receive again."[9]

---

7. Classification of these witnesses by the date at which the manuscript was copied yields the following list: the *Ordo* of Cologne (Cologne, Cathedral ms 123, fol. 80[r]), the *Ordo* of Subiaco (Subiaco 163, fol. 183[v]), the *Ordo* of Saint-Martial in Limoges (Paris, B. N. lat. 1240, fol. 16[r]), the *Ordo* of the Vatican (Bibl. Vatic., Ottobonianus lat. 312, fol. 151[v]), the Sacramentary of Lorsch (Bibl. Vatic., Palatinus lat. 485, fol. 58[v]), the Leofric Missal (Oxford, Bodleian ms. 579, fol. 246[r]), the Romano-German Pontifical (Monte Cassino cod. 451, fol. 203[r]), the Sacramentary of Arezzo (Bibl. Vatic., Vaticanus lat. 4772, fol. 163[r]), the Ritual of Jumièges (Rouen, B. M. Y 127, fol. 54[r]), the *Ordines* of Northern Italy (Milan, Bibl. Ambros. T 27 sup., fol. 42[v]), the Hamburg Missal (Rome, Vallicellana B 141, fol. 2[v]), the *Disciplina Farfensis* (Bibl. Vatic., Vaticanus lat. 6808, fol. 106[r]), the Roman Pontifical of the twelfth century (London, British Library, Add 57528, fol. 151[r]), the Rituals of the Veneto, Siena, St. Florian, Fontavellana, etc.

8. "Mox ut eum viderint ad exitum propinquare communicandus est de sacrificio sancto, etiamsi comedisset ipso die quia communio erit ei defensor et adiutor in resurrectione iustorum, Ipsa enim resuscitabit eum. Post communionem perceptam, legendae sunt passiones dominicae ante corpus infirmi a presbyteris vel a diaconibus quousque egrediatur anima de corpore." — For a critical edition of the *ordo* and its variants I refer the reader to my book, *La liturgie de la mort dans l'Eglise latine, des origines à la réforme carolingienne* (LQF 63; Münster: Aschendorff, 1978), 36–42. It is from this edition that I reprint the text of the *Ordo* here; for this text I prefer the convergent evidence of the tenth-century *Ordines*— those of St. Martial in Limoges, Subiaco, and Cologne—to the text published by Andrieu, *OR* XLIX (Andrieu, *OR* 4).

9. *Codex Juris canonici auctoritate Johannis Pauli PP II promulgatus* (Vatican City: Libreria Editrice Vaticana, 1983), can. 921 § 2. ET: *Code of Canon Law. Latin-English Edition*, translation prepared under the auspices of the Canon Law Society of America (Washington, D.C.: Canon Law Society of America, 1983), 345. Latin text: "Etiamsi eadem die communione refecti fuerint, valde tamen suadetur ut qui in vitae discrimen adducti sint, denuo communicent."

It may come as a surprise, on the other hand, that the legislators of the new Code thought it advisable to suppress mention of the precept concerning viaticum and thus change the formula that the Ritual of 1972 had taken over from the Instruction *Eucharisticum mysterium* of 1967 and the Code of 1917.[10] Yet the idea that viaticum is a duty had been approved by a unanimous tradition dating from at least the fourth century. It is true, of course, that while no longer appealing to a precept, the Code of 1983 does require the faithful in danger of death to be strengthened by communion in the form of viaticum.

The early liturgical rituals presented communion in the form of viaticum as an indispensable provision for the journey ("sine viaticum non exeat," "communicandus est"). The expressions used: "sacrificium sanctum," "corpus et sanguinem," referred to communion under both species. After saying "communicandus est de sacrificio sancto," several witnesses give the formula: "corpus domini nostri Jesu Christi sanguine suo tinctum conservet animam tuam in vitam aeternam."[11] But the word "sacrificium" by itself already signifies the two species in the Old Gelasian Sacramentary.[12] The sentence in the discourse on the Bread of Life, from which the Roman evangeliaries take two of their four pericopes *in agenda mortuorum*,[13] probably had an influence on the giving of both species in communion received as viaticum, in order that this communion might be seen as a clear pledge of resurrection. Those who receive communion as they are dying see the Eucharist exercising its power to raise them up to glory ("in resurrectione iustorum. Ipsa enim resuscitabit eum").

Another common element in the early rituals for viaticum is the atmosphere of expectation of "the hour of death": "Primitus ut adpropin-

---

10. The Code of 1917 said in can. 864 § 1: "In periculo mortis, quavis ex causa procedat, fideles sacrae communionis recipiendae praecepto tenentur"; this is cited in *Eucharisticum mysterium*, no. 39, and in the *Rite of Anointing*, no. 27. In can. 921 § 1 of the 1983 Code this becomes: "Christifideles qui versantur in periculo mortis, quavis ex causa procedenti, sacra communione per modum Viatici reficiantur" ("The Christian faithful who are in danger of death, arising from any cause, are to be nourished by Holy Communion in the form of Viaticum," p. 343).

11. This is true, for example, of the *Ordines* of Northern Italy, the Hamburg Missal, the Collectarium in CV 134 of the Chigi collection, and the Ritual of the Veneto: "May the body of our Lord Jesus Christ, impregnated with his blood, protect your soul for eternal life."

12. This is clear if we compare the final rubric for Holy Thursday: "Communicant et reservant de ipso sacrificio in crastinum unde communicent" (no. 390 in the Mohlberg edition), with the rubric of Good Friday: "Procedunt cum corpore et sanguinis domini quod ante die remansit et ponunt super altare" (no. 418).

13. See Th. Klauser, *Das römische Capitulare Evangeliorum 1. Typen* (Münster: Aschendorff, 1935). The four pericopes are John 11:21-27; John 5:21-24; John 6:37-40; John 6:51-54. "Qui manducat meam carnem et bibit meum sanguinem, habet vitam aeternam; et ego resuscitabo eum in novissimo die" is verse 54 of John 6.

quaret hora exitus"; "Mox ut eum viderint ad exitum propinquare." The connection between viaticum and the closeness of the death that is to be celebrated as a passover or passage is clear. On this point these *ordines* are perhaps witnesses to the ancient practice (not to be considered universal) that wanted the faithful to die immediately after having received the sacrament in their mouths.[14] This expectation of the hour of death is characteristic of communion received as viaticum and distinguishes it in particular from communion received by the sick. Gradually, however, the two came to be put in the same category in the Church. This was true of the Ritual published in 1614 and still in use in 1971. Communion received as viaticum had here lost its original character as celebration of death and preparation for the resurrection and was even located before the anointing of the sick. When completely cut off in this way from the liturgy of death and separated still further from it by the ritual of anointing, communion as viaticum had become in the Roman Ritual a communion of the sick rather than the sacrament of death, as it had been in the early liturgical traditions. The manner in which the rites were organized had affected the understanding of the doctrine involved.

These ancient liturgical traditions spoke to us still as a setting for viaticum, a reading of the passion, and a litany. The reading of the passion, which had been obligatory in the Roman *ordines* I have described, was to become optional in later manuscript witnesses and hypothetical in the Roman Ritual of 1614; in the Roman Ritual of 1972 it is mentioned only in the list of various texts with which the document ends.[16] The action of the ordained minister (priest or deacon) in the old Roman liturgical traditions became an act of private devotion in a family setting.[17] It had

---

14. The least debatable witness to this practice seems to be the account of the death of St. Ambrose by Paulinus, his deacon: "Quo accepto [corpore Domini] ubi glutivit, emisit spiritum, bonum viaticum secum ferens" (PL 14:43). The texts often cited from the *Vita Basilii* or the life of Melania the Younger are of doubtful authenticity. See D. Gorce, *Vie de Saint Mélanie* (SC 90; Paris: Cerf, 1962), 100–101. Only in the Latin text (tenth century) of the life of this saint do we find the sentence that is often cited: "Consuetudo autem est Romanis ut cum animae egrediuntur, communio Domini in ore sit." The Greek text, which seems closer to the original (see Gorce 53), has nothing corresponding to this statement. On this subject Cardinal Rampolla cited: V. Bolland, *Acta SS. Junii, ad diem 14, De vita s. Basilii apocrypha; Vita s. Basilii* 4 (PG 24:315); Balsamon, *In canone LXXXIII Conc. Trull.*; Gregory the Great, *Dialogorum* II, 24; II, 37; IV, 15; IV, 35; Amalarius, *De officiis ecclesiasticis* IV, 41; *Vita s. Othmani* (PL 121:783). See M. Card. Rampolla, *Santa Melania giuniore, senatrice romana*, Nota XL: "Sulla consuetudine della Chiesa Romana di dare nell'ora estrema la communione eucaristica ai moribondi," pp. 254–56.

15. *Rituale Romanum* (1953), tit. VI, cap. VII, 5: "poterit legi."

16. *Rite of Anointing*, chap. VII, nos. 224–29: "If desired, readings may also be taken from the passion of the Lord . . ." (*Rites* 1:634).

17. See A. G. Martimort, "Comment meurt un chrétien" (above, note 4), 6–7; D. Sicard, *La liturgie de la mort* (above, note 8), 40–42.

been instinctive for Stephen, the first martyr, to die while gazing upon and imitating Christ in his passion and death (Acts 7:55-60).

Beginning in the tenth century and in a Gallican milieu, the penitential section that had been vaguely suggested by the litany in the *Ordo* in Phillipps 1667 became rather extensive; the recitation of the seven penitential psalms made its appearance, as did the litanies for the dying and all the prayers that would subsequently be part of the *Ordo commendationis animae*, of which I shall speak further on. In the twelfth century the Cluniac rituals and the monastic traditions would supplement these Gallican traditions in several ways: the brethren were to keep an unbroken watch over the dying man; the dying man was to be placed on a bed of ashes and was to don a hairshirt; even more, the community and, if possible, the dying man himself were to sing the Creed in a solemn manner.

II. THE NEW RITUAL OF VIATICUM

In a reaction against the doctrinal and pastoral consequences of the way in which viaticum had been organized in the Roman Ritual that had been followed since the Council of Trent, Vatican II decreed that the Church must return to the reception of viaticum as the sacrament of Christian death. "In addition to the separate rites for anointing of the sick and for viaticum, a continuous rite shall be drawn up, structured so that the sick person is anointed after confessing and before receiving viaticum."[18] This is why the new Ritual, unlike that of 1614,[19] has separate chapters on the visitation and communion of the sick, the anointing of the sick, viaticum, and a continuous rite that includes penance, anointing, and viaticum. Three points emphasized in the new ritual of viaticum deserve attention:

1. *The Mass of Viaticum*

"When possible, viaticum should be received within Mass so that the sick person may receive communion under both kinds."[20] This directive in the Introduction to the new ritual determines the organization of Chapter III, which states: "Viaticum may be given during Mass, if the ordinary allows the celebration of the eucharist for that purpose (no. 26), or out-

---

18. *VSC* 74 (*DOL* 1 no. 74).

19. As I pointed out, the Ritual of 1614 placed viaticum before the anointing of the sick and in the chapter on the communion of the sick. See *Rituale Romanum* (1953), tit. V, c. IV, *De communione infirmorum*, nos. 16, 19, 21.

20. *Rite of Anointing*, no. 26 (*DOL* 410 no. 3346). Latin text: "Viaticum, si fieri potest, intra Missam recipiatur, ita ut infirmus sub utraque specie communicare possit."

side Mass, according to the rites and norms below."[21] The first section of this chapter is entitled "Viaticum during Mass" (nos. 97–99). This way of beginning the chapter indicates a preference and advocates a practice. The usual way of administering viaticum should include the celebration of Mass in the presence of the sick person. The ritual thus gives practical form to the possibilities allowed by the Motu Proprio *Pastorale munus* of November 30, 1963 (no. 7), and the Instruction *Eucharisticum mysterium* of May 25, 1967 (nos. 32, 6, and 39). The new outlook of the Roman Ritual of 1972 on this point becomes obvious when we recall the successive medieval prohibitions against celebrating Mass in the homes of the sick that are set down in the Gelasian Sacramentary and the Bobbio Missal[22] or again in the Code of 1917 (can. 822 §4) and the restrictions the latter placed on Masses celebrated outside of a church.[23]

2. Communion Under Both Kinds

This second point is connected with the first in the statement from the Introduction that I cited above. The first reason for urging the celebration of Mass in connection with viaticum is that the sick person may receive under both kinds. Moreover, when the sick cannot receive communion under the species of bread, Mass in their homes is recommended so that they may receive under the species of wine alone (*Rite of Anointing*, no. 95). Fidelity to the word of God that is recalled in the Introduction, no. 26 (where John 6:54 is cited), combines with the reason given in the Instruction *Eucharisticum mysterium*, no. 32:

> Holy communion has a more complete form as a sign when it is received under both kinds. For in this manner of reception . . . a fuller light shines on the sign of the eucharistic banquet. Moreover there is a clearer expression of that will by which the new and everlasting covenant is ratified in the blood of the Lord and of the relationship of the eucharistic banquet to the eschatological banquet in the Father's kingdom (see Mt 26:27-29). (*DOL* 179 no. 1261).

---

21. *Ibid.*, no. 94 (*Rites* 1:608). Latin text: "Viaticum infirmo ministrare licet sive intra Missam si, de iudicio Ordinarii, eucharistica celebratio apud illum habeatur (no. 26) sive extra Missam."

22. See Vat. Reg. lat. 316, nos. 1535–38; Bobbio Missal, nos. 379–81.

23. The Code of 1983, can. 932, did away with these restrictions: "Celebratio eucharistica peragatur in loco sacro, nisi in casu particulari necessitas aliud postulet; quo in casu, in loco honesto celebratio fieri debet. Sacrificium eucharisticum peragendum est super altare dedicatum vel benedictum; extra locum sacrum adhiberi potest mensa conveniens, retentis semper tobalea et corporali" ("The celebration of the Eucharist is to be performed in a sacred place, unless in a particular case necessity demands otherwise; in such a case the celebration must be done in a respectable place. The Eucharistic Sacrifice is to be performed upon a dedicated or blessed altar; a suitable table can be used outside a sacred place, always retaining the use of a cloth and a corporal": *Code of Canon Law. Latin-English Edition*, 347).

3. *The Profession of Faith*

Among the liturgical acts urged by the new ritual, the renewal of the profession of baptismal faith is the one that, after the Mass of viaticum in the home, has most caught the attention of pastors. On the day of baptism the "giving back of the creed" (*redditio symboli*), of which the early catecheses spoke,[24] is required of the catechumens, or of the parents in the case of small children. All of the faithful are also called to make this profession each year during the Easter Vigil. In France the "solemn communion" of young people includes it as well. Now the celebration of viaticum is likewise turned into a more solemn communion that looks toward the sick person's "passage with Christ," toward his or her *transitus ad Patrem*.

III. A PASTORAL PRACTICE CENTERED ON VIATICUM

Is it likely that in the present sociocultural situation the new ritual of the sick and dying can help toward, or even restore, a Christian way of preparing for death?

Even in the best of circumstances it can only be one element in the implementation of a renewed pastoral practice that is adapted to the changing world in which human beings continue to live, suffer, and die. Beyond a doubt, nothing would be more contrary to the conciliar mind and to the spirit of the new ritual than to regard the latter as a stereotyped collection of invariable rites or magical formulas. The death of human beings today and the understanding they can have of their death certainly depends on the way in which they live and on the political, cultural, social, and economic responses that they accept, reject, formulate for themselves, or endure in meeting their everyday personal or interpersonal problems.

On the other hand, the liturgical reform envisaged by Vatican II emphasizes the importance of making adaptations to the sociocultural differences found in today's world.[25]

It is not impossible, however, that the ritual of viaticum should help open up new perspectives for a Christian vision of death. On the contrary, this goal seems quite attainable provided the needed pastoral effort is made to recover the meaning of communion received as viaticum.

---

24. The *Explanatio symboli* of St. Ambrose (333–97) was familiar with this *redditio symboli* (no. 9), but it did not indicate either the precise moment for it nor the rite to be followed. See *De sacramentis, Des mystères*, ed. B. Botte (SC 25bis; Paris: Cerf, 1961), 25.

25. VSC 37–40, 63b (*DOL* 1 nos. 37–40, 63b). See X. Seumois, "Commentaire des n°. 37–40 de la Constitution Conciliaire," *LMD* no. 77 (1964) 74–106.

Like all the Eucharists we celebrate in our lifetime, communion received as viaticum "proclaims the death of the Lord until he comes" (1 Cor 11:26), but it does so beyond any other communion. Each Eucharist subjects us to a kind of anticipated death and acts as a pledge of resurrection. For it is our union with Christ that enables us to pass, like him and with him, through death to resurrection. As sacrament of the dead and risen Christ, the Eucharist received as viaticum is a sacrament of our own passage from this world to the Father (John 13:1). Even for Christ, death was the supreme act of detachment, the supreme renunciation. The Eucharist received as viaticum in preparation for our human death enables us to overcome this death. Christ did not do away with death but incorporated it into a sacramental setting so that we might succeed in our passage to the Father. Communion received as viaticum is the true sacrament of death, just as anointing is the sacrament of illness. It is doubtless because the Church is convinced of this that it has at all times (as the Council of Nicaea already attests) refused to set conditions for giving viaticum to any who ask for it.

In our present situation, however, a recovery of the meaning of communion received as viaticum seems to require two things: instruction given over the course of time but also given in a specially emphatic way each year in connection with communion on Good Friday; and the reception of viaticum while fully conscious (as the new ritual desires and as the Code of 1983, can. 922, reiterates[26]). To promote this kind of reception the wise suggestion has been made that the idea of "viaticum" be distinguished from that of "last communion'; the reason is that in most instances persons do not sense, nor do doctors know, when they are going to die. Submission to death, a real acceptance of it in the light of professed faith, the trusting of oneself to Christ in one's passage to the Father—all this supposes that one is still in full possession of one's faculties.[27]

§2. The Celebration of Death in Community

BIBLIOGRAPHY ON AID TO THE DYING

L. Gougaud, "Etude sur les *Ordines commendationis animae*," EL 44 (1935) 12–13 and 24–26.

A. G. Martimort, "L'*Ordo commendationis animae*," LMD no. 15 (1948) 143–60.

---

26. Code of 1983, can. 922: "Sanctum Viaticum infirmis ne nimium differatur; qui animarum curam gerunt sedulo advigilent, ut eodem infirmi pleni sui compotes reficiantur" ("Holy Viaticum for the sick is not to be delayed too long; those who have the care of souls are to be zealous and vigilant that they are nourished by Viaticum while they are fully conscious": *Code of Canon Law*, 345).

27. See *Rite of Anointing*, no. 27 (*Rites* 1:588).

_____, "L'iconographie des Catacombes et la catéchèse antique," *Rivista di archeologia cristiana* 25 (1949) 105–14.

J. C. Didier, *Le Chrétien devant la maladie et la mort* (Paris: Fayard, 1960), 107–20.

D. Sicard, "Preparation for Death and Prayer for the Dying," in *Temple of the Holy Spirit: Sickness and Death of the Christian in the Liturgy*, trans. M. J. O'Connell (New York: Pueblo, 1983), 239–46 (notes: 318–20).

_____, "La mort du Chrétien et sa communauté," *LMD* no. 144 (1980) 59–64.

The whole emphasis in Chapter VI ("Rite for the Commendation of the Dying") of the 1972 Ritual is on making it clear to the dying that the Christian community is united with them as they face the fear of death that is inborn in all human beings. "Charity toward one's neighbor urges Christians to express fellowship with a dying brother or sister by praying with him or her for God's mercy and for confidence in Christ."[28]

The Christian's passage is not meant to be made in isolation. The concern that the Christian's monastic, ecclesial, or familial community should accompany him or her at death has left a profound mark on the Church's liturgical tradition.

I. THE EARLY LITURGICAL WITNESSES

Two of the most important eighth-century Gelasian sacramentaries, those of Gellone and Rheinau,[29] contain an exhortation of commendation of the dying that was to become widespread in the Roman liturgical books of the tenth to the thirteenth centuries, the monastic texts of the eleventh and twelfth, and the Ambrosian texts of the eleventh to the thirteenth.[30] The exhortation, which was known by its opening words, "Proficiscere anima christiana de hoc mundo," was still being used in the Roman Ritual of 1952, where the text was almost unchanged from the Gellone Sacramentary, which I cite here:

> Go forth from this world, O Christian soul,
> in the name of God the almighty Father who created you;
> in the name of Jesus Christ, the Son of the living God, who suffered for you;
> in the name of the Holy Spirit, who has been poured forth upon you;
> in the name of the angels and archangels. . . .
> May your dwelling be established in peace this day and your home in
>   the heavenly Jerusalem.

---

28. *Rite of Anointing*, no. 138 (*Rites* 1:622). Latin text: "Caritas erga proximum urget christianos ut exprimant communionem cum fratre vel sorore moriente, cum eo et pro eo misericordiam Dei et fiduciam in Christo implorantes."

29. Sacramentary of Gellone, Paris B. N. lat. 12048, fol. 246ᵛ–247ʳ; Sacramentary of Rheinau, Zürich, Zentralbibliothek, cod Rh 30, fol. 151ᵛ–152ᵛ.

30. For a list of these witnesses and their variants see D. Sicard, *La liturgie de la mort* (above, note 8), 361–69.

An immense cortège is thus summoned for a final journey that is to be made in the festive atmosphere proper to the individual's "passing over" and to the assembly over which the Triune God presides amid the angels and saints.

The exhortation was followed by a lengthy litanic prayer: "O Lord, receive your servant into blessings. . . . Deliver him as you delivered Noah from the flood. . . ."

The manuscripts listed in this manner between ten and eighteen biblical instances of God's servants who had been delivered; the Church invoked these in the hour of agony or death struggle just as it had invoked them in behalf of the catechumens in the ancient rites of initiation. The *Proficiscere* made it clear that in their deaths the dying were bringing their baptism to fulfillment. The exhortation addressed them as travelers who were being welcomed, brought into peace, and set free as part of the great divine plan of salvation. In baptism they had been buried in Christ for a dying.[31] The liturgy of the agony was the liturgy of a second and definitive baptism; conversely, as Karl Rahner says, 'baptism is the sacramentally visible beginning of that death which is not the culmination of sin but of the sin-suppressing appropriation of salvation.'[32]

The *Proficiscere* was being copied from as early as the end of the eighth century, and the inspiration at work in it certainly goes back to the beginnings of Christianity.[33] But only in the second half of the ninth century do we find a rubric that makes the prayer obligatory in the Frankish kingdom of Charlemagne from the ninth to the twelfth century: "When the soul appears to be entering into the struggle of its departure through the dissolution of the body, the brethren or all the other faithful will do their best to come together. . . ."[34]

The summoning of the *fratres* suggests a clerical or monastic community, but a gathering of "all the other faithful" can only have referred to a much larger community. Nonetheless, as before the ninth century, so after the thirteenth we find no liturgical reference to the presence and role of this community. Perhaps the presence was too much taken for granted for mention to be made of it. The documents that do speak of this gathered community ask them to sing the seven penitential psalms and the litany of the dying. The latter ended, when death had occurred, with a sum-

---

31. See Rom 6:3-4.

32. K. Rahner, *On the Theology of Death*, trans. C. H. Henkey (Quaestiones Disputatae 2; New York: Herder & Herder, 1961), 82–83.

33. See my study of the origin of the *Proficiscere* in *La liturgie de la mort* (note 8), 369–72.

34. "Cum anima in agone sui exitus dissolutione corporis visa fuerit laborare, convenire studebunt fratres vel ceteri quique fideles." For the text, its witnesses, and its variants, see D. Sicard, *La liturgie de la mort* (note 8), 445–46. See also "La mort du chrétien et sa communauté," *LMD* no. 144 (1980) 59–64.

mons to all the saints and orders of angels: "Come to meet him (her), saints of God; hasten, angels of God, to receive his (her) soul and offer it in the presence of the Most High."

The prayer of commendation, which was the only specifically Roman prayer for death,[35] concluded the communal celebration of death at the moment of the final breath:

> God, in whom all mortal things have their life, and in whose sight our bodies, when we die, do not perish but are changed to a better state, we plead with you to accept the soul of your servant. Let the angels take it in their hands to the bosom of your friend Abraham the patriarch, and let it rise to new life on the final day of the great judgment. In your goodness forgive and wash away whatever stain it may have contracted at the devil's prompting while it sojourned in the mortal world. Through Jesus Christ.[36]

II. THE RITUAL FOR THE COMMENDATION OF THE DYING

The Roman Ritual used from 1614 to 1972 had brought together for the final moments of the dying person a rather disparate and composite collection of prayers upon which each successive period of history had to some extent left the mark of its own spirituality.[37] The Ritual of 1972,[38] after some valuable rubrics (nos. 138–42) in which it explains the pastoral reasons for its choices, gives first a series of short formulas for the use of the sick person, then a reading from Sacred Scripture, a short version of the *Proficiscere* and the *Commendo te*, a very abbreviated *Commendamus tibi*, the *Salve Regina*, the *Subvenite*, and the Gregorian prayer *Tibi Domine commendamus*, which had replaced the old Roman prayer in the Ritual of 1614.[39] Readings from the Word of God are normally to occupy the larger part of the service. The *Proficiscere* is suggested for the moment of death, but "depending on the Christian dispositions of the dying person."

---

35. See A. Chavasse, *Le Sacramentaire gélasien,* 58–60; D. Sicard, *La liturgie de la mort,* 79–102.

36. *Ge* 1627.

37. *Rituale Romanum* (1952), tit. VI, c. VII, *Ordo commendationis animae* et c. VIII, *De exspiratione.* See the commentary in J. Ch. Didier, *Le Chrétien devant la maladie et la mort* (Paris: Fayard, 1960), 109–18. Some prayers come from the Old Gelasian Sacramentary, the *Proficiscere* from the Sacramentary of Gellone, the *Commendamus* and the *Delicta iuventutis* from the eleventh-century Hamburg Missal, the *Commendo te* from St. Peter Damien, who died in 1072; the addresses to the Blessed Virgin and St. Joseph date from 1919 and 1922; etc.

38. *Rite of Anointing,* chapter VI, *Rite for the Commendation of the Dying.*

39. On the prayer *"Tibi Domine commendamus"* see D. Sicard, *La liturgie de la mort* (note 8), 355–58.

The point is that if the *Proficiscere* and the eleventh-century version of the *Commendamus tibi* are to be used in the final conscious hours of the dying person, they presuppose a prior knowledge of the Bible and a prior experience of Christian community. A more remote preparation for death is indispensable. The anointing of the sick and the reception of viaticum while in a state of full consciousness can make this earlier preparation bear fruit and enable the dying to celebrate death in a communal setting.

The modern practice of gathering the sick and dying into hospitals and nursing homes where they are cut off from their natural communities, and the impact of urbanization on relationships and on the social fabric required for human development:[40] these give a new pastoral form to the abiding problem of loneliness in the face of death.

When the Ritual of 1972 encourages priests and deacons to join the relatives of the dying in bearing witness to the communion that is the Church, it is aware of how difficult it will be for them to do so. It therefore urges them to train laypeople for this ministry of assisting the dying with the liturgy of commendation.[41] In this way there might emerge a clearer picture of the ministries proper to the local pastor (penance, Mass of viaticum) as distinct from the familial ministries of presence at the death struggle, celebration of death, prayer vigils, and even funeral services.

The 1983 Code of Canon Law points out that "in order to fulfill his office in earnest the pastor should strive . . . with generous love . . . to help the sick . . . particularly those close to death, refreshing them solicitously with the sacraments and commending their souls to God."[42] Among the functions especially entrusted to the pastor, it lists "the administration of Viaticum and the anointing of the sick . . . as well as the imparting of the apostolic blessing."[43]

It does not seem necessary to lay special emphasis on this apostolic blessing *in articulo mortis*. The Ritual of 1972 mentions it, without any special emphasis, as one way of concluding the penitential act that begins

---

40. See Pope Paul VI, Letter *Octogesima adveniens* to Cardinal Maurice Roy (May 14, 1971), no. 10: "Man is experiencing a new loneliness; it is not in the face of a hostile nature which it has taken him centuries to subdue, but in an anonymous crowd which surrounds him and in which he feels himself a stranger" (trans. in J. Gremillion [ed.], *The Gospel of Justice and Peace: Catholic Social Teaching Since Pope John* [Maryknoll, N.Y.: Orbis, 1976], 490).

41. *Rite of Anointing*, no. 142.

42. *Code of Canon Law*, can. 529 § 1 (p. 201). Latin text: "Officium pastoris sedulo ut adimpleat, parochus . . . aegrotos, praesertim morti proximos, effusa caritate adiuvet, eos sollicite sacramentis reficiendo eorumque animas Deo commendando."

43. Can. 530 (p. 203). Latin text: "Functiones specialiter parocho commissae sunt quae sequuntur: . . . 3° administratio Viatici necnon unctionis infirmorum . . . atque apostolicae benedictionis impertitio."

the ritual of viaticum when this is celebrated outside of Mass; it repeats it, in the same spirit, in the *Ritus continuus*.[44] This plenary indulgence at the moment of death, which the popes customarily granted from the fourteenth century on and which Benedict XIV included in the ritual in the eighteenth, is henceforth given by one or other of the two prayers provided.

But the part played by the priest, the pastor of the community, on the occasion of a Christian's death, should not cause us to overlook or minimize the role of the community itself. If it be true that "God did not create men to live as individuals but to come together in the formation of a social unity" and if "he willed to make men holy and save them, not as individuals without any bond or link between them, but rather to make them into a people,"[45] then solitude in the face of death should be replaced for Christians by solidarity and communion. Death "in the communion of the Church" was the ideal that the lives of saints, the liturgical texts, and the homilies of the great bishops vie with one another in attesting. The prayers for the recommendation of the dying, like the revival of family liturgies and the repair of houses and staircases, are elements in the reconstruction of a social fabric in which "the individual can escape from isolation and form anew fraternal relationships."[46] But this supposes that in our socialized, anonymous world[47] Christians continue to foster bonds of brotherhood, build communities, and follow the Lord's commandment. Is this not the sign by which they are to be recognized?

§3. The Liturgical Celebration of Funerals

BIBLIOGRAPHY ON FUNERALS

To the general bibliography add:
P. M. Gy, "Le nouveau rituel romain des funérailles," *LMD* no. 101 (1970) 15–32.
J. Potel, *Les funérailles, une fête?* (Rites et symboles 1; Paris: Cerf, 1973).
R. Rutherford, *The Death of a Christian: The Rite of Funerals* (New York: Pueblo, 1980).
V. Saxer, *Morts, martyrs, reliques en Afrique chrétienne aux premiers siècles* (Théologie historique 55; Paris: Beauchesne, 1980).
M. Amigues, *Le Chrétien devant le refus de la mort* (Paris: Cerf, 1981).

---

44. *Rite of Anointing*, no. 106: "At the conclusion of the sacrament of penance or the penitential rite the priest may give the plenary indulgence for the dying." See no. 122.

45. Vatican II, Pastoral Constitution *Gaudium et spes*, no. 32 (Flannery 931); Dogmatic Constitution *Lumen gentium*, no. 9 (Flannery 359).

46. Pope Paul VI, Letter *Octogesima adveniens* to Cardinal Naurice Roy (above, note 40), no. 11.

47. See R. Daille, "Mort et funérailles dans la société moderne," in *Célébration chrétienne de la mort* (Lyons: Chalet, 1972), 13–43; P. Ariès, "La mort inversée," *LMD* no. 101 (1970) 57–89, and *The Hour of Our Death*, trans. H. Weaver (New York: Knopf, 1981).

The promulgation of the *Ordo exsequiarum* of the Roman Ritual in 1969 and of the French-language Ritual in 1972 was the occasion for numerous publications that make it unnecessary to embark on lengthy explanations here.[48] Is a funeral anything more for a Christian than a complement of death? It gives expression to the unchanging maternal attitude of the Church, that is, its determination to fill with prayer the time between death and burial and to bring out "the paschal character of Christian death."[49] Let us look at the liturgical tradition on funerals.

I. THE EARLY LITURGICAL WITNESSES

The *Ordines romani* dealing with death offer a continuous ritual of funerals. This ritual is a prolongation of the Church's unbroken presence to the dying person who had celebrated his or her own death. The *Ordines* describe successively:

a) the funerary rites in the home, including the preparation of the body, its shrouding, and the antiphons and psalms for these rites;

b) the procession to the church where the funeral is to be celebrated, with the psalms and antiphons provided for this transfer of the body;

c) the prayer service in the church, this being comparable to Matins in its organization;

d) the burial, often preceded by another procession with psalms and antiphons and performed to the accompaniment of the paschal Psalm 118, "Confitemini domino" and its antiphon, "Aperite mihi portas."

The paschal character of death is emphasized by the choice of psalms,[50] among which Psalms 114, "In exitu," and 118, "Confitemini," which Jews had sung at the beginning and end of a Passover meal, had a special place.

---

48. To the works listed in the bibliography the following may be added: *Des chrétiens découvrent le nouveau Rituel des funérailles* (Paris: Centurion, 1972); Cl. Duchesneau, "Célébrer les funérailles en Eglise," in *Célébration chrétienne de la mort* (Lyons: Chalet, 1972), 85–105; J. Th. Maertens, "La liturgie de la mort et son langage," *Le Supplément* no. 108 (1974) 46–92; P. M. Gy, "La *Lex orandi* dans la liturgie des funérailles," *Communio* 6/1 (1981) 72–77; and many other publications, special issues of journals, etc.

49. *VSC* 81: "Ritus exsequiarum paschalem mortis christianae indolem manifestius exprimat."

50. The psalms most commonly used were: 114, "In exitu"; 120, "Ad Dominum"; 25, "Ad te Domine levavi"; 4, "Cum invocarem"; 116, "Dilexi quoniam"; 143, "Domine exaudi"; 139, "Domine probasti"; 23, "Dominus regit me"; 93, "Dominus regnavit"; 33, "Gaudete iusti"; 43, "Judica me"; 132, "Memento Domine David"; 51, "Miserere"; 42, "Quemadmodum"; 65, "Te decet"; 15, "Domine quis habitabit"; 22, "Deus, Deus meus"; 121, "Levavi oculos"; 146, "Lauda anima mea"; 118, "Confitemini Domino." For a detailed study of the Roman funeral rites I refer the reader to D. Sicard, *La liturgie de la mort* (note 8), 102–239.

The atmosphere created by the antiphons or responses—"Subvenite," "Suscipiat," "Chorus angelorum," "In Paradisum," 'In regnum Dei"—was the same as that of the old Roman prayer (cited earlier) at the moment of death, "Deus apud quem omnia morientia." The atmosphere was that of the parable of Lazarus and the rich man (Luke 16:22) and of the dialogue between Jesus and the thief (Luke 23:42-43). The "In Paradisum," which was the special song of the Roman procession to the place of burial, described the three stages in the journey of the deceased Christian:

> May the angels lead you into Paradise.
> May the martyrs welcome you at your coming
> and take you into Jerusalem, the holy city.

In the eyes of the community, which continued to speak to God *in persona defuncti*, those who died in the communion of the Church were incorporated into the great family of the saints, and their death was a summons to confidence and to the peaceful joy of rest and unfading light.

Gallican liturgical traditions laid greater emphasis on God's redeeming mercy to the person who has just died: death is a long and dangerous journey; the person must be set free from the world of sin. The dead person is destined, nonetheless, to share the life of the community that includes all of our ancestors in the faith; to this end the Church prays and pleads for her deceased. At the end of a lengthy historical development the Roman Ritual of 1614 tried to integrate the varied contributions of the centuries, and to produce a rite marked by restraint and brevity; it succeeded only imperfectly in this task. This is why Vatican II ordered that "the paschal character of Christian death" should be more clearly expressed in the rite of funerals.[51]

II. THE RITE OF FUNERALS

a) *The vigil for the deceased.* — The rite of 1969 devotes its first chapter to the vigil or wake to be held in the home of the deceased or in a funeral parlor or even in a church, and to the prayer when the body is placed on the bier. These human gestures are very important to the bereaved family, and the ritual suggests readings and prayers that may help them.

b) *The funeral.* — This may be organized in three different ways, depending on country and local custom. There may be three stations: in the home (or funeral parlor), in the church, and at the cemetery; there

---

51. For a detailed study of the Romano-Gallican rituals of death I refer again to D. Sicard, *La liturgie de la mort*, Part 2: "Des Rituels romano-gallicans de la mort à la réforme carolingienne," 259–418.

may be two stations: in the cemetery chapel and at the burial site; or there may be only one station: in the home of the deceased.

A funeral has four main parts: the welcome and greeting of faith to the dead person's relatives and to the various other people present;

—the Liturgy of the Word, wherein a wide selection of readings allows for the needed adaptations;

—the Celebration of the Eucharist, provided it is not excluded by pastoral considerations or local reasons;

—the farewell to the deceased, or commendation of the deceased to God.

The ritual urges that the celebration of the funeral include a certain number of gestures or rites that emphasize the paschal character of death and Christian faith in the resurrection (lights, the cross, the alb, the liturgical vestments. . .). It offers a fairly wide selection of prayers to fit situations, ages, and functions in the Church. It advocates singing, which can be that of the assembly as it uses song to express its faith, its grief, and its hope.

It is characteristic of the 1969 ritual for funerals that it contains prayers not only for the deceased but for the living who have suffered this loss.

Modern anthropological, sociological, economic, and political interpretations of death have challenged the language Christians use of death, especially in recent times. The 1969 ritual has taken over and revised liturgical formulas inherited from the ancient sacramentaries, but it has also created new prayers. Its approach deserves to be carried further.

c) *At the cemetery.* — Especially in the second type of funeral (it is one that is becoming frequent in our increasingly urbanized Western world), the religious service takes place exclusively in the cemetery or place of cremation. The ritual provides for this type of funeral, at which laypersons can lead the prayers in the absence of a priest or deacon.[52]

d) *The funerals of little children.* — In obedience to the will of Vatican II,[53] the 1969 ritual devotes its fifth, seventh, and eighth chapters to the ceremonies, readings, and prayers for the funerals of children who were baptized or who died before baptism. Like the ritual for the baptism of little children, the rite for the funerals of such children give a great deal of attention to the relatives directly concerned and to their pain and grief.

e) *Prayer for all the deceased brothers and sisters.* — At the Sunday Eucharist the various Eucharistic prayers urge the Christian community

---

52. *Rite of Funerals*, no. 51 (*Rites* 1:679).

53. VSC 82 (*DOL* 1 no. 82): "The rite for the burial of infants is to be revised and a special Mass for the occasion provided."

not to forget to pray for its dead. Depending on custom, a commemorative service is often celebrated (month's mind, anniversary) and usually includes the Eucharist. Each year, moreover, the feast of All Saints is followed by the Commemoration of All the Faithful Departed; the practice began in about the year 1030, at Cluny, when St. Odilo was abbot.[54] These opening days of November are the occasion for visits to the cemeteries. Such visits are only to be encouraged, since they provide an opportunity for prayer and intercession and help the living to see more clearly the eschatological dimension of all human life as it moves toward the Father.

---

54. *The Church at Prayer* IV:117.

Chapter IX

Processions, Pilgrimages, Popular Religion

J. Evenou

Although "true worshipers . . . worship the Father in spirit and truth" (John 4:23), the Church has never interpreted these words of Christ as opposing a universal human tradition, namely, the cult of places, which is the origin of rites of procession and pilgrimage. To those Jews who had become Christians, Jerusalem with its temple, feasts, and solemn processions remained the holy city. The Acts of the Apostles show Peter and John going up to the temple (Acts 3:1) and Paul undertaking a ritual pilgrimage to Jerusalem (Acts 21:26-27). Did not Jesus himself "go up" to Jerusalem for Passover, the Feast of Huts, or the Dedication?

The destruction of the temple, the period of persecutions, and the opposition of Christians to the theater and to the feasts connected with pagan cults could not but put restrictions on external manifestations of faith during the first three centuries. But Christianity is not a disincarnate religion and was simply waiting for a favorable opportunity to express itself outwardly in places of worship. Over the centuries and despite many changes, processions and pilgrimages have answered profound religious needs of the human psyche; they have taken forms in which the liturgy is combined with popular religion and in which religion and faith live in a close relationship that must, however, always be tested for its authenticity.

§1. Processions

BIBLIOGRAPHY

W. Dax, "Bittprozession," *RAC* 2 (1954) 422-29.
Les processions: LMD no. 43 (1955).

The procession, which is a religious, communal, solemn march, is a form of cult found in all religions. Its simplicity and adaptive flexibility give it an eminently popular character. The Jewish liturgy in the time of Christ was familiar with it,[1] as were the pagan cults of the Roman world (*pompa*), and the Church endeavored to match or christianize such pagan processions as it could not suppress.[2]

I. DEFINITION

A procession is a liturgical assembly on the move. The constant elements of a procession are the gathering of a local community with its pastor at an appointed place and an orderly advance behind the cross,[3] accompanied by prayers and songs, to another place that is the appointed goal in space. It is a form of solemn supplication that is motivated by some striking event and is experienced as an especially intense moment of liturgical life.

The prayer finds expression in song; in particular, the psalms, sung with a refrain or in alternating verses, are the characteristic accompaniment of Christian processions, just as they established the rhythm of religious processions in the Old Testament.[4] To the psalms was later added the litany, a very popular form of song in which the crowd gives a short

---

1. On the principal feasts: see R. de Vaux, *Ancient Israel: Its Life and Institutions*, trans. J. McHugh (New York: McGraw-Hill, 1961), 511–12.

2. The Roman procession on April 25 seems to have replaced the Robigalia: L. Duchesne, *Origines du culte chrétien* (Paris: E. de Boccard, 1920[5]), 304–5; see G. Dumézil, *La religion romaine archaïque* (Paris: Payot, 1974), 168–70, 269. The procession of February 2 may have replaced the Amburbale, and Rogation Days the three days of Ambarvalia: D. de Bruyne, "L'origine de la Chandeleur et des Rogations," *RBen* 34 (1922) 14–26; on these two Roman purificatory processions see G. Dumézil, *ibid.*, 239–42. In Gaul, too, there was a triduum of litanies at the beginning of January, "quod ad calcandam gentilium consuetudinem patris nostri statuerunt" (Council of Tours, 567, can. 18, ed. C. De Clercq, CCL 148A:182); on this pagan custom and the Church's opposition to it see J. C. Baroja, *Le Carnaval* (Bibliotheque des histoires; Paris: Gallimard, 1979), 168–80.

3. The carrying of more or less numerous crosses is attested in the earliest descriptions of processions in Rome, Byzantium, and Tours. Subsequently, one that was more valuable was singled out to be carried before the celebrant and his ministers and, after the procession, to be placed standing opposite the altar. See Socrates, *Historia ecclesiastica* VI, 8 (PG 67:690); Sozomen, *Historia ecclesiastica* VIII, 8 (PG 67:1538); Justinian, *Novellae* 123, c. 32; Gregory of Tours, *In gloria confessorum* 20: "radiantibus cereis crucibusque"; OR XX, 7; XXI, 10; XLI, 28; Andrieu, OR 3:241–43; *Missale Gothicum* (ed. Mohlberg), no. 336: "invictum hoc signum cum plebium cuneis praeferentes"; Benedictus Canonicus, *Liber politicus* 29 (ed. Fabre-Duchesne 2:148): "subdiaconus regionarius more solito portat crucem ad altare."

4. The singing of psalms during processions is attested by St. Ambrose, *Ep.* 40, 16 (PL 16:1107); the psalms, together with their antiphons, were the main songs used at burials according to OR XLIX; today the psalms are still assigned to, or suggested for, funerals.

and unvarying response to invocations sung by one or more soloists.[5] Some of the hymns of Frankish poets, which included a refrain by the crowd, have survived to our day (*Gloria laus, O Redemptor*, and others) and have inspired composers of hymns to the Blessed Sacrament. Finally, the monastic and canonical tradition created still another genre of processional song, one that is made up of ornate antiphons and responses and does not provide for any participation of the people.[6]

The celebrant sometimes offers a prayer at the end of a procession. In any case, all processions end with Mass, except for the Corpus Christi procession, which is Eucharistic and can only be a continuation and prolongation of the Mass that precedes it.[7]

Depending on their purpose, processions are either festive or penitential; they are clearly distinguished from one another by the color of the vestments worn by celebrant and ministers and even more by the character of the songs, since a penitential procession does not permit hymns and songs of joy. The penitential character of some processions was even more strongly emphasized in antiquity and the Middle Ages: the marchers walked barefoot, clad in sackcloth and with heads either veiled or covered with ashes; in addition, there were fasts and lengthy stations for prayers. Festive processions, on the other hand (Palm Sunday, Corpus Christi, translation of relics, and so on), call for very extensive display: decorations along the route, banners, choirs and musical instruments, light and colors.

II. LOCAL ORIGINS OF PROCESSIONS

Even in the age of persecutions some actions of the communities became external manifestations of faith. After the martyrdom of St. Cyprian in 258, for example, the transfer of his body to the cemetery was done "with candles and torches, in the joy of a true victory procession."[8] After the Peace of Constantine, Christian worship became an organized affair and developed in ways that made it accessible to the masses of new Christians. As recent converts, the latter needed to find in the Christian liturgy a brilliance and splendor comparable to that of the pagan feasts they had

---

5. On these acclamations see Gregory of Tours, *Historia Francorum* X, 1 (ed. Krusch-Levison, MGH [1951²], 1:481; Eginhard, *Translatio s. Marcellini* 31 (PL 104:555).

6. This tradition, which bulks large in the Processionals, has almost disappeared from the Roman rite: a lengthy response is indicated for the end of the procession on Palm Sunday; some recent suppressions ("Adorna thalamum" on February 2; "Ave Rex noster" on Palm Sunday) may be thought regrettable.

7. *Caeremoniale episcoporum* ed. 1984, n. 387.

8. *Acta proconsularia de martyrio s. Cypriani* 6 (CSEL 3:cxiii).

known. Processions, being collective activities that were filled with song and allowed the body to pray as much as the heart, were one of the forms of worship that made Christianity a religion of the people.

1. *Jerusalem*

At Jerusalem, the liturgy meant a reliving of the gospel in its orignal setting.[9] The Christian community and the pilgrims whom it welcomed were careful to commemorate the gospel events in the places, real or supposed, where they had occurred. The stational liturgical services were "suitable to the place and the day."[10] Bethlehem and the cave of the Nativity, the upper room of the Last Supper and Pentecost, the Mount of Olives, Golgotha, and the empty tomb were places rich in memories, where the gospel narratives connected with them became startlingly real. Movement from place to place was necessary if the community was to follow Christ day after day during the great week of the passion. The procession with palms in the time of Bishop St. Cyril deeply impressed Egeria, who was a pilgrim in Jerusalem in about 380:

> When three o'clock comes, they go up with hymns and sit down at the Imbomon, the place from which the Lord ascended into heaven. (For when the bishop is present everyone is told to sit down, except for the deacons, who remain standing the whole time.) And there, too, they have hymns and antiphons suitable to the place and the day, with readings and prayers between them. At five o'clock the passage is read from the gospel about the children who met the Lord with palm branches, saying, "Blessed is he that cometh in the name of the Lord."
>
> At this the bishop and all the people rise from their places, and start off on foot down from the summit of the Mount of Olives. All the people go before him with psalms and antiphons, all the time repeating, "Blessed is he that cometh in the name of the Lord." The babies and the ones too young to walk are carried on their parents' shoulders. Everyone is carrying branches, either palm or olive, and they accompany the bishop in the very way the people did when once they went down with the Lord. They go on foot all down the Mount to the city, and all through the city to the Anastasis, but they have to go pretty gently on account of the older women and men among them who might get tired. So it is already late when they reach the Anastasis; but even though it is late they hold Lucernare when they get there, then have a prayer at the Cross, and the people are dismissed.[11]

Egeria describes not only this procession, in which liturgical anamnesis becomes historical recollection (and how could it be otherwise in Jerusa-

---

9. A. Renoux, *Le Codex arménien Jérusalem 121* (PO 35/1 [1969]; 36/2 [1971]).

10. *Egeria's Travels* 31, 1, trans. J. Wilkinson (London: S.P.C.K., 1971), 132. Latin: "Apta diei ipsi vel loco" (in: Egérie, *Journal de voyage*, ed. P. Maraval [SC 296; Paris: Cerf, 1982], 272).

11. *Ibid.*, 31 (Wilkinson 132–33; SC 296:273–75).

lem?)[12] but also the processions of the Easter octave. These belonged to another genre, since in them historical imitation gave way to mystagogical instruction of the newly baptized, who were accompanied by the faithful and the clergy:

> On the first Sunday, Easter Day itself, they assemble in the Great Church, the Martyrium, and similarly on the Monday and Tuesday; and when they have had the dismissal, there they always go with singing from the Martyrium to the Anastasis. But on the Wednesday they assemble on the Eleona, on the Thursday in the Anastasis, on the Friday on Sion, on the Saturday Before the Cross, and on the eighth day, the Sunday they assemble once more in the Great Church, the Martyrium.
>
> On each of the eight days of Easter the bishop, with all the clergy, the "infants" who have been baptized . . . and any of the people who wish, go up to the Eleona. . . . When the psalms and prayer are finished, they go down with singing to the Anastasis in time for Lucernare. And this happens on each of the eight days; but on a Sunday at Easter time, after the people have been dismissed from Lucernare at the Anastasis, they all lead the bishop with singing to Sion.[13]

Two kinds of procession were thus to be found at Jerusalem from the fourth century on: one emphasized the places where Christ was born, lived, and suffered; the other used the places and shrines to serve pastoral needs. The same two types of procession would be found elsewhere as well.

2. *Rome*

At Rome, pastoral need took precedence in the organization of the stations; between the fifth and the eighth century the city was gradually divided into regions by means of *tituli* where at regular intervals inscribed in the calendar the bishop summoned clergy and people to assemble. The Tridentine Missal continued to name the stational churches for each day of Lent, the other days of fasting, and some feasts. The point of the whole plan was to have each neighborhood of Rome participate in turn in the common Eucharist. The great churches meanwhile were reserved for the most important gatherings:[14] for example, the Lateran Basilica for the feasts

---

12. The liturgical and the historical were still seen as a unity and as dimensions of the "mystery," in the Pauline sense of the term; see R. Taft, "Historicisme: une conception à revoir," *LMD* no. 147 (1981) 61–83, especially 77–79.

13. *Egeria's Travels* 39 (Wilkinson 139–40; SC 296:293). On the fortieth day after Epiphany the procession met at the Anastasis.

14. See H. Grisar, *Das Missale im Lichte römischer Stadtsgeschichte* (Freiburg: Herder, 1925); J. P. Kirsch, *Die Stationskirchen des Missale Romanum* (Freiburg: Herder, 1926); *idem*, "L'origine des stations liturgiques du Missel Romain," *EL* 41 (1927) 137–50; R. Hierzegger, "Collecta und Statio," *ZKT* 60 (1936) 511–54; G. G. Willis, "Roman Stational Liturgy," in his *Further Essays in Early Roman Liturgy* (Alcuin Club Collections 50; London: S.P.C.K., 1968); A. Chavasse, "L'organisation stationnale du carême romain avant le VIIIe siècle. Une organisation 'pastorale,'" *RevSR* 56 (1982) 17–32.

connected with Easter, the Vatican Basilica (until the ninth century), and the Liberian (St. Mary Major) for Christmas.

The gathering (*collecta*) of clergy and faithful took place at an appointed church from which they then went in procession, amid the singing of psalms and litanies, to the stational church where the pope celebrated Mass.

The Roman stational system with its procession followed by the Eucharist was imitated in Milan and Ravenna, Gaul and Germany.[15]

Rome had other processions, both penitential (February 2 originally, the major litany on April 25) and festive: on the *dies natalis* of the Roman martyrs, the people went to their churches and processions were organized, especially for the Apostles Peter and Paul on June 29, as a hymn attributed to St. Ambrose attests: "Armies in close ranks traverse the streets of that great city. On three different routes they celebrate the holy martyrs. One would think the whole world was in procession."[16]

3. *Gaul*

In around 370, St. Mamertus, bishop of Vienne, appointed the three days before Ascension for fasting and processions of supplication.[17] The first Council of Orléans (511) extended this arrangement to all of Gaul. The Rogation Days, which perhaps took the place of ancient spring agrarian rites, would continue down to the mid-twentieth century to be one of the important times of the liturgical year in countries still essentially rural. The passage of the cross through the streets turned the parish into a sacred area; and the community that followed the cross in petitionary prayer offered to God the labors of the field and the fruitfulness of the earth.

4. *Constantinople*

Processions, probably organized originally by St. John Chrysostom in response to the parades of the Arians, were the characteristic feature

---

15. In eighth-century Metz, for example, thirty-five churches in the city or outside the walls served as stations for Lent and Easter week: see. V. B. Pelt, *Etudes sur la cathédrale de Metz*. 1. *La liturgie* (Metz: Imprimerie du Journal Le Lorrain, 1937), 29–35. See also U. Berlière, "Les stations liturgiques dans les anciennes villes épiscopales," *Revue liturgique et monastique*, 1920, 213ff.

16. St. Ambrose, *Hymni* LXXI, 25–30 (PL 17:12–15). The three different routes led to the Vatican, the basilica on the Ostian Way, and the Basilica Apostolorum on the Appian Way.

17. St. Avitus of Vienne, *In rogationibus homilia* (PL 59:289–91); Sidonius Apollinaris, *Ep.*, V, 14 (PL 58:544). — In Milan these processions took place during the week before Ascension; in Spain, after the Council of Gerona (517), they were held in the week after Pentecost. In Gaul there were other rogations on the first three days of January; see above, note 2.

of the stational liturgy at Constantinople.[18] From the fifth to the seventh centuries, each important, that is, stational, Eucharistic liturgy had to involve a liturgical procession. As late as the tenth century there were sixty-eight such processions in the course of the year, though they were now reserved to the most important occasions.[19] They were spaced out through the year in dependence on the sanctoral and the commemoration of important events of the city's life; they were often several kilometers long, and were given a popular character by the use of silver crosses and candles and the antiphonal singing of psalms, troparies, and litanies. These processions ultimately left their mark on the opening rite of every Eucharist, with its three antiphons, litany and Trisagion.

III. DEVELOPMENT AND VARIETY OF PROCESSIONS

Because processions have their roots in the people and in specific localities, it is difficult to classify them in a systematic way. The most that can be done is to put them into a few categories based on some characteristic elements.

1. *Processions Connected with a Date*

Some processions marked down in the general or local calendars are closely connected with the liturgical celebration of the mystery of salvation (the Easter cycle) or the saints. The present Roman liturgy has few such processions. In the order of the calendar these are: on February 2, the procession in which the faithful, candle in hand, go to meet Christ the Light;[20] — the Palm Sunday procession, which was modeled on the procession at Jerusalem, underwent an extraordinary expansion in the Middle Ages, and turned into a triumphal homage to Christ the King; — the procession of the assembly behind the Easter Candle at the beginning of the Easter Vigil, symbolizing in a striking way the passage from darkness to light; the procession was restored in 1951, but it is far from having recovered in the West the splendor it has always had in the Eastern Churches; — in place of the (Roman) major litany on April 25 and the (Gallican) Rogation processions on the three days before Ascension, the episcopal conferences can henceforth decide on the date and manner of celebrations of petition for the productivity of the earth;[21] it is not pos-

---

18. J. Baldovin, "La liturgie stationnale à Constantinople," *LMD* no. 147 (1981) 85–94.

19. J. Mateos, *Le Typicon de la Grande Eglise* (2 vols.; OCA 165–66; Rome: Pontificio Istituto Orientale, 1962–63).

20. The candles blessed on this occasion and carried lit in the procession gave the feast of the Presentation its popular name, Candlemas (French: Chandeleur, from *candelorum*).

21. *GNLYC* 45–47 (*DOL* 442 nos. 3811–13).

sible to transfer to an urbanized world and to any and every region of earth what was originally intended for the rural world of Western Europe; — the procession of the Blessed Sacrament, which was a fourteenth-century development of the feast of Corpus Christi, has become so impressive and lavish in both city and countryside that it is known in France simply as *Fête-Dieu*, the "Celebration of God."

The Middle Ages and the modern period have known many other processions that are national or local traditions. Examples of the former in France are the procession on August 15 that is known as "the procession in fulfillment of Louis XIII's vow" and commemorates the consecration of France to Our Lady in 1638,[22] and the procession to the cemetery on All Saints' Day. At the local level every patronal feast has its procession. Until the end of the last century, and in some cases even more recently, many parishes had a procession to the baptistery during Vespers on Easter.[23] Until the eighteenth century some churches had a procession on Easter morning. In France, the Ascension was also the occasion for a solemn procession that is attested as early as the sixth century.[24]

Many diocesan rituals also provided for a procession every Sunday before the high Mass; it was initially intended as a march outside the church,[25] but it most often took the form of a homage to the cross and lent solemnity to the Lord's Day.[26]

2. *Processions Connected with a Rite*

A good many processions were intended to lend solemnity to a movement already required by the performance of rites;[27] they were thus "functional." By attaching some splendor and display to the movement and

---

22. Documentation on this procession in the *Rituel de Bellay* (1830), 3:200–5.

23. P. Jounel, "Les vêpres de Pâques," *LMD* no. 49 (1957) 96–111.

24. Gregory of Tours, *Historia Francorum* V, 11.

25. In the monasteries this procession made its way around the entire precincts, at least in the beginning, as is clear from the eighth-century Gelasian sacramentaries (*Liber sacramentorum Gellonensis*, ed. A. Dumas [CCL 159; 1981], 452–53) and the books that depend on them (the Aniane Supplement: *Gr* 1473–76; *PRG* nos. 178–79, 194–211 [2:332, 356–61]). See E. Martène, *De antiquis monachorum ritibus*, lib. II, c. 3 (4:46–49 in the Venice edition); A. Franz, *Die kirchlichen Benediktionen im Mittelalter* 1 (Freiburg: Herder, 1909), 633–44.

26. P. Le Brun, *Explication . . . des prières et des cérémonies de la messe . . .*, 1:85–93 (in the Liège ed. of 1777). The procession followed upon the Asperges. From the seventeenth to the nineteenth century many French dioceses published their own *Processionale*: these books often contained a wealth of responses and collects which gave color to each feast and liturgical season.

27. A procession can become an independent rite; examples of this are the procession of the Blessed Sacrament at Lourdes and the daily torch procession held there during the pilgrimage season.

involving the entire assembly in it, the Church highlighted the objective of the movement and enabled the faithful to express their devotion toward it. This type of procession includes: the procession with the viaticum or with Easter communion for the sick; the solemn translation of relics, especially for the dedication of a church;[28] funeral processions (the aim here is to bring out the full Christian meaning of a human gesture and turn it into an ecclesial act); the transfer of the reserved Eucharist to the repository on Holy Thursday; the first entrance of a bishop into his episcopal city.[29]

Of the same type are other processions that are likewise required by a liturgical action but are more limited in scope since they involve the movement of only part of the assembly: the entrance of the ministers at a solemn Mass; the "little entrance" of the Eastern rites and the procession with the gospel in the Roman rite; the "great entrance" of the Eastern rites, the "administration" of the Lyons rite, the offertory procession of the Roman rite; the communion procession; the procession with the holy oils at the Chrismal Mass; the procession for the showing and veneration of the holy cross on Good Friday; the procession of the newly baptized from the bapistery to the altar.[30]

3. *Extraordinary Processions*

Certain processions have retained their exceptional character, connected as they are most often with times of disaster or public misfortune: war,[31] destructive rains,[32] or epidemics.[33] The Roman Ritual of 1614 thus

---

28. *Ordo dedicationis ecclesiae et altaris* (1977), cap. 2, nos. 29, 31, 35 (compare with the old *Ordo* of 1961, nos. 26–31). First testimonies from Constantinople under Constantius, from Milan in the time of St. Ambrose; see H. Delehaye, *Les origines du culte des martyrs* (Brussels: Société des Bollandistes, 1933²), 55–57, 65–67. For the development of the translation, showing, and procession of relics see N. Hermann-Mascard, *Les reliques des saints. Formation coutumière d'un droit* (Paris: Klincksieck, 1975), 193–234.

29. Already attested at the end of the fourth century, e. g., by Sozomen, *Historia ecclesiastica* VIII, 14 (PG 67:1552–53).

30. This procession, appointed today for the baptism of children (see the *Rite of Baptism for Children*, no. 67; *Rites* 1:210), was regarded as especially important in the baptismal instructions of the Fathers; e.g., St. Ambrose, *De sacramentis* 4, 5–7; *De mysteriis* 43, 2 (SC 25bis:104 and 178).

31. For example, the processions organized by Theodosius as he was attacking Eugene: Rufinus of Aquileia, *Historia ecclesiastica* II, 33 (PL 21:539); or that ordered by Childebert at the siege of Saragossa: Gregory of Tours, *Historia Francorum* III, 29 (ed. Krusch-Levison, 1:125–26). In 601 St. Gregory the Great, *Registrum epistolarum* XI, 31 (ed. Ewald, 2:301), exhorted the bishops of Sicily to hold processions twice a week amid the calamities caused by invasion.

32. Litany urged at Constantinople in 399: St. John Chrysostom, *Contra ludos et theatra homilia 1* (PG 56:265).

33. The plague at Nantes: Gregory of Tours, *Historia Francorum* X, 30 (Krusch-Levison 525) and at Rome (*lues inguinaria*) after the floods of 589. In order to ward off disaster at

provided for a certain number of extraordinary processions or supplications (tit. 10): to plead for rain (c. 6) or good weather (c. 7), to turn away storms (c. 8), in time of shortage or famine (c. 9), in an epidemic (c. 10) or a war (c. 11), and for any other tribulation (c. 12). These processions are penitential, and their principal chant is the litany of the saints, whence their ancient name "Litany."[34]

In the Mass that is celebrated at the end of the procession, the formulary is to be used that best corresponds to the intention of the procession.[35]

Sometimes the procession takes the form of a visitation of places in order to exorcise or sanctify them. Thus a procession with holy water is part of the rite that inaugurates the building of a church.[36]

Sometimes, however, a procession is occasioned by an auspicious event; for example, the torchlight procession that began in many different parts of Rome and converged on St. Peter's Square on the evening of October 11, 1962, for the opening of the Second Vatican Council.

§2. Pilgrimages

BIBLIOGRAPHY

    B. Kötting, *Peregrinatio religiosa. Wallfahrten in der Antike und das Pilgerwesen in der alten Kirche* (Forschungen zur Volkskunde 33–35; Münster: Stenderhoff, 1980²).

    A. Dupront, "Pèlerinages et lieux sacrés," *Encyclopedia Universalis* 12 (1976) 729–34.

    J. Chelini and H. Branthomme, *Les chemins de Dieu. Histoire des pèlerinages chrétiens des origines à nos jours* (Paris: Hachette, 1982).

I. CHARACTERISTICS OF A PILGRIMAGE

The people of God in the Old Testament were a people on the move: from Egypt to Canaan and, later, from exile back to Jerusalem. The jour-

---

Rome, St. Gregory the Great, who had just been elected bishop of the city in 590, ordered processions to march from each of the city's seven "regions" to St. Mary Major: Gregory of Tours, *Historia Francorum* X, 1 (pp. 477–81). — St. Gregory the Great, *Registrum epistolarum* XIII, 2 (Ewald 2:367), describes an almost identical procession in 603. The procession with the reliquary of St. Genevieve in Paris was also a response to exceptional circumstances (seventy-seven times between 856 and 1789): see *Caeremoniale Parisiense* (1703), 262–73.

34. On *litaneia* see Simeon of Thessalonica (fifteenth century), *De sacra precatione* 339 and 353 (PG 155:615, 655). The term had already been used by St. John Chrysostom (see note 32 for reference). It was transliterated as *letania* in Latin and is frequently found in the letters of St. Gregory the Great; the writers of Gaul use *rogationes* for the same idea.

35. *GIRM* 331 (*DOL* 208 no. 1721); *GNLYC* 47 (*DOL* 442 no. 3813).

36. *Rite of Dedication of a Church and an Altar* (1977), chap. 1, no. 25 (*Rites* 2:199).

ney of this caravan, especially in its most decisive stages, is described in the Bible as a great festive procession with singing, musical instruments, and banners.[37] The God of Israel was present with his people, sharing their nomadic life until they should enter his temple.[38] Even after the return from exile, the Jews of Jerusalem continued to be pilgrims as they obeyed the periodic rhythm of ascent to Jerusalem and return to their homes. Even more than the people of the Old Testament, the new people of God is a people on the move, advancing after Jesus toward the kingdom. This fundamental situation of the Church finds popular expression in pilgrimages.

Like processions, Christian pilgrimages imply an advance, undertaken in a spirit of penance, thanksgiving, or devotion toward a sacred place that is its goal.

But a pilgrimage has its own specific characteristics as well. To begin with, it is essentially a leaving behind and an estrangement: a breaking away from ordinary time, a breaking out of everyday space, a leaving home (*peregrinus*: the same Latin word means both "pilgrim" and "stranger" or "foreigner"). Next, a pilgrimage means a journey: a road to be taken, usually on foot, serves as a necessary test—more or less lengthy and painful—to be passed. Finally, the goal is a holy place where the divine power is made manifest and the believer encounters God. The extreme eschatological form of pilgrimage is one from which the person does not return: the traveler's goal is reached in death at the end of the journey, and the encounter with God is definitive.

II. PLACES OF PILGRIMAGE

In the Christian view, no place is sacred in itself; if places have become the goal of pilgrimages, it is because God or a saint have manifested their presence there in a special way.

The oldest pilgrimage, and the one that remains the model of all others, is the pilgrimage to the holy places, to the land where Christ lived and where people experience most intensely the presence of the God who became man. This is the pilgrimage whose goal—the empty tomb of the risen Christ—is at the very heart of the Christian faith.[39]

After the Holy Sepulcher, the cult of the bodies of the saints doubtless provides the greatest number of places of pilgrimage; the tombs of the

---

37. Num 9:10; Josh 6; Ps 105; 114; 126; Isa 52:12; 60; Ezra 3. — See F. Louvel, "Les processions dans la Bible," *LMD* no. 43 (1955) 5–28.

38. 2 Sam 6; 1 Kgs 8; 2 Chron 6:40-42; Ps 24; 68; 118; Neh 12:31-38. — See F. Louvel, *ibid.*

39. On pilgrimages to the holy places during the first nine centuries see H. Leclercq, "Pèlerinages aux lieux saints," *DACL* 14/1 (1939) 65–176.

martyrs and then of the other saints have always been places of grace and signs of immortality for pilgrims. Rome can display the glorious memorials of the Apostles Peter and Paul,[40] and the journey *ad limina Apostolorum* has brought crowds not only from Italy[41] but from all over the world.[42] The Santiago route, strewn with monasteries and hostels that serve as stopping-places, leads to the supposed tomb of another apostle at Compostella. To speak only of the West, the cult of St. Michael the Archangel at Mont-Saint-Michel[43] and that of St. Mary Magdalene at Vézelay[44] have drawn throngs of pilgrims; in the modern period more recent saints have had their turn (St. Francis and St. Clare at Assisi, St. Therese at Lisieux, St. Bernadette at Nevers). Relics—real, supposed, or simply representative—are at the origin of pilgrimages or have subsequently given these a new dimension or have justified them. Sacred images (icons or statues) have in their turn been the basis of pilgrimages, especially to places dedicated to the Virgin Mary, whether the image was obtained by a miraculous discovery (the medieval Black Virgins; the "found," usually modern Virgins) or has been the object of special devotion (Our Lady of Pity) or is a reminder of an appearance (Lourdes, La Salette, Pontimain, and others).

The pilgrimage center is often defined by an enclosure that contains churches, chapels, tomb, sacred spring, and calvary, the whole constituting a sacred space that is cut off from the space around.[45]

The Holy Land and Rome have always been favorite places of pilgrimage; other places, however, have had periods of great popularity followed by periods of neglect due to shifts in the collective outlook. For more than a century now Lourdes has drawn pilgrims, just as the tomb of St. Martin at Tours did at one time.[46] The stream of pilgrims remains but it moves in a new direction.

In the Middle Ages pilgrimages were sometimes prescribed as public,

---

40. Testimony of Gaius, a Roman priest at the beginning of the third century, preserved by Eusebius of Caesarea, *Historia ecclesiastica* II, 25, 7 (ed. G. Bardy, SC:31:92–93).

41. In the fifth century Prudentius was already describing pilgrimages from areas near Rome: "From the gates of Alba come long processions, advancing in white lines through the countryside. . . . The inhabitants of the Abruzzi and the peasants of Etruria come at the same time" (*Peristephanon* XI, 203–6 [PL 50:552]).

42. For the first eight centuries see H. Leclercq, "Pèlerinage à Rome," *DACL* 14/1 (1939) 40–65.

43. See *Millénaire monastique du Mont Saint-Michel 3. Culte de Saint Michel et pèlerinage au Mont* (Paris: Lethielleux, 1971).

44. V. Saxer, *Le culte de Marie-Madeleine en Occident des origines à la fin du Moyen Age* (2 vols.; Clavreuil, 1959).

45. The description applies, for example, to the Grotto area at Lourdes.

46. E. Delaruelle, "La spiritualité du pèlerinage de Saint-Martin de Tours du Ve au Xe siècles," in *La piété populaire au Moyen Age* (Turin: Bottega d'Erasmo, 1975).

though not solemn penances; this type of pilgrimage caused many abuses that the Church took some time to curb.[47] On the other hand, the Church has promoted certain pilgrimages that it judged to meet the needs of a given age; one example is the practice, rather widespread at one time, of an annual procession of the parishes of a diocese to their mother church, the cathedral, during Pentecost week;[48] a modern example would be the national and international Eucharistic congresses.

III. THE PILGRIMAGE EXPERIENCE

Each place of pilgrimage creates forms of expression and participation that are adapted to the place, the age, and the pilgrims. Whether pilgrims come individually or in groups, they are caught up in ritual celebrations and in requirements of sacramental practice that are the concern of the Church but that also make use of traditional expressions, individual or collective, of devotion. At the end of the journey, as they are about to enter the place of pilgrimage, the participants must continue to advance, but now in an orderly and solemn manner: a procession thus crowns the journey and thereby creates a transitory sacred space that often links different sanctuaries.

Certain other gestures are required as spontaneous expressions of the encounter that the pilgrims are seeking in the holy place; thus we find at all sanctuaries, Christian or non-Christian, such practices as touching or kissing a tomb, a reliquary, an image, or a rock on which an appearance took place, drinking from or even bathing in a sacred spring, making an offering that signifies self-detachment, and leaving a trace of one's presence (candle, ex-voto, graffiti) or, on the contrary, taking away a souvenir of the holy place. The Church has never rejected such gestures because they are from the outset fully human; it requires only that they help pilgrims in their pursuit of the essential, namely, conversion of heart and openness to God.

The history of liturgy and contemporary pastoral theory cannot overlook the important part played by pilgrimages, today as in the past, in effecting liturgical exchanges between various regions, as well as the influence of some places of pilgrimage on the spread of rites, books, songs, and on the prestige enjoyed by works of art.[49]

---

47. C. Vogel, "Le pèlerinage pénitentiel," *RevSR* 38 (1964) 113–53.

48. U. Berlière, "Les processions de croix banales," *Académie royale de Belgique. Bulletins de la classe des Lettres,* 5. serie, 8 (1922) 419–46.

49. *Le Pèlerinage* (Cahiers de Fanjeaux 15; Toulouse: Privat, 1980); M. M. Gauthier, *Les routes de la foi. Reliques et reliquaires de Jérusalem à Compostelle* (Paris: La Bibliothèque des Arts, 1983).

Because of the throngs of pilgrims that visit them, the liturgy must be celebrated with greater care and beauty at places of pilgrimage. Moreover, the nature of some of these places requires that the praise of God be celebrated almost unceasingly, as at Jerusalem in the fourth and fifth centuries, at Rome after the establishment of the urban monasteries, and at other shrines such as Tours and Arles. At the very least, the faithful should find in these places the atmosphere required for a profound encounter with the Lord; they should see the catholicity of the Church manifested there and be introduced to a more active and intelligent participation in the liturgy.

IV. JUBILEES

BIBLIOGRAPHY

H. Thurston, *The Roman Jubilee: History and Ceremonial* (London: Sandes, 1925).
R. Foreville, "Jubilé," *Dictionnaire de spiritualité* 8 (Paris: Beauchesne, 1974) 1478–87.

A jubilee, which is an institution described in the Book of Leviticus, is an extraordinary year that recurs every fifty years or at the end of seven weeks of years. It is a year of blessings granted by God to his people, and the prophets speak of it as a prefiguration of the messianic age. Jesus points to himself as the one who reveals the full meaning of the ancient jubilee.[50]

In 1300 Pope Boniface VIII undertook to introduce this Old Testament institution into the life of the Church, linking it to a pilgrimage to the shrines of Rome.[51] Jubilees (or holy years) were originally intended only for centenary years and bestowed their blessings only in Rome. Gradually, however, the time between them was shortened (first to every fiftieth, then to every twenty-fifth year), and the place where they became operative was extended: not Rome alone, but the entire Catholic world was to benefit from them for an entire year.[52] Sometimes an extraordinary event

---

50. Lev 25; Luke 4:16-21; G. Lambert, "Jubilé biblique et jubilé chrétien," *Nouvelle revue théologique* 72 (1950) 234–51.

51. Bull *Antiquorum habet* (February 22, 1300), in *Extravagantes comm.* V, IX, 1. In 1220 Honorius III had granted Stephen Langton a jubilee for the fiftieth anniversary of the death of St. Thomas Becket; see R. Foreville, *Le Jubilé de saint Thomas Becket du XIIIe au XVe siècle (1220–1470). Etudes et documents* (Paris, 1958). The idea of a jubilee was a good bit older: R. Foreville, "L'idée de Jubilé chez les théologiens et canonistes (XIIe–XIIIe s.), avant l'institution du Jubile romain (1300)," *RHE* 56 (1961) 401–23. On the true meaning of a jubilee see Clement VIII, Bull *Annus Domini* (1599), in Cherubini, *Bullarium . . .* 3:82–85.

52. One exception: Paul VI decided that the jubilee of 1975 should be celebrated locally during the preceding year (*Documentation catholique* 55 [1973] 502).

gives rise to an extraordinary jubilee (the jubilee of 1802 in France after the restoration of Catholic worship; the jubilees of redemption for the entire world in 1933 and 1983).

In Rome the beginning and end of a holy year are signaled by a symbolic gesture: the opening and closing of one of the doors of the four major basilicas, a "holy door" reserved for pilgrims in a jubilee year.[53]

There are also local jubilees that are limited to a city or a shrine; for example, the jubilee of Compostella, which occurs when July 25 falls on a Sunday,[54] or the jubilee of Our Lady of Puy, when March 25 falls on Good Friday.[55]

When the Church celebrates pilgrimages with special pomp for an entire year and when it extends a more urgent invitation to the faithful to visit the holy places during that time, it is urging them primarily to conversion. Jubilees have gradually been replaced by plenary indulgences, which have the same meaning and purpose; the granting of these indulgences calls to mind the ancient penitential discipline, but puts it at the service of a broader and more positive intention: spiritual renewal in fidelity to the gospel, and the pursuit of justice and charity. Holy years periodically remind Christians that they must be a holy people, for a jubilee is simply an ordinary year that is lived in an extraordinary way.[56]

§3. Popular Religion

BIBLIOGRAPHY

P. Wiertz, "Volkskunde und Liturgiewissenschaft. Aufgaben der religiösen Volkskunde nach dem II. Vatikanischen Konzil," *ALW* 9 (1966) 429–36.
Religion populaire et réforme liturgique = *LMD* no. 122 (1975). Reprinted as a volume with the same title (Rites et symboles 4; Paris: Cerf, 1976).
B. Plongeron and R. Pannet (eds.), *La religion populaire. Approches historiques* (Bibliothèque Beauchesne, Religions société, politique 2; Paris: Beauchesne, 1976).
La piété populaire au Moyen Age (Actes du 99ᵉ Congrès national des sociétés savantes; Paris: Bibliothèque nationale, 1977).
La religion populaire (Paris: Editions du C.N.R.S., 1979).
Y. M. Hilaire (ed.), *La religion populaire. Aspects du christianisme populaire à travers l'histoire* (Centre interdisciplinaire d'études des religions de l'Université de Lille III; Lille, 1981).
F. A. Isambert, *Le sens du sacré. Fête et religion populaire* (Le sens commun; Paris: Editions du Minuit, 1982).

---

53. This ceremony was begun by Alexander VI for the jubilee of 1500.

54. Approved by Leo XIII, November 1, 1884 (*Ubi primum*).

55. Approved by Pius XI in a letter of January 31, 1932; the jubilee lasts from Holy Thursday evening to the third Sunday of Easter.

56. John Paul II, Apostolic Constitution *Aperite portas Redemptori* Proclaiming the Holy Year of Redemption 1983–84 (January 6, 1983), in *The Pope Speaks* 28 (1983) 152–63.

In adapting types of prayer and worship that have been practiced in other religions (processions, pilgrimages), the Church satisfies a constant, inborn need of *homo religiosus*. Popular religion thus consists of a collection of behaviors and ritual practices that are more or less in harmony with the prescriptions of the hierarchic authorities. The attitude of the Church to popular religion has varied, in different periods and countries, from a tolerance meant to show receptivity[57] to a weakness that lets itself be overrun[58] or, at the other extreme, a severity that condemns and seeks to purge.[59] Only in the post-Tridentine period was a clear distinction made between what is liturgical and what is not.

I. RULES AND EXPERIENCE

When, beginning in the fourth century, the Church welcomed a throng of new converts, then the barbarian peoples, and then those of the New World, it had to regulate the religious behavior of populations that were only very imperfectly christianized or even, at times, reverting to paganism. The result has been a long and often uneven battle between the Church and an ancestral fund of beliefs felt to be safeguards, unacknowledged survivals of pagan worship, and superstitious or magical practices.

The liturgical books point out the kind of behavior that is expected by prescribing rites and prayers, codifying certain practices, and excluding others. But if we are to see how these prescriptions were or were not received and how the liturgy was actually carried out in a given period and country, we must turn to other sources. Reminders of proper behavior, bans, and the repeated denunciations issued by councils and synodal statutes and found in rituals and sermons: all these give us a more accurate insight into the concrete life of the Christian people.

Participation in the sacraments has constantly changed its character, even while the ritual may have remained the same: from the solemn baptism of adults in the midst of the community during the Easter Vigil to the widespread practice of infant baptism *quam primum*; from confirmation celebrated along with baptism to confirmation administered only when the bishop comes; from reception of the Eucharist every Sunday or even every day to annual communion; from public and nonrepeatable penance

---

57. J. Jungmann, *The Early Liturgy to the Time of Gregory the Great* (Notre Dame: University of Notre Dame Press, 1959), chapters XI–XIII.

58. When a rite drifts towards superstition, magic, and syncretism (as in the case of voodoo). See J. B. Thiers, *Traité des superstitions qui regardent les sacrements . . .* (1751).

59. In each period of reform in the Church: the Carolingian reform, the Gregorian reform, the Tridentine reform; but even back in the fifth century: see St. Gelasius, *Lettre contre les Lupercales*, ed. G. Pomarès (SC 65; Paris: Cerf, 1959).

to frequent confession of devotion. The meaning of Sunday Mass is seen differently by those who attend it regularly and those who come to church only once a month or a few times a year.[60]

II. VITAL RITES AND FEASTS

1. *The Principal Moments of Human Life*

In every civilization celebrations and rites have lent special solemnity to birth, puberty, marriage, and death. In the Christian world baptism finally came to coincide with birth. Thus Pascal observed that "today people enter the Church at the same time as they enter the world . . . so that when reason begins to operate it no longer makes any distinction between these two very opposed worlds." Beginning in the seventeenth century, under the influence of St. Vincent de Paul, first communion, which was now put off until about the age of twelve, became a solemn affair, yet the profession of faith that it was intended to be often went unnoticed: the celebration had become a rite of passage from childhood to adolescence.[61] The familial and societal activities connected with marriage gradually provided the gestures for the Christian ritual of marriage.[62] Finally, for their funerals Christians adopted the funerary rites of the Romans, while permeating them, sometimes imperceptibly, with their own radically new faith in the resurrection.[63] Furthermore, the gestures that thus surrounded these key moments of human life have varied according to culture and historical period; consequently, to grasp the evolution of the Christian outlook at any given time we must study places and manners of burial, funerary inscriptions and meals, announcements and processions, testaments and elements in the display of grief, and so on.[64] When we deal with collective mentalities or outlooks, we find that those of clergy and people are more or less indistinguishable.

---

60. *Se rassembler le dimanche* = *LMD* no. 130 (1977).

61. H. Chéry, *La communion solennelle en France* (Rencontres 37; Paris: Cerf, 1951); *Communion solennelle et profession de foi* (LO 14; Paris: Cerf, 1952).

62. See above, Chapter VI.

63. See C. Vogel, "Le banquet funéraire paléochrétien," in B. Plongeron and R. Pannet (eds.), *La religion populaire. Approches historiques* (Bibliothèque Beauchesne, Religions société, politique 2; Paris: Beauchesne, 1976), 61–78. The feast of the Chair of Peter on February 22 succeeded the domestic commemoration of the dead in ancient Rome (*Cara cognatio*).

64. J. Potel, *Les funérailles, une fête?* (Rites et symboles 1; Paris: Cerf, 1973; P. Ariès, *The Hour of Death*, trans. H. Weaver (New York: Knopf, 1981); M. Vovelle, *Mourir autrefois. Attitudes collectives devant la mort aux XVIIe et XVIIIe siècles* (Archives 53; Paris: Gallimard, 1974); P. Chaunu, *La mort à Paris, 16e, 17e, 18e siècles* (Paris: Fayard, 1978); *En face de la mort* = *LMD* no. 144 (1980).

The Second Vatican Council was careful to respect the traditions of the various peoples when they are compatible with the Christian faith (the same respect was not always shown in the past).[65] Thus in baptism "it is lawful . . . to allow . . . those initiation elements in use among individual peoples, to the extent that such elements are compatible with the Christian rite of initiation."[66] Following the lead of the Council of Trent, Vatican II also allows, and even desires, that in the celebration of marriage, other praiseworthy customs and ceremonies be retained; more than that, the episcopal conference of each country is free "to draw up . . . its own rite, suited to the usages of place and people."[67] The rite of funerals, for its part, "should correspond more closely to the circumstances and traditions of various regions."[68]

2. *Daily and Seasonal Rhythms*

As the daily Office became increasingly the preserve of monks and clerics, the Christian people turned to added devotions for an equivalent means of sanctifying the day: the Angelus in the morning and at noon and evening, the rosary with its one one hundred and fifty *Aves* corresponding to the Psalter.[69]

In cultures on which Christianity has left its mark, the rites are echoed even in daily activities and gestures: evening prayer as a family, blessing at table, sign of the cross over the loaf of bread, decoration of the furnishings and the house.

The rhythm of the seasons, which is so important in rural civilizations, led to the institution of the Ember Days at the beginning of each season; to the christianization of agrarian rites that were deeply rooted in custom: major litany and rogations, the original procession on February 2, the blessing of eggs, beans, new fruits, grapes, each activity being connected with a different Christian feast; and to the substitution of Christian feasts for the feasts of the winter (Nativity of Christ) and summer (St. John the Baptist) solstices, although this did not prevent the continuation of pagan customs on these two dates.[70] The transition from one year

---

65. *VSC* 37–40 (*DOL* 1 nos. 37–40).

66. *VSC* 65 (*DOL* 1 no. 65).

67. *VSC* 77 (*DOL* 1 no. 77).

68. *VSC* 81 (*DOL* 1 no. 81).

69. On the Angelus see *The Church at Prayer* IV:143, 177. For a recent attempt at renewal of this devotion see *Angelus Domini. Celebrazione dell'Annuncio a Maria* (Rome: Curia generalis OSM, 1981). Since the eighteenth century manuals of devotion have made popular a formulary for morning and evening prayers that is attributed to Fénelon.

70. See T. J. Talley, "Liturgical Time in the Ancient Church: The State of Research," in *Liturgical Time: Papers Read at the 1981 Congress of Societas Liturgica* (Rotterdam, 1982), 34–51.

to the next has always been the object of festivities that are often accompanied by a collective inversion of the social order. The Church had a good deal of trouble in resisting the merrymaking on the first of January.[71] Many of the customs that at one time made their way into the churches (feast of simpletons, feast of fools, feast of the ass) may have been connected with this temporary inversion of the social order.

Despite exaggerations and deviations, the Church has endeavored to give a gospel meaning to practices that are not clearly Christian and, by means of blessings that may embrace any and every human activity, lead those who request such blessings to make acts of faith.

3. *The Veneration of the Saints*

In this context the veneration of the saints is especially important. The saints have been venerated as much, if not more, for their powers as wonderworkers, as for the witness of Christian life that they have given. Their patronage is sought for countries, parishes, confraternities, trade associations, and even domestic animals; the relationship gradually comes to be marked by informality on the clients' side. The saints whom the Church regards as the most important have not always enjoyed the same popularity among the faithful: St. Anthony of Padua, for example, is better known than an apostle like St. Bartholomew. The saints most cultivated are those who have a reputation as protectors and healers.[72] The local feast of a saint is the occasion for liturgical celebrations that are prolonged by festivities outside the church: Mass and fair go together.[73] Relics, images, and statues may occupy a disproportionately large place in devotion, and the veneration of the saints can include quite unorthodox practices[74] in which survivals of ancient pre-Christian rites connected with springs, trees, and fire can be seen.[75] The Church's watchfulness in this area has not always been blessed with lasting success, as St. Augustine observed in his day: "We teach one thing, but we are compelled to tolerate another."[76]

---

71. See St. Leo the Great, *Sermons*, ed. R. Dolle (SC 22bis; Paris: Cerf, 1964²), *VIIᵉ sermon pour Noël* 4, pp. 156–61; St. Caesarius of Arles, *Serm.* 33, 4 (CCL 43:146). The lighting of St. John's Fires has continued down to the present day.

72. For one diocese see R. Lecotte, *Recherches sur les cultes populaires dans l'actuel diocèse de Meaux* (Mémoire de la fédération folklorique d'Ile-de-France, 1953).

73. This was already true in the fifth century; see, e.g., the account of the feast of St. Justus at Lyons in Sidonius Apollinaris (PL 58:547–48).

74. See V. Saxer, *Morts, martyrs, reliques en Afrique chrétienne aux premiers siècles* (Théologie historique 55; Paris: Beauchesne, 1980); St. Caesarius of Arles, *Serm.* 192 (CCL 44:779–82).

75. For one province see A. Van Gennep, *Culte populaire des saints en Savoie* (Archives d'ethnologie française 3; Paris: Maisonneuve et Larose, 1973).

76. *Contra Faustum* XX, 21 (CSEL 25:563; PL 42:385).

III. THE POWER OF CUSTOM

Popular religion dislikes change and resists it, or accepts it only after a slow evolution of mentalities. It thinks of rites as meant to be repeated in the form they have always had, even if their meaning is now obscured. Those believers who practice least are the ones most upset by changes in ritual; they refuse to admit that the changes are justified and attribute them to the arbitrary will of the clergy. We see this at every liturgical reform: the reform of the calendar led to schism in Russia and in Greece; the liturgical reform decreed by Vatican II has been regarded by some as an unacceptable disruption, even when it has dealt only with seemingly minor matters like the calendar.

Collective memory ensures the retention through the centuries of local ritual practices that are unknown to the liturgical books and have sometimes been disapproved to no avail by the clergy: the "showing" of the relics of the saints every seven years in the Limousin; the great *troménie* at Locronan (Finistère) every six years;[77] the procession of dancers at Echternach (Luxembourg) on Pentecost Monday in honor of St. Willibrord. Each region could contribute its own item to the list.

IV. EXPRESSION IN DRAMA

Signs, gestures, and formulas play a very important part in the lives of simple folk. Rosaries, medals, holy pictures, candles, and signs of the cross are vehicles of a faith that is clumsy in expressing itself but can be deep or can degenerate into religiosity. Words attract gestures that accentuate them: the account of the institution of the Eucharist that used to be said in silence but was almost mimed by the priest and, at the same time, underscored by the ringing of the bells in the tower or at least of a handbell and by a whole set of ceremonial actions by the ministers around the altar; the entrance of the Palm Sunday procession into the church after a threefold knocking on the door with the shaft of the cross. The singing of the Passion by three deacons likewise reflected an effort at dramatization. Today the young Churches of Black Africa find it quite natural to dance and clap as a way of giving a rhythm to the celebrations. The quest of the spectacular can even take first place, as in the Holy Week processions in Seville, where the connection with the liturgy is a rather loose one.

Between the tenth and the thirteenth centuries the major feasts of the year gave rise to liturgical dramas.[78] These were sacred plays acted by

---

77. D. Laurent, "La Troménie," in M. Dilasser (ed.), *Locronon et sa région* (Paris: Nouvelle Librairie de France, 1979), 194–223.

78. G. Cohen, *Anthologie du drame liturgique en France au Moyen-Age* (LO 19; Paris: Cerf, 1955); R. Donovan, *The Liturgical Drama in Medieval Spain* (Studies and Texts 4;

clerics at a fixed point in the service and depicted the personages of the gospel (or of legend). At Christmas time there was the procession of the prophets, the scene of the shepherds at the crib, the adoration of the Magi, the Office of the star or, again, the weeping of Rachel. At Easter there was the Office of the holy sepulcher, the three Marys at the tomb, the pilgrims at Emmaus, and the raising of Lazarus. The lives of the saints likewise provided subjects, as in the St. Nicholas play or the play about Daniel in the lions' den. Liturgical drama gradually adopted the vernaculars, and its productions became longer and introduced more characters; finally it was separated from the liturgy and the sanctuary and turned into theater or mystery play.

The need of visualizing the content of the liturgical feasts would, however, find other ways of expressing itself. The crib in the churches, the procession of the shepherds, the placing of the infant Jesus in the crib by the celebrant during the night of Christmas are actions that even today spring from the same source.

V. FROM DEVOTION TO LITURGY

Many popular customs had their origin in the feasts of the Church (Christmas tree, Kings' Cake, Candlemas pancakes, Corpus Christi bouquet, various sayings). When the liturgy becomes obscure or foreign to the people, they seek its equivalent in devotions. By adapting itself to the uneducated, the allegorical interpretation of the Mass at least enabled them to see in the Eucharistic celebration an actualization of the sacrifice of Christ. The way of the cross, which was a simplified version of the pilgrimage to Jerusalem, was more meaningful to generations of Christians than the Good Friday liturgy, which was beyond their understanding.[79]

The liturgical services celebrated by the clergy and the books of Hours and offices adapted for use by the laity were succeeded, or overlaid, by other, nonliturgical devotions that were nonetheless more appreciated by the people. This was true in particular of Benediction of the Blessed Sacrament, which developed from the seventeenth century on as an increasingly standard addition to Sunday Vespers and even as an independent service.[80] Songs in the vernacular found a place at "low" (that is, not sung) Masses, where they overlaid the texts of the Missal.

Toronto: Pontifical Institute of Mediaeval Studies, 1958); D. Dolan, *Le drame liturgique de Pâques en Normandie et en Angleterre au moyen âge* (Paris: Presses Universitaires de France, 1975); B. D. Berger, *Le drame liturgique de Pâques* (Théologie historique 77; Paris: Beauchesne, 1976).

79. M. J. Picard, "Croix (chemin de)," *Dictionnaire de spiritualité* 2/2 (1953) 2576–2606.

80. For example, C. Thuet, *Appendix à la pratique du catéchisme romain, contenant certaines prières eucharistiques et solennels saluts. . . . Composé en faveur des Eglises . . .*

The danger that the liturgy may be stifled by devotions is not an illusory one. There was a time when First Fridays established a monthly pattern of piety that was independent of the liturgical year; the month of St. Joseph was in competition with Lent; the Easter season disappeared behind the Month of Mary; Sundays were often obscured by feasts of the saints.

On the other hand, devotions may find a place within the liturgy. Very important feasts such as those of the Trinity, the Blessed Sacrament, and the Sacred Heart of Jesus had their origin in special devotions and owed their development and their inclusion in the Church's calendar to the echo they awakened in the Christian people.

Sometimes a devotion introduces a regrettable distortion into a liturgical feast, as when Palm Sunday becomes more important than Easter or the feast of All Saints is overshadowed by the commemoration of the dead. Sometimes, too, the Church must forbid new devotions that it considers useless or dangerous to the faith of the Christian people.[81]

The Second Vatican Council acknowledges the validity of devotions and exercises of piety but it also assigns them their proper place: they are not to be substitutes for the liturgy but rather must "be so fashioned that they . . . accord with [it], are in some way derived from it, and lead the people to it, since, in fact, the liturgy by its nature far surpasses any one of them."[82]

lesquelles depuis quelques années cette dévotion ayant commencé, se continue et amplifie
. . . (Paris, 1634), 348.

81. A. de Bonhome, "Dévotions prohibées," *Dictionnaire de spiritualité* 3 (1957) 778–95.

82. *VSC* 13 (*DOL* 1 no. 13).

Chapter X

Blessings

P. Jounel

To "bless" (*benedicere, eulogein*) is to "say a good word" that is addressed to God on behalf of human beings or to human beings on behalf of God. To bless is to praise God, invoke him, and receive from him a manifestation of his attentive presence at our side. But while the blessing of God descends on human beings, it also extends to the other works of his hand, as it does to the whole of nature, which is at his service: "Blessed be you, Lord" (Dan 3:52-56); "May the Lord bless you" (Ps 134:3). This twofold movement proper to blessing fills the liturgy. Benediction-as-praise finds its central expression in the Eucharist and the Liturgy of the Hours. The blessing that descends on persons and things includes both everyday life and the annual cycle, and leaves its mark on the great stages of Christian life. From their reception into the catechumenate to their death struggle, with marriage as a milepost in between, Christians receive the blessing of God. The priest invokes this blessing on the congregation at the end of every Mass. Throughout the year there are the blessing of candles on February 2, the blessing of ashes and palms, the blessing of the oils by the bishop on Holy Thursday, and the blessing of fire and water during the Easter Vigil.

I shall not deal in this chapter with those blessings that are a constitutive part of the celebration of the Eucharist and the other sacraments or of the unfolding liturgical year. Nor shall I deal with other blessings already discussed: those that confer a ministry or establish persons in a state of life or dedicate churches and altars. Alongside these major blessings, however, there are many other blessings. Some are given directly to persons, others to places where Christians carry out their many activities, and still others to objects located in churches or intended to promote the devotion of the faithful. In thus providing a broad range of blessings, the Church gathers up a euchological heritage and a collection of popular practices that have their roots in the Bible and have been passed on to the Church down the centuries.

§1. Blessing in the Bible

BIBLIOGRAPHY

H. W. Beyer, "Eulogeō," *TDNT* 2 (original = 1935) 751–63.
J. P. Audet, "Esquisse historique du genre littéraire de la bénédiction juive et de l'eucharistie chrétienne," *Revue biblique* 65 (1958) 371–99.
P. Van Imschoot, "Bénédiction et malédiction," *Dictionnaire encyclopédique de la Bible* (translated from the Dutch) (Turnhout: Brepols, 1960).
A. Stuiber, "Eulogia," *RAC* 6 (1966) 900–28.
G. Lukken, "Was bedeutet *benedicere*?" *Liturgisches Jahrbuch* 27 (1977) 5–27.
G. Braulik, " 'Durch dich sollen alle Geschlechter der Erde Segnung erlangen,' " *Bibel und Liturgie* 52 (1979) 172–76.
H. Reifenberg, "Sichtbares als Offenbarung und Preisung. Pastorale Aspekte zum Benediktionale," *ibid.*, 177–82.

Blessing, understood both as gift from God and as praise of God, occupies an important place in the Bible. The two aspects are there seen as closely dependent on each other. Thus it is already a divine blessing that human beings are able to bless their creator: "May those whom God has blessed bless his most holy Name" (Tob 13:18).

I. BLESSING IN THE OLD TESTAMENT

In the Semitic world, a blessing (*berakah*), like a curse, is a power-laden action that human beings can perform. The power to bless, which can be passed on to others, especially from father to son, comes from God, the Blessed One (Gen 49:25). There is one word that beyond all others sums up the content of blessings: *shalom*, "peace."

God's blessing is always bestowed with complete freedom. He gives his blessing either to individuals or to the people as a whole. The Lord is often depicted as himself directly blessing (Gen 1:22, 28; 2:3; Ps 45:2; 67:7). His blessing rests upon all of creation but preeminently upon human beings. His first action after creating man and woman is to bless them (Gen 1:28). The object of this blessing is the promise of a numerous posterity (Gen 12:2; 13:6), but also fruitfulness for soil and animals and increased possessions (Deut 28:1-13). The divine blessing extends to institutions such as the sabbath (Gen 2:3; Exod 20:11). Among human beings the patriarchs are the recipients of a special blessing (Gen 17:7ff.; 26:3). The same is to be said of Moses, the leader whom God chose for his people. Once the covenant at Sinai has been struck, God's blessing is always linked to the fidelity of the people to the Law, that great gift that he has given to Israel. From this point on, God, who respects human freedom, offers his people a choice between blessing and curse (Deut 11:26-29).

The importance of God's blessing in the life of the people inevitably found expression in cult. It was in worship that believing Israelites had their privileged experience of the divine blessing, which was transmitted to them by priests or the king (Gen 14:19; Deut 33:1-29; Josh 14:13; 2 Sam 6:18; 1 Kgs 8:14, 55). In time, the bestowal of the blessing became the prerogative of the Levites and priests. The blessing given by Aaron served as prototype for theirs: "The Lord bless you and keep you: The Lord make his face to shine upon you, and be gracious to you: The Lord lift up his countenance upon you, and give you peace" (Num 6:24-26).

Once blessings came to be used in worship, they also became a formula of praise, glorification, and thanksgiving that human beings addressed to God. Even in Genesis, we see Eliezer, Abraham's servant, blessing the Lord (Gen 24:48). Blessing takes the same form in the prescription given by Moses in Deuteronomy 8:10, in the Song of Deborah (Judg 5:2-9), and in the ending of the Book of Tobit (Tob 12:6). It is however in the psalms, many of which have a cultic origin, that we most often find the exhortation to bless God (for example, Ps 16:7; 33:2; 68:26). Some psalms are hymns of blessing (71:18-19; 89:52; 103:2, 20, 21, 22). Words of blessing erupt in the canticle in Daniel, which praises God and urges all of creation to praise him (Dan 3:52-87).

The Book of Nehemiah contains a real liturgy of blessing: "Ezra blessed the Lord, the great God; and all the people answered, 'Amen, Amen,' lifting up their hands; and they bowed their heads and worshiped the Lord with their faces to the ground" (Neh 8:6). This tradition was taken over into the liturgy of the synagogue, which combined prayer of blessing with the proclamation of God's Word.

The Old Testament thus shows an evolution in the idea of blessing. The starting point is a primitive exchange with mysterious forces that bestow a power for good and for evil; but blessing eventually becomes the expression of a spiritual bond linking human beings with God, whose benefits they experience throughout their lives and to whom they feel urged to respond with praise and thanksgiving.

II. BLESSING IN THE NEW TESTAMENT

The New Testament received its concept of blessing from the Old. We see Jesus blessing children (Mark 10:16) and blessing his apostles as he departs from them (Luke 24:50). The Gospel According to Luke opens with the *Benedictus* of Zechariah (Luke 1:68) and ends with a glimpse of the apostles "continually in the temple blessing God" (Luke 24:53). Although the word "bless" does not occur in Matthew's text, it is certainly a prayer of blessing that Jesus utters when he says: "Father, I proclaim your praise (*exomologoumai*), for you have hidden these things from the wise and intelligent and revealed them to little ones" (Matt 11:25).

Jesus and his disciples faithfully attended the synagogal liturgy (Luke 4:16), the main part of which was the "Eighteen Blessings" (this according to testimonies that are from a later time but seem to be deeply rooted in the tradition). Even the proclamation of God's Word was accompanied by blessings. Mention must be made also of meals, at which a blessing is attested as early as the time of Samuel (1 Sam 9:13). Here the bread was blessed first and then an initial cup of wine; then, at the end of the meal, the cup of blessing was shared. The Passover meal was the most outstanding of the entire year; especially to be noted among its rites was the singing of the Hallel, in which the acclamation "Alleluia" is itself a summons to bless the Lord.[1]

It is in this context that we must locate the words and actions of Jesus at the first multiplication of the bread and fish, at the Last Supper, and at Emmaus. As he was about to multiply the loaves and fishes, he "said the blessing" (Matt 14:19; Mark 6:41). At the Last Supper he broke the bread "having pronounced the blessing" (Matt 26:26; Mark 14:22), and he did the same at table in Emmaus (Luke 24:30). "The bread is not blessed; rather a blessing is spoken over the bread in recognition of the sovereign rule of God."[2] Jesus did bless persons but he never blessed things. In his instructions to his disciples he told them to bless those who cursed them (Luke 6:28), and promised that if they were faithful to his commandment of love, they would receive the supreme blessing when they entered the kingdom: "Come, you blessed of my Father" (Matt 25:34).

St. Paul repeats the command of Jesus: "Bless those who persecute you; bless and do not curse them" (Rom 12:14), and he claims to put it into practice in his own life (1 Cor 4:12). Blessings addressed to God flow spontaneously from his pen (Rom 1:25; 9:5; 2 Cor 11:31). He takes part in meals at which they bless "the cup of blessing" (1 Cor 10:16), as Jesus had done. He reminds the Galatians that as children of Abraham they inherit the blessing that the Lord had given to him: "Those who are men of faith are blessed with Abraham who had faith" (Gal 3:9). The opening of the Letter to the Ephesians combines in a single sentence the two aspects of blessing: "Blessed be the God and Father of our Lord Jesus Christ, who has blessed us in Christ with every spiritual blessing in the heavenly places"

---

1. Ch. Perrot, "Le repas du Seigneur," *LMD* no. 125 (1975) 29–46.
2. *Ibid.*, 33.

(Eph 1:3). The apostle goes on here to explain the riches contained in the blessing with which we have been favored in Christ. Christ is in his person the fullness of the blessing that God has bestowed on humankind.

But if the Lord Jesus is God's blessing in living form, he is also, with the Father, the object of the blessing that rises up from all of creation: "Worthy is the Lamb . . . to receive . . . glory and blessing!" (Rev 5:12).

§2. The Liturgy of Blessings

BIBLIOGRAPHY

Martène, Lib. 2, *De sacris benedictionibus*, M 821–44.

J. Catalani, *Rituale Romanum . . . perpetuis commentariis exornatum* (Padua: J. Manfre, 1760²), 2:1–150.

A. Franz, *Die kirchlichen Benediktionen im Mittelalter* (2 vols.; Freiburg: Herder, 1909; reprinted: Graz: Akademische Druck, 1960).

J. Baudot, "Bénédictions," *DACL* 2 (1910) 670–84.

P. De Meester, *Liturgia bizantina. Studi di rito bizantino . . .*, Libro II, Parte 6: *Rituale-Benedizionale bizantino* (Rome: Tipografia Leoniana, 1930).

M. Sodi, "Benedizione," *Nuovo dizionario di liturgia* (Rome: Ed. Paoline, 1984), 174–75 (extensive bibliography).

On some particular blessings:

Bell: M. Righetti, *Manuale di storia liturgica* 4 (Milan: Ancora, 1959), 523–25; P. Jounel, *Consécration d'une cloche* (Paris: Desclée, 1963) (with translations by A. M. Roguet).

Episcopal blessings of the people: E. Moeller, *Corpus benedictionum pontificalium* (4 vols.; CCL 162, 162A, 162B, 162C; Turnhout: Brepols, 1971–79).

Exorcism: Righetti, *ibid.*, 532–45.

King (queen): Righetti, *ibid.*, 492–99; Martène M 770–82 (with bibliography); M. Clausel de Coussergues, *Du sacre des rois de France* (Paris, 1825).

Ordeals: H. Leclercq, "Ordalie," *DACL* 12 (1936) 2377–90; Righetti, *ibid.*, 546–54; Martène M 883–903 (wth bibliography).

Pilgrims: Righetti, *ibid.*, 499–501.

Table: J. Baudot, "Bénédiction de la table et des aliments," *DACL* 2 (1910) 713–16.

Water: P. de Puniet, "Bénédiction de l'eau," *DACL* 2 (1910) 685–713; M. Righetti, *ibid.*, 525–32.

In the time of St. Justin, as in the apostolic age, candidates for baptism went down into the water in order to be "renewed by Christ and consecrated to God," without any preceding prayer.[3] Soon, however, as Tertullian attests, the minister would "call God down" upon the water before having the candidate descend into it, "for at once the Spirit comes down from heaven and stays upon the waters, sanctifying them from

---

3. St. Justin, *Apologia I* 61, ed. L. Pautigny (Textes et documents 1; Paris: Picard, 1904), 126.

within by himself, and when thus sanctified they absorb the power of sanctifying."[4] Then, he adds, "we come up from the washing and are anointed
with the blessed unction, following that ancient practice."[5] This invocation of God upon the water and this use of oil began a chapter in the history of Christian worship that would lead to developments impossible to
foresee. The Western liturgy of our day includes over two hundred blessings of persons and things. Not only would later Christians multiply blessings, but from the Middle Ages on they would believe that nothing is to
be used for the glory of God and the service of human beings unless it
has first been blessed. The prayer of praise or invocation, together with
its accompanying gesture, paid homage to the sovereign lordship of the
creator and of him whom the creator has established as king of the universe. But the practice was not without ambiguity. Blessings could become rites whose primary purpose was to rescue persons and things from
the dominion that the demon was regarded as exercising over the world.
In this pessimistic vision of creation a simple prayer was no longer enough,
and an exorcism would often precede the blessing proper. The evolution
of mentalities can be seen in the stages through which the ritual of blessings has passed in its development.

I. THE FIRST PRAYERS OF BLESSING

The first collection of blessings makes its appearance in the *Apostolic
Tradition* of St. Hippolytus.[6] The first blessings are of oil for the sick,
of cheese, and of olives (chapter 5–6); they come after the Eucharistic
Prayer. At a baptism "a prayer is first to be said over the water"; the bishop
then "gives thanks" over the oil of thanksgiving and exorcizes the "oil of
exorcism"; during the Eucharist that follows upon baptism he gives thanks
"over the mixed milk and honey" and over the water, both of which are
to be given to the neophytes together with the consecrated bread and wine
(chapter 21). In his description of the community's evening meal, Hippolytus refers to the bishop's prayer of thanksgiving over the lamp; the
bread that the bishop gives to the faithful at this meal is a "eulogy," a
bread that has been blessed (chapters 25–26). Finally, there is the blessing
of the fruits of the soil that are presented to the bishop; there is even a
specification of which fruits can be blessed and which cannot (chapters
31–32). In the prayers of blessing, intercession plays a part but thanks-

---

4. Tertullian, *De baptismo* IV, 4; text and trans. in E. Evans, *Tertullian's Homily on
Baptism* (London: S.P.C.K., 1964), 11.

5. *Ibid.*, VII, 1 (Evans 17).

6. *La Tradition apostolique de saint Hippolyte*, ed. B. Botte (LQF 39; Münster: Aschendorff, 1963).

giving predominates. It is even prescribed that "these words are to be used in every blessing: 'Glory to you, Father and Son with the Holy Spirit in the holy Church, now and always and through endless ages. Amen'" (chapter 6).

The structure of prayers that is thus established to embrace the whole of life is not thought of as something added to the sacraments, because the entire celebration is regarded as sacramental. The practices mentioned, and even the formulas to be used with them, have Jewish antecedents, but there is also a lively awareness that Christian worship has an eschatological dimension. Thus the milk and honey that are blessed for the newly baptized do not simply symbolize the entrance of these new Christians into the true Promised Land; they also serve the same function, but by antithesis, as the bitter herbs that recalled the Exodus from Egypt in the Jewish Passover ritual. Again, while Christian prayers of blessing rise up, as does Jewish prayer, to the Almighty One, their decidedly Trinitarian character underscores their essential newness.

The Syrian *Apostolic Constitutions*[7] also have prayers over the *myron* (VII, 27), the oil of anointing and the baptismal water (VII, 42-43), ordinary water and the oil of exorcism (VIII, 29), and over the first fruits (VIII, 40). The work bears witness to the Christian use of Aaron's blessing (II, 57). In all of these prayers the element of thanksgiving is quite predominant. As far as the minister of blessing is concerned, the *Apostolic Constitutions* flatly reserve this function to bishops and priests (VIII, 28). Finally, the book describes the way in which the bishop is to bless the people: After the deacon has asked them to bow their heads, the bishop stretches his hands out over them while saying the prayer of blessing (VIII, 41).

The *Euchologion of Serapion*[8] shows that the blessing was given in the same way in Egypt (chapter 4). More importantly, it provides many prayers for blessing catechumens (chapters 3–4), the people (5), laypersons (6), the sick (7–8), the land that it may be fruitful (9), offerings of oil and water (17–18), baptismal water and chrism (19, 25), and the oil, bread or water given to the sick (29). To be noted is the importance assigned to the blessing of water in Egypt.

II. THE SACRAMENTARIES AND EUCHOLOGIA

1. *Rome*

The earliest witness to the Roman liturgy of blessings is undoubtedly

7. F. X. Funk (ed.), *Didascalia et Constitutiones Apostolorum* (2 vols.; Paderborn: Schöningh, 1905), vol. 1.
8. *Ibid.*, 2:158–95.

the prayer "Per quem haec omnia" of the Canon. It is between the end of the prayer "Nobis quoque" and this final formula that the sacramentaries insert various blessings: for the oil of the sick on Holy Thursday (*Ge* 381–82; *Gr* 333–34), the milk and honey given to the newly baptized during the baptismal vigils of Easter and Pentecost (*Le* 205), the first new beans at Ascension (*Ge* 577), and the first new grapes on the feast of St. Sixtus (August 6; *Gr* 631). In the Middle Ages many blessings were added at the "Per quem haec omnia." The *Sacerdotale* of Alberto di Castello (or Castellani) would still have the blessing of the Easter lamb and Easter eggs at this point. By inserting the blessings of various foods before the doxology of the Canon, Roman practice emphasized the bond uniting the food of human beings with the bread of life and cup of salvation.

In reading the sacramentaries we must bear in mind that the words *benedictio* and *consecratio* did not yet have the juridical meaning that would be assigned to them from the twelfth century on. The two terms are used indifferently, especially in speaking of the ordination rites. Also to be noted is the difference in style between the blessings in the sacramentaries and those in older documents. Henceforth the element of invocation clearly takes priority over thanksgiving. The latter still has its place in various important formularies, such as the blessing of the Easter candle and, to a lesser degree, in the opening section of the prayers of ordination or the prayer for the consecration of virgins. Most blessings, however, are satisfied to invoke God's protection on an individual or specific group of persons.

The so-called Leonine Sacramentary has the blessing for the ordination of bishops, priests, and deacons, as well as the blessing that accompanied the giving of the veil to a virgin or a wife; it ends, moreover, with the blessing of the baptismal font.[9] The manuscript is incomplete, however, and we must go to the Gelasian and Gregorian sacramentaries for the blessings connected with the celebration of Christian initiation.

2. *Frankish Territory*

The Gelasian and Gregorian sacramentaries contain a number of blessings that seem to have been added in Frankish territory. This applies, in the Gelasian, to the blessing of water to be used in sprinkling homes (*Ge* 1556–65), the blessing of water and salt to be used in exorcisms against lightning (*Ge* 1568), and the blessings of a new threshing floor (*Ge* 1569–70), new fruits (*Ge* 1603–4), apples (*Ge* 1605), and trees (*Ge* 1606). In the Carolingian Supplement to the Gregorian Sacramentary we find, among other things, the Easter *Exsultet* (*Gr* 1021), the blessings for doorkeepers, lectors, exorcists, acolytes, and subdeacons (*Gr* 1792–1805), the

---

9. *Le* 942–54, 1103–10, 1331.

blessings for table and for the cloistered areas of monasteries (*Gr* 1465–86), and, above all, a sizable collection of blessings that the bishops of Gaul gave to the people at Mass after the Our Father (*Gr* 1738–77). Among the latter is the blessing of Aaron (*Gr* 1777), the Christian use of which had already been attested in Syria by the *Apostolic Constitutions*. Most of these blessings already had a place in the eighth-century Gelasian sacramentaries (*Gell* 2815–81).

3. *Spain*

The old Spanish liturgy had a type of blessing in which, consistently with the Spanish genius, the prayers were much more fully developed. Exorcisms sometimes occupied a disproportionate place. Thus the blessing of the oil for the sick that begins the *Liber ordinum* concentrates throughout on the "impetum daemonum" that is the cause of sickness.[10] Similarly, the blessing of water begins with a lengthy exorcism first of the salt, then of the water itself. The priest turns westward to expel the demon, then eastward to invoke the Lord. The participation of the people in the prayer takes the form of frequent "Amens." These "Amens" were required especially in the blessing that, in Spain as in Gaul, was given at Mass after the Our Father.

4. *The Byzantine East*

The Byzantine euchologion is almost contemporary with the Romano-Frankish and Spanish sacramentaries.[11] It contains a large number of blessings connected with rural and maritime life: sowing, first fruits of the harvests, planting of vines, vintage, new wine, boats, fishing nets. Among the blessings connected with domestic life (betrothals, pregnant women, women who have just given birth) one in particular is to be noted: the splendid formulary for blessing a newly adopted child. But, apart from the confection of *myron*, which is reserved to the patriarch, the most solemn blessing of the year is the blessing of water on Epiphany, the day when the baptism of the Lord is celebrated. The blessing begins with five readings from the Bible (three from the Book of Isaiah) and a lengthy litanic prayer. Then, after three extensive prayers filled with Old Testament types, come the solemn blessing of the bowed people and the blessing of the water, into which the priest dips the cross three times. He then sprinkles the water toward the four points of the compass. The people then

---

10. *Le Liber Ordinum*, ed. M. Férotin (Paris: Firmin-Didot, 1904), cols. 7–24.

11. *Euchologion sive Rituale Graecorum*, ed. J. Goar (Paris, 1647). See the translation of the Great Blessing of the Waters in the selection by A. Nelidow and A. Nièvre, *Euchologe ou Rituel de l'Eglise orthodoxe* (Le Bousquet-sur-Orb [Herault], 1979) 133–40.

come forward to kiss the cross, be sprinkled, and drink a mouthful of the newly blessed water.

5. *The Medieval Pontificals and Rituals*

A study of blessings in the medieval pontificals would require a great deal of space. I shall limit myself, therefore, to mention of the largest collection, the one in the Romano-German Pontifical of the mid-tenth century. This was to be the main source for many later pontificals and for the rituals; this is true first and foremost with the Roman liturgy.[12]

The Romano-German Pontifical is a compilation, made in Mainz, of many rites already in use in the Frankish and German territories. Its redactor was therefore a witness rather than a creator; consequently, his work is of vital interest to us. Various blessings are provided for such basic foods as water, salt, and bread, depending on the use to be made of them (thus there are blessings of water intended for sprinkling the people or for purifying a house or fields that have been seeded, water to counteract eye problems or the demon, water for the dedication of a church, the water in this case being mixed with salt, wine, and ashes). Three categories of blessings call for attention because of the mentality they display.

First, there are the blessings of candles for the procession on February 2, of ashes for the beginning of Lent, and of palms (this last is already attested for Spain by the *Liber ordinum*[13]). Previously it had been thought sufficient simply to go in procession carrying candles or palms or to bestow ashes on penitents. Henceforth, however, it seems that no object can have a cultic use unless it has first been withdrawn from the profane world by a preceding blessing. Furthermore, the candles and palms, which have now become blessed objects, are kept throughout the year as pledges of divine protection. The thing has become more important than the action.

A second series of blessings to be noted comprises the rites for the crowning of a king, queen, or emperor. These bear witness to the ascendancy of the Church over civil society. The rites themselves are older than the tenth century. The first royal coronation known to us is that of a king of Scotland in 574. A crowning of the Visigothic kings at Toledo in 672 is also attested. A century later, Pepin the Short was crowned king of the Franks by St. Boniface in 751 and then by Pope Stephen II at Saint-Denis in 754. The pope crowned not only Pepin but with him Queen Bertrada and their two sons. In 800 Pope Leo III crowned Charles emperor of the West. All of Charlemagne's successors would be obliged, like him, to have their power consecrated by the pope in a rite of coronation. At a much

---

12. *PRG* 3:44–55.
13. *Liber Ordinum* (ed. Férotin), cols. 179–84.

more modest level we find blessings being given to knights, swords, and battle flags.

The Romano-German Pontifical thus shows the ascendancy of the Church over society in the age of the barbarians. On the other hand, we also find the Church accepting the atrocious practices of the time by giving ritual form to ordeals or "judgments of God."[14] This Pontifical contains lengthy *Ordines* for blessing red-hot iron (*PRG* 246), the boiling water (*PRG* 247) or the ice-cold water (*PRG* 248) into which an accused person was thrown, and the bread and cheese used to ferret out a thief (*PRG* 249–52). The popes followed St. Gregory the Great in opposing these tortures that originated in Germanic law, but the practice of them lasted for centuries in countries north of the Alps. In the ninth century Archbishop Agobard of Lyons had assailed the practice, but Hincmar of Rheims had justified it. Not until the fourth Council of Lyons (1215) would the liturgical blessing of such practices, if not the practices themselves, finally disappear.

Beginning in the twelfth century the monastic rituals made their appearance and, in the fourteenth and fifteenth, rituals for parishes. The former often contain the blessings given in the old sacramentaries and pontificals. The latter, however, at least outside of Germany, include hardly any of them. On the other hand, the blessings found in the parochial rituals constitute a real treasury of local liturgies and provide choice material for studying the concrete life and outlook of the populations whose lives they sanctified.[15]

III. BLESSINGS FROM THE COUNCIL OF TRENT TO THE SECOND VATICAN COUNCIL

1. *Castellani's Ritual*

The Fathers of the Council of Trent used a *Liber sacerdotalis* that had been published at Venice in 1523 by Alberto di Castello or Castellani and that had been successful enough to be reprinted a number of times.[16] This ritual contains not only the blessings connected with the celebration of the sacraments but a further collection of over fifty others. It opens with a *Prooemium* that uses Scripture to explain the several meanings of "blessing": on the one hand, praise and thanksgiving to God and, on the other,

---

14. A bibliography on ordeals is given in A. G. Martimort, *La documentation liturgique de dom Edmond Martène* (ST 279; Vatican City, 1978), 427–28.

15. P. M. Gy. "Collectaire, Rituel, Processional," *Revue des sciences philosophiques et théologiques* 44 (1960) 441–69.

16. *Liber sacerdotalis* (Venice: M. Sessas and P. de Ravanis, 1523).

a rite for sanctifying persons and things. In keeping with tradition, the editor tells his readers that the act of blessing is reserved to bishops and priests. On a number of occasions, Castellani's Ritual refers to Venetian usages; in fact a number of his blessings must have been influenced by them. We find in his collection a blessing of the waters on the eve of Epiphany that shows Byzantine influence; blessings of St. John's wine, bread, wine and fruits associated with St. Blaise, St. Agatha's bread, and seeds on the day of St. Mark; blessings for a caritative meal, for pilgrims departing and returning, and all the blessings connected with rural life and with canonical or monastic life in community.

2. *The Ritual of Paul V*

The first official ritual published at Rome was that of Paul V in 1614; it was to remain in use until shortly after the Second Vatican Council. This ritual, which was less influenced than Castellani's had been by the traditions of the northern regions, contained only eighteen common blessings and eleven others reserved to a bishop or a priest appointed by him. The common blessings are those of water for sprinkling, candles (except on February 2), homes (on Holy Saturday and at other times), places generally, new houses, bedrooms, new ships, grains and vines, and pilgrims to the Holy Land. These are followed by various blessings for foods, especially during the Easter season. The collection of eighteen nonreserved blessings was to remain unchanged until 1952. The collection of reserved blessings was increased by only three further prayers.

3. *Diocesan Rituals*

The voluminous appendixes added to the diocesan rituals in many regions brought together a large number of blessings that the Roman Ritual had left out. These other blessings, which had been inherited from the Middle Ages, often met pastoral needs, since the populations of the regions were attached to the traditions connected with the blessings. These various *Collectiones rituum* were also a storehouse that would be drawn on to fill out the Roman Ritual in the twentieth century.

In the eighteenth and early nineteenth centuries, real diocesan rituals were developed in France that were characterized above all by their collections of blessings. These collections increased the number of blessings and made an effort to organize them according to a logical plan. We may take as an example the Ritual of Belley, which the Curé of Ars used and which went through a number of editions between 1830 and 1843.[17] The bishop who published it says that he "looked through the most recognized

---

17. *Rituel du diocèse de Belley*, published by Mgr A. R. Devies (Lyons, 1843).

rituals of France and Italy for the special blessings contained in each."[18] The collection begins with Benediction of the Blessed Sacrament; then come fourteen blessings of persons, fifteen of buildings, six of animals, sixteen of objects connected with agriculture, eleven of things that serve as food, nine of remedies, and eighteen nonreserved blessings of objects of devotion. The section of reserved blessings contains twenty-three formularies, the most recent being for the blessing of a railroad. A careful study of these one hundred and thirteen blessings would reveal a keen sensitivity to the needs of the people of that day.

4. *1925 and 1952 Editions of the Roman Ritual*

In 1925 Pope Pius XI published an edition of the Roman Ritual *ad normam Codicis Iuris Canonici accommodatum*. The 1917 Code of Canon Law had not introduced any major changes in the chapter on blessings (can. 1144–49). Following the lead of the Code, Title VIII of the new Ritual notes first that any priest can give blessings, except for those that are reserved, but that deacons and lectors can give only those expressly allowed them by law. Turning then to the validity of blessings, it introduces a distinction between constitutive blessings and invocative blessings. The former resemble consecrations in that they give to the persons, objects, and places on which they are bestowed a kind of sacredness that withdraws them from all secular use; invocative, or simple, blessings, on the other hand, do not change the nature of the person or object to whom the Lord is asked to grant some spiritual or corporeal effect. The Code of 1983 does not keep this distinction, but speaks simply, in canon 1171, of "res sacrae, quae dedicatione vel benedictione ad divinum cultum destinata sunt" ("sacred things which are destined for divine worship through dedication or a blessing"). Finally, in keeping with the 1917 Code, the Ritual of Pius XI states that while blessings are meant primarily for Catholics, they can also be given to catechumens and even to non-Catholics, unless the Church has a prohibition against it.

The edition of 1925 left the previous collection of blessings practically untouched, but it added an enormous appendix of one hundred and fifty blessings, seventy-one not reserved and seventy-nine reserved. In this compilation, which includes good and not so good things, we find, to begin with, a certain number of medieval blessings that had survived in local rituals, then the blessings that the Holy See had approved over the course of a century to meet the new needs of a technological world (railroad, airplane, seismograph). But a sizable part of this appendix is devoted to

---

18. Among the bishop's sources are said to be "an old Ritual published by St. Francis de Sales" and "a collection of blessings printed at Padua in 1797" (*Rituel du diocèse de Belley* 2:167).

the fifty-two blessings peculiar to various religious Orders.[19] Here we find such strange devotions as the chastity belt of St. Thomas Aquinas and the ring of St. Joseph or the simultaneous wearing of the five scapulars of the Blessed Trinity, the Lord's Passion, the Immaculate Conception of Mary, the Seven Sorrows, and Mount Carmel; the piling up of these in the space of ninety pages could only bring discredit upon the Ritual in various parts of the world.

A further step was taken in the edition of 1952, which was published by Pius XII. Here the appendix became part of the body of the Ritual, whose collection of one hundred and seventy-nine blessings (ninety-five of them reserved) was arranged according to a rational plan.[20]

The Instruction *Inter Oecumenici* of September 26, 1964, did away with the reservation of blessings, except for the seven listed in article 77.

§3. The Reformed Liturgy of Blessings

The Book of Blessings is one of the sections of the Roman Ritual that has been revised in accordance with the Liturgical Constitution of Vatican II.[21]

I. BLESSINGS IN THE CONSTITUTION *SACROSANCTUM CONCILIUM*

In speaking of blessings, the conciliar document is satisfied with decreeing that "reserved blessings shall be very few; reservations shall be in favor only of bishops and Ordinaries."[22] Meanwhile, since the document follows custom and places blessings among the sacramentals, it thinks of them as "sacred signs bearing a kind of resemblance to the sacraments: they signify effects, particularly of a spiritual kind, that are obtained through

---

19. A first collection of blessings peculiar to some religious orders was published by the Congregation for the Propagation of the Faith as an *Appendix ad Rituale Romanum . . . in usum et commoditatem Missionariorum Apostolicorum* (Rome, 1864). It contained only eighteen blessings. The edition of the *Rituale Romanum* published at Tournai in 1893 had an *Appendix* and a *Supplementum*, with their own pagination and containing thirty-four formularies of blessing approved by Cardinal Goossens, archbishop of Malines. This seems to have been the chief source for the *Appendix* in the Ritual of 1925. Most of these blessings came from French diocesan Rituals by way of indults granted to these dioceses when they began using the Roman books once again.

20. E. Viale commented on the *Rituale Romanum* of 1952 in *LMD* no. 34 (1953) 164–67.

21. The new *Benedictionale* was published in 1985. A summary presentation of it had been given in *Notitiae* 19 (183) 320–22.

22. *VSC* 79 (*DOL* 1 no. 79).

the Church's intercession. They dispose people to receive the chief effect of the sacraments and they make holy various occasions in human life."[23] At work in them is the "divine grace that flows from the paschal mystery of Christ's passion, death, and resurrection." Consequently, "there is hardly any proper use of material things that cannot be . . . directed toward human sanctification and the praise of God."[24] In order that this purpose may be attained, "the sacramentals are to be reviewed in the light of the primary criterion that the faithful participate intelligently, actively, and easily; the conditions of our own day must also be considered."[25] The Constitution adds that when rituals are revised, new sacramentals may be added as need requires and that provision is to be made "that some sacramentals, at least in special circumstances and at the discretion of the Ordinary, may be administered by qualified laypersons."[26]

II. THE BOOK OF BLESSINGS

The collection of about fifty *Ordines* that makes up the Book of Blessings is preceded by a theological and pastoral introduction. This explains the nature of blessings, the organization of the rites to be used in them, the ministers who can bestow them, and, finally, the adaptations that are within the power of the episcopal conferences.

1. *The Ministry of Blessing That Is Entrusted to the Church*

God, who is blessed beyond all else, is the origin and source of every blessing. He favored the human couple with his blessing when he created them, and he has not ceased to bless humankind after the Fall, as the lives of the patriarchs and the history of the Israelite people, especially of their priests, Levites, and kings, attest. But the supreme blessing that God has given is the sending of his Son, who blessed the Father in the name of human beings and brought the Father's blessing to all, but especially to the lowliest. By his death and resurrection and his sending of the Spirit he poured out upon the race the fullness of divine blessing. The Church, which shares in the cup of blessing (1 Cor 10:6), continues to bless the

---

23. VSC 60 (*DOL* 1 no. 60). This article of the Constitution repeats the definition of sacramentals given in the 1917 Code of Canon Law (can. 1144), but replaces the vague expression, "res aut actiones" with the idea of sign, which is so basic: "sacramentalia sunt signa sacra." The Code of 1983 repeats the conciliar definition verbatim (can. 1168). This definition is quite different from the idea that the Church still had of sacramentals in the thirteenth century. See A. M. Roguet, "Qu'est-ce qu'un sacramental?" *LMD* no. 2 (1945) 24–26.

24. VSC 61 (*DOL* 1 no. 61).

25. VSC 79 (*DOL* 1 no. 79).

26. *Ibid.*

Lord in Christ and, having been given the ministry of sanctifying human beings, has established the various forms of blessing whose nature and effects are explained in the conciliar constitution.

The Church's blessings are liturgical actions. It is therefore fitting that their celebration be a community action. The most important of them call for participation by the diocesan or parochial community. All require the participation of at least some of the faithful. It is therefore indispensable that the faithful receive some appropriate instruction on the nature and effects of blessings. This will put them on guard against any superstitious interpretation of the rite.

As an exercise of the priesthood of Christ, the ministry of blessing can be carried out by any member of the people of God in accordance with the character of the blessing in question. It is for the bishop to preside at the most solemn ones that concern the entire diocesan community. He can, however, always delegate a priest to take his place. It is for priests to preside at blessings intended for the communities of which they have charge, unless the bishop is present. All the blessings contained in the Book of Blessings can be given by a priest. The *De benedictionibus* (Praenotanda 18 c) has this to say about deacons: "As aides to the bishop and his presbyterium in the ministries of word, altar, and charity, deacons are permitted to preside at certain celebrations, as will be indicated at the proper place. But whenever a priest is present, it is appropriate that he preside, while the deacon serves him by exercising his own proper ministry in the liturgical function." Many blessings, which are likewise enumerated, can be given by laypersons, men or women, by reason of their special responsibility (parents, for example, in relation to their children) or of a ministry entrusted to them in the Church (for example, acolytes and readers or, again, extraordinary Eucharistic ministers and catechists).[27]

2. *The Structure of the Rite of Blessing*

The celebration of a blessing has two main parts. The first is the reading of God's Word, the second is praise of God's goodness and petition for his aid. The whole ceremony usually begins and ends with special rites. To promote participation by the people, the Ritual prescribes not only exhortations and an explanation of the rites but also songs, a period of silence, and a prayer of the faithful that may either precede or follow the formula of blessing.

---

27. The Code of 1983 (can. 1168) says simply: "Quaedam sacramentalia, ad normam librorum liturgicorum, de iudicio loci Ordinarii, a laicis quoque, congruis qualitatibus praeditis, administrari possunt" ("In accord with the norm of the liturgical books and according to the judgment of the local ordinary, some sacramentals can be administered by lay persons who are endowed with the appropriate qualities": *Code of Canon Law* 422–23).

It is fitting that the blessing be accompanied by meaningful gestures such as the raising of the hands in prayer or their imposition, the sign of the cross, a sprinkling with holy water, or an incensation. On the other hand, lest a stimulus be given to a superstitious interpretation, objects and places ought not to be blessed by a simple gesture that is not related to the Word of God and not accompanied by a prayer of intercession or praise.

For each rite of blessing the Ritual indicates whether it may be linked to the celebration of the Eucharist. Several blessings may be given in a single celebration, as, for example, the blessing of a house and the blessing of the holy pictures to be venerated therein; but one of the blessings takes precedence over the others, which are then included in the main one.

3. *Adaptations*

More than any other liturgical book, the Book of Blessings must take local traditions into account. Many of the rites of blessing proposed in the typical edition will be useless for most countries; on the other hand, some countries will look in vain for formularies that they would find very useful. The needs of a primarily agrarian civilization are not those of an industrialized region. The *Ordo* for the blessing of church doors may have a purpose in Italy, where craftsmen continue to cast splendid bronze doors, but it will hardly be of use anywhere else. On the other hand, the Book understandably does not contain many blessings used in Germanic lands, especially Bavaria and Austria, where many customs connected with the course of the year have always been given a sacral dimension: for example, Advent wreaths, St. John's wine, St. Blaise candles, and Assumption wreaths.

The Book of Blessings grants episcopal conferences the authority to introduce into the Ritual, after ratification by the Holy See, all the adaptations and additions that seem appropriate in the light of local traditions. They can also add other prayers to those proposed as optional; they can choose new readings and authorize translations that are adapted to their respective countries. The Book of Blessings, which is secondary in importance to the Missal and the *Ordines* of the sacraments, thus offers a privileged terrain for application of the Constitution *Sacrosanctum Concilium*, no. 40, which urges a fuller adaptation of the Roman liturgy to cultures that are alien to the Western world.

4. *The Arrangement of the Book of Blessings*

The Book gives first the blessings bestowed directly on persons: various blessings connected with domestic life; blessings of the sick, of missionaries setting out to proclaim the gospel, of catechists, of societies whose purpose is to help in public need; blessings of pilgrims and travelers.

The second part contains blessings bestowed on buildings and various forms of Christian activity: blessing of the cornerstone of an important building, except for a church (this blessing is part of the rite of dedication); blessings of a new house, a new seminary, a new religious house, a new school or university, a new library; blessings of a new hospital or old-age home, a workplace, an exercise center, and various media of communication (printing office, cinema, radio and television studios); blessings of certain technological machinery (power stations, aqueducts) and tools; blessings of animals, fields and pastures, and new fruits; blessing at table.

The third part brings together blessings of objects contained or erected in churches: blessings of a new baptismal font, a new tabernacle, a new door, a new cross, and images of the Lord, the Blessed Virgin Mary, or the saints that are intended for veneration by the faithful; blessings of a bell, an organ or other musical instruments, objects destined for use in the liturgy, water, and stations of the Cross; blessing of a cemetery.

In the fourth part are blessings of objects whose purpose is to foster the devotion of the Christian people: blessings of water or other elements in honor of the Blessed Virgin or the saints; blessings of medals, small crucifixes, pictures, rosaries, scapulars.

The collection ends with a blessing given in thanksgiving and a blessing for various situations.

§4. Blessings and Popular Religion (by J. Evenou)

BIBLIOGRAPHY

> A. van Gennep, *Manuel de folklore français contemporain* (7 vols.; Paris: Picard, 1943–58), volume 1.
> F. X. Weiser, *Handbook of Christian Feasts and Customs: The Year of the Lord in Liturgy and Folklore* (New York: Harcourt, Brace, 1952).
> J. P. Audet, "Le sacré et le profane: leur situation en christianisme," *Nouvelle revue théologique* 79 (1957) 33–61.
> D. Dubarle, "L'invention du sacré," *LMD* no. 123 (1975) 126–34.

As part of its biblical heritage, the Church has retained the prayer of blessing that can embrace all of creation and each of its parts but is now addressed to the Father through Christ, because everything was created through him and for him and has been reconciled by the blood of his cross (see Col 1:15-20). According to the *Apostolic Tradition*, "in everything we take, we are to give thanks to the holy God by taking it for his glory."[28]

---

28. *Traditio apostolica* 32 (Botte 78–79).

But in acting in this way the Church also takes into account a need felt in the religious depths of human beings; this need has always been a main constituent of popular religion, but it must constantly be "evangelized."

I. BLESSING UPON THE WHOLE OF LIFE

In ages when civilization was primarily rural, the Western Church threw a net of blessings over the whole life of human beings and over all their individual and collective activities. Christians were trained to trace the sign of the cross on themselves with holy water every morning and night, to bless the food at table and make the sign of the cross over the loaf of bread,[29] and to receive blessed bread each Sunday when they did not receive communion. But they also expected the Church to bless each stage of their lives, from before birth to beyond death: blessing of women during pregnancy and at their churching; blessing of children on fixed occasions and when they fell ill; blessings connected with betrothal and marriage or other states of life; blessing when setting out on a journey and returning from it; blessing of the dead and their graves.

Individuals and societies knew they were also dependent on the universe and the rhythms of the natural world. Consequently, the seasons and their labors had to have their rites of sanctification, propitiation, and thanksgiving, in which blessings and processions were geared to the feasts of the Lord and the saints. After having been waved in the procession on Palm Sunday the blessed palms were planted in graves and fields or tied to the crucifix in the home as a sign of life, exorcism, and protection. The three Rogation processions were understood as an extended act of blessing that embraced homes, fields, and meadows, vines and grain crops, human beings and animals.[30] Other blessings accompanied the popular celebrations connected with dates in the liturgical calendar, thus linking the life of the countryside with the cult of the saints: blessing of bread, wine, water, and fruits for St. Blaise on February 3; of crosses to be planted in the fields and among the vines on May 3 (Discovery of the Holy Cross); of fire on the feast of St. John the Baptist in the summer;[31] of grapes on the feast of St. Sixtus (August 6); of harvested grains on August 15 and seeds on September 8; and so on. Do we not find in the *Apostolic Tradi-*

---

29. On Christian customs at meals and their relation to the Eucharist see *LMD* no. 18 (1949): *Le repas, le pain et le vin.*

30. Local customs bring out this meaning more clearly: the procession must cover the entire area of the parish; the priest must give his blessing right and left and from the highest spot; he must bless especially the springs of water.

31. This joyous fire has not always and everywhere had a blessing.

tion, back in the third century, formulas for blessing oil, cheese, olives, and produce generally, and even flowers?[32]

There were blessings for the animals too, or at least for those that had become the working companions of human beings and a valued but always endangered possession. These blessings might be given in time of epizootic disease or on fixed occasions, namely, the feasts of saints who were regarded as patrons and protectors of livestock.[33] Nor was the environment of the animals forgotten.[34]

The setting in which human beings lived and the tools they used were also blessed: houses when first built and, on Holy Saturday, boats, fishing and hunting.[35]

II. BLESSING AS SUPPLICATION

In the difficult world of the medieval West, human beings were at the mercy of climatic disturbances, poor harvests, and epidemics; they knew their helplessness and relied on the providence of God. Given these conditions, it is quite understandable that in blessings the element of petition—and indeed petition chiefly for advantages of a temporal kind (protection, prosperity, fruitfulness)—immediately took precedence over the element of praise, to the point of becoming almost exclusive.

The result, however, was a dangerous imbalance. The idea of blessing was easily put on a pagan religious level, where magical thinking was in control. People believed that there existed higher powers from which came strength, well-being, and life, and others that produced evil and misfortune. Added to this was a sense of the presence of demons in the world and its elements, a presence that had to be exorcized by calling on the omnipotence of God. Consequently, as can be seen in the exorcisms that accompanied a number of blessings, as well as in use of holy water,[36] certain blessed objects, and the sign of the cross, there was so strong an em-

---

32. Above, pp. 263–69.

33. Or of a category of animals, each region having its specialized saints.

34. In fact, it even seems that provision was made for every detail: stables, animals generally, flocks, sick animals, their food (salt and oats), farmyard animals, bees and their hives, silkworms . . .: *Rituale Romanum* (ed. 1952), tit. IX, c. 5; c. 6, n. 20; c. 7, n. 9.

35. *Ibid.,* c. 6 and c. 8. The sanctification of space, like that of time, was carried as far as possible in monasteries where all rooms were regularly visited in order to bless them adequately: *Gell* 466–82.

36. Even the gestures that accompanied the blessing of baptismal water on Holy Saturday and were intended to emphasize the symbolism were not proof against a quasi-magical interpretation. The same may be said of blessings that were reduced to a simple sign of the cross; these were the privilege of cardinals and some priests.

phasis on driving out the spirit of evil as to suggest that creation had been radically corrupted or that Christ's victory over evil was not total.

III. THE OBJECTS BLESSED

The same mental and religious outlook led to a materialization of blessings. They were thought to contain a concrete, almost palpable element, which, as it were, filled the human beings or things that received the blessings and enabled them in turn to communicate this power to others.

In the Christian West this attitude assigned a privileged place to those who bless. In order to emphasize the greatness of the priesthood, blessings soon came to be reserved to bishops and priests; the *Apostolic Constitutions* are already a witness to this development.[37] Prayers and gestures of blessing that were performed by laypersons were regarded as peripheral acts of devotion, while the ever increasing number of reserved blessings intensified the impression that priests, bishops, and the pope were possessors of special powers rather than ministers of the kindness of God.

The idea that the value in a blessing is transferred to the object blessed gave rise at a very early date to the custom of "eulogies," which is already attested in the *Apostolic Tradition*.[38] Little loaves, cakes, fruits, sometimes wine, objects of devotion, and even relics were blessed quite specially and exchanged among bishops or monasteries as signs of the charity that bound them together.[39] This custom has continued down to our own time in the form of *Agnus Dei*s and the Golden Rose, which the pope blesses and sends to an important person or a church,[40] and even more in the form of the blessed bread that is substituted for the Eucharist in the case of catechumens and those of the faithful who do not receive communion.[41]

But this custom was much more widespread in the past: blessed objects (eulogies, relics and substitutes for them, blessed oil or water) were

---

37. *Constitutiones Apostolorum* VIII, 28 and 46 (Funk 1:530 and 560).

38. A "eulogy" was the piece of bread that the faithful received from the hand of the bishop at an agape: "It is a eulogy and not a eucharist, which is a symbol of the Lord's body": *Traditio apostolica* 26 (Botte 66–67); see 28 (Botte 72–73).

39. The canons of Laodicea (second half of the fourth century) decree that the Eucharist (*ta hagia*) is no longer to be sent as a eulogy in the Easter season (can. 14) and that the eulogies of heretics are no longer to be accepted since they are really "alogies" or curses (can. 32). Text in H. Bruns, *Canones apostolorum et conciliorum* 1 (Berlin: Reimer, 1839), 75–77.

40. On the blessing and conferral of the Golden Rose and *Agnus Dei*s see J. Catalani, *Sacrarum caeremoniarum sive rituum ecclesiasticorum sacrae Romanae ecclesiae libri tres* . . . 1 (Rome, 1790), 265–76, 281–90; 2 (Rome, 1791), 277–80; see also J. Kreps, "La rose d'or," *QL* 11 (1926) 71–104, 149–78.

41. See H. Leclercq, "Eulogie," *DACL* 5:733–34; J. Gaillard, "Eulogies," *Catholicisme* 4 (Paris: Letouzey, 1954) 685–86.

regarded, and used, as protections against sickness, the perils of travel, the danger of fire, or any other misfortune. These objects were considered to have special powers, which varied according to place and period: Candlemas candles as protection against lightning; hawthorn branches on Rogation days to protect livestock and cultivated fields; crosses made of ears of wheat to protect the harvest in the granaries. Nowadays the same attitude shows in the use of medals, rosaries, Lourdes water, and so on.[42] These practices and many others may be evidence of a spirit of true faith and trust in the providence of God, but they may also represent a superstitious quest of an effectiveness unconnected with faith.

IV. BLESSINGS IN A TECHNICIZED WORLD

Unless we return to their original meaning, blessings are likely to disappear from the Christian purview, along with the agrarian world and sacral universe in which they flourished.[43] The progress of science and technology even in rural life, the growing mechanization and urbanization, a better knowledge of the laws of nature, and an increased control of its energies have caused many blessings to become anachronisms or to lose a large part of their Christian meaning. The blessings that have been adapted to new needs seem artificial to many: the blessing of horses gave rise to picturesque processions, but how can the same happen with tractors?

Most significantly, Christians have become habituated to prayer of petition and no longer know how to bless God with praise and thanksgiving. It is indeed a good thing to ask God to bless the things we use so that they may serve our true good and his glory. It is still more important, however, to recognize, before we use things to our advantage, that all of them, even after they have been transformed by human genius, come ultimately from God and derive an unfailing goodness from him. This first meaning of blessing has found expression in the Roman Canon ever since the fourth century: "Through him [Christ], O Lord, you constantly create all these good things, you sanctify them, endow them with life, bless them, and give them to us." In the Missal of 1970 the prayer said at the preparation of the gifts conveys the same meaning: "Blessed are you, Lord, God of all creation. Through your goodness we have this bread to offer . . . ." When thus focused on praise and admiration rather than on petition, our blessings will once again be in the biblical tradition that Jesus followed in his own prayer.

---

42. Lourdes water belongs in the category of miraculous waters that need no special blessing to produce their effect; they are blessed by their nature.

43. The Church itself has worked to suppress certain usages as being tainted with superstition.

Chapter XI

Monastic Rites and Religious Profession

A. Nocent

§1. Monastic Profession in the West

BIBLIOGRAPHY

O. Casel, "Die Mönchsweihe bei St. Benedikt," *JLW* 5 (1925) 1–45.

P. de Puniet, *Le Pontifical Romain, histoire et commentaire* 2 (Paris: Desclée, 1931), 63–95. ET: *The Roman Pontifical: A History and Commentary*, trans. M. V. Harcourt (New York: Longmans, Green, 1932f.).

P. Oppenheim, "Mönchsweihe und Taufritus," in *Miscellanea liturgica in honorem L. Cuniberti Mohlberg* 1 (Rome: Edizioni liturgiche, 1948), 259–82.

H. Frank, "Untersuchungen zur Geschichte der benediktinischen Professliturgie im frühen Mittelalter," *Studien und Mitteilungen zur Geschichte der benediktiner Ordens und seiner Zweige* 63 (1951) 93–139.

M. Righetti, *Manuale di storia liturgica* 4 (Milan: Ancora, 1959²), 477–81.

A. de Vogüé, *La Règle du Maître. Text, traduction et notes* 2 (SC 106), 360–67, 370–79.

_____, *La Règle de saint Benoît. Commentaire historique et critique* 6 (SC 186), 951–61.

In the beginning, monasteries did not have rites of their own but followed the liturgical practice of the diocese in which they were located. They did, however, have some usages peculiar to them, which were set down in customaries (*Consuetudines*).[1]

Monastic life produced a ritual of profession, the essentials of which are described in the Rule of the Master and then in the Rule of St. Benedict.

---

1. The main published sources for a study of monastic profession are: *Ge* 1571; *Gell* 2581; *Gr* 1311; *PRG* 1:70–76; Andrieu, *PR* 1:174–76, 296–300; 2:413–14; 3:397–98; E. Martène, *De antiquis ecclesiae ritibus* and *De antiquis monachorum ritibus*, M 718–30, 1138–1200; *Corpus consuetudinum monasticarum*, directed by K. Hallinger (Siegburg: F. Schmitt, 1963ff.), vols. 1–10.

The Rule of the Master is very concerned about the poverty of the candidate, and we see in it a real care to draw up a list of his property, actual or potential, which he is to make the object of an act of donation. The candidate is to make a promise of stability in his own hand, adding to it an inventory of his property, and he is to offer himself to God in the oratory of the monastery. The document is to be countersigned by religious witnesses and by the bishop, a priest, a deacon, and other clerics of the territory. If the candidate has no present possessions he is to be received after an inquiry; he is to vouch for his perseverance by stipulating at the end of his written promise that any property coming to him later on will belong to the monastery. In view of profession the abbot is to inquire into the brother's dispositions. The next day, after Prime, the candidate asks the abbot to receive him and petitions the community to remain in the oratory and pray for him. The community engages in a fairly long period of prayer, which the abbot brings to an end in the name of all. The brother then asserts his intention of giving himself to God and the monastery. With his own hand he puts the list of his possessions on the altar, together with a formula expressing the total gift of himself. He then sings "Suscipe me, Domine. . . ." In reply the abbot sings: "Confirma hoc, Deus, quod operatus es in eo." All then give the kiss of peace to the newly professed. The abbot brings the ceremony to an end and takes from the altar the monk's list of possessions and document of self-donation.[2]

The Rule of St. Benedict, in its fifty-eighth chapter, also has a ritual for monastic profession. It follows the ritual in the Rule of the Master quite closely, but it also shows a certain independence and, more importantly, is on a more spiritual level.

If after a two months' stay in the monastery a postulant promises perseverence, he is to be shown the kind of life that awaits him: "Ecce lex, sub qua militare vis; si potes observare, ingredere; si vero non potes, liber discede."[3] Ten months later, in the oratory and in the presence of all, the novice promises stability, fidelity to monastic life, and obedience. He is to write out this promise in his own hand, sign it, and place it on the altar. After putting it there he sings the verse: "Suscipe me, Domine, secundum eloquium tuum et vivam" (Ps 118[119]:116). The community repeats it three times and ends with a *Gloria Patri*. The novice then prostrates himself at the feet of each of the brethren and asks them to pray for him.

---

2. *La Règle du Maître* 87, 25–75; 89, 1–35; ed. A. de Vogüé (SC 106), 360–67, 370–79.

3. See *RB 1980: The Rule of St. Benedict in Latin and English with Notes*, ed. T. Fry (Collegeville: The Liturgical Press, 1981), 267–69: "This is the law under which you are choosing to serve. If you can keep it, come in. If not, feel free to leave."

He is then stripped of all his own clothing and clad in garments belonging to the monastery.

Although St. Benedict states that the profession is to be made in the oratory, he does not mention a celebration of the Eucharist or specify any liturgical celebration during which the profession takes place. Nonetheless, by the end of the seventh century, tradition required that the abbot himself celebrate the Mass and recite the prayers over the newly professed. This seems to have been the practice in the Roman monasteries.[4] Depending on the place, profession was made at the beginning of Mass before the Introit,[5] between the epistle and the gospel,[6] or after the gospel or Creed;[7] this last was the most common practice and finally prevailed.[8]

The various rituals would take over and expand the elements provided especially by St. Benedict.

I. EXAMINATION OF THE MONK

The inquiry with which the ritual of profession began put the emphasis primarily on the freedom with which the candidate commits himself. This point is, of course, of the greatest importance. Thus the monks of Fulda wrote to Charlemagne, protesting that no one can be forced into monastic life.[9] Moreover, the Council of Aix-la-Chapelle in 817 judged that children who had been offered by their parents were not bound by the vows.[10] A number of twelfth-century rituals made provision for an examination.[11]

---

4. O. Casel, "Die Mönchsweihe bei St. Benedikt," *JLW* 5 (1925) 13. Theodore of Canterbury speaks of this obligation of the abbot as if it were already traditional: *Paenitentiale* 3, 3 (PL 99:928). Dom Casel shows how the early rituals heaped up formularies under the title of *Ordinatio monachi ex canone Theodori*, canons sometimes attributed to St. Gregory.

5. This was the practice at Farfa and Cluny, for example, according to B. Albers, *Consuetudines monasticae* 1 (Stuttgart: Roth, 1900), 130–40; *The Customary of the Eynsham*, ed. A. Grandsen in *Corpus consuetudinum monasticarum* 2:59, shows the practice of making profession either at the Introit or after the gospel; the *Decreta Lanfranci*, ed. D. Knowles, *ibid*, 3:88, offers the same options.

6. *Le Liber ordinum*, ed. M. Férotin (Monumenta Ecclesiae liturgica 5; Paris: Didot, 1904), col. 85.

7. Except for the *Consuetudines* that give the option of making profession either at the Introit or after the gospel or Creed, many put the rite after the gospel or Creed. One example among many others: *Consuetudines Beccenses*, ed. M. P. Dickson, in *Corpus consuetudinum monasticarum* 4:181.

8. It was adopted by the Benedictines, Cistercians, and Carthusians, and the present-day ritual of religious profession assigns it to this point.

9. B. Albers, *Consuetudines monasticae* 3 (Montecassino, 1912), 74.

10. *Synodi secundae Aquisgranesis Decreta authentica*, ed. J. Semmler, in *Corpus consuetudinum monasticarum* 1:473.

11. *The Customary of the Eynsham* (note 5, above), 2:27. — B. Albers, *Consuetudines monasticae* 3:134.

At Monte Cassino, however, the examination omitted this canonical aspect and took the form of a baptismal scrutiny.[12] Here the abbot reminded his hearers of how Christ had given an example of the practice of humility and penitence;[13] he then asked the one making profession about his resolve to renounce the world and seek conversion.[14] There was an evident tendency here to asssimilate the ritual of profession to the ritual of baptism, to which profession was willingly compared.[15] The Romano-German Pontifical says: ". . . quia secundus baptismus est, vel iuxta iudicium Patrum, et omnia peccata dimittuntur sicut in baptismo."[16] Examination in the form of a baptismal scrutiny was often adopted in later or modern rituals. The Roman Pontifical, however, followed its predecessors and did not include it.[17]

II. COMMITMENT OF THE MONK

The monk should logically have made his commitment immediately after the examination. This was what a twelfth-century ritual of Monte Cassino prescribed[18] and what was done at Cluny.[19] The Roman Pontificals of the twelfth and thirteenth centuries contained a litany and prayers[20] that were doubtless intended to follow upon the monk's oral promise, as was customary at Monte Cassino.[21] But the Roman Pontifical of 1596, followed by the rituals most commonly used in our own time, ordered these prayers said immediately after the examination and before the promise. The wordiness of the prayers[22] and the fact that one of them is ad-

12. Andrieu, *PR* 1:295–96.

13. "Dominus noster Iesus Christus . . . pietate sua ostendit nobis humilitatis et penitentiae modum . . ." (Andrieu, *PR* 1:295).

14. "Vox ergo, filii, qui relicto saeculo confugium fecistis ad Deum, ecce coram eo et coram hoc sacrosancto altari stantes ante praesentiam fratrum qui hic consistunt, proprio ore dicite si vultis abrenuntiare saeculo huic et pompis eius. Respondeant Volumus. . . . Vultis assumere conversionem morum vestrorum. . . . Volumus. Vultis profiteri oboedientiam. . . . Volumus" (Andrieu, *PR* 1:295–96).

15. The Eastern rituals would emphasize this parallelism; see below, p. 298.

16. *PRG* 1:72. See Casel, "Die Mönchsweihe . . .," 34.

17. Andrieu, *PR* 1:174; 2:413; 3:397–98.

18. *Ibid.*, 1:206.

19. B. Albers, *Consuetudines monasticae* 1:139.

20. Andrieu, *PR* 1:174; 2:413; 3:397. See also G. Hürlimann, *Das Rheinauer Rituale* (Spicilegium Friburgense 5; Fribourg, 1959), 144–46. In this twelfth-century ritual the reading of the profession is followed by a short *Kyrie* litany and prayers.

21. See note 18.

22. "Deus indulgentiae Pater . . ."; "Deus, qui per coaeternum Filium . . ."; "Domine Iesu Christe, qui es via . . ."; "Sancte Spiritus, qui te Deum. . . ."

dressed to the Son and another to the Holy Spirit betray a late and non-Roman origin.[23]

The act of profession was twofold: an oral commitment and a written commitment. The old written commitment, or *petitio*, is used nowadays to ask the community, some time in advance, for admission to vows. In most monasteries today, only the oral commitment is put in the written profession. The formulary for the written document took and still takes quite varied forms.[24] In about 790 Paul the Deacon cited the one he believed to have been in use "among the ancients."[25] The formula most widely used today contains, first, the vow of stability in a specific monastery, then the vow to seek conversion of life, and finally the vow of obedience.[26]

After signing the document, the monk places it on the altar; the gesture is a very meaningful sign of his determination to be incorporated into Christ's offering to his Father.

III. THE SINGING OF THE *SUSCIPE* AND THE PRAYERS

The monk's gesture of self-giving is underscored by the thrice-repeated singing of the verse: "Suscipe me, Domine, secundum eloquium tuum et vivam, et non confundas me ab expectatione mea," which is taken up by all the monks present around the newly professed, as they pray that their brother's offering may be acceptable. All conclude the singing with the *Gloria Patri*.

At the end of the seventh century, as we saw, it was already a tradition that the abbot should celebrate the Mass and recite the prayers over the professed.[27] These prayers are found in the old liturgical books but

---

23. These prayers are to be found in the Rheinau Ritual (note 20). In his *Monumenta veteris liturgiae Alemannicae* 2 (St. Blasien, 1779), 93–95, M. Gerbert published an *Ordo* from the eleventh-century Rheinau Pontifical, in which these prayers are also found. Perhaps they passed from there into the Roman Pontifical. See Andrieu, *PR* 1:174, note.

24. R. Molitor, "Von der Mönchsweihe in der lateinischen Kirche," *Theologie und Glaube* 16 (1924) 584–612, cites many examples of written formulas.

25. "Exemplar promissionis, sicut solebant antiqui monachi regulam promittere: In nomine Domini promitto me ego ille in sacro monasterio beati martyris sive confessoris illius secundum instituta beati Benedicti coram Deo et sanctis angelis eius praesente etiam abbate nostro illo, omnibus diebus meis in hoc sancto monasterio amodo et deinceps perseveraturum et in omni oboedientia quodcumque mihi praeceptum fuerit oboediturum. Ego ille talis hanc promissionem a me factam manu propria coram testibus scripsi et roboravi": in *Theodomari Epistola ad Karolum regem*, ed. J. Winandy and K. Hallinger, in *Corpus consuetudinum monasticarum* 1:174.

26. "Ego frater N . . . promitto sollemniter stabilitatem, conversationem morum meorum et oboedientiam secundum Regulam sancti Benedicti et Constitutiones a Sancta Sede approbatas in hoc venerabili monasterio."

27. *Ge* 1574 (p. 229): *Oratio pro renuntiantibus saeculo*, is perhaps representative of the original form. — See O. Casel (note 4) 33–36, 41.

vary in number. The modern rituals have reduced them to two: the first, "Clementissime dominator, Domine," asks that the monk may have the virtues and qualities required by his profession; the second, "Omnipotens et misericors Deus, totius sanctae religionis origo," which is sometimes in the form of a preface, contains many allusions to the Rule and asks divine help for this person who is undertaking a difficult kind of life.

IV. CLOTHING OF THE MONK

In the ritual set down by St. Benedict in chapter fifty-eight of his Rule, the clothing brings the celebration to an end, being the sign of a definitive self-giving and incorporation into a new world. Later rituals have introduced a blessing of the garments; this was unknown to St. Benedict but is already mentioned in the *Ordinatio monachi ex canone Theodori*[28] as well as in the Romano-German Pontifical and the Roman Pontificals of the twelfth and thirteenth centuries.[29] The paschal and Pauline theme of "putting on Christ" is part of this blessing, at least from the twelfth century on: ". . . ut hic famulus tuus, qui hoc usus fuerit, te induere mereatur."[30]

V. OTHER RITES

At the present time, it is after the clothing, and not before (as in St. Benedict's intention), that the monk prostrates himself at the feet of each of his brethren and asks them to pray for him. At this point there was introduced, at a very early date, the kiss of peace that the newly professed receives from his brothers after asking for their prayers; the Rule of the Master had already prescribed this greeting.[31] First, however, the abbot expresses the meaning of this fraternal kiss in a very short address, the wording of which is already determined and which Durandus of Mende boldly attributed to St. Augustine.[32] The same Pontifical of William Durandus has this ceremony accompanied by the singing of the antiphon: "Confirma hoc, Deus, quod operatus es in nobis." According to other rituals, the monks are also to sing the psalms that begin "Magnus Dominus et

---

28. Casel 34.

29. *PRG* 1:70–71; Andrieu, *PR* 1:175; 2:414; 3:397. The same is true of the twelfth-century ritual of Monte Cassino: Andrieu, *PR* 1:296.

30. For example, Andrieu, *PR* 1:175.

31. *Regula Magistri*, ed. A. de Vogue 2 (SC 106) 376.

32. Andrieu, *PR* 3:399.

laudabilis nimis" and "Ecce quam bonum et quam iucundum habitare fratres in unum."[33]

Various extras, usually from a late period, that were inspired by a questionable allegorism, came in time to weigh down the original ritual; one such addition was the prostration of the newly professed, sometimes even covered with a pall, during the remainder of the Mass until communion.[34] A felicitous effort to return to the simplicity of the sources seems to have successfully eliminated these symbolisms, which were often in bad taste, from the modern rituals.

Today most monasteries follow the very sober ritual whose main lines I have been describing. However, when temporary vows were introduced by the Code of 1917, each monastic Congregation also composed as simple a rite as possible for this profession; everything is removed from it that might suggest a definitive profession. The celebration takes place after the gospel or Creed. After a short examination the man who is about to profess his temporary vows reads his formula of profession and signs it; often he does not place it on the altar. Then everyone joins in singing the "Suscipe" once, and, as need requires, the professed dons the insignia of the rank he now occupies.

§2. Religious Profession in the West

BIBLIOGRAPHY

Ordo professionis religiosae, editio typica (Vatican Polyglot Press, 1970). ET: *Rite of Religious Profession*, trans. International Committee on English in the Liturgy (Washington, D.C.: United States Catholic Conference, 1971). New translation of the Introduction in *DOL* 392 nos. 3230–48.

A. Duval, "Quelques données et réflexions historiques sur l'engagement religieux," in *Engagement et fidélité* (Paris: Cerf, 1970), 69–115.

P. Raffin, "Liturgie de l'engagement religieux: le nouveau rituel de la Profession religieuse," *LMD* no. 104 (1970) 151–66.

M. Auge, "I riti della professione religiosa," *Rivista Liturgica* 60 (1973) 326–44.

E. von Severus, "Der neue *Ordo professionis religiosae*," *Heiliger Dienst* 27, no. 3 (1973) 121–26.

A. Mayer, "De formula professionis religiosae," *Notitiae* 9 (1973) 283.

Until the appearance of the *Ordo professionis religiosae*, the various religious orders and congregations all used rituals of their own that were more or less original and connected with their manner of life. The *Ordo*

---

33. Ps 48 and 133.

34. R. Molitor, "Symbolische Grablegung bei dem Ordenprofess," *Benediktinische Monatschrift* 6 (1924) 54–57.

professionis religiosae, which was promulgated on February 7, 1970,[35] does not intend simply to do away with these rituals. It is presented rather as a normative blueprint that is to be respected but that also allows for many adaptations. When Vatican II called for the preparation of such a ritual,[36] its intention was not at all to do away with local rituals; it was aware, however, that some of the latter contained prayers or rites hardly compatible with authentic liturgy. Thus, for example, the new ritual is quite strict with regard to profession at the moment of communion: it forbids it without qualification for rituals to be composed in the future and urges institutes that already follow this practice to discontinue it, since it is out of harmony with a true understanding of the liturgy.[37]

In Part IV of its Introduction the *Ordo* takes up the question of adapting the ritual to the various institutes. In such adaptations, a distinction must always be made between temporary vows and perpetual vows. Unless a different practice is permitted by a particular law (and if it is, the institute should be urged to change it, as I noted above), profession is to be made during Mass and after the gospel or Creed.[38] Any adaptation must respect the following points: the rite is to take place after the gospel; the arrangement of the parts of the ritual must be kept unchanged, although one or other may be omitted or replaced by a similar one; a distinction must be kept between perpetual profession and temporary profession or renewal of vows; in some cases, the formula of profession must be changed.[39] The Congregation of Religious has set down very clear rules with regard to the formula of profession: it is not to be left to the initiative of the individual professed; it must be substantially identical throughout each institute; every formula of profession must express the vows of poverty, chastity, and obedience according to the Rule and Constitutions, mention the name or office of the person receiving the profession in the name of the Church, and, finally, state the date of the profession.[40]

I. STRUCTURE OF THE RITE

Before giving the rituals of temporary and perpetual profession, the *Ordo* gives the ritual for entrance into the novitiate, which I shall not dis-

35. *Ordo professionis religiosae*, editio typica (Vatican Polyglot Press, 1970); ET: *Rite of Religious Profession*, trans. International Committee on English in the Liturgy (Washington, D.C.: United States Catholic Conference, 1971).

36. *VSC* 80 (*DOL* 1 no. 80).

37. *Ordo professionis religiosae*, Introduction 15 (*DOL* 392 no. 3244).

38. *Ibid.*, 14 (*DOL* 392 no. 3243).

39. *Ibid.*

40. SCR, *Reply* of February 14, 1973, in *Notitiae* 9 (1973) 283 (*DOL* 393 nos. 3249–51).

cuss here. It goes on then to the rituals of temporary and perpetual profession. I shall study the latter as being the most complete.

It will be clear that this ritual has been extensively influenced by the ritual of monastic profession. The rite always takes place during Mass and after the gospel or Creed. In an appendix the *Ordo* gives three Mass formularies that are suitable for temporary profession, perpetual profession, or the renewal of vows. These Masses are also included among the ritual Masses in the Roman Missal.

The rite is simple in its structure: calling of the candidate—homily—examination of the candidate by the celebrant or the superior—petition in the form of a litany that replaces the General Intercessions. The central part of the rite is the profession, for which the *Ordo* gives a model formula in an appendix. It suggests that the typically monastic *Suscipe* be sung after the profession.

In the new *Ordo* these various parts are followed by a blessing or consecration of the professed. This is something entirely new, and the formulas have been composed expressly for the purpose; the *Ordo* offers a selection. This consecration has raised some problems, and questions have inevitably been asked about its value by comparison with the consecration of virgins.[41] I shall note here only that this "consecration" is given to religious men as well as to religious women. Just as the nuptial blessing, which in the past looked only to the wife, nowadays looks to the husband as well, so also this religious consecration is given to men as well as to women. It is not, however, given to men who live in the world and are not religious. It is to be noted that this blessing or consecration can be given only after the profession of perpetual vows.

Depending on the tradition observed in the various religious institutes, the blessing is followed by the giving of the symbols of profession; they express the person's complete self-giving to God. For religious women the symbol is to be a ring, which expresses her irrevocable betrothal to Christ. It is noted that nothing is said of clothing, which played such an important part in the rituals of the Middle Ages; in the course of time the habit came to be given at entrance into religious life, in a ceremony known precisely as "clothing." In the present *Ordo*, however, the habit is given at the first temporary profession.[42] In the various institutes some article of clothing is usually reserved to be given at perpetual profession.

The rite ends with a few words from the celebrant or the superior or with a greeting of the newly professed person by the community.

---

41. See the explanatory note by the Relator of the study group that prepared both rites, in *Notitiae* 7 (1971) 107–10 (*DOL* 395 no. 3262, footnote R2).

42. *Ordo professionis religiosae* p. 20, no. 31; p. 59, no. 17. *Rite of Religious Profession*, p. 12, no. 31; p. 37, no. 17.

II. THEOLOGY OF THE RITUAL

In the new *Ordo* a very rich lectionary has greatly expanded the didactic aspect of the rite: it offers eight readings from the Old Testament,[43] sixteen from the New,[44] and fifteen from the gospel.[45] In addition, the prayers of the ritual seek to show religious life as a following after Christ. The prayer often takes the form of a "blessing" and follows the outline of the Christ-centered history of salvation that is still going on and in which religious life has its place as a following of Christ in his salvific activities. The history of salvation had already provided models of religious life in the Old Testament: the new *Ordo* refers to them and especially to Abel,[46] Abraham, Samuel, Elijah, and Elisha.[47] The Blessed Virgin is a model of perfect obedience in following Christ through a complete sharing of his passion.[48] The choice of the gospel of the Annunciation is doubtless to be explained by this motif of Mary's perfect obedience to the divine plan for her.[49]

Especially to be noted is the synthesis given in the prayer of consecration, "Deus omnis sanctitatis fons et origo." The holiness of God has manifested itself despite the sin of Adam; it made itself limpidly clear in Abel and in the other holy persons God has raised up, and most clearly in the Virgin Mary. Christ has rebuilt the world through his paschal mystery, and the action of the Spirit draws human beings to a more demanding following of Christ. Religious life thus has its point of departure in the Old Testament, while its model is Christ; it is thus fully incorporated into the history of the world's salvation and into Christ's body, the Church, for which it is as it were a channel of vital breath.[50]

Because it thus plays a part in the history of salvation, religious life cannot be looked upon as a kind of private specialization that is organized under a Rule. It is essentially bound up with the Church; Vatican II strongly emphasized this link between religious life and the Church.[51] The bond exists because religious life works to increase the holiness of the Church.[52]

---

43. *Ordo*, p. 40, nos. 91–94; p. 83, nos. 98–105. *Rite*, p. 26, nos. 91–94; p. 55, nos. 98–105.

44. *Ordo*, pp. 40–41, nos. 95–109; pp. 83–84, nos. 106–21. *Rite*, p. 26, nos. 95–109; pp. 55–56, nos. 106–21.

45. *Ordo*, pp. 42–43, nos. 125–36; pp. 86–87, nos. 138–52. *Rite*, p. 28, nos. 125–36; pp. 57–58, nos. 138–52.

46. *Ordo*, p. 30, no. 67. *Rite*, p. 20, no. 67.

47. *Ordo*, p. 40, nos. 91–94. *Rite*, p. 26, nos. 91–94.

48. *Ordo*, p. 25, no. 57; p. 31, no. 67; p. 68, no. 62; p. 74, no. 72. *Rite*, pp. 16–17, no. 57; pp. 20–21, no. 67; pp. 44–45, no. 62; pp. 48–49, no. 72.

49. Luke 1:26-38; *Ordo professionis religiosae*, p. 86, no. 145. *Rite*, p. 57, no. 145.

50. "Ecclesiae sanctitatem augeant": first Mass for perpetual profession, *Ordo*, p. 114. ET: "Let them . . . increase the holiness . . . of your Church": *Rite*, p. 75.

51. Dogmatic Constitution *Lumen gentium* 44.

52. Above, note 50.

That is why it requires its members to grow constantly in fervent love and more perfect worship.[53] The life of consecration "builds up" the Church;[54] it is a logical step in the life of those who have been baptized and confirmed: "Beloved sons (daughters), in baptism you have already died to sin and been consecrated to the Lord; are you resolved to deepen this consecration through perpetual profession?"[55]

§3. Monastic Profession in the East

BIBLIOGRAPHY

J. M. Besse, *Les moines d'Orient antérieurs au Concile de Chalcédoine* (Paris, 1900), chapter VI: "Les engagements monastiques" (131–46).

B. Evetts, "Le rite copte de la prise d'habit et de la profession monastique," *Revue de l'Orient chrétien* 10 (1906) 10–73, 130–48.

J. Villecourt, "Le rite copte de la profession monacale pour les religieuses," *Bessarione* 26 (1909) 35–49, 301–47.

P. de Meester, *Liturgia bizantina. Studi di rito bizantino . . .*, Libro II, Parte 6: *Rituale-Benedizionale bizantino* (Rome: Tipografia Leoniana, 1930), 7–72.

_____, "Le rasophorat dans le monachisme byzantin: Ses origines, ses développements, sa signification," in *Sbornik. Receuil dédié à la memoire du Professeur P. Nikov* (Sofia, 1940), 323–32.

_____, *De monachico statu iuxta disciplinam byzantinorum* (Codificazione canonica orientale, Fonti II, 10; Vatican Polyglot Press, 1942), 83–93.

A. Vielleux, *La liturgie dans le cénobitisme pachomien au IVe siècle* (Studia Anselmiana 57; Rome: Herder, 1968).

M. Wawryk, *Initiatio monastica in liturgia byzantina: Officiorum schematis magni et parvi necnon rasophoratus exordia et evolutio* (OCA 180; Rome, 1968).

P. Raffin, *Les rituels orientaux de la profession monastique* (Spiritualité orientale 4; Bellefontaine, 1974).

The Eastern liturgy shows great variety in its various rituals for religious profession, and there can be no question of studying all of them here. They do, however, have a common structure, and this fact makes it possible to get a fairly accurate idea of the Eastern ritual and its theological content.

I. THE TIME AND PLACE OF PROFESSION

Profession is not always made during the celebration of the Eucharist, but it is always connected with the altar. Pseudo-Dionysius shows that in his time and his Church, profession was made during the Eucharistic

---

53. Dogmatic Constitution *Lumen gentium* 44.
54. *Ordo* p. 31, no. 67; p. 35, no. 76. *Rite*, pp. 20–21, no. 67; p. 23, no. 76.
55. *Ordo*, p. 25, no. 57; p. 68, no. 62. *Rite*, pp. 16–17, no. 57; pp. 44–45, no. 62.

celebration. Unfortunately it is hardly possible to locate these practices in a concrete time and place; there are difficulties in saying anything more than "in the fifth and sixth centuries." In his writings we find a brief but adequate description of the rites. The priest stands at the altar and recites invocations over the monk, who stands behind him. After consecrating him, the priest asks him whether he is resolved to live the monastic life. The new monk ratifies his commitments, and the priest makes the sign of the cross over him and then cuts his hair while calling upon the Blessed Trinity; he takes his old garment from him and puts a new one on him; he, and all those present, give him the kiss of peace; finally the priest gives the new monk the Eucharist.[56] In the writings of Pseudo-Dionysius on baptism there are analogies, in terminology and ritual, with monastic life, but we do not know where this life was being lived or under what Rule.[57] It is to be observed that a priest and not the bishop received the profession and consecrated the monk.

The *Ordinatio monachi ex canone Theodori* shows that in the Greek liturgy profession was incorporated into the Eucharist at a very early date.[58] The Armenian[59] and Eastern Syrian[60] rituals show the same practice. Codex Barberini 336 makes it clear that profession is always connected with the altar.[61] At the present time, profession is made in front of the holy doors in the Armenian and Greek rites,[62] but in the Syrian rite of Antioch the tonsure and clothing take place in the nave of the church, in the area where the monks celebrate the Divine Office.

The priest's role is to consecrate the monk; the superior of the monastery also has a part to play, but it is difficult to specify what it is.

II. THE STRUCTURE OF THE RITES

The Eastern rituals show two different ways of viewing and carrying out monastic profession. Despite the opposition of Theodore of Studios

56. Pseudo-Dionysius, *Hierarchia ecclesiastica* (PG 3:533); see R. Roques, "Eléments pour une théologie de l'état monastique selon Denys l'Aréopagite," in *Théologie de la vie monastique. Etudes sur la tradition patristique* (Théologie 49; Paris: Aubier, 1961), 285–96.

57. L. Bouyer, *The Spirituality of the New Testament and the Fathers*, trans. M. P. Ryan (History of Christian Spirituality 1; New York: Seabury, 1963), Chapter XVI: "Pseudo-Dionysius and the Mysticism of the Fathers" (395–421).

58. Above, note 4.

59. The two rituals for monastic profession were published by F. C. Conybeare, *Rituale Armenorum* (Oxford: Clarendon, 1905).

60. I. M. Vosté, *Pontificale iuxta ritum Ecclesiae Syrorum orientalium, id est Chaldaeorum*, Pars IV (Vatican Polyglot Press, 1938), 308–87.

61. This codex was probably written around 800. For the text see J. Goar, *Euchologium sive Rituale Graecorum* (Venica: Javarina, 1730; reprinted: Graz, 1960), 382–411; see 390.

62. F. C. Conybeare (note 59), 136–44.

to a double ritual (since he regarded the self-giving of monks as in every case the same[63]), the distinction prevailed, and we find among the Byzantines two offices (*akolouthia*): one for the "little habit" that makes the candidate a *mikroschēmos* or *staurophoros* (the monk is consecrated with the rite of the little habit and receives a cross which he is to wear on his breast); the other for the "great habit" that makes the candidate a *megaloschēmos* or "perfect monk" (*teleios monachos*). The monk may, however, remain permanently in the first of these two states, since profession in the East is always definitive. The giving of the monastic habit and profession are one and the same act that includes clothing and tonsure.

Before being admitted to profession the candidate must spend three years in probation and receive the garb of a novice. There is an intermediate state between novitiate and profession; it is called the "rasophorate" because the monk wears a black *rason* (a kind of roomy cloak), which is more voluminous than that of novices, and a *kamilavchion* (a cylindrical black hat with a little brim at the top). The person may remain in this state throughout his life.

a) *Preparatory rites*. — In the Byzantine Rite both offices—those of the little and the great habit—were originally celebrated in the narthex; they now take place before the holy doors at the beginning of Mass; in the case of the *megaloschēmos* the Divine Office, beginning with Vespers, serves as preparation for the profession. In the other rites there is a real office comprising prayers, readings, and songs. The Armenian Rite has two ways of celebrating this preparatory part: in the first, the hygoumen examines the candidate; in the second the candidate removes his garments and receives tonsure before entering the church. As a result these rituals resemble those of the catechumenate and emphasize the penitential aspect of monastic profession.

b) *Readings*. — In the Byzantine Rite the readings are those of the Mass, but in the other rites the readings associated with profession are done at a different time. In the second canon of the Armenian Ritual (that is, the second way of celebrating a profession) we find an original and thought-provoking selection: three groups of readings are given: (1) *Isa 35:3-8*: The Messiah comes to restore the universe; profession is thus seen in its cosmological aspect and linked to redemption; *Eph 6:10-18*: Monastic life is a struggle and a spiritual battle; *Matt 5:1-6*: The beatitudes. — (2) *Isa 56:1-5*: The Lord welcomes proselytes; *1 Pet 5:6-11*: Be sober and keep watch; *John 16:33—17:8*: The priestly prayer of Jesus for unity. — (3) *Lam 3:22-45*: The solitary sits in silence; *1 Pet 2:1-10*: The new priesthood; *2 Tim 1:6-14*: Stir up the gift received through the laying on of

---

63. Theodore of Studios, *Testamentum* (PG 99:1820); *Epist. Lib.* 1 (PG 99:941).

hands; *Luke 10:17-24*: The seventy-two disciples are sent on a mission. This little sample is enough to show how stimulating these lectionaries are.[64]

c) *Consecration of the monk*. — The two main actions are clothing and tonsure; the prayers accompanying these rites differ from ritual to ritual, but all the rituals have them. The examination of the monk with regard to his renunciation and promises is indeed not secondary, but on the other hand it is not an essential part of the consecration, as it is in the West. Furthermore, the formula of profession and the examination regarding stability, chastity, obedience, and poverty are points introduced at a later time into the Byzantine Rite.

d) *Rite of tonsure*. — The shears and monastic garb are often placed first at the foot of the altar; in the Byzantine Rite the acts of tonsure and clothing themselves signify monastic consecration. The prayers and rites of tonsure differ from ritual to ritual.

e) *Clothing*. — The rite of clothing is the sign of definitive self-giving and entrance into a new world. The habit is sometimes blessed, and its various components are usually donned in successive actions accompanied by suitable prayers that bring out their symbolism: tunic, cincture, headdress, cloak, a kind of scapular or blouse (for the *mikroschēmos* or *megaloschēmos* respectively), and sandals.

f) *Secondary rites*. — These are of some interest because their symbolism is at times baptismal. The two Syrian rites and the Byzantine Rite include a signing, which Pseudo-Dionysius connects with baptism. The giving of a cross is also practiced among the Byzantines, Syrians, and Copts. In the Byzantine Rite the newly professed also receives a candle; this again is reminiscent of the baptismal rite. Among the Copts both monks and nuns are anointed on the forehead with holy oil as a sign of purification and incorruptibility.

g) *Rites of introduction into the community and religious life*. — All the rituals except the Coptic include the kiss of peace to be given by all the brethren to the newly professed. In the Byzantine Rite, the new monk is brought to the refectory to the singing of a troparion that recalls the return of the Prodigal Son and the banquet celebrated for him. In the East Syrian Rite the newly professed prostrates himself at the feet of each of his brethren and asks for their prayers; in the West Syrian Rite the feet

---

64. See the references given in P. Raffin, *Les rituels orientaux de la profession monastique* (Spiritualité orientale 4; Bellefontaine, 1974), 145–50.

of the newly professed are washed by the superior and the priests and deacons.

h) *Closing rite.* — The Byzantine and Armenian rites have a concluding action like the one we saw earlier in some Western monastic rituals: the newly professed remains in the church for eight days; after the eighth day the superior takes the man's cowl from his head and loosens his cincture.

III. THE RITUAL FOR NUNS

Among the Byzantines the ritual of the rasophorate for nuns, which seems to have been in use back in the fifteenth century,[65] is the same as for monks, the troparies alone being adapted.

A fifteen-century euchologion contains an adaptation of the office of the "little habit" for nuns. The more recent euchologion likewise has an adaptation.[66] As far as the office of the "great habit" is concerned, the euchologion in Barberini 336 anticipates that it will be transposed for the use of nuns, but it adds six prayers in this case.[67]

The Armenian Rite has a *Canon faciendi monachum iuxta tonsuram Aegyptorum et Sancti Montis Palestinae, virorum ac mulierum qui assumunt virginitatem in Christo.*[68]

The West Syrians likewise use the same rites (with the necessary adaptations) for nuns as for monks.[69] Here, however, special readings are provided for nuns.[70] The same is true of the East Syrians[71] and the Copts; among the latter there is a rite for the bestowal of the headdress on the nun;[72] once again, it has special readings.

---

65. M. Wawryk, *Initiatio monastica in liturgia byzantina. Officiorum schematis magni et parvi necnon rasophoratus exordia et evolutio* (OCA 180; Rome, 1968), 260–61.

66. *Ibid.,* 257–59.

67. *Ibid.,* 251–56.

68. F. C. Conybeare (note 59), 136–55.

69. O. Heiming, "Der *Ordo* des heiligen Mönchsschema in der syrischen Kirche," in *Vom christlichen Mysterium. Gesammelte Arbeiten zum Gedächtnis von Odo Casel* (Düsseldorf: Patmos, 1951), 152–72. — idem, "Der nationalsyrische *Ritus tonsurae* im Syrerkloster der ägyptischen Skete," in *Miscellanea Giovanni Galbiati* 3 (Fontes Ambrosiani 27; Milan, 1951), 123–74.

70. See the list in P. Raffin (note 64), 149.

71. I. M. Vosté, *Pontificale iuxta ritum Ecclesiae Syrorum Occidentalium, id est Antiochiae,* Pars 3 (Vatican Polyglot Press, 1942). The list of readings is given in P. Raffin (note 64), 150.

72. O. H. E. Burmester, "Rites and Ceremonies of the Coptic Church," *Eastern Churches Quarterly* 10 (1954) 217–29; L. Villecourt, "Le rite copte de la prise d'habit et de la profession monacale pour les religieuses," *Bessarione* 26 (1909) 35–49, 309–47.

IV. THEOLOGICAL CONTENT OF THE EASTERN RITE
OF MONASTIC PROFESSION

A comparison of the Armenian Ritual with the *Mystagogical Catecheses* of Cyril of Jerusalem shows quite clearly that a deliberate parallel is being drawn between monastic profession and baptism.[73] The ritual as such unfolds in a single continuous action, and we find in it rather an advance toward a summit than any specific moment that would be the center of the whole: the rite in its entirety is a consecration. The fact that monastic life is paralleled with baptism in this way serves to locate it within the life of the gospel and the ongoing history of salvation: the monk and nun are renewed persons who, like renewed creation, make it clear today that the history of the world's restoration is still going on.

§4. The Blessing of an Abbot in the Latin Liturgy

BIBLIOGRAPHY

J. Baudot, "Bénédiction d'un abbé et d'une abbesse," *DACL* 2 (1910) 723–27.
P. de Puniet, *Le Pontifical Romain, histoire et commentaire* 2 (Paris: Desclée de Brouwer, 1931), 113–42. ET: *The Roman Pontifical: A History and Commentary,* trans. M. V. Harcourt (New York: Longmans, Green, 1932ff.).
P. Salmon, *Etude sur les insignes du pontife dans le rit romain* (Rome: Officium libri catholici, 1955).
G. Roggi, *La benedizione degli abati nella Chiesa romana* (Vallombrosa, 1958).
M. Righetti, *Manuale di storia liturgica* 4 (Milan: Ancora, 1959²), 481–84.
R. Somerville, "*Ordinatio abbatis* in the Rule of St. Benedict," *RBén* 77 (1967) 246–63.
A. Vielleux, "La théologie de l'abbatiat cénobitque et ses implications liturgiques," *Vie Spirituelle: Supplément* no. 86 (September, 1968) 351–93.
Ordo benedictionis abbatis et abbatissae, typical edition (Vatican Polyglot Press, 1971). ET: *Rite of Blessing of an Abbot and an Abbess* in *The Rites of the Catholic Church* 2 (New York: Pueblo, 1980), 115–24 and 125–31. New translation of the Introductions in *DOL* 399 nos. 3277–91.
U. Bomm, "Der neue Ritus des Abts- und Äbtissenenweihe," *Heiliger Dienst* 27 (1973) 148–52.
A. Nocent, "L'ordo benedictionis abbatis et abbatissae," *Rivista Liturgica* 60 (1973) 321–25.

I. THE EARLY RITUAL

If we judge by the oldest documents, the early rite for the blessing of an abbot was very brief. But the Rule of the Master already gives a fairly

---

73. See P. Raffin 161–66.

detailed description of the ritual it prescribes. The bishop of the place is the one who gives the blessing. He himself writes in the diptychs the name of the abbot-elect, which will be read out during Mass. Only after that, and outside of the oratory, does the celebration begin. It takes place in the presence of the bishop and his curia and of the community. The ceremony in this case is the blessing of an abbot who succeeds a former abbot. The latter gives the Rule to his successor, along with the key to the larder, an inventory of the property of the monastery, and so on. A lengthy formula accompanies the transmission of the Rule. The outgoing abbot then leads the abbot-elect into the oratory and has him take the abbot's place. He now gives his successor his cloak as well. The bishop then pronounces a prayer of blessing over the abbot-elect (the text is not preserved for us); the new abbot then places the Rule on the altar. At this point the community prays for its new abbot. The latter then prostrates himself along with the entire community and the bishop says a second prayer; the abbot then kisses the knees of the bishop, who lifts him up and gives him the kiss of peace. The new abbot in turn gives the kiss of peace to the members of the episcopal curia and then to his own community.[74]

St. Benedict did not put any of these regulations into his own Rule, but he does emphasize in his second chapter the important part played by the abbot: ". . . sciat quam difficilem et arduam rem suscepit, regere animas . . ." ("He must know what a difficult and demanding burden he has undertaken: directing souls . . .").

The first official formulary made its appearance in the Gregorian Sacramentary. It consists of a single prayer: "Concede, quaesumus, omnipotens Deus, et famulum tuum ill. vel illam, quem ad regimen animarum eligimus, gratiae tuae dono prosequere, ut te largiente, cum ipsa tibi nostra electione placeamus."[75]

In the eighth century and in Frankish territory the rite tended to vary and become more complex. The Sacramentary of Gellone has the Gregorian prayer just cited, but it adds three others under the title *Oratio quando abbas vel abbatissa ordinatur in monasterio*.[76] We may therefore legitimately suppose that the rite was somewhat different when the blessing was conferred in, for example, a cathedral. The first of these three

---

74. *Regula Magistri* 93, 1–78, ed. A. de Vogue, *La Règle du Maître* 2 (SC 106) 424–41, especially 424–31.

75. *Gr* 996 (p. 342): "Almighty God, be pleased to bestow the gift of your grace on your servant whom you have called to direct souls, so that through your generosity our choice of him may be pleasing to you." See also a Mass *Pro abbate et congregatione* in *Gr* 1308–10 (pp. 435–36). — *Ge* has only a Mass *Pro sacredote sive abbate (defuncto)* (nos 1638–42).

76. *Gell* 2576 (p. 399): *Oratio ad abbatem faciendum:* "Concede, quaesumus, omnipotens Deus, et famulum tuum. . . ." — *Gell* 2577–79: *Oratio quando. . . .*

prayers, "Cunctorum bonorum institutor," is very restrained: it is a prayer for the person who has accepted the responsibility of directing monks or nuns. The second, *Item alia benedictio*: "Omnipotens sempiterne Deus, affluentem illum spiritum," contains a clause that was to have considerable influence on later liturgical books, and this right down to the new ritual of Vatican II: "ut qui per nostrae manus impositionem hodie abbas constituitur." The gesture involved indeed only one hand and not both: "nostrae *manus* impositionem," but it was nonetheless to some extent ambiguous and might suggest a sacramental consecration. The third prayer, *Item alia benedictio*: "Domine Deus omnipotens, qui sororem Moysen Mariam . . .," is for an abbess.

II. EXPANSION OF THE RITUAL IN THE ROMAN-GERMAN PONTIFICAL OF THE TENTH CENTURY

This Pontifical shows a determination to give the blessing of an abbot or abbess the outward form of a sacrament and to make its celebration an imitation of episcopal consecration. It anticipates two possible cases: an *ordinatio* and a *consecratio*.

An *ordinatio*[77] is given to an abbot who is dependent on the authority of the bishop; it is celebrated in the cathedral church. Consequently, it cannot be given to an abbess. After the collect of the Mass, the bishop tells the faithful that an abbot is to be blessed, and he performs the ceremony before the gospel. In imitation of the "handing over" of the Book of the Gospels at the consecration of a bishop, the Romano-German Pontifical introduces a "handing over" of the Rule to the abbot, together with the mission of seeing to its observance. Then comes the *traditio baculi*, a non-Roman usage that iconography shows to have existed in ninth-century Gaul.[78]

A *consecratio*,[79] on the other hand, is given in the monastery church and is bestowed on abbesses as well as abbots. It includes the prayer "Cunctorum bonorum operum" and the prayer "Omnipotens sempiterne Deus, affluentem spiritum," which refers to an imposition of the hand and is here sung in the manner of a preface. This is followed by another (*alia*), very short prayer, a third *Pro adepta dignitate*: "Omnium Deus fons bonorum iustorumque," and a final one, *Item alia*: "Deus cui omnis potestas et dignitas famulatur." The *Te Deum* is sung and the people use the accla-

---

77. *PRG* 1:62–67.

78. The Sacramentary of Marmoutiers (Autun, Bibl. Municip., ms. 9) speaks of the abbot as carrying a pastoral staff and giving the blessing.

79. *PRG* 1:67–69.

mation "Kyrie eleison." The blessing ends with the prayer, 'Deus aeternae lucis inventor." The Mass then continues.

The Pontifical adds a further prayer for the blessing of an abbess: "Domine Deus omnipotens, qui sororem Moysi," which is from the Gellone Sacramentary.[80] It also gives a Mass for an abbot; this includes episcopal blessings before communion.[81]

III. FROM THE TWELFTH CENTURY TO VATICAN II

The twelfth-century Pontifical of the Roman Curia clearly represents a return to ancient simplicity;[82] on the other hand, it still has the prayer "Omnipotens sempiterne Deus, affluentem spiritum," with its accompanying imposition of the bishop's hand. And yet in this same twelfth century, Yves of Chartres was reminding others of the simplicity that ought to mark the blessing of an abbot: ". . . in qua nec fit manus impositio, nec consecratio, sed simpliciter benedictio."[83]

The thirteenth-century Pontifical of the Roman Curia continues the complications of the past.[84] William Durandus, working in around 1294, made further additions,[85] and most of the expansions he introduced were to be part of the Roman Pontifical down to the new ritual of Vatican II.

Before the blessing Durandus provides for a—very formal—kind of examination conducted by the bishop, who wants assurance that the election has been properly carried out. Subsequent pontificals show the bishop being given the *Mandatum apostolicum* that authorizes him to bless the abbot; he then requires the new abbot to take an oath of submission to the Holy See. These new elements of the rite evidently reflect a concrete situation of the period.

A series of questions imitates the examination that precedes the consecration of a bishop.

After the singing of the Alleluia or Tract and before the gospel, the abbot, clad in priestly vestments, comes before the bishop. The seven penitential psalms are then recited, in accordance with a practice inherited from Cluny.[86] These are followed by the litany of the saints, the Our

---

80. *PRG* 1:69. — *Gell* 2579 (p. 400).
81. *PRG* 1:69–70.
82. Andrieu, *PR* 2:170–74.
83. Yves of Chartres, *Ep. 73 ad Bernardum abbatem* (PL 162:94).
84. Andrieu, *PR* 1:408–13.
85. *Ibid.*, 3:400–8.
86. E. Martène, *De antiquis monachorum ritibus*, Lib. 5, c. 1, no. 46 (M 1149). — In this work Martène transcribes a series of manuscripts that give the blessing of an abbot and an abbess. M 707–17 studies their date and the place where they originated and were used. Other important sources to be examined are the monastic customaries; see B. Albers, *Consuetudines monasticae* (note 9, etc.), and the *Corpus consuetudinum monasticorum* (note

Father, some verses, the old prayer "Concede" from the Gregorian Sacramentary, and the prayer "Cunctorum bonorum institutor" from the Sacramentary of Gellone. The bishop then sings the preface, "Omnipotens sempiterne Deus, affluentem spiritum," which is from the Sacramentary of Gellone, but has been changed in its opening part. During the preface he lays his hand on the abbot's head. Next come two prayers of thanksgiving: "Deus cui omnis potestas et dignitas famulatur" and "Omnium Domine fons bonorum," which are from the Romano-German Pontifical of the tenth century. The Pontifical of 1596 was to add a third prayer, "Exaudi, Domine, preces nostras," which expresses the role of the abbot and which Durandus of Mende had prescribed for after the Mass.[87] Finally, the new abbot receives the Rule, the pastoral staff, and the ring, each accompanied by a prayer.

At the offertory the abbot offers two loaves of bread, two small casks of wine, and two candles; this practice was introduced by the Pontifical of the Roman Curia.[88]

At the end of the Mass the bishop leads the abbot to his chair and enthrones him; the *Te Deum* is sung, and during it the monks pledge their obedience.

The Roman Pontifical of the closing Middle Ages added to this rite a kind of mock concelebration. From the beginning of the Mass to the gospel, the abbot celebrated at a side altar while the bishop was celebrating at the main altar. From the offertory on, the abbot knelt in the presbyterium and in a low voice joined the bishop in reciting all the prayers except for the words of consecration.

In the course of time abbots received the various pontifical insignia, the bestowal of which was provided for in the ritual of abbatial blessing. The oldest of these insignia is the pastoral staff. The giving of a ring, together with the formula "Accipe anulum fidei," made its appearance in the twelfth-century Pontifical of the Roman Curia,[89] in which we also see the new abbot donning stockings, sandals, and tunicle. At the end of Mass he also receives gloves and miter. Finally, he blesses the throng during the procession from the church. These insignia were honorary in the case of abbots and are to be explained by the service that the latter rendered, since they helped the bishops and celebrated pontifical Mass in their stead when they were absent.[90]

---

1). A complete study of the extant manuscripts is being made by B. Johnson as a dissertation for the Pontifical Institute of Liturgy at San Anselmo in Rome.

87. Andrieu, *PR* 3:405.

88. *Ibid.*, 2:409; 3:407.

89. *Ibid.*, 2:413.

90. P. Salmon, *Etude sur les insignes du pontife dans le rit romain* (Rome: Officium libri catholici, 1955), 49ff.

In the old Pontificals the blessing of an abbess was identical with that of an abbot.[91] The more recent Roman Pontifical, however, omitted the giving of the pastoral staff, nor was a ring given to an abbess since she had worn one since her consecration as a nun. Except for the reading of the *Mandatum apostolicum,* the saying of one of the prayers and the penitential psalms, and the rites of quasi-concelebration, the prayers were identical with those in the blessing of an abbot.

IV. THE BLESSING OF AN ABBOT AND AN ABBESS SINCE VATICAN II

It was clear that the ritual for the blessing of an abbot and an abbess had undergone the influences of successive periods and that the theology proper to it had become distorted, so that rather serious confusions could result.

Three criteria were followed in restoring the ritual to its proper form: (1) it was not to be impoverished but rather modified; any suppression had to be justified as necessary by serious reasons; (2) its authenticity was to be ensured by avoiding everything that could lead to a confusion of the ordination of a bishop with the simple blessing of an abbot; (3) the formularies, which at times were overly juridical, were to be revised and given a more deeply spiritual and monastic content.

Here are the most obvious characteristics of this new ritual that was published on November 9, 1970:

1) The blessing is celebrated during Mass, but after the gospel, as in the new rituals for ordination, consecrations, and blessings.

2) In the old ritual the new abbot-elect was presented to the bishop by two other abbots, in an intentional imitation of the ritual for the ordination of a bishop. The point in episcopal ordination, however, was to emphasize episcopal collegiality, and this had no meaning in the case of abbots. Ordinarily, therefore, two religious who had been members of the electing chapter are appointed to present the abbot-elect to the bishop.

3) The concelebration is now real and not fictive. Any priests who are present also concelebrate with the bishop and the new abbot.

4) In what is perhaps a reflection of the ritual of episcopal consecration, an abbot who is blessed in his own abbey by another abbot may preside over the celebration from the offertory onward; otherwise he takes first place after the principal concelebrant.

5) The ring and pastoral staff are blessed before the celebration.

---

91. For example, *PRG* 1:76–82.

6) There is no longer any imposition of the hand on the new abbot; this rite is now reserved for sacramental ordinations.

7) The formula of the blessing has been composed in light of the spiritual teaching about abbots that is given in the Rule of St. Benedict. Three other optional formulas are provided. All express in different ways the essential responsibility of an abbot: to guide monks in their search for God.

8) The giving of the ring and the miter is optional; an abbot may, however, wear them later on, even if they have not been given to him at the time of his blessing. Nowadays many abbots are no longer elected for life; it would therefore be an inauthentic gesture to give them a ring, which symbolizes the definitive bond between monastery and abbot. The oldest of all gestures, the giving of the Rule, has of course been retained. The giving of a pastoral staff has also been kept as being ancient and still meaningful, but since the formula that used to accompany the bestowal of the staff expressed a purely juridical and disciplinary outlook, it has been replaced by one with a more positive content.

9) If the abbot has no territorial jurisdiction, he is no longer enthroned, nor does he pass among the faithful and give his blessing.

The blessing of an abbess is likewise very simple without being impoverished. It has the same structure as the blessing of an abbot, with the necessary adaptations. After the gospel, two nuns present the abbess-elect to the bishop, who conducts a brief examination. The singing of the litanies is followed by the blessing, in which one of three optional formulas is used. The new abbess is then given the *Rule* and also a ring if she did not receive one at her profession.

Among the ritual Masses of the Roman Missal there is one for the blessing of an abbot or an abbess. The Lectionary provides two readings from the Old Testament, five from the New, and three from the gospel.

V. THEOLOGICAL CONTENT OF THE BLESSING OF AN ABBOT OR AN ABBESS

One aim of the new ritual is to prevent any confusion of this blessing with a sacrament. At the same time, however, it strives to make clear the role of an abbot (or abbess), for it is this that justifies a blessing and distinguishes him (her) from other superiors.

To this end the content of the examination by the bishop has been changed. The emphasis is now on the essential role of an abbot, which is to lead his brethren to love of God, an evangelical life, and fraternal charity. He is urged to be an exemplar of monastic life and not simply a teacher of doctrine; to be concerned first and foremost with the salvation of his monks; to safeguard the possessions of the monastery and to do so (this is a new emphasis) not only for his brethren but also in order that he may give aid to pilgrims and the poor. If the abbot also has jurisdiction over a territory, reference is made to his mission as pastor.

The prayer of blessing, which is no longer a preface but, as is fitting, simply a prayer, emphasizes the teaching role of the abbot and the care he must take to adapt himself to the various personalities for which he is responsible, and to focus his attention primarily on service and not simply on his own authority. He must teach all to esteem the *Opus Dei* and *lectio divina*, and be careful to lose none of those who have been entrusted to him and for whom he will have to render an account.

It is to be noted that this ritual cannot be used for a titular abbot, who has the title but does not receive the blessing.

§5. The Blessing of a Monastic Superior in the East

BIBLIOGRAPHY

A. Dmitrievskij, *Stavlennik* (Kiev, 1904).

A. Maltzew, *Die Sacramente der orthodox-katholischen Kirche des Morgenlandes* (Berlin, 1908). The texts with a German translation.

J. Pargoire, "Archimandrite," *DACL* 1 (1907) 2739–61.

P. de Meester, *De monachico statu iuxta byzantinam disciplinam* (Codificazione canonica orientale, Fonti II, 10; Vatican Polyglot Press, 1942), 202–4.

_____, "L'archimandritat dans les Eglises de rite byzantin," in *Miscellanea liturgica in honorem L. Cuniberti Mohlberg* 2 (Rome: Edizioni liturgiche, 1949), 115–37.

I shall discuss only Byzantine usage here. The title of archimandrite is no longer used by the Armenians, while among the Chaldeans, Syrians, and Copts there are no special rites that can be compared with this category of blessing.

I. MONASTIC SUPERIORS IN THE EAST

It is indispensable to bear in mind the titles given to superiors of monastic communities.

From the sixth to the eighth century they had the interchangeable titles of higumen and archimandrite. But from the end of the eighth or beginning of the ninth century on, the title of archimandrite was bestowed primarily on heads of major monasteries. There are other titles besides those of higumen and archimandrite:[92] *Abbas, Patēr, Kathigoumenos,* and,

---

92. An "archimandrite" is one "who is at the head of the flock (*mandra*)."

for the head of several united monasteries, *Katholikos*. There are also honorary archimandrites. At one time there were even female archimandrites, at least among major superiors, but instances are rare. In the East no less than in the West there have been abuses both in the wearing of insignia connected with these dignities and in celebrations.

II. THE RITES FOR THE BLESSING OF
A MONASTIC SUPERIOR

The Greek Euchologion has but a single rite for the blessing of either a higumen or an archimandrite.[93] It is the bishop who gives the blessing, which takes place outside the sanctuary.

The candidate is presented to the bishop. The latter exclaims: "May the grace of the Holy Spirit be with you, giving you his light, strength, and understanding all the days of your life!" The deacon then says: "Be attentive!" The bishop imposes his hand and prays:

> O God, who care unceasingly for the salvation of human beings, you gather this flock into unity. Do you, Lord of all things, keep your servant blameless; in your great kindness protect him who keeps your commandments without weakening, so that no lamb may be lost or corrupted by the wolf. It has pleased you to place this servant of yours at the head of this flock: show him to be worthy of your kindness and adorn him with all the virtues, so that in his actions he may give good example to those who are subject to him. May they imitate his irreproachable holiness of life and, being saved from condemnation, stand at his side before your awesome judgment.

This is followed by a litany that ends with a prayer: "Hear our prayer, Lord, and make your servant a faithful superior of this venerable monastery, a prudent steward of the fold which your grace has entrusted to his care. May he do your will in all things and be worthy of the heavenly kingdom."

The bishop then takes the superior's cloak from him and gives him a new one, saying: "Let the servant of God, N., be raised to his chair; let him be superior and pastor of this venerable monastery, N."

All the monks stand and cry: "He is worthy, he is worthy, he is worthy." The bishop then gives him the kiss of peace, and so do all the monks. The bishop then bestows the pastoral staff with the words: "Receive this staff with which you are to guide your wavering flock; for on the day of judgment you must render an account of them to our God."

Everyone wishes him a long term as superior, and the Mass begins.

---

93. See the text in J. Goar (note 61), 395–96; also in J. L. Assemani, *Codex liturgicus Ecclesiae universae* 12 (Rome, 1766; photographic reprint: Welter, 1902), 315.

In the Slavic Pontifical, a distinction is made between the rite for the promotion of a higumen (this is practically identical with the rite just described) and the rite for the blessing of an archimandrite. If the latter is not a higumen, the prayer of blessing for that rank is first recited over him; he is then proclaimed an archimandrite and receives the miter and cross at the time of the Little Entrance of the liturgy. At the end of Mass the bishop gives him the pastoral staff and an instruction.[94]

III. THEOLOGICAL CONTENT

A monastery is looked upon here as a kind of miniature church that is entrusted to the care of the superior. The latter's main concern must be to give an example and to protect his flock. The theology is a very simple one but it expresses the essential thing, namely, that the responsibility of the superior is primarily of the spiritual order: to inspire the monks to vie with him in holiness of life.

---

94. See A. Maltzew, *Die Sacramente der orthodox-katholischen Kirche des Morgenlandes* (Berlin, 1898), 347–74.

Index

The following pages list the people, places, and events about which a pertinent statement is made in this book. By no means should this index be considered a complete listing of the scores of people, places, and events recorded in this book.